Poverty Warriors

THE HUMAN EXPERIENCE OF PLANNED SOCIAL INTERVENTION

THE HOGG FOUNDATION RESEARCH SERIES

WAYNE H. HOLTZMAN, EDITOR

Tornadoes over Texas by Harry Estill Moore
Electric Stimulation of the Brain edited by Daniel E. Sheer
Inkblot Perception and Personality by Wayne H. Holtzman,
Joseph S. Thorpe, Jon D. Swartz, and E. Wayne Herron
Changing Parental Attitudes through Group Discussion
by Carl F. Hereford
Tomorrow's Parents by Bernice Milburn Moore and Wayne H. Holtzman
Across the Tracks by Arthur Rubel
A Future for the Aged by Frances Merchant Carp
Delinquency in Three Cultures by Carl M. Rosenquist and
Edwin I. Megargee

POVERTY WARRIORS

The Human Experience of Planned Social Intervention

BY LOUIS A. ZURCHER, JR.

With a Foreword by GARDNER MURPHY

PUBLISHED FOR THE HOGG FOUNDATION FOR MENTAL HEALTH
BY THE UNIVERSITY OF TEXAS PRESS, AUSTIN & LONDON

International Standard Book Number 0-292-70051-2
Library of Congress Catalog Card Number 70-111391
Copyright © 1970 by the Hogg Foundation for Mental Health
Manufactured in the United States of America

To the Target Neighborhood Officers
and to Susan

How do you fight poverty? Do you walk up to it, grab it by the throat, kick it in the ass, and say, "Get the hell out of my life"? Or do you sit down with it, study on it, and quiet-like chew away at it till it's all gone? I know which way is most fun, but which way works longest and best?

—A TARGET NEIGHBORHOOD OFFICER

FOREWORD

BY GARDNER MURPHY

ACTION RESEARCH, in the sense in which the term was used by Kurt Lewin, has offered huge promise to the social sciences. One could wish that during this period of eager, nervous, governmental experimentation with the plight of the poor and the underprivileged in our cities, towns, and rural areas there might be a more explicit recognition of the possibilities of action research in a newly conceived arena: research in the dynamics and outcomes of massive federal intervention. This conception is quite different from that of "applied social research," or a study of the implications of pure research for practice. It is not enough to provide a "research aspect" for a huge integration program, or, after the expensive study has been completed, to conduct a brief "evaluation" of its outcome. Rather, it is essential that as intervention comes to be conceptualized, the requisite feedback be provided by which the intervention itself can be understood.

Unfortunately, public policy has not yet come to reflect this necessity. It has, however, taken very real and important forward steps in providing for limited social-science evaluation, step by step, of some of our more sharply defined little efforts in medical, educational, and ameliorative programs. The present report by Professor Zurcher describes one such scientific study, one in which the Topeka Office of Economic Opportunity was closely observed, step by step, and its outcome evaluated after a year and a half. It offered Dr. Zurcher an opportunity to watch, at very close range, a kind of research that was, to be sure, not the kind a team of social scientists would have

planned, but one that dealt, nevertheless, with a community effort
in which the day-by-day consequences of fresh social action could
be viewed with great objectivity. This is an unusual kind of social
research, and an important one. As the social scientist conceptual-
izes the action research of all sorts going on in the national arena,
he can reach new conceptualizations of social change.

The explicit formulation of the Topeka oeo, described here as
the "Overlap Model," works within the existing social institutions
through "maximum feasible participation." In a book as genial, direct, and appealing as this volume, it is delightful to find the issues
and the terms defined in the actual words of the various participants
in this urban effort. The phases in social change are documented up
to the hilt, chapter by chapter, page by page. The top leaders and
middle-level leaders, the rank and file, all are seen as they grope,
week by week, toward the solution of urgent problems and the rec-
tification of social ills. Their many grass-roots hunches and many
judgments of outcomes are recast by Dr. Zurcher as "hypotheses to
be tested," and "outcomes to be evaluated." With minimal intervention of his own, he observed the community elements of each level
being drawn into the phases of action which took shape realistically,
disappointments ushering some methods *out*, fresh hopes ushering
other methods *in*.

The present volume aims constantly to be rich, concrete, specific,
and above all, *personal* in its message to the reader. When a point
has been made three or four times by different members of a small
group, we may come to a long and charming interview in which
essentially the same points are again made. This is simply because
we are allowed, in this way, to see each person thinking, feeling,
and acting.

Two generalizations, while not unexpected, stand out among the
conclusions. (1) Those who are chosen to "represent" the poor
find themselves in a stressful and often impossible situation. They
cannot get for their "constituents" everything that is wanted and
needed, and they are then cast in a painful role of conflict, being
regarded as members of an elite, or as renegades and deserters.
(2) The Overlap Model inevitably involved, as active participants,

very few of Topeka's "poor." Indeed, none of the so-called "hard-core poor" assume positions of indigenous leadership. The personal failures of individuals, though relevant, are not the central issue here. The whole picture of the social structure makes it plain why it is difficult for the centers of community power to really know very much about the struggle being carried out at the level of the OEO. Nevertheless, documentation for the reasons for helplessness and disappointment, as seen from a lower middle-class or lower-class point of view, will be bared to the reader, and the components of everyday bureaucracy will be recognized even when a rather bold new adventure is being tried out.

Among the many virtues of this book is the charmingly direct form and human way in which these successes and failures are spelled out. The author concludes that few definitive conclusions can be drawn regarding the feasibility of the effort at "maximum feasible participation," but this study leaves little doubt that in Topeka, at least, the effort was decidedly worthwhile. Here and there are seen new hope and new self-image capable of rectifying the futile and unhappy place of the poor in society. Such encouragements, and also the concomitant discouragements, as seen in this book and other current studies of poverty intervention can contribute to bolder and more challenging intervention conceptualizations.

PREFACE

IN 1964, CONGRESS passed the Economic Opportunity Act and declared the "War on Poverty." Under a section providing for the development of local community-action programs, the Act stated that such programs were to be "developed, conducted, and administered with the maximum feasible participation of residents of the areas and members of the groups to be served."[1] The mandate for participation of the poor in the decision-making processes of poverty programing generally stimulated considerable controversy within participating communities.

Twenty years ago, Kurt Lewin described the forces that serve to maintain social systems in a state of "quasi-stationary equilibrium."[2] He outlined complex dynamics underlying the formation of group standards and group-determined social habits, and demonstrated those standards and habits generally to be resistant to change. When social change did occur, there had been an "unfreezing" of significant components of the social system, engendered by an increase in the forces for, or a decrease in the forces against, change. Since such forces and such systems are the result of human interaction, the process of "unfreezing" can be stressful to at least some of the system's members.

A community is a social system, and frames a complicated network of social groups and associated norms, values, and role expectations. A person may be a member of any number of social groups,

[1] Economic Opportunity Act of 1964, 78 Stat. 508, Sec. 202 (a).
[2] Kurt Lewin, "Problems of Group Dynamics and the Integration of the Social Sciences: I, Social Equilibria," *Journal of Human Relations* 1, 1 (1947), 5–41.

broadly defined, that vary in size, degree of formalization, cohesiveness, openness, tolerance for change, and member characteristics. The individual enacts his membership role within a specific group in accordance with his interpretation of what is expected of him and what he expects of himself. Similarly, he learns to anticipate certain behaviors from others, depending upon whatever roles he perceives them to be enacting in association with whatever social groups. Those behavioral expectations sustain for him a degree of predictability of, and control over, events in his social world. Thus he may become distressed, to the extent delimitated by his personality structure, when changes in the social system or incidences of atypical behavior interfere with the sense and order of things as he perceives them. Also, the learning of new roles, insofar as those roles require the abandoning or modification of accustomed behavior, may be stressful to the individual. Related to this is the stress-producing conflict that may result when two or more of the multiple roles the person enacts, by virtue of his membership in a multiplicity of social groups, are perceived by him or others significant to him to have conflicting behavioral expectations.

Social change is, by definition, a process in which the boundaries of groups are reshaped, behavioral expectations are redefined, new social roles are learned, and roles in transition come into conflict. To the community, depending upon the rapidity of, and its tolerance for, change, this can mean a struggle between those social forces that perpetuate the quasi-stationary equilibrium and those that strive to recenter the balance of social power. To the individual, depending upon his needs to maintain the *status quo* and his tolerance for role assimilation and role strain, the process of change can be unsettling and psychologically painful.

Much community social change can be associated with such impelling factors as technological and industrial development, ideological and religious influence, immigration and emigration, and cultural diffusion. However, *controlled* and *planned* intervention for community social change, particularly concerning the amelioration of poverty, has with the passage of the Economic Opportunity Act become a national technique. Poverty-intervention organizations, most of them supported by the Office of Economic Opportunity, purport directly to restructure those community social habits and standards that account for institutionalizing a cycle of poverty. Needless to say, such intervention, if it effectively "unfreezes" community social structures and mobilizes change, must challenge some of the human value orientations, role expectations, and group identifications that comprise the forces sustaining the quasi-stationary equilibrium of the community.

The following pages present some of the experiences of men and women, poor and not poor, who participated in a community's OEO poverty program. The research upon which this book is based was not the survey type typically utilized in evaluations of planned social change. That is, the research did not primarily concern itself globally with the material impact upon the community of all the subcomponents of the local poverty program. Rather, the focus was upon those subcomponents which best revealed the process experiences of the participants. The study was concerned with three major components of the local poverty program: (1) the Topeka Office of Economic Opportunity and its staff; (2) the Economic Opportunity Board and its members; and (3) the Target Neighborhood Committees and their indigenous leaders.

More specifically, the research sought answers to such questions about the poverty-intervention organization as: How was it developed and by whom? What were its structure, function, and goals? Was there a discernible organizational model? What were the characteristics of the staff members, and how did they view the social-intervention task? What was the nature of the staff role, what were the rewards and stresses associated with the role, and how were the stresses resolved? What was the community reaction to the poverty-intervention organization? How did the staff recruit and maintain citizen participation and accomplish organizational goals? Did organization and staff change over time?

Concerning the Economic Opportunity Board, the study inquired: Who were its members? What were the decision-making processes for poverty programing? Were there significant social-psychological differences between poor and not-poor members of the Board, and if so, what part did such differences play in the decision-making processes? How did the members interact? What were the sources of conflict and of consensus? Did the attitudes of members change as a result of Board participation? How did members view their association with the poverty program?

About the Target Neighborhood Committees, the research asked: What were the group dynamics of the committees? Were there discrete stages of development for the committees, and if so, what was the relation of such stages to social and personal change? What processes governed the emergence of indigenous leadership? What were the characteristics of indigenous leaders, and what were their expectations of their followers and the staff of the poverty-intervention organization? What rewards and stresses did they encounter and how did they accommodate stresses? How did the indigenous leaders view the poverty program, and did those views change over time?

These questions, among others intended to highlight the experiences of poverty warriors and their "maximum feasible participation," are dealt with in considerable detail throughout the book. Parts I, II, and III detail, respectively, the poverty-intervention organization, the Economic Opportunity Board, and the Target Neighborhood Committees. Within each of these parts, chapters describe the structure and processes of the poverty-program components, and the impact of participation upon the individuals who were involved. Part IV presents an overview and some conclusions.

Since the research intention was to assess as closely as possible the elements of the participants' process experience, my assistants and I acted on the methodological assumption that there is no substitute for "being there." Although structured interviews and questionnaires, described in the appendices, were used, the richest data were gathered by our observation in the meetings of the Board and Target Neighborhood Committees and through our close association and unstructured interviews with the staff of the Topeka Office of Economic Opportunity and its citizen participants (Appendix A presents a detailed discussion of the research role, the research staff, and the Research Committee). Data are drawn from the poverty program of a single community and therefore generalization of findings is left to the judgment of the reader. However, I believe that the emphasis of our research upon the human process rather than upon program content, and the affirmations we have received from other poverty researchers and social planners in numerous symposia and consultations, encourage extrapolation and further comparative research.

I have attempted to present the findings in a format and style which would be useful to planners as well as implementers, practitioners as well as theorists, students as well as professors, and basic as well as applied researchers. Also, I have tried to avoid casting interpretations of the data in other than an interdisciplinary framework. My methodological and conceptual biases are nonetheless quite apparent, and, I might add, not unwillingly so. I am taken with the value of studying social and psychological processes in natural settings, and heartily agree with those of my colleagues who are convinced that as social scientists we must turn more research attention to the contemporary social problems of human beings and to their intended solutions.

L.A.Z., Jr.

The University of Texas
Austin, Texas

ACKNOWLEDGMENTS

I AM DEEPLY INDEBTED to a number of persons for their assistance and to several organizations for their financial support throughout this research project. In particular, the suggestions and encouragements of Gardner Murphy, William Key, and James Taylor were invaluable in conceptualizing and implementing the study, as well as in the interpretation of data. Director Robert Harder and Assistant Director Simon Martínez generously, and not always comfortably, kept the poverty program in their charge open to research. William Simons, Fred Hill, Rosanne Barnhill, Basil Keiser, Janis Boldridge, and Marilyn Simons were exemplary research assistants and helpful critics. Ivan Belknap, Charles Bonjean, Dale McClemore, and Norval Glenn offered many constructive suggestions during the preparation of the manuscript. Lolafay Coyne organized and performed the statistical analyses. Robert Blauner, Jack Otis, Wayne Holtzman, Bernice Moore, and Bert Kruger Smith stimulated the revision and strengthening of the final draft. Susan Lee Zurcher somehow managed to be a full-time wife and companion at the same time she was a part-time research assistant.

The Menninger Foundation, through the consideration of Roy Menninger, supported this research with seed funds during its early phases. The Office of Economic Opportunity subsequently funded the project (Grant 66-9744), and William Lawrence served as an advisor as well as a grant administrator. I would like to express my appreciation to Robert Sutherland and the Hogg Foundation for a grant facilitating the writing of the manuscript. Carolyn Campbell, with the help of Barbara Pickett, Adreain Kirkpatrick, and Linda

Grenadier, diligently and patiently typed and retyped the manuscript through various stages to its final form.

The members of Topeka's Economic Opportunity Board, and in particular the Target Neighborhood Officers, not only contributed the substance of this report, but stimulated and educated its author. For their friendship, candidness, and insight I am profoundly grateful.

Several of the chapters in this book contain material from papers that I have previously published elsewhere: (with William H. Key) "The Overlap Model: A Comparison of Strategies for Social Change," *Sociological Quarterly*, 8, 4 (Winter, 1968), pp. 85–97 (Chapters 1 and 2); "Implementing a Community Action Agency," in Milton F. Shore and Fortune B. Mannino (eds.), *Community Mental Health: Problems, Programs and Strategies.* New York: Behavioral Publications, 1969 (Chapter 1); "Functional Marginality: Dynamics of a Poverty Intervention Organization," *(Southwestern) Social Science Quarterly*, 48, 3 (December, 1967), pp. 411–421 (Chapters 2 and 3); "The Poverty Board: Some Consequences of 'Maximum Feasible Participation,'" in press, *Journal of Social Issues* (Chapters 5 and 9); "Stages of Development in Poverty Program Neighborhood Action Committees," *Journal of Applied Behavioral Science*, 5, 2 (April, 1969), pp. 222–258 (Chapter 12); "Poverty Program Indigenous Leaders: A Study of Marginality," *Sociology and Social Research*, 53, 2 (January, 1969), pp. 147–162 (Chapters 11 and 15); "The Leader and the Lost: A Case Study of Indigenous Leadership in a Poverty Program Community Action Committee," *Genetic Psychology Monographs*, 76 (August, 1967), pp. 23–93 (Preface and Chapter 13); (with Alvin E. Green) *From Dependency to Dignity: Individual and Social Consequences of a Neighborhood House.* New York: Behavioral Publications, 1969 (Chapter 14).

The permission of the publishers to reproduce the material in modified form is gratefully acknowledged.

CONTENTS

TABLES

FIGURES

Poverty Warriors

THE HUMAN EXPERIENCE OF PLANNED SOCIAL INTERVENTION

PART I
The Poverty-Intervention Organization

▚▚

Part I focuses upon the development, implementation, and subsequent dynamics of the Topeka Office of Economic Opportunity, a poverty-intervention organization, and upon the characteristics and stresses of its staff.

In Chapter 1, the community setting, as a base for poverty intervention, is described. The individuals and events influential in establishing the Topeka Office of Economic Opportunity are discussed, with particular attention given to the evolution of intervention goals and rationale. The "Overlap Model," a term that appropriately summarizes the local planners' working assumptions concerning poverty intervention, is outlined and contrasted with a dramatically different intervention model.

The structure of the Topeka Office of Economic Opportunity, designed to implement the Overlap Model, is described in Chapter 2. A complex of committees introduced by the Topeka Office of Economic Opportunity is discussed as its attempt to guarantee "maximum feasible participation" of the poor and to obtain the optimum mixing of all participants. The Topeka Office of Economic Opportunity is described as striving to maintain an operating position, termed herein "Functional Marginality," between the poor and the not-poor in the community, in order to serve as a "bridge" to facilitate the interaction of both groups toward the amelioration of poverty. The characteristics of the staff of the Topeka Office of Economic Opportunity are presented, and are related to the division of labor employed during the urgent initial task of recruiting program participants—a division of labor that was maintained throughout later staff operations.

Chapter 3 details the conflicts inherent in the Overlap Model and Functional Marginality, and the differences in program expectations between poor and not-poor participants. The strain of reconciling "maximum feasible participation" of the poor with the operating realities of the Topeka Office of Economic Opportunity is discussed. The stresses upon the staff resulting from goal conflicts, differences in expectations, and demands to sustain co-ordinative efforts are reported, with attention given to the methods by which staff members express and/or resolve those stresses. A final note is added on the travails of managerial succession in a poverty-intervention organization, and described is the "ideal" staff member as depicted by participants who were poor.

A brief inventory of the tangible program accomplishments of the Topeka Office of Economic Opportunity (for example, programs funded, implemented, persons served, etc.) during the period of the study is presented in Chapter 4.

CHAPTER I

The Planners

As PART OF ITS EFFORT to implement the Economic Opportunity Act of 1964, the Office of Economic Opportunity offered local communities financial and technical assistance to develop and support antipoverty programs if those communities gave evidence of determination to: (1) Mobilize their own public and private resources for the attack. (2) Develop programs of sufficient scope and size to give promise of eliminating causes of poverty. (3) Involve the poor themselves and co-ordinate the community-action programs through public or private nonprofit agencies or a combination of these. Specifically, funding was available for the development of poverty-intervention organizations ("Community Action Agencies," in OEO terms) and for a network of individual programs such as remedial reading, job training, counseling and homemakers' services, vocational rehabilitation, job development, health services, day-care centers, and family planning. The poverty-intervention organization would develop, implement, and co-ordinate the assorted programs within their respective communities. The federal government would pay up to 90 per cent of the cost of the local programs during their first two years of operation. The balance, to be furnished by the community, could be in cash or in kind (services and facilities).[1]

The Office of Economic Opportunity intended that the community-action programs would enable communities to attack their local poverty problems in a positive and co-ordinated manner. The OEO clearly indicated the belief that local leaders in business, labor, and civic organizations would be important factors in the formation and support of all antipoverty projects, and suggested that appropriate voluntary and government agencies be brought together to determine how they could help in the total antipoverty effort. The appeal for an all-out "War on Poverty," and the offer of support, went to communities throughout the nation. One of the thousands of communities to respond was Topeka, Kansas.

COMMUNITY SETTING

Topeka, the capital of Kansas, has a population of approximately 125,000 persons, of whom 8 per cent are Negro-Americans, 3.5 per cent are Mexican-Americans, and 0.8 per cent are American Indians. As reported in the 1960 census, less than 2 per cent of Topeka's citizens are unemployed and less than 1 per cent are on welfare. The median annual income for the Topeka family is $6,000, with 16 per cent of families earning less than $3,000 per year. There are no crowded tenements, no shanty towns, at this writing no organized protests, nor any of the other more dramatic and headline-making evidences of chronic poverty. However, a comparative neighborhood-by-neighborhood analysis of socio-economic conditions in To-

[1] Office of Economic Opportunity, "Community Action Program Fact Sheet," Washington, D.C., 1965, mimeograph.

peka yields a more revealing set of statistics. Some of the neighborhoods have 10 per cent of their residents unemployed, 20 per cent
on welfare, and 30 per cent living in housing considered substand-
ard.[2] Perhaps typical of many other rural and small urban communities in the Midwest, Topeka sustains quiet, relatively unseen
poverty pockets.

According to a demographic and power-structure analysis of
Topeka conducted in 1963, it is

a stable, slowly growing community, which only in recent years has attracted some manufacturing plants of national corporations to augment
the blue collar jobs provided by the Santa Fe Railroad and a number of
small home owned organizations. It can be described as "lightly" indus-
trialized. Since World War II it has developed extensive psychiatric facilities organized around the famed Menninger Foundation and its School
of Psychiatry. The state of Kansas and the federal government are major
employers. This pattern of economic expansion has brought about an increase in the proportion of both blue collar and professional groups in
the population.

The community "power structure" is dominated by the usual combination of financial, real estate, communication, and business leaders whose
primary organizational affiliations are: the Chamber of Commerce, the Topeka Country Club, and the Rotary Club. Conservative in outlook, they
have avoided being regressive, though their political rhetoric still contains
references to states' rights, rejection of Federal expansion, an emphasis
upon individualism, a rejection of a welfare ideology, and a general dis-
taste for the direct use of government to promote socially acceptable ends.

The values of the businessmen are mirrored by those of the middle
class majority, much more than would be true in a larger or a more cos-
mopolitan American community, although the pattern of population
growth described above has resulted in some dilution of generally
strongly Republican conservatism.[3]

---

[2] Topeka-Shawnee Regional Planning Commission, "Neighborhood Analysis
for the Topeka-Shawnee County Regional Planning Area," Master Plan Report
No. 5, Topeka, Kansas, September, 1965.

[3] William H. Key, "An Urban Renewal Relocation Program," in Milton F.
Shore and Fortune B. Mannino (eds.), *Community Mental Health: Problems,
Programs, and Strategies*, pp. 22–37.

Key discusses the existence of poverty in Topeka, and comments that the poor have manifested

almost no organized protest. The NAACP, after being in an urban renewal struggle, lost a charismatic leader and has only a nominal membership. The city has no active chapter of CORE. About a year ago it was rumored that the Black Muslims made an abortive attempt to organize Topeka Negroes. At the time of this writing, there are no pickets, no boycotts, and no demonstrations.[4]

Prior to the Economic Opportunity Act of 1964, therefore, Topeka is depicted as a relatively stable, quiet, complacent, and basically conservative community which had indices of poverty, but which was making no concerted dramatic effort toward its amelioration.

THE TOPEKA WELFARE PLANNING COUNCIL

In November of 1964, the Topeka Welfare Planning Council became interested in the poverty programs available through the Economic Opportunity Act. The Council, a volunteer-citizens group of approximately two hundred community leaders, mostly professionals or businessmen, had with support from the United Fund demonstrated some prior interest in Topeka's social problems. A Council Subcommittee was formed to investigate the possibility of establishing an OEO poverty-intervention organization in Topeka. The Subcommittee consisted of nine members: two city commissioners, the executive director of the United Fund, the director of the Topeka Human Relations Commission, the city director of recreation, the superintendent of schools, the president of the Topeka Welfare Planning Council, a research associate in the Menninger Foundation, and the chairman of the Department of Sociology at Washburn University.

After considerable deliberation, the Subcommittee decided to apply for a one-year OEO Planning and Development Grant, and received commitment from the Topeka Welfare Planning Council for

4 *Ibid.*

the mandatory 10 per cent "local share" of total program funding. Although it would have been possible for the Council to have been awarded large amounts of poverty money immediately by direct application for specific poverty programs, it intentionally chose the slower Planning and Development Grant provided by OEO. The Subcommittee strongly felt that since the poor were only indirectly represented in the Topeka Welfare Planning Council, and since there was little organization among the poor in the community, the hurried acquisition of funds for operating programs would have allowed, at best, only token representation from among the poor in the development and administration of the programs. The Subcommittee was much impressed with, and determined to implement, the "maximum feasible participation" mandate of the Economic Opportunity Act. Furthermore, members of the Subcommittee were impressed with OEO's suggestion that the antipoverty efforts be a coordinated community effort, and they felt that a Planning and Development Grant would provide them with time to structure a poverty-intervention organization which would encourage community-wide effort.

The intentions of the Topeka Welfare Planning Council are best represented in the section on "Goals" in their application for a planning grant to the Office of Economic Opportunity (copy on file with the Topeka Office of Economic Opportunity):

The Planning period would be devoted to assessing the needs of the poverty stricken and, based on that assessment, we would define and chart the steps for an effective, comprehensive, and broad-ranging attack on the problem of poverty in Topeka. We feel that this is a rare opportunity to systematically assess our community needs and resources, and we wanted to develop a planning outline to guide our welfare efforts over the next ten to twenty years.

While definitive answers await the outcome of the planning period, the following seems to characterize the existing situation. Past efforts to deal with poverty in Topeka, as elsewhere, have been fragmented and poorly coordinated. Many needs have not been met, while other needs have been met only sporadically or ineffectively. Needed are groups of social innovations which provide a total rehabilitation effort, pushing towards an enrichment of opportunities and capacities among the impoverished. Program planning will attempt to deal with a wide range of needs, starting in the pre-school years, and extending to the problems of the aged. It is anticipated that plans will be made for nursery schools, for neighborhood centers, for training institutions whose efforts are integrated with local industrial needs, for part-time job opportunities that give a reentry into the world of work, for the development of indigenous leadership and social action programs among the poor, and for augmenting the economic opportunities and welfare services available to the aged.

Two aspects of the planning seem especially important: (1) It will attempt whenever possible to develop sub-professional roles and indigenous leadership among the impoverished; and (2) It will, from the very beginning, have built into it a research and evaluation component.

The grant application also outlined the Topeka Welfare Planning Council's intended "Steps in Planning":

While the Welfare Planning Council is aware of many unmet needs, and can sketch out certain possible innovations which are likely to meet the needs, much more work is needed before an operational plan can be submitted. Several major steps are anticipated. First, it is necessary to define more specifically the nature and scope of the problems, and the specific needs of specific groups among the impoverished. Such a "mapping" will require a comprehensive review of present agency records, and further fact-finding procedures in which the impoverished themselves will be involved wherever possible. We anticipate, therefore, that survey research carried out among and by the more impoverished will be an important step in the planning. Second, it is necessary to enlist the participation of both the indigenous poor and of the total community in setting up innovative programs. We need to build involvement and commitment, both in the neighborhoods and among participating agencies. Third, the specifics of various programs need to be planned. We need to develop new administrative procedures for new kinds of agencies and workers; we need to develop requirements for staff; we need to develop initial program plans; and we need to integrate new programs, if any, into the present community structure. The latter point seems especially important; if new agencies and services are to be viable, they must somehow come to be part of ongoing commitments in organizations.

The Council then determined that the first phase of the planning period would be used to structure and staff a skeleton poverty-intervention organization and to develop a rationale and strategy for the amelioration of poverty which would involve the whole community and would encourage program consistency. The skeleton organization then would co-ordinate the assessment of community needs, and of currently available resources to meet those needs. The third phase called for focusing upon ways and means of enlisting participation from among both the poor and the not-poor, and of gaining co-operation and support from already existing community agencies. The final phase of the planning was to set the stage for solidifying and expanding the poverty-intervention organization and for beginning the acquisition of additional OEO-funded programing.

The members of the Topeka Welfare Planning Council Subcommittee spent many hours discussing, among themselves and with national and local consultants, the form and direction they could anticipate for the Topeka program. Those discussions and consultations clearly and continually reflected two primary orientations: a social-science orientation, and a political orientation. The social-science orientation, much influenced by the sociologist member of the Subcommittee and the other members' frequent contact with the staff of the Menninger Foundation, emphasized the importance of the participation of the poor for its potential socialization and social-therapy impact. The importance of their participation for effective group process and for facilitating social change was taken to be a fact.

The political orientation emphasized the need for understanding the distribution of responsibility for welfare endeavors among various community organizations, and the place the new poverty-intervention organization would have in that complex. The power "facts of life" were assessed, and consideration was given to ways whereby the intended organization, as a broker for the poor, could upgrade social services and extend the outreach of already existing agencies.

A particular point of view seemed to emerge from the Subcommittee's deliberations—a general method of operation, a *raison d'être*, or what I have labeled and refer to herein as the "Overlap Model" for the amelioration of poverty or social change.

THE OVERLAP MODEL

Mayer Zald has written that a major stage in the thinking about organization for community action is a development of a general model of the enabling process—a model of planned change through client–change-agent relations.[5] Severyn Bruyn agrees, indicating that the idea, concept, or model for the community action came first in the programs he studied, then came the action.[6]

Although the Subcommittee of the Topeka Welfare Planning Council did not explicitly speak of "models" for the amelioration of poverty or social change, its formulations for the proposed Topeka program provide discernible evidence that such a model did in fact evolve. Perhaps the best way to illustrate that implicit model is to present some of its characteristics, as manifested by the expectations of the Subcommittee, and at the same time to contrast its elements with those of another quite different poverty-program model.

Frank Riessman has written that social-action programs which seek to organize the poor on their own behalf could be viewed as falling within one of two camps: those "within the system," and those "outside of the system." Riessman then presents a systematic comparison of two "outside of the system" action programs (The New Student Left and the approach of Saul Alinsky) on such variables as target groups, goals, methods, and philosophic roots. It is Riessman's conclusion that "social actionists functioning outside of the system, and various social planners functioning within the system, have much to gain from mutual contact and exploration. From this union a much more rounded, meaningful strategy of change may emerge together with the necessary theoretic base."[7]

---

[5] Mayer N. Zald, *Organizing for Community Welfare*, p. 34.
[6] Severyn T. Bruyn, *Communities in Action: Pattern and Process*, p. 133.
[7] Frank Riessman, "A Comparison of Two Social Action Approaches: Saul Alinsky and The New Student Left," Albert Einstein College of Medicine, Department of Psychiatry, New York, September, 1965, mimeograph, p. 9.

The model for the poverty program put forth by the Topeka Welfare Planning Council will be presented here as one which purported to work largely "within the system," as an organization funded by the Office of Economic Opportunity, yet intended to bring together disparate components of the community into a single program for social change. I conceptualize that social-action approach as the Overlap Model, shall present its components, and for further clarification, contrast it with the Saul Alinsky Model as summarized by Riessman.[8]

Both the Overlap and the Alinsky Models for poverty intervention stressed the social-therapeutic aspects of active involvement of the poor in endeavors that affected their lives. The Alinsky Model, however, assumed that contrived and open conflict between the poor and some specified "enemies" among the not-poor served to build the self-esteem and confidence of the poor by their awareness of new-found power. To paraphrase one Alinsky organizer:

> The have-nots are entitled to freedom, and to dignity, and to justice just as any other human beings are so entitled. The have-nots should have the same rights and freedoms as the haves. In order to get these rights and privileges, since the consciences and moral beliefs of most of the haves are not operative, then the have-nots must take, as Mr. Alinsky says, "The low road to morality." They must seek ways of gaining power, real power, in the community, and through the gaining of this power, *take* dignity and respect and justice for themselves. It is our intention to provide ways that they can acquire the kinds of powers that they deserve to have as citizens in a democracy.[9]

The tactics which operationalize the Alinsky Model are "whatever serves the purpose": picketing, sit-ins, demonstrations, boycotts, and special harassing techniques (e.g., mailing a box of dead rats from a housing project to the mayor's office, to dramatize the squalid living

---

[8] For a more detailed elaboration of the general poverty-intervention approach of Saul Alinsky, see Saul D. Alinsky, *Reveille for Radicals*, and Saul D. Alinsky, "The War on Poverty—Political Pornography," *Journal of Social Issues*, 21 (January, 1965), 41–48.

[9] Squire Lance, in a speech to the Catholic Interfaith Council, Catholic Chancellory, Kansas City, Missouri, March 23, 1966.

conditions; dumping mounds of garbage collected from the streets
of a poverty district onto the front lawn of the superintendent of
City Sanitation, to protest neglectful garbage service). The philosophic roots for this organizational style, according to Riessman, are
the old cio strategies and leftist tactics.[10]

The Overlap Model, by comparison, expects self-esteem and confidence to grow among the poor as they expand the number and variety of their social roles through active participation in the complex
of the proposed Topeka poverty program. It expects a "we-feeling"
to grow among the Target Neighborhood people as they shape their
action committees, and a sense of power and control to develop as
they evolve expertise in *using* the Establishment to meet their needs
and goals. Furthermore, the Overlap Model expects members of the
various social-economic strata to influence each other, breaking
down stereotypes and opening new lines of communication, as they
work jointly to implement oeo community-action proposals. The
not-poor, as well as the poor, are expected to learn from their participation.

The Overlap Model, like the Alinsky Model, appears to recognize
the social functions of nonviolent conflict, and assumes that such
conflict would be an expected by-product of, and could be a stimulus to, ameliorative social change.[11] However, the perimeters of the
arena for conflict distinguish the two models. The Alinsky approach
assumes a social benefit to the poor by their "digging in" against the
Establishment and "rubbing raw the sores of discontent." The Overlap Model holds that there might be valuable and usable "within
the system" opportunities that could be lost to the poor by more direct "conflict" methods (e.g., agency co-operation, 10 per cent local
funding for community-action proposals, services in kind, job-training programs, housing programs, etc.). Furthermore, directly attacking the Establishment might result in further alienation of the poor,
cutting them off from the opportunity to expand their social roles by
participation in community affairs—a socialization process assumed
to be essential in the Overlap Model. The Overlap Model antici-

[10] Riessman, "A Comparison of Two Social Action Approaches," p. 3.
[11] See Lewis Coser, *The Social Functions of Conflict.*

pates that conflict would be engendered when the poor, as they became more confident and began to realize the power of their participation, would inevitably want to move "too fast" for the co-operating community agencies. The question of *how much* control and *how much* power the poor could take is also seen to be a source of potential conflict. But the Overlap Model assumes that the organizational structure which would operationalize it would provide a "within the system" setting for such struggles, and maintain a climate of give-and-take that in itself would have a socialization effect upon all the participants.

Both the Overlap and Alinsky Models emphasize the organization of residents in poor neighborhoods, including all socio-economic levels, ethnic and religious groups, and educational levels within these neighborhoods. But operationally the Alinsky organization consists primarily of low-income members of ethnic minorities in a specific neighborhood. The Overlap Model intends not only that broad representative participation would be obtained from within each low-income neighborhood, but also that participation and commitment would be obtained on a community-wide basis. The Overlap Model views the community as a dynamic totality in which the neighborhood is a functional part, and expects poverty intervention to be a mutual, interlocking, and concerted effort.

The Alinsky Model encourages rapid, hard-hitting intervention, with little consideration about the direction that social change might take beyond a three-year term of local gains. The Overlap Model hopes to espouse a poverty-intervention organization which, intended increasingly to be run by beneficiaries of the program, can look for the slower, more cumbersome socialization processes to create, in the long run, more enduring and stable community social change. Community agencies are not to be labeled as "enemies," but are to be invited to grow and challenged to be flexible. In the Alinsky view, agency change under such circumstances would be improbable, since the poor do not possess the necessary "clout" to influence change. The Overlap Model's use of a loud and well-timed "We invite you to participate with the neighborhood people" is thought to have considerable and ever increasing "clout" because poverty has become a national issue, and ameliorative programs quite in vogue. Many of the potentially participating local agencies, whose counterparts in other communities have been targets of protest groups, are expected by the Overlap Model to see that approach as less threatening. Since those agencies are not protest-oriented, the poor in Topeka are expected to be able to use their more moderate approach with advantage, to "get more flies with honey."

In other words, according to the Overlap Model, there may be times when the poor find it necessary to try to "beat the system," but also times when, instead, they should try to "use the system." Essentially, the choice of action model is taken to depend upon the characteristics of the community itself.

The Alinsky Model holds that there is only so much power available in a given community. For the poor to have some, the not-poor must lose some.[12] The Overlap Model assumes a community to be a relatively open power-system, and contends that power does not necessarily have to be taken from the Establishment to empower the poor. Rather, the development of leadership among the poor, and their increased facility in "within the system" social roles, would add to the sum total of community resources.

The Alinsky Model avoids guarantees to the *status quo* that might be built into a poverty-intervention program imposed upon a community "from above." "Within the system" OEO programs often have fallen prey to various political machinations. The Topeka program was to be funded by Washington and advised by a staff of federal employees and thus would be, in that sense, imposed from above. However, the Overlap Model purports to provide system expertise and meaningful participation to representatives from low-income areas, and to invite their increasing control as they become more and more expert.

The Alinsky Model, in communities where it has been successful, has involved more neighborhood people faster than was expected by the Overlap Model. The degree to which the people would be involved, and the stability of their involvement in community as well

[12] Riessman, "A Comparison of Two Social Action Approaches," p. 5.

as neighborhood affairs, was considered to be another question. The hypothesis was that the Overlap Model, in Topeka as an appropriate community, would provide wider and more stable involvement toward more lasting social change.

The Subcommittee members of the Topeka Welfare Planning Council felt that the approach of Saul Alinsky, along with his Industrial Areas Foundation, was unsuitable for Topeka. On the other hand, neither did they think that a totally "City Hall" approach to the amelioration of poverty would be appropriate. They wanted an approach which would be somewhere in between, one which would implement the mandates of the Economic Opportunity Act and give opportunity for representative community involvement—with special emphasis upon the benefits of involving the poor in determining the program.

The Overlap Model, the term with which I have labeled the crystallization of the Subcommittee's endeavors, is similar in many ways to the models for action typologized by observers in other community settings. It is similar to the "co-determination" strategy advocated by Shostak,[13] the "third party" antipoverty intervention suggested by Rein and Riessman,[14] the "assertive" strategy observed by Witmer and Winter,[15] and the change strategy outlined by Bredemeier.[16] Further, the Overlap Model seems to include what Ross

[13] Arthur B. Shostak, "Promoting Participation of the Poor: Philadelphia's Anti-Poverty Program," *Social Work*, 11 (January, 1966), 65–72; and Arthur B. Shostak, "Containment, Co-Optation, or Co-Determination?" *American Child*, November, 1965, 1–5.

[14] Martin Rein and Frank Riessman, "A Strategy for Anti-Poverty Community Action Programs," *Social Work*, 11 (April, 1966), 3–12.

[15] Lawrence Witmer and Gibson Winter, "Strategies of Power in Community Organizations," Chicago, University of Chicago, 1968, mimeograph.

[16] Harry C. Bredemeier, "Suggestions to Communities for Participation in the War on Poverty," Rutgers University, Urban Study Center, New Brunswick, New Jersey, 1964, mimeograph. For additional discussions of models for community action and social change, see George M. Beal, "How Does Social Change Occur?" Iowa State University, RS-384, Cooperative Extension Service, Ames, Iowa, February, 1962; Wendell Bell and Maryanne Force, "Urban Neighborhood Types and Participation in Formal Associations," *American Sociological Review*, 21 (February, 1956), 146–156; Harry C. Bredemeier, "New Strategies for the War on Poverty," *Trans-Action*, 2 (November–December, 1964), 3–8;

refers to as the "reform," "planning," "process," and "therapy" orientations of social intervention[17] and the "medicalizing" and "normalizing" orientations toward the poor delineated by Rainwater.[18]

The Subcommittee members of the Topeka Welfare Planning Council thought the rationale for the Topeka poverty program, presented here as the Overlap Model, was the most sensible and potentially most workable for the community in which they lived. Fur-

---

Bruyn, *Communities in Action*; Edmund Burke, "Citizen Participation in Renewal," *Journal of Housing*, 23 (January, 1966), 18–25; Robert Chin, "The Utility of System Models and Developmental Models for Practitioners," in Warren G. Bennis, Kenneth D. Benne, and Robert Chin (eds.), *The Planning of Change: Readings in the Applied Behavioral Sciences*, pp. 201–214; Amitai Etzioni and Eva Etzioni (eds.), *Social Change: Sources, Patterns and Consequences*; William A. Gamson, "Community Power Research and Community Action," paper given at the American Sociological Association, San Francisco, California, 1967; Arnold Gurin and Joan Levin Ecklein, "Community Organization for What? Political Power or Service Delivery?" Brandeis University, Waltham, Massachusetts, mimeograph; Michael Harrington, *The Other America: Poverty in the United States*; Floyd Hunter, Ruth C. Schaffer, and Cecil G. Sheps, *Community Organization: Action and Inaction*; William H. Key, "Controlled Intervention—The Helping Professions and Directed Social Change," *American Journal of Orthopsychiatry*, 36, 3 (April, 1966), 400–409; Richard T. LaPiere, *Social Change*; Sar A. Levitan, "The Design of Antipoverty Strategy," in Ben B. Seligman, *Aspects of Poverty*, pp. 238–287; Ronald Lippitt, Jeanne Watson, and Bruce Westley, *The Dynamics of Planned Change*; Eleanor Maccoby, Joseph Johnson, and Russell Church, "Community Integration and the Social Control of Juvenile Delinquency," *Journal of Social Issues*, 14, 3 (1958), 38–51; S. M. Miller and Martin Rein, "The War on Poverty: Perspectives and Prospects," in Ben B. Seligman, *Poverty as a Public Issue*; Peter Rossi and Robert A. Dentler, *The Politics of Urban Renewal: The Chicago Findings*; Christopher Sauer, John Holland, Kenneth Tiedke, and Walter Freeman, *Community Involvement*; Philip Selznick, *TVA and the Grass Roots*; Roberta Sigel, "Citizen Committees—Advice vs. Consent, *Trans-Action*, 4 (May, 1967), 47–52; Hans B. C. Spiegel, *Citizen Participation in Urban Development*, Vol. 1, *Concepts and Issues*; Roland L. Warren, *The Community in America*; Roland L. Warren, "Types of Purposive Social Action at the Community Level," No. 11, *Papers in Social Welfare*, pp. 17–30; James Q. Wilson, "Planning and Politics: Citizen Participation in Urban Renewal," *Journal of the American Institute of Planners*, 29 (November, 1963), 47–52.

[17] Murray G. Ross, *Case Histories in Community Organization*.

[18] Lee Rainwater, "Neutralizing the Disinherited: Some Psychological Aspects of Understanding the Poor," Washington University, St. Louis, Missouri, 1967, mimeograph.

thermore, they felt that the goals they had set for the local poverty program were very much in keeping with the expectations of the Office of Economic Opportunity.

On May 1, 1968, the Topeka Welfare Planning Council received the Planning and Development Grant from the Office of Economic Opportunity. The Subcommittee members now were faced with the task of designing a poverty-intervention organization which would operationalize the rationale and goals, reflected in the Overlap Model, they had determined for the Topeka poverty program.

CHAPTER 2

The Topeka Office of Economic Opportunity

As soon as the oeo Planning and De-
velopment Grant funds had been transferred to the community,
the Topeka Welfare Planning Council began to implement the poverty program. The Council Subcommittee formally established a
skeleton poverty-intervention organization with the name "Topeka
Office of Economic Opportunity" (toeo), and leased office space
in one of the low-income neighborhoods. The Subcommittee hired
a director (a white Methodist minister, three times elected from a
poverty area to the Kansas State Legislature, a former research
associate in the Menninger Foundation, and a Council Subcommittee member), an assistant director (a Mexican-American working
man who had fifteen years' experience as a union and civil-rights

organizer and official), and an office manager (a Negro housewife-secretary who had been a leader in local youth and church programs). Together with Subcommittee members, the new TOEO staff began to design the intervention organization, and to plan in greater detail the community's "War on Poverty."

In line with the Overlap Model, the staff of the TOEO proclaimed the purposes of that poverty-intervention organization to be:

(1) To give a voice to the voiceless and a face to the faceless; (2) To provide an opportunity for low-income persons to develop their programs; (3) To provide a working exchange between members of all socio-economic classes—an exchange that will hopefully engender social change; and (4) To contribute to the developing theories of social change.[1]

To accommodate those goals, to provide machinery for planning and implementing community-action proposals, and as a means for encouraging community participation, the TOEO staff and the Council Subcommittee developed a complex of committees. The first of these, considered to be temporary and called the "City-wide Committee," was composed of the TOEO staff, the Subcommittee, and twenty representatives from the community at large.

Through the City-wide Committee, the TOEO then established a set of eleven "Study Committees," whose titles indicate their functions: Education, Housing, Recreation, Employment, Health, Community Social Services, Legislative Change, Ongoing Structure and Application Review, Public Assistance, Rural Affairs, and Small Business Loans. Each committee was to deal only with its own specific topic, have its own elected officers, and have a membership of persons who were specialists in that particular field and of representatives from low-income areas. The committees were to assess community needs and resources, and make suggestions about future poverty programing.

Concerned that the complex of committees still did not afford the poor enough opportunity for participation, the TOEO staff, through the City-wide Committee, designated twelve "Target Neighbor-

[1] Topeka Office of Economic Opportunity, *Annual Report for 1965–1966*, Topeka, Kansas, p. 11.

hoods," which had by census and agency reports manifested high indices of poverty and blight. Each of these geographic areas was to have a "Target Neighborhood Committee" composed of residents, with elected officers, which through at least monthly meetings would serve as a forum for neighborhood needs and problems. The TOEO staff stated that it would depend upon the Target Neighborhood Committees to provide "a channel for communication and activity" between the poor and the not-poor, to act as "a training ground for activity, citizenship, and leadership" among the poor, to "look clearly at their own Neighborhood to see not only problems but also possible solutions," and to initiate action proposals.[2]

Lastly, it was determined that the City-wide Committee would evolve into "The Economic Opportunity Board of Shawnee County, Kansas, Inc." The Board would be composed of no more than seventy-five voting members: the chairmen and vice-chairmen (Target Neighborhood Officers) of Target Neighborhood Committees, the chairmen of Study Committees, representatives from local agencies, and, under the heading "citizens at large," business and professional men, religious and civil-rights leaders, and other concerned persons.

As structured, the Board would have at least one-third elected representation from among the poor (the Target Neighborhood Officers), and would be empowered with final approval of all poverty-program budgetary, personnel, and programing matters. As soon as the Board was legally incorporated, members of the TOEO staff were to become its employees and the Topeka Welfare Planning Council was to terminate its role as a steering body.

The TOEO staff and the Subcommittee developed the committee complex on three assumptions: (1) That the over-all structure would best implement the mandate of the Economic Opportunity Act and would provide meaningful participation of the poor. (2) That the *process experience* of the indigent participants would increase their social roles and skills, whereby they might acquire more power or control vis-à-vis those community elements which af-

2 *Ibid.*, pp. 2–7.

fected their lives. (3) That the equal-status pursuit of mutual goals (community-action proposals) by members from disparate socio-economic levels, working together in structured social situations (Board and Study Committee meetings), would break down stereotypes, encourage communication, broaden understanding, and engender social change. The Director of the TOEO wrote about his poverty-intervention organization as follows:

What is the Topeka program trying to do? What makes the Economic Opportunity Program different from the many hundreds of other committees already in existence?

The TOEO is not going to supplant or eliminate existing social services. Its purpose is to highlight the positive benefits which can be derived from the Economic Opportunity Act and the many other programs which are geared to upgrading the individual and his family. These benefits include education, job counseling, day-care services, Head Start and others. This unusual legislation is trying to encourage advance planning for the increasing number of social problems which are facing our rural-to-urban society. The TOEO is available for Topekans who wish to help themselves, their neighborhood, and their community.

The Economic Opportunity Act is different from the many other Federal programs because it involves the receivers or the beneficiaries of the program in the planning, developing, and executing of any community action projects. The Act also emphasizes the need for a high degree of cooperation between private and public helping agencies. The Topeka plan is designed to carry out the intent of the Act.

This is a program involving social change. The Topeka plan, however, does not see any lasting importance in helping one or two persons over a period of several months. It is interested in bringing about those changes which will affect a significant number of low-income persons over an extended period of time.

The Topeka plan is styled along the lines of grass roots democracy, combining a New England town meeting with the Kansas House of Representatives. The power of the people is not seen as a threat, but rather as a necessary and desirable weapon in the war on poverty. People living together in cities or on farms develop problems which cannot be solved in isolation or by simple, individual effort. The Topeka plan provides the opportunity for citizens to participate actively in the transactions of society, and to school them in the benefits of our society which have not been possible before this time.

Through its massive committee structure and its generously sized Board, there is the opportunity to set up lines of communication which have previously been broken. . . .

The Topeka Plan is a New England town meeting in the sense that through its Neighborhood and Study Committee meetings any person who is interested in the program or has problems can come and freely express his thoughts. The Study and Neighborhood Committees sift ideas as do the Standing Committees and the House of Representatives. In each case the committees are responsible for making recommendations to the larger body. In each situation, an element of learning takes place as each person bumps his ideas against those of other persons. In this exchange ideas are refined and redefined in the public arena.

The Economic Opportunity Board functions in the same way as the House of Representatives as it passes on legislative matters. The Board is called upon to debate, demand, and then approve or disapprove the recommendations coming from the neighborhood or study committees. Through this kind of inter-relationship, the persons working in the new Economic Opportunity Program will indeed see that there is a new-found freedom of expression and action through the program, which is at the same time coupled with a high degree of responsibility. People in the program should begin to assume a more active and creative part in society.

No effective and comprehensive program such as OEO can continue without understanding what it is about, where it is going and how it is going to function. What can be accomplished by bringing together people with enduring hardships and people of good will and positions of power? What can be done in a spirit of cooperation, compromise, and negotiation?

From the beginning of the Topeka program the assumption was made that effective and long-term social change requires far more than the lower class person talking to the low-income person, or middle class people or an agency personnel getting together to cluck about the problems of poverty in Topeka. A new kind of organization was needed which would draw together people of diverse background and experience from segments of the city of Topeka under one umbrella. The governing body of OEO in Topeka must be truly representative of the city to build on the good base of cooperation which already exists between the citizenry, the agencies, organizations, and institutions. The Board is structured in such a way that the low-income person works *together* with the comfortable.

Through this cooperative exchange, feelings of distress can be replaced with feelings of trust, suspicion replaced with confidence, disrespect replaced with respect and dignity. Who can better teach middle-class ways of living and striving than the middle-class persons? Who can better break down false impressions and ideas of low-income persons than the person himself!

The Topeka program operates in a free and open way encouraging all interested persons to participate. OEO did not come into the city on a white charger to strike down the foe of "the establishment." OEO developed with a spirit of cooperation and a desire to supplement existing social services. The objective is to involve persons from the Target Neighborhood, agency personnel, and citizens-at-large in the shaping of the program. These representative persons serving on a county-wide Board are called upon not to endorse the *status quo* nor to march militantly on city hall.

This is an accurate picture of the Board which is not interested in short term gains, but is much more concerned with changing attitudes, modifying agency procedures, developing more openness toward low-income persons, bringing in new programs to work directly with low-income persons, and finally, making the opportunities of American society available to the maximum number of people in Topeka.[3]

The TOEO staff outlined the process by which they expected various community-action proposals to be developed through the committee structure. Ideas for specific projects to meet specific needs were to flow from the Study Committees and Neighborhood Committees. The TOEO would make an initial write-up of a proposal, which then would be reviewed by the Target Neighborhood Committees. The Ongoing Structure and Application Review Committee of the Economic Opportunity Board would evaluate the proposal, and, if it approved, would recommend that the TOEO write it up in final form. The final form would be presented to the Board for vote. If the vote was favorable, the proposal would be forwarded to the regional Office of Economic Opportunity, and, if appropriate, to the Office of Economic Opportunity in Washington, D.C. Funded proposals would then be reviewed by the governor of Kansas, who

[3] *Ibid.*, pp. 7–9.

would in turn notify the TOEO that funding for the project was available. The project then would be implemented in the Target Neighborhoods, with the co-operation of the Target Neighborhood Committees.[4]

"ON MIDDLE GROUND"

The structure and intended functions of the TOEO very much reflected the expectations of the Overlap Model. Furthermore, the organizational style of the TOEO reflected the legislative experience of its Director. According to him, the "key words" for "the Topeka Plan" were "Compromise, Communication, Negotiation, Cooperation, Evolution, and Representative Democracy."[5] His references to a "New England town meeting" and the "House of Representatives," as analogous to different committee structures in the TOEO, further indicated the influence of his political experience. The Director wrote:

An all out effort to keep "everyone" on board is needed to achieve program ends. To keep "everyone" aboard means that everyone is genuinely involved in the total process of decision making. The "ins" and "outs" must hobnob together. The University President needs to sit down with the janitor. The social scientist needs to visit with the carpenter. The housewife needs to get to know the cook. The agency person needs to get caught in the cross fire of generations of resentment. The persons from the Target Neighborhoods need to see, sense, and know that social change takes time. . . . The Topeka program rests on middle ground, reaching out and including all actions and efforts for social change.[6]

The TOEO was thus planned to occupy and sustain a marginal position between the community poor and the not-poor, and to provide a vehicle for their functional interaction toward poverty programming. Earlier, I conceptualized the poverty-program rationale and goals that evolved from the deliberations of the Topeka Welfare Planning Council as the "Overlap Model." Now I conceptualize the

[4] *Ibid.*, p. 14.
[5] *Ibid.*, p. 10.
[6] *Ibid.*, p. 10.

marginal position of the TOEO, the poverty-intervention organization designed to operationalize that model, as "Functional Marginality." It was expected that the TOEO, by maintaining a "middle ground" between the poor and the not-poor, and particularly between the officers of the Target Neighborhood Committees and agency representatives, would be able to stimulate and implement an effective amelioration of poverty and bring about lasting social change.

In a case study of another poverty program, Wilson and Bennett describe a poverty-intervention organization as a coalition intended to provide a transitional framework, in which a range of groups can contribute toward limited objectives. They suggest that a coalition so developed must attempt to provide the basic conditions for each participant to balance his inducements for participation with his contributions through participation. They further suggest that poverty-intervention organizations are generally negotiated into existence by choosing objectives that to some extent serve the goals of all participants.[7] The TOEO similarly was intended to encourage a

[7] Charles E. Wilson and Adrienne S. Bennett, "Participation in Community Action Organizations: Some Theoretical Insights," *Sociological Inquiry*, 37, 2 (Spring, 1968), 191–203. For other discussions of the organizational characteristics of poverty-intervention organizations, see Burtram M. Beck, "Knowledge and Skills in Administration of an Anti-Poverty Program," *Social Work*, 11, 3 (July, 1966), 102–106; George Brager and Frances P. Purcell (eds.), *Community Action Against Poverty*; Martin L. Cohnstaedt and Peter Irons, "A Head Start for Community Organizations," paper presented to the Society for the Study of Social Problems, American Sociological Association Meetings, Miami Beach, Florida, August, 1966; Louis A. Ferman, Joyce L. Kornbluh, Alan Haber (eds.), *Poverty in America*; Leo Fishman (ed.), *Poverty Amid Affluence*; Florence Heller Graduate School for Advanced Studies in Social Welfare, "Community Representation in Community Action Programs," Report No. 1 (February, 1968), Brandeis University, Waltham, Massachusetts; Margaret Gordon, *Poverty in America*; Berton H. Kaplan (ed.), "Poverty Dynamics and Interventions," *Journal of Social Issues* (entire issue), 21 (January, 1965), 1–153; Howard B. Kaplan, "Implementation of Program Change in Community Agencies," *Milbank Memorial Fund Quarterly*, 45 (July, 1967), 321–332; Kirschner Associates, "A Description and Evaluation of Neighborhood Centers," Albuquerque, New Mexico, December, 1966, mimeograph; Ralph M. Kramer, *Participation of the Poor*; Ralph M. Kramer and Clare Denton, "Organization of a Community Action Program: A Comparative Case Study," *Social Work*, 12, 4 (October, 1967), 68–80; Elliott A. Krause, "Functions of a Bureaucratic Ideology: 'Citizen Participation,'" *Social Problems*, 16 (Fall, 1968), 129–143;

28 Poverty Warriors

coalition among representatives from different socio-economic levels of the community, and intended to do so by assuming a position of Functional Marginality amid those representatives.

RECRUITING POVERTY WARRIORS

As the TOEO Director and Assistant Director attempted to enlist members of the community to serve on the various committees, they discovered a recruitment dilemma. The pervading attitude to TOEO's early efforts was community indifference. The first response of several of those individuals who did show interest (other than the Council Subcommittee members) was concern with the *intervention* angle of the program. The TOEO, intervening in the "quasi-stationary equilibrium" of the community, was warily viewed by: (1) Some local-government officials who perceived it to be a potential "federal power grab." (2) A few welfare professionals who saw it as a threat to their competencies. (3) A number of traditional mediators for the poor (e.g., ministers, officers of civil-rights groups) who perceived it to be a threat to their mediation role. (4) Some not-poor members of the community who saw it potentially "stirring up trouble" and "turning loose *those* people on the community." (5) Many of the poor themselves who suspected a "con job," and

---

Peter Marris and Martin Rein, *Dilemmas of Social Reform: Poverty and Community Action in the United States*; Hanna H. Meissner (ed.), *Poverty in the Affluent Society*; Melvin B. Mogulof, "A Developmental Approach to the Community Action Program Idea," *Social Work*, 12, 2 (April, 1967), 12–20; Daniel Patrick Moynihan, *Maximum Feasible Misunderstanding: Community Action in the War on Poverty*; Frank Riessman, Jerome Cohen, and Arthur Pearl, *Mental Health of the Poor*; Aaron L. Rutledge and Gertrude Zemon Gass, *Nineteen Negro Men*; Shostak, *Social Work*, 11 (January, 1966), 65–72, and *American Child*, November, 1965, 1–5; Arthur B. Shostak and William Gomberg (eds.), *New Perspectives on Poverty*; Ben B. Seligman, *Poverty as a Public Issue*; Ben B. Seligman, *Aspects of Poverty*; Hans B. C. Spiegel, *Neighborhood Power and Control: Implications for Urban Planning*, Document No. PB 183176, U.S. Department of Commerce, Springfield, Virginia, 1967; John B. Turner and Arthur Blum, "Action and Knowledge Gaps in Neighborhood Organization," paper presented at the National Association of Social Workers' Council on Community Planning and Development, Cleveland, Ohio, December 4–6, 1968; Witmer and Winter, "Strategies of Power in Community Organizations."

perceived it to be nothing different from, nor less manipulative than, any other agency in which they had no say. Furthermore, and rather paradoxically, there seemed to be a "Let's not rock the boat" attitude among residents of the low-income areas, an attitude which also, at least in part, probably accounted for the general lack of militancy in that group.[8]

Those staff strategies which often convinced agency, business, or government officials to co-operate with the TOEO seemed to be those which discouraged the poor from becoming involved. To get representatives from the community power-structure "aboard," the TOEO staff talked of policy, guidelines, "paced" social change, standardized procedures, spheres of operation. The members of the staff represented themselves as competent *agency* officials, who knew and used the language and practices of bureaucracy.[9] The impersonality, abstract rationales, and distant policies seem, however, mainly to have convinced the poor that the TOEO would be "just another one of those agencies that tell us what we can have and what we can do." On the other hand, the Target Neighborhood residents seemed to respond when the staff members made an effort to become known to them as persons rather than as titled officials.[10]

The TOEO Director and Assistant Director solved their recruitment dilemma by a division of labor. The Director, drawing upon his experience as a legislator and a minister, concentrated primarily upon the community power-structure. His political ability and bureaucratic expertise eventually won the co-operation and participation of most of the city's key agency and government officials. The Assistant Director, drawing upon his experience as a union organ-

---

[8] For discussions of similar resistances in other settings, see George Brager, "Organizing the Unaffiliated in a Low-Income Area," in Ferman, Kornbluh, and Haber (eds.), *Poverty in America*, pp. 390–395; George Criminger, "A Neighborhood House Leads the Way," in R. Franklin (ed.), *Patterns of Community Development*, pp. 97–104; and Frances Piven, "Participation of Residents in Neighborhood Community Action Programs," *Social Work*, 11, 1 (January, 1966), 73–80.

[9] A "universalistic" approach. See Talcott Parsons and Edward A. Shils (eds.), *Toward a General Theory of Action*, pp. 76–79.

[10] A "particularistic" approach, *ibid.*

izer, gradually gained the confidence and participation of Target Neighborhood residents because he was "a regular guy, just like us, and we got to know him as a person."

During their efforts to attract participants to the developing TOEO committee complex, both the Director and Assistant Director manifested considerable charismatic behavior. The Assistant Director more closely enacted the classic Weberian charisma when recruiting Target Neighborhood residents. He eschewed confining organization and rigid rules, preached the urgency of "changing times" and the "Great Society," enthusiastically and dramatically proclaimed the new cause heralded by "maximum feasible participation," exhorted all to "get on the band wagon," and emphasized the *process goals* of the TOEO. The Director, though he appealed to the not-poor with such bureaucratic abstractions as "increased agency outreach" and "maximization of services" and emphasized the *content goals* of the TOEO, seemed, nonetheless, charismatic in his interactions with agency and local-government officials. The Director's behavior might be representative of a leadership or authority type generated in and by modern bureaucracy, a type which might be called "bureaucharisma."[11]

By October, 1965, six months after the TOEO had been established, it was fully operational as a poverty-intervention organization. All the Study Committees had been formed, were meeting, and were contributing to a general assessment of community needs. Most of the Target Neighborhood Committees had elected officers, and were regularly conducting meetings. The Economic Opportunity Board had been incorporated, was operating as the major decision-making body of the poverty program, and had filled sixty-four of the seventy-five member slots allotted. By the end of the next month, two OEO community-action proposals (one for a day-care center and the other for an extension-worker program) had, as intended, slowly coursed through the entire committee complex and were submitted to Washington for approval and subsequent funding. The pro-

[11] For a general discussion of the characteristics of charisma, see Hans H. Gerth and C. Wright Mills (trans. and eds.), *From Max Weber: Essays in Sociology*, pp. 196–204.

cedure for reviewing the local proposals was slow—"inefficient" by bureaucratic standards—but it did allow greater participation of the poor in decision-making than might have a more "streamlined" procedure. Approximately five hundred participants, most of them poor, had at differing levels participated in the preparation of the proposals.

CHAPTER 3

Dilemmas and Staff Stresses

SOME THEORISTS have postulated that it is a prerequisite for goals to concur before community action can occur. Bruyn, for example, writes that "community sentiment" and a consensually validated "set of beliefs" are necessary "for any association to survive in effective operation in the community."[1] Holland, Tiedke, and Miller state that "in order for action to take place at all, there must be some convergence of interests of those actors in the social system who had appropriate sentiments, beliefs, and/

[1] Severyn T. Bruyn, *Communities in Action: Pattern and Process*, pp. 128–129.

or rationally calculated purposes with references to a problem."² The TOEO, striving to operationalize the Economic Opportunity Act and the Overlap Model, introduced two distinct sets of goals for which it sought community consensus: the program *content* available through OEO community-action proposals, and the "maximum feasible participation" *process* experience for the poor. Both of those goals were foreign to established patterns of community action. In such case, the model of consensus–then action–then change is not an accurate theoretical sequence for the TOEO. To seek consensus for the goals of innovative content and process impinged upon entrenched attitudes, role expectations, social habits and organizational policies, and was, *in itself,* action with potential for social change.

The TOEO's dual goals of program *content* and participation *process,* and the diversity of membership in its committee complex, make it difficult to isolate as a specific type of formal organization. The TOEO does, however, seem to fall into Etzioni's category, "multipurpose organization," and manifests the goal conflicts and staff-role strain he sees as unavoidable in that type.³ Perhaps the complexity of the TOEO as a type of formal organization is best revealed by considering Blau and Scott's four classifications based upon "prime beneficiary": (1) "mutual benefit associations," in which the prime beneficiary is the membership; (2) "business concerns," in which the owners are prime beneficiaries; (3) "service organizations," in which the client group is the prime beneficiary; and (4) "commonweal organizations," in which the prime beneficiary is the public at large.⁴ If one considers the process experiences of the poor when participating in decisions which determine the conduct of the TOEO, the organization becomes a "mutual benefit associa-

---

² John B. Holland, Kenneth E. Tiedke, and Paul A. Miller, "A Theoretical Model for Health Action," *Rural Sociology,* 22 (June, 1957), 149–155. See also James W. Green and Selz C. Mayo, "A Framework for Research in the Actions of Community Groups," *Social Forces,* 31 (May, 1953), 323–326.

³ Amitai Etzioni, *Modern Organizations,* pp. 14–16.

⁴ Peter M. Blau and W. Richard Scott, *Formal Organizations,* p. 43.

tion." When one observes the do-*for*-the-poor inclinations of agency and local-government participants, and the services rendered to the poor not participating in the committee complex, the TOEO becomes a "service organization." If one considers the staff rewards for management efficiency and positive cost-benefit analysis, the TOEO loosely becomes a "business concern." Finally, if the poverty program is seen to be a benefit to the entire community, the TOEO becomes a "commonweal organization." The diversity of the TOEO indicates the many hats that had to be worn by its staff, and the vast complexity of expectations for the staff from among members of the community at large.

Bruyn describes two ideal models for community action: the "community council" approach and the "self-study" approach.[5] Zald describes community-action organizations according to the goal dimensions of "change orientation" and "service orientation."[6] The TOEO incorporates characteristics of both of Bruyn's ideal types and Zald's orientations, further indicating its operational complexity, and the challenges to its staff. Wilson and Bennett observe that community-action organizations, specifically poverty-intervention organizations, are "generally negotiated into existence by choosing objectives that to some extent serve the goals of all the participants. . . . There is no best set of rules for negotiating goals for a community action organization. It is reasonably clear, however, that negotiations must recognize the aspirations, the relative power positions, and internal structure of the various groups."[7] It was the TOEO staff's task, by no means an easy one, to "negotiate" the implementation of goals, and to recognize such aspirations, power positions, and internal structures—as well as to accommodate the expectations underlying those factors. Writing about the disparity between the formally stated goals of the Economic Opportunity Act and the real-

[5] Bruyn, *Communities in Action*, p. 41.
[6] Mayer N. Zald, *Organizing for Community Welfare*, p. 46.
[7] Charles E. Wilson and Adrienne S. Bennett, "Participation in Community Action Organizations: Some Theoretical Insights," *Sociological Inquiry*, 37, 2, (Spring, 1968), 195.

istic expectations of what a poverty-intervention organization can do within a given time, Mogulof states:

> Those who are enraptured with "innovation" and "social change" must also recognize that it is crucial for the community action agency to deal initially with the need to establish and maintain itself. It must demonstrate its credibility as an agency by winning funds; it must legitimate itself with the organizations in its environment (some of whom have won their own legitimacy by creating the illusion of effectively dealing with the problems of poverty).

> It is highly likely that a community action agency subjected to such expectations will be under severe strain. On the one hand it is expected to achieve such goals as "innovation," "social change," "coordination," and "comprehensiveness"; at the same time its organizational tasks deal with "establishment," "maintenance," "credibility," and "legitimation."[8]

The TOEO staff, by implementing the Overlap Model through Functional Marginality, was constantly resolving the dissonance between "reality" and the diverse expectations of program participants. During meetings of the Economic Opportunity Board, TOEO staff members were in the middle of exchanges between members. They were in the middle of squabbles among agency officials, and between those officials and Target Neighborhood Officers concerning the implementation of poverty programs. They were central in the group dynamics throughout the stages of development of Target Neighborhood Committees. The staff members were under the scrutiny of citizens in the community at large, the local press, the regional and national OEO, and research observers. The TOEO Director and Assistant Director, as a rule and not an exception, spent sixteen or seventeen hours a day amid the controversy and conflict endemic to planned social intervention.

---

[8] Melvin B. Mogulof, "A Developmental Approach to the Community Action Program Idea," *Social Work*, 12, 2 (April, 1967), 14. See also Ralph Segalman, "Dramatis Personae of the Community Action Program: A 'Built-In' Conflict Situation," *Rocky Mountain Social Science Journal*, 4 (October, 1967), 140–150; and Burtram M. Beck, "Knowledge and Skills in Administration of an Anti-Poverty Program," *Social Work*, 11, 3 (July, 1966), 102–106.

"FEELING OUT OF TOUCH"

Earlier it was mentioned that the TOEO Director assumed responsibility for recruiting participants from among the not-poor members of the community. The Assistant Director had the responsibility
of recruiting indigenous participation (leaders from among the
poor). That division of labor proved efficacious for "getting people
on board," but it later engendered staff stresses within the TOEO. If
the Target Neighborhood residents made an autonomous program-
move that was perceived by an agency to be inappropriate, the Director often would be criticized by that agency for "not being able
to control the program." If Target Neighborhood Committee members felt their plans had been restricted by an agency, they usually
accused the Assistant Director of "being more interested in pleasing
the agencies than in working with us." The strategies which appeared to stimulate initial participation of the poor and the not-poor
seemed also, until the new roles were more clearly understood, to
develop unrealistic expectations for power and control of the program among both the poor and the not-poor alike. The frustrations
of unfulfilled expectations typically were vented upon the TOEO staff.

It was impossible for the Director and Assistant Director continu-
ously to maintain their contrived division of labor. For example, at
Board meetings they had to interact with both poor and not-poor
participants. Merton noted that any single position involves the individual in not one but a whole set of role relations and expectations,
inherent in which is the possibility for conflicting expectations. He
further observed that a person usually avoids conflicting demands
by the fact that he does not have contacts with all members of his
role-set at once. Thus he can live up to the expectations of some at
one time, and others at another time.[9] Clearly the positions of the
TOEO Director and Assistant Director supported role-sets which contained conflicting expectations of the publics served. Further, the
TOEO rationale of bringing together members from disparate socio-
economic components of the community encouraged the likelihood

    [9] Robert K. Merton, "The Role-Set," *British Journal of Sociology*, 8 (June,
1957), 106–120.

of the staff's experiencing conflicting expectations. Goldner reported that "boundary roles," like those of the Director and Assistant Director, could facilitate an individual's ability to "bridge" disparate publics, but could also result in his being held suspect by those publics.[10]

The Director was acutely aware of the importance of the "maximum feasible participation" of the poor in the poverty program. Yet often his attempts to involve the poor, particularly in meaningful levels of program control, brought anxious comments from agency officials: "You're moving the program too fast; slow down, or you're going to lose middle-class participation." "It's a poor administrator who doesn't run programs through proper channels." Realistically, the Director knew that he needed agency co-operation not just to implement the Overlap Model, but to acquire the cash and services in kind which would make it possible for the community to acquire OEO's 90 per cent of program funding. Topeka is a fairly small city, and such funds and services in kind were very hard to come by. Therefore, the Director spent a good proportion of his time in conference with agency officials, professionals, and local businessmen, frankly courting their help. On the other hand, he felt that in his pursuit of middle-class participation he was losing contact with the poor. He stated, disappointedly:

"I think the Target Neighborhood residents are feeling out of touch with me. They don't want to look upon me the same way they look upon the mayor, as someone distant and far away. I think they need more personal contact than that, and I think I should get more involved in the Neighborhoods."

A few of the Target Neighborhood Officers, during interviews, verified the Director's intuition. Said one, "I don't know, but it seems the Director's changed somehow since he took the job. When he

---

[10] Fred H. Goldner, "Organizations and Their Environment: Roles at Their Boundary," paper read at the meeting of the American Sociological Association, New York, 1960. See also Robert L. Kahn, Donald M. Wolfe, Robert P. Quinn, J. Diedrick Snoek, and Robert A. Rosenthal, *Organizational Stress: Studies in Role Conflict and Ambiguity.*

was a minister, we used to see a lot of him around here. Now we don't see him so much, and we wonder why." Another commented, "I notice we call him 'Doctor' now. We used to call him 'Reverend,' but he was closer to us then."

The Assistant Director, although his task was primarily to work with Target Neighborhood residents, felt a similar frustration. As the TOEO grew in size, and its portfolio of programs increased, he had to spend more time in the office with what he referred to as "that damned paper work." At one point, after the TOEO had been in operation for almost two years, he angrily commented, "Damn it! My job description says I'm supposed to spend 65 per cent of my time in the Neighborhoods. But I can't get away! I can't get out of this office! I probably don't spend 15 per cent of my time in the Neighborhoods anymore." He continued:

"I'm beginning to lose it with the Neighborhood Officers. They used to say things to me much more directly, but I don't think they do anymore. Hell, one of them teased me the other day because I was out of the office. He told me if I wasn't careful that fresh air would kill me!"

The division of labor, so long as it held up, also engendered some conflict between the Director and Assistant Director themselves. To deal successfully with the agencies, the Director had to think primarily in terms of program balance, rigid scheduling, and traditional techniques. On occasion, he felt that a similar approach might be useful in the Target Neighborhoods. The Assistant Director felt that precise scheduling was difficult, and complained:

"The Director wants me to have things done in the Target Neighborhoods by a set date, just like the Kansas Legislature. But that can't be done, because the people in the Target Neighborhoods aren't legislators, and they aren't used to doing things by certain deadline times. I can't push them. If I do, I lose them. You've got to play the game by their rules, not by rules you've set up. The Director's a minister and he's used to finishing sermons on schedule. He was also a legislator and used to having certain legislative moves completed at the end of a session. It's not that way in the Target Neighborhoods. Things don't run on schedule that way. You've got to play it by ear."

The Director, on the other hand, was under enormous pressure from the regional and national Offices of Economic Opportunity to "meet criterion deadlines." Furthermore, he was responsible for establishing, on schedule, bench marks which would lead to further funding for the program.

The Assistant Director, influenced by his union-organizing experience, was on occasion tempted to "mix it up" with agency officials. He at times felt restricted by the Director, who counseled him to "play it cool" and let solutions evolve through negotiation. This difference in attitude was nicely illustrated in a discussion between the Director and Assistant Director concerning the intervention approach of Saul Alinsky. The Assistant Director thought the Alinsky approach has merit:

"Maybe it's not right for Topeka, but I think it's a good approach in general. There's one good thing in particular about Alinsky. He lets the people go all the way. Here in OEO I get the feeling that we restrict the people, so they can't really get with it. We tell them to get involved, but then we put limits on how far they can go."

The Director disagreed, "I don't think it's appropriate. There's no room for compromise in the Alinsky approach." The Director and Assistant Director on occasion disagreed about the degree of autonomy that Target Neighborhood Committees should have. The Assistant Director generally felt, "Let them go, wherever they want!" The Director, referring to "organizational cohesiveness," wanted to "keep them within the fold."

These points of disagreement between the Director and Assistant Director are not meant to indicate a working difficulty between them. On the contrary, they were close personal friends and worked in harmony throughout their association with the TOEO. Rather, the differences are to be seen as resulting in some part from their earlier job experiences, but in large part from the division of labor they were forced to establish in order to recruit program participants, maintain program funding, and operationalize the Overlap Model.

"THE ROAD ALWAYS SEEMS BUMPY!"

When an organization is young, changing, or relatively informal, its day-to-day operating procedures are more likely to be influenced by the personal managerial philosophy of key staff.[11] The Director, commenting on the lack of precedents for a poverty-intervention organization, reflected:

"When I leave this job, I'll really have an education. In this job you really find out what you can do, how far you can stretch your abilities: The thing about this job is that there are no guidance lines. No right or wrong way that you know how to move. You just have to go ahead and do it, and hope for the best."

The Director drew heavily upon his previous political experience as he guided the TOEO. The political slant of its organizational style seemed to fit well with the Overlap Model for social change and did provide Target Neighborhood representatives with chances to experience participative democracy, particularly in the Neighborhood Committee meetings. However, as the TOEO grew, some incongruities could be perceived between participant democracy as might be seen in the Kansas State Legislature and participant democracy as it was in the TOEO committee complex. Most apparent was the fact that the poor were not politicians. Arguments and debates were not so abstract or effectively neutral in the committee meetings as they often were in the Legislature. Conflict centered around powers and controls that were meaningful to the poor in terms of their everyday lives, and not a distant constituency. The Director's own experience with the developing poverty program prompted him to comment:

"It's not really working like the Legislature, as I'd hoped. There, proposals are presented, discussed, voted upon, and we'd move on. Here, proposals often become less important than the debate itself.

---

[11] Blau and Scott, *Formal Organizations*, p. 6. See also Joseph A. Litterer, *Organizations: Structure and Behavior*, p. 34.

he participants stay worked up even after an issue is voted upon
d off the agenda. The road always seems bumpy!"

When the TOEO was enacting its purported Functional Margin-
lity, it could be expected that the content of a specific community-
ction proposal often would appear secondary, especially for the
oor, to the participative and power-experiencing process of devel-
ping and implementing it. To sustain the organizational style which
ermitted the "road to be bumpy" was stressful to the TOEO staff,
articularly at the beginning when the members drew upon their
rior experiences with more conventional kinds of organizations.

The Director was particularly frustrated when members would
esign from the Economic Opportunity Board, when citizens who
were "on board" would no longer participate in the programs. The
withdrawal of an active participant was a threat to the "city-wide"
outreach intended for the poverty program, and, in terms of the political orientation of the Director, the loss of a valuable constituent.
His ministerial experiences also influenced his perception of participant withdrawal. "I guess I'm too much of a minister," he stated,
"to feel comfortable when a member of the congregation leaves, no
matter what the reason."

ACTION Now!

The not-poor who were participating in the committee complex
were accustomed to long-range planning and the slow but systematic processing of proposals through bureaucratic machinery. The
TOEO often was pressured to make its major material task the winning of federal funds through community-action programing—a
task which also demanded long-range planning and patient processing. In contrast, the Target Neighborhood residents generally insisted upon immediate results and were vociferously impatient with
delays. The poor's demands for *action now* indicated more than a
desire for programs or funds per se. Their behavior seemed to manifest an indifference to future orientation, and an urgency to achieve
quickly results for which they themselves were at least somewhat
responsible. The Target Neighborhood residents had continually

been told that *"the poverty program is your program,"* and many of them were eager to test the promise.

The TOEO's Functional Marginality was severely challenged during arguments between the poor and not-poor participants concerning action-timing. If community-action proposals, particularly those involving delegate agencies, moved more quickly than the agencies could comfortably accommodate, the TOEO staff would be pressured to "keep things in line." If the proposals bogged down for any reasons beyond their control, the Target Neighborhood residents would become angry, or worse, disillusioned, and the TOEO staff would be held accountable for "selling them out."

FROM "CLIENTS" TO "COLLEAGUES"

As the poor increasingly exercised their prerogative to participate in decision-making concerning the conduct of the poverty program, some of the representatives from agencies traditionally accustomed to doing *for* the poor were challenged to shift, at least during committee meetings, their perceptions of the poor from "clients" to "colleagues." To be consistent with its proclamations for equal-status interaction among the participants, the TOEO staff had to encourage agency officials to decrease their role-distance from the poor—sometimes with the result that jealously guarded professional statuses were threatened. Further, the TOEO staff on occasion suggested that an agency make formal or informal policy changes to accommodate the poor's expectations for the program and their participation in it. Such encouragements and suggestions often brought "interloper" criticisms from officials who felt they had been dealing with social problems and the poor much longer than had the TOEO staff.

How MUCH POWER?

When the Target Neighborhood participants became more comfortable with, and practiced in, new social roles in the committee complex, the issue of power introduced another TOEO dilemma. Specifically, how much power could the poor have within the poverty program? What were the limits of "maximum feasible participation"? Who set the ceiling of power for the poor, and who reset that ceiling when inevitably it was reached? The TOEO staff attempted to implement a particular structure and style, determined the balance of votes on the Board, and thus set the extent of organizational control available to the poor. But what if the power and control available to indigenous participants cannot keep pace with the growing skills, confidences, and desires anticipated by the Overlap Model? Will the poor be forced to leave the program and form splinter groups, or stay with it but "keep their place"? Will the participating poor pressure the TOEO staff to restructure, yielding more formal control to them? What would be the not-poor participants' reactions to increased power for the poor? Paradoxically, the TOEO may, over time, grow more bureaucratic, more identified with agencies and government, and become less favorable toward "participative democracy."[12] It is assumed that the "overlap" experience will allow power shifts within the poverty program—the not-poor increasingly yielding to the more clearly focused and presented desires of the poor. Precisely that appeared to be happening during the course of our research. However, if the assumption is incorrect, or if the Overlap Model demands more time than the participants are willing to wait, then the TOEO staff will increasingly be hard pressed to remain "on the middle ground." At this writing, the question "how much power?" was increasingly being asked by some of the Target Neighborhood participants.

GROWTH TOWARD AUTONOMY

The TOEO political slant implied an attempt toward organizational solidarity. The Director felt that all the components of the committee complex should remain "within the fold." Thus the Target Neighborhood Officers were to consult with TOEO staff concerning the scheduling of meetings, elections, agenda, developing of community-action proposals, etc. But as the participating poor became more familiar with the poverty program, some of them felt the need to act, in small ways at first, more independently and to be less

12 The TOEO may follow the means-end goal displacement discussed in Sheldon L. Messinger, "Organization Transformation," *American Sociological Review*, 22 (February, 1965), 3–10.

accountable to the TOEO. The conflict between what was perceived by TOEO staff to be "organizational integrity," and the potentially increasing Target Neighborhood push for autonomy, developed into a dilemma which, like the ceiling-of-power problem, was a recurring one for the TOEO staff.

THE PARADOX OF TOEO SUCCESS

Like any organization that must be funded externally and recurrently, the TOEO had to be concerned with *demonstrating* its efficiency. The most tangible evidence for efficiency was the technically correct and successful preparation and implementation of OEO community-action proposals. An extension of that criterion, one stimulated by the political slant of the organization, was the rapid passing of a proposal through the TOEO committee complex. The proposal-producing was a wordy business. According to the *Annual Report*, the written information distributed to participants was "not measured by the sheet but by the inch."[13] The participating poor, not so practiced as the not-poor in skimming over such materials but nonetheless wanting to know what was happening in "their program," often impeded the "efficiency" of the proposal machinery. The poor's desire for "action now" did not mean action to the exclusion of their having their "say" in determining programs. Therefore, another dilemma faced the TOEO. On the one hand, a commitment had been made to involve the poor in the decision-making process. On the other hand, their involvement decreased the TOEO's major measurable index of efficiency.[14] The TOEO generally was forced to favor the efficiency horn of the dilemma by the rather insistent prompting of higher levels of OEO management to "get more programs going." The Director stated, with noticeable despair:

"I'm in sympathy with participation of the poor, but sometimes I have to get things done—now! I can't wait, or we'll lose the oppor-

13 TOEO, *Annual Report for 1965–1966*, Topeka, Kansas, p. 5.
14 Blau points out that an organization excessively concerned with efficiency easily becomes impatient with the slowness of the democratic process. Peter M. Blau, *Bureaucracy in Modern Society*, pp. 105–110.

tunity to fund a program, and keep things going. So I have to take short cuts, and sometimes those short cuts mean cutting down on the time the Target Neighborhood residents can spend considering the programs themselves. It's disturbing, but it's a fact of life."

The shifting expectations of the national Office of Economic Opportunity often dramatically disrupted the TOEO's efforts to implement the local program. As the national "War on Poverty" grew older, specific organizational requirements, regulations, and procedures deluged poverty-intervention organizations. Often the mandates for procedural changes would be issued after an organization had struggled more or less on its own to establish a comfortable mode of operation. No doubt many of those mandates were necessary to bring local programs into accord with the expectations of the Economic Opportunity Act. However, poverty-program directors were nonetheless harassed when they had to change the tack to which community members had become accustomed. A clear case of this problem emerged when the TOEO staff was directed by national and regional OEO to restructure the Economic Opportunity Board in accordance with the legislative changes (the Quie Amendment to the Economic Opportunity Act). The intention of the legislation was, among other things, to guarantee that at least one-third of the Board membership would be comprised of low-income persons. Apparently, a significant number of communities were not providing for adequate participation of the poor. The Topeka program, on the contrary, had been careful from the onset to include at least one-third low-income membership on all of the committees, and particularly on the Economic Opportunity Board. Nevertheless, the TOEO Director had to modify the Board membership in accordance with the specific letter of the legislation, which meant removing some of the low-income persons and some of the not-poor members and replacing them with others. The proportion of poor to not-poor Board members would not be changed. The distraught Director complained:

"We worked for months to recruit participants for the Topeka program, and finally convinced a significant number of persons to get on board. We had a working balance of representatives from all walks of life in the community, and a good socio-economic distribution. The Board members had finally begun to work together, had realized each other's potentials, had become familiar with one another, and were starting to come to meaningful conclusions. Then, bang! We have to change the whole Board, and we weren't even in violation of the spirit of the legislation! It makes me sick!"

A number of the participants who were removed from their membership slots were openly angry, and the TOEO staff bore the brunt of that anger.

Community evaluation of the TOEO's activities also presented a paradoxical criterion for success. When the TOEO accomplished no social change—and then actually would be failing—the worst the staff could expect was community indifference. When change was brought about and consequently some anxieties and resistances aroused, the staff might be unfavorably evaluated by some community members. Ironically, the mark of the TOEO success for social change in many cases was its unpopularity—a situation that was extremely stressful to the staff members who identified with, and had "roots" in, the community.

"I Feel like Getting Away"

The Director and Assistant Director were under almost continuous stress as they attempted to implement and maintain the Topeka poverty program. Their jobs kept them involved seven days a week and, as mentioned earlier, usually sixteen or seventeen hours a day. Only rarely did either man have an entire night free to spend with his family, since almost every night of the week had a scheduled session of one or another committee. They often talked of expanding the size of their staff, but during most of their tenure of office the funding situation was such that it would have been difficult to do so.

Since the office of the research staff was in the same set of buildings with the TOEO office, the Director and Assistant Director often would visit with members of our staff. Sometimes they would just sit quietly and have a cup of coffee. Other times they would excitedly "let off steam" concerning some specific problem that was facing them at the moment. Both men expressed the feeling that the research office was "a place where we can get away from the rat race" that was taking place in the TOEO office.

On the other hand, sometimes the Director and Assistant Director perceived our research to be an additional source of stress to them. The Director, for example, commented:

"I feel that I've shifted from a 'colleague' to a 'subject' in this operation. I don't know if I like being under a microscope. I know I'm making some mistakes in this program, and I don't know if I like having people around recording those mistakes. Eighteen months from now maybe I could be more objective about it, but right now I don't like the idea that somebody knows about the mistakes I'm making."

On occasion I would match the Director's frustration with frustration of my own, and with righteous indignation that the carefully designed neutral research stance was being interpreted as "pressure" on the poverty-intervention organization and its staff. Those mutual misunderstandings could have ended the research rapport that existed between our staffs.[15] However, the Director and I made every effort to "talk out" the problems associated with action/ research, and despite a few uneasy moments we did maintain a profitable association. After listening to him, I would gain more insight to the way that our research, particularly the Research Committee (see Appendix A), might contribute to staff anxiety. After listening to me, the Director would conclude, for example:

"I'm very tired and many things have been happening over the last week, so maybe that's part of the reason I'm saying the things

---

[15] For discussions of staff/researcher conflict, see the following chapters in Richard N. Adams and J. J. Preiss (eds.), *Human Organization Research*: Robert K. Bain, "The Researcher's Role: A Case Study," pp. 23–28; John Gullahorn and George Strauss, "The Field Worker in Union Research," pp. 28–32; Steven A. Richardson, "A Framework for Reporting Field-Relations Experiences," pp. 124–139; and Rosalie H. Wax, "Twelve Years Later: An Analysis of a Field Experience," pp. 166–178.

I'm saying, and I'm blaming you for things that don't have anything to do with you. You happen to be the person closest around that I can get after."

After the research staff gained experience in our interaction with the TOEO staff, the message became very clear to us: the Director and Assistant Director simply needed a place to relax, a place to "sound off," a place where they could gripe and otherwise express themselves without undue harassment, a place where they could escape the crushing dilemmas seemingly built into the TOEO's Functional Marginality and Overlap Model. Very often, the Director and Assistant Director would talk about quitting their jobs, and taking "anything else that comes along." They would muse about "the worth of it all," and wonder whether they were getting anywhere with this program." The Director commented, meditatively:

"Last Friday night I had a chance to go to a movie with the family. It seemed so special, a common thing like that. But then I counted back and realized that's the first time that I'd been to a movie with the family since I took the job as Director, and that was over eighteen months ago! I began to wonder if it's worth it!"

The Director indicated the tone of his experience in the poverty program, and his view of the staff role as stress-associated, when he chose the following quote (attributed to Theodore Roosevelt) as an introduction to the first *Annual Report* of the TOEO:

It is not the critic who counts, not the man who points out how the strong man stumbled, or where the doer of deeds could have done them better. The credit belongs to the man who is actually in the arena; whose face is marred by the dust and sweat and blood; who strives valiantly; who errs and comes up short again and again . . . who knows the great enthusiasms, the great diversions, and spends himself in a worthy cause; who, at the best, knows in the end the triumph of high achievement; and who, at the worst, if he fails, at least fails while striving greatly, so that his place shall never be with those cold and timid souls who know neither victory nor defeat.

The Assistant Director, in a less literary but perhaps more poignant manner, commented after a particularly hectic week:

"I haven't been sleeping too well. I keep having this nightmare that people're chasing me. I guess I'm worrying about this program too much. One of these days pretty soon I'm just going to take a vacation and try to forget all about it. Yes, that's what I'm going to do. Next month, I'm going to take three days off and go out pheasant hunting, and get out there where you can forget about things. I want to get out there where there're trees, and where there's room to move around. Hell, maybe one of these days I'm going to do more than that. Maybe I'll just tell my wife to pack up things and we'll go down to the Sierra Madres in Mexico, where everything is quiet."

MANAGERIAL SUCCESSION

On November 29, 1966, the TOEO Director gave notice of his resignation, to become effective on January 16, 1967. At that time, he would take a staff position with the Kansas governor-elect. A new director was not picked until February, and did not begin work until March. During that interim, the Assistant Director served in the capacity of Acting Director, and found himself facing a whole new set of stress-producing situations. During managerial succession a poverty-intervention organization is particularly vulnerable to disruption—whether instigated inadvertently by sudden changes in community support or national policy, or advertently by power struggles among participants with vested interests.

The Assistant, now Acting, Director found himself in the midst of an Economic Opportunity Board squabble over the choice of a new man for the permanent director position. Target Neighborhood Officers wanted an indigenous director. Agency representatives wanted a professionally trained director. Some Board members, particularly Negro-Americans, wanted a Negro-American director, period. Others argued for specific men on the basis of what they perceived to be admirable qualifications—whether those qualifications be education, experience, political affiliation, friendship, or some combination. The Acting Director was himself ineligible for the permanent position because he did not meet the educational requirements in the job description. However, he was quite ambivalent about wanting the position of permanent director. His comments ranged from "If they change the regulations and ask me, I'll take it," to "I wouldn't have the job if they handed it to me on a silver platter!"

The Acting Director's tenure was indeed hectic. During that period the Economic Opportunity Board was struggling through the reorganization of membership demanded by the mandate of the national Office of Economic Opportunity. The Board president, who had been a Target Neighborhood Officer, struggled with considerable clamor to enact the leadership role as he perceived it (see Chapter 6). A number of half-finished proposals, several wanting for the 10 per cent local share, were facing deadlines. A team of federal auditors was investigating the TOEO books on a report (later to be discounted) that they were not in order. The Acting Director began in earnest to look for another job, but agreed to stay on until a permanent director was hired.

In March, 1967, the Director had been selected and began to operate the TOEO, concentrating primarily upon the development and expansion of an interoffice cadre. Shortly thereafter, following several disagreements concerning operation of the program, the Assistant Director, former Acting Director, left his position to take a job in private industry. Several weeks later he commented to me, "Say, you know, I'm not having those nightmares anymore!"

STAFF NEEDS

What kind of persons must the director and assistant director of a poverty-intervention organization that plays the role of Functional Marginality be? Obviously, as demonstrated in the TOEO, they are expected to be durable, flexible, to have a high frustration tolerance, to be committed to the Overlap Model, and to view their job as temporary.

Some of the Target Neighborhood Officers expressed opinions about the characteristics of an "ideal" TOEO staff:

"Above all, they should be men who can delegate responsibility, because that's what this program's all about."

"They should be learned and experienced—not just with book learning, though that's important—about the facts of poverty life."

"They should be able to work with people of all religions and colors and wages, so that none of them can say 'They're for them and against us.'"

"They better be sincere about wanting to work with us, because we can tell the phonies. Also, they have to be sincere, because they could probably make more money doing something else."

"One thing for sure. They have to be dedicated. It takes dedicated men to stay with this program as it goes along."

"The director and assistant director of this program have to have lived here for a good spell of time, so they can be sensitive to the needs of the people here."

"They've got to be eager—but not too eager—so they won't steamroll us who might be slower at first."

"The director in particular must be a good administrator, because there's money involved. What I mean is, he's got to be able to administrate, but not administrate us right out of the program, like has happened in other cities."

"They've got to be guys who don't try to snow us, man, with bigdeal promises. We know the score. We know there's some good stuff in the poverty program, but there's no sense trying to con people with the promise of some big miracle. Tell it like it is, that's what they should do."

"They have to have broad shoulders, because they're going to be carrying other people's troubles."

"I don't know if I can say what I mean. The staff has to know the difference between getting ideas from the poor and letting the poor *give* their ideas to them. You know what I mean?"

"When we talk about the ideal director, we say 'he.' Can't it be a *she?* If it was a she, you'd know one thing for sure, and that is, program would go through the Board too fast because she'd ma sure there was a lot of talking about it!" (Laughter)

"The way we've been talking, it sounds like we need some peo like Superman. You know, he isn't real *either!*"

The ideal staff member, then, would be fair, sincere, dedicat(eager but sensitive, educated but practical, emphatic, a local a knowledgeable resident, an able administrator who could deleg; authority and ensure participation, and be able to "tell it like it He (or she) would be all these things—in a context of organi tional, professional, and task ambiguity and uncertainty!

The TOEO Director and Assistant Director had come to their j(with perhaps more relevant past-employment experience than staff members of most poverty-intervention organizations. Yet t still at times had difficulty living with the role of "change age: The regional and national Office of Economic Opportunity provi(both men with an abundance of information and training concern program *content* and organization procedures, but provided tl with little information relevant to the *process* aspects of their j(The Office of Economic Opportunity expected the TOEO staff to change agents *and* administrators, but it educated and inforr primarily the administration facet of that dual task. Our resea staff's interaction and discussions with the TOEO Director and As ant Director met some of that need, but not to the extent that a n legitimized OEO training program for the staff could have done. the training programs should be continuing, not one-shot or casional. New stresses and dilemmas emerge with each incremer social change. The staff members need not only information to them cope with such program change, but they need also a recep and supportive audience with whom they can express, discuss, perhaps resolve their sources of stress.

To maintain Functional Marginality and keep the Overlap M operating, the TOEO was expected to be durable under recu: stress and crises, to remain flexible and innovative, and to be a(able in expectations and assumptions so that it could accomm(

the social change it purported to stimulate. When operating as planned, the TOEO had to expect to be a vortex of community controversy and had to be able to resist resultant pressures and temptations to identify exclusively either with the poor or with the power structure. It had to be considered temporary, someday to be obsolete, and therefore it had to avoid the goal displacement that usually accompanies longevity and expansion of an organization. The TOEO had to be, therefore, an atypical organization as changeable as the change it hoped to stimulate. The expectations for, and challenges to, poverty-intervention organization were, of course, extended to the staff that had responsibility for directing it.

CHAPTER 4

The Programs

THE FOCUS OF THIS BOOK is upon the *human experience* of planned social intervention, and thus upon the process of a poverty program rather than upon its content. However, I shall now present a few summary statistics to indicate the logistic scope and nature of the Topeka endeavor.

Prior to and by the end of our research (September, 1965–May, 1967), the TOEO and its committee complex implemented the following major community-action proposals:

Planning and Development Grant: Carried out the planning phase of the TOEO, and organized the Target Neighborhood Committees.

The Programs

Head Start, summer, 1965:	Provided a prekindergarten educational experience for 319 poverty children.
Neighborhood Youth Corps Program, 1965:	Provided 104 needy students work; maximum of 15 hours per week, at $1.25 per hour.
Head Start Follow-through Program, 1965–1966:	Corrected physical, dental, and psychological problems detected in participants during the summer program, 1965.
Adult Basic Education Program:	Provided basic adult-education classes, equivalent to public-school grades 1–8, for 155 persons.
Neighborhood Youth Corps Program, summer, 1966:	Provided 125 needy students work; maximum of 32 hours per week, at $1.25 per hour.
Neighborhood Youth Corps Program, 1966–1967:	Provided 125 needy students work; maximum of 15 hours per week, at $1.25 per hour.
Medicare Alert Program:	One thousand persons, age 65 and over, in Shawnee County were informed by indigenous workers about, and subsequently signed up for, Medicare.
Day Care Services and Family Center Program:	Provided full day-care services for 32 preschool children, and educational and counseling opportunities for 500 young adults.
Neighborhood Extension Worker and Neighborhood Aide Program:	Provided "bridges of services" to the 15,000 low-income persons in the Target Neighborhoods.
County Beautification Project:	Provided full-time employment for 30 unemployed men, whose work was to improve and make more safe Shawnee County roads and bridges.

Conduct and Administration Operation Grant for the TOEO Office:	Provided funding for the TOEO to co-ordinate and be responsible for all OEO programs in Shawnee County. Enabled the TOEO to provide information to interested citizens, and to work in the Target Neighborhoods.
Neighborhood House Program:	Provided an on-site facility to serve the needs of persons in the Highland Park–Pierce Neighborhood.
Head Start, summer, 1966:	Provided prekindergarten educational experience for 450 poverty children.
City Beautification Project:	Provided full-time employment for 20 unemployed men, whose work was to improve the parks of Topeka.

These and a few smaller programs (such as the Neighborhood Survey Project conducted to determine poverty characteristics in the Target Neighborhoods, and the Emergency Worker Project, which provided jobs to low-income people for reconstruction tasks following a Topeka tornado), employed nearly 250 Target Neighborhood residents and provided services to several thousands of others. Just before the completion of our research, another summer Head Start Program and a $200,000 Manpower Training and Development Program were implemented.

Indicating the degree of co-operation between the TOEO and other community entities, the following seventeen agencies and organizations were among those that contributed cash and/or services in kind toward the local share of federal OEO funding:

Topeka Public Schools
City-County Health Department
Kansas State Cooperative Extension Service
University of Kansas Graduate School of Social Work
Topeka Human Relations Commission

Shawnee County Welfare Department
Topeka Recreation Commission
Topeka Day Care Association
Board of Directors—United Fund
Urban Renewal Agency
Menninger Foundation
Legal Aid Society
Social Security Administration
Washburn University
Topeka Chapter of the National Association of Social Workers
Topeka Park Department
Shawnee County Commission

The total budget for the Topeka poverty program during this period, including OEO funding and local share, was slightly over $1,000,000.

PART II
The Poverty Board

▀▄

Part II focuses upon the structure of, and processes within, the Economic Opportunity Board, the major decision-making body of the Topeka poverty program. It further focuses upon some significant demographic and social-psychological characteristics of Board members, and how those characteristics related to decision-making and the interaction of members. Part II is also concerned with Board members' opinions of the program after their participation, and whether that participation influenced any measurable change in the characteristics of members.

In Chapter 5, the hypothesis that the poor (Target Neighborhood Officers) and the not-poor (agency representatives and citizens at large) will differ significantly in important demographic and social-psychological characteristics is tested, and is reported as being supported. It is postulated that the Overlap Model was therefore operationalized in the Economic Opportunity Board. The social-psychological differences, taken to reflect contrasting views of self-in-society generated by adaptation to idiosyncratic exigencies of social environ-

ment, are discussed as providing sources of conflict between pc
and not-poor Board members concerning poverty programmi
Variation in the differences among Board members are also discuss
as they relate to sex and ethnic group.

To illustrate the kinds of conflict concerning poverty programi
that can develop among Board members, a typical Board meeting
recorded through its minutes and is reconstructed and discussed
Chapter 6. The setting of the meeting, its attendance, seating patte
agenda, and minutes are presented in detail, and are intersper
with research-observer reconstructions and interpretive comme
The duration of the meeting, hidden agenda, organizational inc
sistencies, vested interests, and members' expectations and role p
ceptions are discussed as influencing the direction of Board proce
ings. The relation of Target Neighborhood Officer Board partici
tion (statements made during the meetings) to tenure as a Bo
member is described. The role strain experienced by a Target Nei
borhood Officer elected to the position of Board president is rep
ed, and the sources and impact of that strain discussed.

In Chapter 7, the responses of agency representatives and citiz
at large to formal interview questions concerning the poverty
gram are presented. The questions are listed in the order asked, e
followed by the distribution of responses, representative quotes,
interpretive discussion. The responses of members, sampled a
they had experienced considerable program participation, incl
their opinions of: Board membership; "maximum feasible partic
tion" of the poor; community change as a result of the poverty
gram; other Board members; Board and program efficacy; pers
and organizational impact of participation; growth of formal
informal contacts through participation. The role of the local p
as an evaluator is illustrated and discussed.

Chapter 8 presents the responses of Target Neighborhood Offi
to essentially the same set of formal interview questions aske
agency representatives and citizens at large. As in Chapter 7,
questions are listed in the order asked, each followed by the di
bution of responses, representative quotes, and interpretive dis

sion. The responses of Target Neighborhood Officers are contrasted with those of agency representatives and citizens at large.

The hypothesis that "maximum feasible participation" of the poor in the poverty program will significantly modify social-psychological characteristics taken to represent a view of self-in-society is tested, and reported as being supported, with important exceptions, in Chapter 9. The relation of kind and perception of participation to the direction and degree of social-psychological change is discussed. Variations in change among Board members are also discussed as they relate to sex and ethnic group.

CHAPTER 5

Portrait of the Poverty Board

As mentioned in the Preface, the
Economic Opportunity Act insisted that community-action programs
be "developed, conducted, and administered with the maximum
feasible participation of residents of the areas and members of the
groups to be served."[1] Both the origin and the meaning of that mandate were, at least initially, rather unclear.[2] As the Act was implemented across the nation, *ad hoc* interpretations of the degree and
kind of participation open to the poor spawned dramatic controversy,

[1] Economic Opportunity Act of 1964, 78 Stat. 508, Sec. 202 (*a*).
[2] Lillian Rubin, "Maximum Feasible Participation: The Origins, Implications
and Present Status," *Poverty and Human Resources Abstracts*, 2 (November–
December, 1967), 5–18.

particularly concerning the representation, selection, and decision-making power of the poor on the policy-formulating "poverty boards" which governed local community-action programs.[3] Congress subsequently attempted to resolve the question of how many poor constituted "maximum feasible participation" by amending the Economic Opportunity Act (Quie Amendment) and declaring that no community-action program would be funded unless at least one-making power of the poor on the policy-formulating "poverty boards" At the same time Congress attempted to clarify this criterion for board membership, specifying that "the representatives of the poor shall be selected by the residents of areas of concentration of poverty, with special emphasis on participation by residents of the area who are poor."[5]

Rubin suggests that the "maximum feasible participation" idea had a social history prior to its becoming a legislative mandate.[6] Involvement of the beneficiaries in determining the program, the emphasis upon "self-help," and the importance of local autonomy and responsibility were all conceptual cornerstones and practical realities in, for example: the U.S. Projects for Underdeveloped Coun-

[3] See, for example: Barbara Carter, "Sargent Shriver and the Role of the Poor," *The Reporter*, 35 (May 5, 1966), 18–19; Richard A. Cloward, "The War on Poverty: Are the Poor Left Out?" *The Nation* (August 2, 1965), 55–60; Woody Klein, "People vs. Politicians: Defeat in Harlem," *The Nation* (July 27, 1964), 27–29; Erwin Knoll and Jules Whitcover, "Fighting Poverty—And City Hall," *The Reporter*, 32 (June 3, 1965), 19–22; Erwin Knoll and Jules Whitcover, "Policies and the Poor: Shriver's Second Thoughts," *The Reporter*, 33 (December 30, 1965), 23–25; Ralph M. Kramer, *Participation of the Poor*; Elliott A. Krause, "Functions of a Bureaucratic Ideology: 'Citizen Participation,'" *Social Problems*, 16 (Fall, 1968), 129–143; Daniel Patrick Moynihan, *Maximum Feasible Misunderstanding: Community Action in the War on Poverty*; David Sanford, "The Poor in Their Place," *The New Republic*, 153 (November 20, 1965), 5–6; William C. Selover, "Federal Pressure Felt: U.S. Poor Gain Foothold in Local Programs," *Christian Science Monitor* (August 2, 1966), p. 10; William C. Selover, "Old Ways Bind Poverty Drive," *Christian Science Monitor* (August 3, 1966), p. 1; and Hans B. C. Spiegel, *Citizen Participation in Urban Development*, Vol. 1, *Concepts and Issues*.

[4] Economic Opportunity Amendments of 1966, 80 Stat. 1451, Sec. 203 (*c*) 2.

[5] *Ibid.*, (*c*) 3.

[6] Rubin, *Poverty and Human Resources Abstracts*, 2 (November–December, 1967), pp. 7–9.

ies,[7] the militant civil-rights movement,[8] and in domestic commun-
y-development programs such as those of Saul Alinsky,[9] the Ford
oundation, [10] Harlem Youth Opportunities Unlimited,[11] and Mobil-
ation for Youth.[12]

The Economic Opportunity Board was intended to be the high
oint of "maximum feasible participation" of the poor in the Topeka
overty program. Also, the Board was to be the primary focus of
he Overlap Model, where members from different socio-economic
trata in the community could interact on an equal-status basis with
ne vote each, and come by way of consensus to decisions governing
pecific community-action proposals. It was therefore implicitly as-
umed that those Board members who were representatives of the
oor would differ significantly from its other members in social-
sychological variables, often associated with socio-economic status,
which were indicative of a general sense of competence and confidence vis-à-vis society, broadly defined. The Overlap Model's intention to provide social therapy for the poor—as a result of their
participation in the program—took for granted, as did the "maximum
feasible participation" mandate of the Economic Opportunity Act,
that there are some social-psychological characteristics which need
changing.

That assumption, for the purposes of this study, was taken as an
hypothesis. More specifically, it was hypothesized that those Board

7 Peter Kuenstler, "Urban Community Center Work in Underdeveloped
Countries," *Community Development*, 1 (1958), 27–31; Ibrahim Shamin, "The
Role of Lay Leaders," *Community Development*, 3 (1959), 81–87.
8 John H. Wheeler, "Civil Rights Groups—Their Impact Upon the War on
Poverty," *Law and Contemporary Problems*, 31 (Winter, 1966), 152–158.
9 James Ridgeway, "Saul Alinsky in Smugtown," *The New Republic*, 152
(June 26, 1965), 15–17; Frank Riessman, "A Comparison of Two Social Action
Approaches: Saul Alinsky and The New Student Left," Albert Einstein College
of Medicine, Department of Psychiatry, New York, September, 1965, mimeograph; Charles E. Silberman, *Crisis in Black and White*, pp. 308–355.
10 *American Community Development: Preliminary Reports by Directors of
Projects Assisted by the Ford Foundation in Four Cities and a State; Stirrings
in the Big Cities: The Great Cities Projects.*
11 *The Federal Delinquency Program: Objectives in Operation Under the
President's Committee on Juvenile Delinquency and Youth Crime.*
12 *Ibid.*

members who were representatives of the poor would be significantly *lower* than the other members in annual family income, membership in voluntary associations, formal education, activism, achievement orientation, and future orientation, and significantly *higher* in
anomie, integration with relatives, isolation, normlessness, powerlessness, alienation, and particularism.[13]

THE MEASURES

After fourteen months of observation, unstructured interviews, and
rapport-building in the Topeka poverty program, the research staff
decided it would be permissible and timely to administer a brief
questionnaire to the members of the Economic Opportunity Board.
We wanted to test the hypothesis of social-psychological differences
between the poor and not-poor members, and to see whether the
fairly consistent patterns of Board conflict that we had observed (in
the seven meetings held during the fourteen months) had any relation to those differences. At this time, we also decided to readminister (and in fact did readminister) the questionnaire seven months
later to assess member changes in the social-psychological characteristics as a result of their participation. In this chapter I shall discuss
only the findings of the first administration, and shall discuss the
change data later (Chapter 9). It was assumed, of course, that the
fourteen months' participation already passed had had some impact
for change upon the members, as our observations indicated. But to
administer the questionnaire had not, in our opinion, been advisable
earlier than November, 1966.

The questionnaire, administered individually to the Board members, contained demographic items, questions assessing the extent
of program participation, and the following scales:

a) *Kahl Activism Scale* (sense of mastery over the physical and
   social environment)[14]

---

[13] Because of the space required to bring together some previous studies that
illustrate various social-psychological characteristics of the poor, documentation,
for this note only, is found at the end of this chapter as note 13ª.
[14] Joseph A. Kahl, "Some Measurements of Achievement Motivation," *American Journal of Sociology*, 70, 6 (May, 1965), 669–681.

b) *Srole Anomie Scale* (social malintegration; the internalized counterpart of social dysfunction)[15]
c) *Kahl Integration with Relatives Scale* (degrees of dependence upon family)[16]
d) *Rosen Achievement Value Orientation Scale* (value for, and motivation toward, academic and occupational achievement, particularly regarding striving for status through social mobility)[17]
e) *Future Orientation Items* (three items drawn from the Kahl Activism Scale which, based upon face validity, were taken to indicate willingness to plan for the future: (1) Nowadays a person has to live pretty much for today and let tomorrow take care of itself. (2) How important is it to know clearly in advance your plans for the future? (3) Planning only makes a person unhappy since your plans hardly ever work out anyway.)[18]
f) *Dean Isolation Subscale* (feeling of separation from the majority group or its standards)[19]
g) *Dean Normlessness Subscale* (feeling of purposelessness; absence of values that might give direction to life)[20]
h) *Dean Powerlessness Subscale* (feeling of helplessness; inability to understand or influence the events upon which one depends)[21]
i) *Dean Alienation Scale* (sum total of Isolation, Normlessness, and Powerlessness Subscales; taken to indicate a general syndrome of alienation)[22]

[15] Leo Srole, "Social Integration and Certain Corollaries: An Exploratory Study," *American Sociological Review*, 21 (December, 1956), 709–717.
[16] Kahl, *American Journal of Sociology*, 70, 6 (May, 1965), 674.
[17] Bernard C. Rosen, "The Achievement Syndrome: A Psychocultural Dimension of Social Stratification," *American Sociological Review*, 21 (April, 1956), 203–211.
[18] Kahl, *American Journal of Sociology*, 70 (1965), 680.
[19] Dwight G. Dean, "Alienation: Its Meaning and Measurement," *American Sociological Review*, 26 (October, 1961), 753–758.
[20] *Ibid.*, pp. 755–756.
[21] *Ibid.*, pp. 754–755.
[22] *Ibid.*, pp. 756–757.

j) *Stouffer-Toby Role Conflict Scale* (value orientation toward institutionalized obligations of friendship [particularism] versus value orientation toward institutionalized obligations to society [universalism]).[23]

A few of the items measuring activism, anomie, achievement orientation, or future orientation were identical on two or more of those scales. For the research administration, such items appeared only once on the questionnaire, but were scored as appropriate for each scale. All questionnaire items were randomly ordered. The responses were then analyzed for statistically significant differences between members who were representatives of the poor and those who were not, and for sex and ethnic differences (see Appendix D for a reproduction of the questionnaire).

THE DIFFERENCES AND SOME CONSEQUENCES

Sixty-one Board members completed the questionnaire. Of the responses, twenty-three were Target Neighborhood Committee Officers (TNOs); thirty-eight were agency representatives or citizens at large (non-TNOs). Of the TNOs, twelve were male, eleven female; eight were Anglo-American, ten were Negro-American, three were Mexican-American, and two were American Indian. The median annual family income for TNOs was from $3,000 to $5,000, with 44 per cent earning less than $3,000 annually. Median level of formal education for TNOs was high-school graduate, with 40 per cent being high-school drop-outs. Of the non-TNOs thirty-four were male, and four female; thirty-two were Anglo-American, three were Negro-American, and three were Mexican-American. The median annual family income was $7,000 plus, and the median level of formal education was college graduate, with 45 per cent having done graduate work. Differences between TNO and non-TNO median family income, level of formal education, and membership in voluntary associations (TNO = 2; non-TNO = 4) were statistically significant (P < .01).[24] TNO medians for age (forty-six

23 Samuel A. Stouffer and Jackson Toby, "Role Conflict and Personality," *American Journal of Sociology*, 56 (March, 1951), 395–406.
24 Wilcoxon Rank Sum Test, one-tailed. See Frank Wilcoxon, S. K. Katti,

TABLE 1. Comparison of TNO and Non-TNO Median Scale Scores
(N = 61)

Scaleᵃ	TNO (N = 23)	Non-TNO (N = 38)	Significance of Differenceᵇ
Activism	17.0	18.5	p < .01
Anomie	6.0	4.0	p < .01
Integration with relatives	2.5	2.0	NS
Achievement orientation	15.0	17.0	p < .01
Future orientation	9.0	10.0	p < .05
Isolation	16.0	13.0	p < .01
Normlessness	10.0	6.0	p < .01
Powerlessness	15.0	12.0	p < .01
Alienation	40.0	32.0	p < .01
Particularismᶜ	1.5	0.0	p < .02

ᵃ Not used as Guttman Scales.
ᵇ Wilcoxon Rank Sum Test, one-tailed. See note 24 of this chapter.
ᶜ Particularism, on this scale, is reciprocally related to universalism.

years), Board attendance (four meetings), length of Topeka residency (twenty-nine years), and tenure as Board member (eight months) did not differ significantly from non-TNO medians for age (forty-three years), Board attendance (four meetings), length of Topeka residency (twenty-one years), and tenure as Board member (ten months).[25]

Table 1 reveals striking and consistent differences between TNOs and non-TNOs in the social-psychological variables measured by the questionnaire. The differences are statistically significant in the directions expected. That is, TNOs scored lower than non-TNOs in activism, achievement orientation, and future orientation, but higher than non-TNOs in anomie, isolation, normlessness, powerlessness, alienation, and particularism. These differences are taken to indicate contrasting views of self-in-society that reflect prior adaptation to the exigencies of differing social environments.

There are more than one thousand OEO poverty boards throughout the United States. Topeka's Economic Opportunity Board is as-

and Roberta A. Wilcox, *Critical Values and Probability Levels for the Wilcoxon Rank Sum Test and the Wilcoxon Signed Rank Test.*
25 Wilcoxon Rank Sum Test, two-tailed. *Ibid.*

sumed to be fairly typical of the others, though it has a larger membership than most. At minimum, boards are similar in that they *must* have no fewer than one-third of their members representatives of, and selected by, residents in poverty areas. Since the remaining members usually are drawn from higher socio-economic strata, it can be hypothesized that social-psychological differences, paralleling those manifested in the Economic Opportunity Board and presented in Table 1, will exist among the total membership of a given board. What effects would such differences have upon board dynamics, particularly the processes of decision-making? How might such differences influence members' perceptions of one another, and their perceptions of board means and ends? Poverty boards have been characterized as "conflict-ridden." To what extent is such conflict a function of disparate member definitions of the situation, influenced by differing attitudes toward self-in-society?

Observation by the research staff in nineteen regular and seventeen executive sessions of Topeka's Economic Opportunity Board, and interviews with the participants, revealed patterns of behavior which reflected TNO/non-TNO differences in the scale variables. Following are some examples of issues around which debate, sometimes heated, centered during early Board meetings. The scale variable (Table 1) which seems most closely related to each issue is indicated in parentheses.

Non-TNOs tended to view the local poverty program as they might any organized community-action program—optimistically, and confident that their efforts would bring results beneficial to the community. They took their participation, and the fact that such participation would be meaningful, for granted. TNOs initially seemed pessimistic about the meaningfulness of their participation, and expressed the feeling that their efforts would most likely not bring results (activism). Non-TNOs, appearing convinced that community officials wanted to help with programs, wanted to invite their co-operation. TNOs seemed to feel that most local officials actually did not care about the poor, and that officials in general are guilty until proven innocent (anomie). Non-TNOs appeared to be influenced by the conviction that, with dedicated and concerted work, these community factors which perpetuate poverty could be changed, and that the local program could be made into the best in the country. TNOs at first seemed neither so certain that the system could be changed, nor that it would be judicious to exert as much energy as the program was calling for, since the rewards at that time were rather unclear (achievement orientation). Non-TNOs appeared quite tolerant of program delays endemic to the bureaucratic process, and argued for the importance of "long-range programing," "feasibility studies," etc. TNOs seemed markedly impatient with such delays, and insisted upon "action now" (future orientation). They seemed often to indicate a perception of a "have *versus* have-not" or an "us *versus* them" struggle, and at the onset to avoid identifying with the community (isolation). Non-TNOs tended to believe that if the Board conformed to OEO standards, if it met the criteria for community need, and if the applications were prepared according to rules and regulations specified by OEO, they could with some confidence expect grants for additional projects (contingent, of course, upon the availability of federal funds). TNO's, on the other hand, did not initially seem willing to invest the rules, regulations, criteria, or procedures with purposeful value, or to accept the relative predictability of outcome from conformity to those norms (normlessness). Non-TNOs appeared to be satisfied with their degree of individual influence in Board decision-making processes, and with the potential impact of those decisions for community change. TNOs did not seem to feel that Board action would change much for the poor, or that their own influence within Board decision-making processes was significant (powerlessness). Non-TNOs tended to accept Board members or co-operating officials on the basis of title and to encourage the impartial and objective hiring of program staff (universalism). TNOs tended to favor the evaluation of others not on the basis of title but rather according to "what kind of guy he is," and to insist that one should give jobs to people he knows or to whom he is related (particularism).[26]

[26] For comparable views of conflict in other poverty boards, see: Ralph Kramer, *Participation of the Poor*; Ralph Kramer, "Ideology, Status, and Power

Similar issues pivotal to controversy and debate might be expected in other poverty boards where TNOs (or their counterparts) and non-TNOs significantly differ in social-psychological variables such as those measured in this study. Also, it might be anticipated that, as was the case in the Economic Opportunity Board, non-TNOs will tend to dominate the early meetings—perhaps not advertently but by virtue of their familiarity with, and skills and attitudes related to, the structure and functions of formal meetings.

TNO/non-TNO differences reported in Table 1 highlight the fact that Board dynamics represented much more than the manifest aspects of program content. The dynamics reflected a fission or fusion of world views, and the travails of socialization. The experience of Board *process*, particularly for TNOs, may well have been more meaningful (or frustrating) than the *content* of Board proceedings.

The differences between TNOs and non-TNOs presented in Table 1 illustrate the complex task confronting a poverty-intervention organization like the TOEO. If the organization has implemented the federal mandate, it will have on its board the poor and the non-poor, and thus probably will have established a social situation in which conflict is inevitable. Such conflict probably is intended to have social benefit and to have potential for engineering social change.[27] But it is nonetheless conflict, and the poverty-intervention organization is expected to be the mediator. The organization, like the TOEO, would purport to be a "bridge" between the poor and the not-poor, and attempt to co-ordinate their efforts in the board and to gain consensus concerning ways and means of poverty programing. Thus, particularly in the beginning phases of board operation, the members of a poverty-intervention organization staff may find themselves

---

in Board-Executive Relationships," *Social Work*, 10, 4 (October, 1965), 107–114; Moynihan, *Maximum Feasible Misunderstanding: Community Action in the War on Poverty*; and Ralph Segalman, "Dramatis Personae of the Community Action Program: A 'Built-In' Conflict Situation," *Rocky Mountain Social Science Journal*, 4 (October, 1967), 140–150.

[27] See, e.g., Lewis Coser, *The Social Functions of Conflict*; and Ralph Lane, Jr., "Sociological Aspects of Mental Well Being," in R. Brockbank and D. Westby-Gibson (eds.), *Mental Health in a Changing Community*, pp. 43–45.

attempting to relate to, and satisfy the demands of, both poor and not-poor members, possibly to the satisfaction of neither.

The OEO training programs for staff and board members might profit by including in their curricula not only discussions of poverty-program content and formal roles for participants, but also discussions of participant interaction, perceptions, and process experiences. Another point for training discussion—and a research hypothesis as well—would be that the kinds of social-psychological differences which exist between the poor and the not-poor might obtain between the chosen leaders of the poor and those poverty-area residents who are not OEO indigenous leaders or who are not participating in OEO activities. Patterns of issue-related conflicts among those groups might parallel conflicts seen between the poor and not-poor board members.

Further analyses revealed that TNO males differed significantly $(p<.05)$[28] from TNO females only in isolation (male median=14; female median = 18.5) and in annual family income (male median =$3,000–$5,000; female median=$0–$3,000. There was no significant difference between male and female non-TNOs. Significant $(p < .05)$[29] ethnic differences were found among TNO medians for activism (A = 17.5; NA = 16.0; MA = 16.5; I = 14.0),[30] normlessness (A = 8; NA = 10; MA = 13; I = 14.5), and powerlessness (A = 16; NA = 17.5; MA = 15; I = 12). No significant ethnic differences were found among non-TNO medians. Although the number of subjects was quite small within each ethnic subdivision, there was enough scale-score variation among the subdivisions to hypothesize for further research that median TNO scale scores may be influenced by the proportion of ethnic representation. The same hypothesis may be offered for the proportion of TNO males and females. If TNO sex and ethnic factors are broadly related to social-psychological variables such as those measured here, then poverty boards

[28] Wilcoxon Rank Sum Test, two-tailed, See note 24 of this chapter.
[29] Kruskal-Wallis One-Way Analysis of Variance. See Sidney Seigel, *Nonparametric Statistics for the Behavioral Sciences*, pp. 184–194.
[30] A = Anglo-American; NA = Negro-American; MA = Mexican American; I = American Indian.

might expect such differences to stimulate controversy on program issues among the poor themselves, as well as between the poor and the not-poor. It has been stated that no significant sex or ethnic differences existed among the non-TNOs. Again, though the number of subjects was very small, it might cautiously be concluded that the differences in social-psychological variables reported here are more closely related to socio-economic factors than to sex or ethnic ones, but that the influence of sex and ethnic factors becomes more apparent among the TNO group.

Table 2 presents correlations among scale variables, age, income, education, and voluntary associations for all Board members. As might be expected, activism, achievement orientation, future orientation, annual family income, formal education, and voluntary-association membership are positively related to one another and negatively related to anomie, integration with relatives, isolation, normlessness, powerlessness, alienation, and particularism. The latter variables are all positively related. The correlation coefficients among anomie, achievement orientation, and future orientation are escalated by those items which the scales have in common. Similarly, the correlation coefficient signifying the relation of alienation to each of its subscales (isolation, normlessness, and powerlessness) reflects the representation of the subscale items in the total alienation scale score. The respondent's age was not remarkably related to the other variables.

These data support the findings of the authors of the scale concerning interrelations among the specific variables measured, and the relations of the variables to socio-economic level. Also, the data further illustrate the directions of differences between TNO and non-TNO Board members.

Although the correlations were not statistically significant and were of a very low order, TNO Board attendance and tenure of membership were positively related to activism, achievement orientation, and future orientation, and negatively related to isolation, normlessness, and alienation. The relations cannot be considered change data, but may indicate the direction of changes which were taking

TABLE 2. Correlations among Scale Variables, Age, Income, Education, and Voluntary Associations for Board Members[a]

	Activism	Anomie	Integration with relatives	Achievement orientation	Future orientation	Isolation	Normlessness	Powerlessness	Alienation	Particularism	Age	Annual family income	Formal education
Anomie	-.71[b]												
Integration with relatives	-.21	.20											
Achievement orientation	.73[b]	-.72[b]	-.34[b]										
Future orientation	.79[b]	-.80[b]	-.28[c]	.72[b]									
Isolation	-.35[b]	.52[b]	.30[c]	-.46[b]	-.46[b]								
Normlessness	-.57[b]	.54[b]	.25[c]	-.56[b]	-.51[b]	.35[b]							
Powerlessness	-.47[b]	.57[b]	.24	-.53[b]	-.48[b]	.65[b]	.62[b]						
Alienation	-.55[b]	.65[b]	.31[c]	-.62[b]	-.57[b]	.80[b]	.77[b]	.92[b]					
Particularism	-.10	.06	.14	-.13	-.04	.09	.20	.21	.20				
Age	-.04	.10	.02	-.16	.07	.02	-.01	.03	.02	.22			
Annual family income	.49[b]	-.48[b]	.04	.55[b]	.42[b]	-.31[c]	-.29[c]	-.42[b]	-.41[b]	-.16	-.19		
Formal education	.30[c]	-.27[c]	-.01	.41[b]	.25	-.19	-.25[c]	-.16	-.23	-.17	-.19	.51[b]	
Voluntary association membership	.13	-.22	-.06	.12	.11	-.19	-.11	-.10	-.16	.05	-.03	.20	.40[b]

[a] Pearson r; N = 61; df = 59.
[b] P < .01.
[c] P < .05.

place as a result of subsequent participation—changes which will be presented and discussed in detail in Chapter 9.

The data indicate that there were indeed significant demographic and social -psychological differences between members of the Economic Opportunity Board who represented the poor and those who did not. Those differences also indicate that, at least on the Board, the Overlap Model was potentially viable, and that the social-therapy assumptions of that model and of "maximum feasible participation" could be tested.

[13a] Richard A. Ball, "A Poverty Case: The Analgesic Subculture of the Southern Appalachians," *American Sociological Review*, 33 (December, 1968), 885–895; H. Beilin, "The Pattern of Postponability and Its Relation to Social Class Mobility," *Journal of Social Psychology*, 44 (August, 1956), 33–48; M. Beiser, "Poverty, Social Disintegration and Personality," *Journal of Social Issues*, 21, 1 (January, 1965), 56–78; W. Bell, "Anomie, Social Isolation and Class Structure," *Sociometry*, 29 (June, 1957), 105–116; B. Bernstein, "Language and Social Class," *British Journal of Psychology*, 11 (1960), 271–276; B. J. Boose and S. S. Boose, "Some Personality Characteristics of the Culturally Disadvantaged,"*Journal of Psychology*, 65 (March, 1967), 157–162; M. Elaine Burgess, "Poverty and Dependency: Some Selected Characteristics," *Journal of Social Issues*, 21 (January, 1965), 79–97; Harry M. Caudill, *Night Comes to the Cumberlands;* A. Cohen and H. Hodges, "Characteristics of the Lower Blue Collar Class," *Social Problems*, 10, 4 (1963), 303–334; M. P. Deutsch, "The Disadvantaged Child and the Learning Process," in A. H. Passow (ed.), *Education in Depressed Areas;* Lamar J. Empey, "Social Class and Occupational Aspirations: A Comparison of Absolute and Relative Measurements," *American Sociological Review*, 21 (December, 1956), 703–709; Louis A. Ferman, Joyce L. Kornbluh, and Alan Haber (eds.), *Poverty in America;* Herbert J. Gans, "Redefining the Settlement's Function for the War on Poverty," *Social Work*, 9, 4 (October, 1964), 3–12; Herbert J. Gans, "Subcultures and Class," in Ferman, Kornbluh, and Haber (eds.), *Poverty in America;* Nona Y. Glazer and Carol F. Creedon, *Children and Poverty;* Margaret Gordon, *Poverty in America;* Rosiland Gould, "Some Sociological Determinants of Goal Striving," *Journal of Social Psychology*, 13 (May, 1941), 461–473; Alan L. Grey, *Class and Personality in Society;* W. C. Haggstrom, "The Power of the Poor," in Frank Riessman, Jerome Cohen and Arthur Pearl (eds.), *Mental Health of the Poor*, 205–223; E. Herzog, "Some Assumptions About the Poor," *Social Service Review*, 37, 4 (December, 1963), 391–402; Lola M. Irelan and Arthur Besner, "Low-Income Outlook on Life," *Welfare in Review*, 3 (September, 1965), 13–19; Berton H. Kaplan, "The Structure of Adaptive Sentiments in a Lower Class Religious Group in Appalachia," *Journal of Social Issues*, 21 (January, 1965), 126–141; Suzanne Keller, "The Social Role of the Urban Slum Child: Some Early Findings," *American Journal of Orthopsychiatry*, 33, 5 (1963), 823–831; L. LeShan, "Time Orientation and Social Class," *Journal of Abnormal and So-*

cial Psychology, 47, 3 (July, 1952), 589–592; Hylan Lewis, "Child Rearing Among Low Income Families," in Ferman, Kornbluh and Haber (eds.), *Poverty in America*; Oscar Lewis, *The Children of Sanchez* and *La Vida*; Elliott Liebow, *Tally's Corner*; H. McClosky and J. Schaar, "Psychological Dimensions of Anomie," *American Sociological Review*, 30, 1 (February, 1965) 14–40; William McCord, John Howard, Bernard Friedberg, and Edwin Harwood, *Life Styles in the Black Ghetto*; Dwight McDonald, "Our Invisible Poor," in Ferman, Kornbluh, and Haber (eds.), *Poverty in America*, pp. 6–24; C. Paul Marsh and Minnie M. Brown, "Facilitative and Inhibitive Factors in Training Program Recruitment Among Rural Negroes," *Journal of Social Issues*, 21 (January, 1965), 110–125; Hanna H. Meissner (ed.), *Poverty in the Affluent Society*; S. M. Miller, "The American Lower Class: A Typological Approach," in Arthur B. Shostak and William Gomberg (eds.), *New Perspectives on Poverty*, pp. 22–40; S. M. Miller, Frank Riessman, and Arthur Seagull, "Poverty and Self-Indulgence: A Critique of the Non-Deferred Gratification Pattern," in Ferman, Kornbluh, and Haber (eds.), *Poverty in America*, pp. 285–302; W. B. Miller, "Focal Concerns of Lower Class Culture," in Ferman, Kornbluh, and Haber (eds.), *Poverty in America*, pp. 261–270; Salvador Minuchin, Braulio Mantalvo, Bernard Guerney, Bernice Rosman, and Florence Schumer, *Families of the Slums*; Walter Mischel, "Preference for Delayed Reinforcement and Social Responsibility," *Journal of Abnormal and Social Psychology*, 62, 1 (January, 1961), 1–7; A. H. Passow (ed.), *Education in Depressed Areas*; Helen Pearlman, "Self-Determination: Reality or Illusion?" *Social Service Review*, 39, 4 (1965), 410–422; Alphonso Pinkney, *Black Americans*; Frank Riessman, "The Strengths of the Poor," in Shostak and Gomberg (eds.), *New Perspectives on Poverty*, pp. 40–47; Frank Riessman, Jerome Cohen, and Arthur Pearl, *Mental Health of the Poor*; Hyman Rodman, "The Lower Class Value Stretch," in Ferman, Kornbluh, and Haber (eds.), *Poverty in America*, pp. 270–284; B. Rosen and A. D'Andrade, "Psycho-social Origins of Achievement Motivation," *Sociometry*, 22 (September, 1959), 185–218; Aaron L. Rutledge and Gertrude Zemon Gass, *Nineteen Negro Men*; Louis Schneider and S. Lysgaard, "The Deferred Gratifiation Pattern: A Preliminary Study," *American Sociological Review*, 18, 2 (April, 1953), 142–149; Ben B. Seligman, *Aspects of Poverty*; Ben B. Seligman, *Poverty as a Public Issue*; R. L. Simpson and M. Miller, "Social Status and Anomia," *Social Problems*, 10, 3 (Winter, 1963), 256–264; Gideon Sjoberg, R. Brymer, and B. Farris, "Bureaucracy and the Lower Class," *Sociology and Social Research*, 50, 3 (April, 1966), 325–337; E. M. Spinley, *The Deprived and the Privileged*; I. Stone, D. Leighton, and A. H. Leighton, "Poverty and the Individual," in L. Fishman (ed.), *Poverty Amid Affluence*, pp. 72–97; M. Strauss, "Deferred Gratification, Social Class, and the Achievement Syndrome," *American Sociological Review*, 27 (June, 1962), 326–335; Charles A. Valentine, *Culture and Poverty*; Donald R. Whyte, "Sociological Aspects of Poverty: A Conceptual Analysis," *Canadian Review of Sociology and Anthropology*, 2, 4 (November, 1966), 175–189; C. Wright and H. Hyman, "Voluntary Association Memberships of American Adults," *American Sociological Review*, 23, 3 (June, 1958), 284–294.

CHAPTER 6

Deliberations, Debates, and Decisions

FROM THE TIME of its incorporation in October, 1965, the Economic Opportunity Board held at least quarterly meetings. The agenda for each meeting was determined by the staff of the TOEO in co-ordination with the Board president, vice-president, treasurer, and secretary, elected by the members from among their number. As the key decision-making unit in the Topeka poverty program, the Board had during its first year of operation considered and acted upon such community programs as: Head Start, Neighborhood Youth Corps, Adult Basic Education, Medicare Alert, Day Care Services and Family Center, a Neighborhood Extension Worker and Neighborhood Aide Program, a City-County Beautification Project, a Neighborhood House, and the conduct and administration of the TOEO. The Board attempted to process those programs in accordance with the purpose put forth in its articles of incorporation:

1. To administer and assure the proper use of money being made available under the Economic Opportunity Act of 1964 and any other amendments added thereto. To serve as the co-ordinating agency for programs under the Economic Opportunity Act.
2. To maintain a continuous, positive, analysis of Shawnee County's community agencies to assure their adequate serving of low-income families and persons.
3. To be sensitive to the total human needs of the people of the city and county and to cooperate with other community agencies in making provisions for present and future needs.
4. To stimulate communication between all segments of the population of Shawnee County so that the most effective and efficient use can be made of human resources.
5. To otherwise enter into contracts and negotiations with any and all agencies operating under the Economic Opportunity Act of 1964 and amendments thereto or any other governmental agency, federal, state, city, quasi-public agencies or any charitable, benevolent, education, nonprofit organization or any other person or organization, for the purpose of accomplishing the objectives for which this nonprofit organization is established.[1]

To illustrate the interactive patterns of Economic Opportunity Board members, and to demonstrate the nature of some agenda items which engendered controversy, the setting and dynamics of a typical Board meeting will now be detailed. The meeting to be presented took place on September 28, 1966, nearly a year after the Board's incorporation, and was the seventh full meeting to date. The meeting was one of those nearest to the time of the administration of our research questionnaire, which had revealed the differences in social-psychological characteristics between the poor and not-poor members (Chapter 5).

[1] By-laws of the Economic Opportunity Board of Shawnee County, Kansas, Inc., pp. 1–2.

THE SETTING

The meeting of September 28 was held, as generally were all Board meetings, in a large, rectangular conference room of the Shawnee County Courthouse. The room had the asphalt-tiled floor, aluminum-framed windows, pastel walls, sound-proofed ceiling, fluorescent lighting, and hissing air conditioning so typical of contemporary government offices. One entered the Courthouse at the basement level, signed in under the scrutiny of a uniformed guard, walked past the sheriff's office to the elevators, and rode to the second floor. The conference room was across from one of the courtrooms. Board meetings were scheduled to begin at 7:30 P.M. Consequently, with the exception of the sheriff's office personnel and a few cleaning attendants, the building was vacated.

At the front of the conference room, near the door, was a small table behind which sat the Board officers and TOEO staff. At the right of the table was a large movable blackboard. Two curving rows of tables with chairs faced the head table, and behind these were five additional rows of about nine chairs each.

A total of fifty-six people attended the meeting on the evening of September 28, forty-two of whom were voting members of the Board. Of these members, sixteen were Target Neighborhood Officers, fourteen were agency representatives, and twelve were citizens at large. Thirty of the voting members were men and twelve were women. There were twenty-three Anglo-Americans, five Mexican-Americans, twelve Negro-Americans, and two American Indians. Among the remaining fourteen people in attendance were six research observers, two TOEO staff members, and six guests. Figure 1 presents the seating arrangements of the participants.

Figure 1 reveals that most of the Target Neighborhood Officers were seated in chairs behind the tables at the front of the room. Most of the agency representatives and citizens at large were seated in chairs in the middle of the room or toward the back. This pattern was more typical of later than of earlier Board meetings. At the earlier meetings, the agency representatives and citizens at large, tending to dominate the meetings, generally sat at the front of the

IGURE 1. Seating Arrangement, Economic Opportunity Board Meeting, ptember 28, 1966

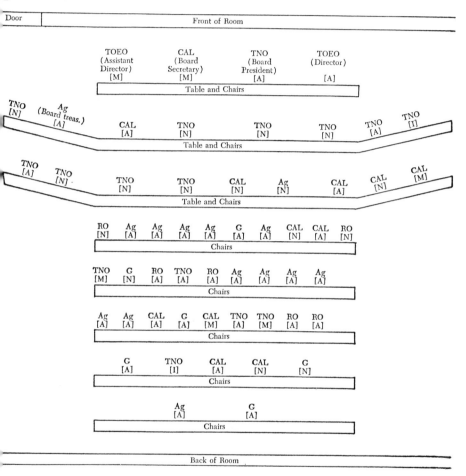

TOEO = Topeka Office of Economic Opportunity
CAL = Citizen at large
TNO = Target Neighborhood Officer
Ag = Agency representative
G = Guest
RO = Research observer

[M] = Mexican-American
[A] = Anglo-American
[N] = Negro-American
[I] = Indian-American

room. The Target Neighborhood Officers, initially less active during the meetings, often took rear seats. Gradually, as the Target Neighborhood Officers became more involved in the meetings, they moved closer to the front. Shortly after the September 28 meeting, the two rows of tables and chairs at the front of the room were reserved for them, at their request.

It is apparent in Figure 1 that Target Neighborhood Officers tended to cluster, as did agency representatives. Citizens at large pretty well distributed themselves around the room. This pattern had emerged by the third Board meeting, and generally was maintained by member choice. Finally, the seating division between Target Neighborhood Officers on the one hand, and agency representatives and citizens at large on the other, was formalized, as just mentioned, by reserving the two rows of tables and chairs for TNO's.

The seating arrangement represented, to a considerable extent, a substantial division between Target Neighborhood Officers and agency representatives. Conflict among Board members usually took the form of TNOs *versus* agency representatives, with the citizens at large siding with one group or dividing their opinions between the two groups. TNOs generally looked more favorably upon citizens at large, feeling that they came to the meetings not because it was their job but because they were actually interested in the problems of the poor.

Agenda

The agenda for the meeting of September 28 had earlier in the week been prepared by TOEO staff and Board officers. Although mimeographed copies had been mailed to all members, additional copies were distributed to the participants shortly before the meeting was called to order. The agenda items, indicating the direction the meeting was intended to take, were as follows:

1. Reading and accepting of the minutes of the last meeting.
2. Treasurer's report.
3. Report and ratifying of action concerning the Highland Park–Pierce Neighborhood House.
4. Report and ratifying of action by Personnel Committee.

5. Report on Beautification Project.
6. Ratifying action concerning Head Start.
7. Report on Out-of-School Neighborhood Youth Corps and Proposed Neighborhood House.
8. Report and ratifying of Work-Study Student Program.
9. Report concerning Budget Review Committee.
10. Unscheduled business.
11. Adjourned to meet for a special called meeting, October 26, 1966.

Since it was the Board's policy not to allow tape recording of its proceedings, a verbatim transcript of the sample meeting was not available. What is narrated here is an edited and condensed reconstruction of the meeting based on the notes of the six research observers who were in attendance. To give the reader an indication of the extent to which the agenda items were followed, and to provide structure to the narrative, the official minutes for each item of business are presented first. The minutes, reproduced here as recorded by the Board secretary (except that participating individuals are identified by type of Board membership rather than proper name), are followed by the observers' reconstruction of the discussion concerning the agenda item. The reconstruction is followed by some analytical comments. It is intended that the *content* of the meeting will be described by the minutes, and that the *process* will be described by the observer's reconstruction and the comments.

THE MEETING

Minutes: A summary of the minutes of the meeting of the Executive Committee during July and August were read by the secretary. An agency representative moved that the minutes be accepted. The motion was seconded and passed.

Reconstruction: Several Board members had already arrived at the Courthouse conference room by 7:10 P.M. although the meeting was not scheduled to begin until 7:30 P.M. There were two or three small clusters of members, engaging in quiet conversation. The Director of the TOEO was talking to the Target Neighborhood Officer who was chairman of the Personnel Committee about his forthcoming report to the Board. The Assistant Director was straightening our chairs, distributing ash trays here and there, and setting up some handouts and mimeographed sheets on a table near the door. The president of the Board, recently elected and a former Target Neighborhood Officer, shuffled through some notes on the table and remarked, to no one in particular, "I'm still pretty new at this game, you know." The president, who as a TNO had worn his working-man's clothes to meetings, now was dressed in a dark-blue suit. He seemed to be having trouble with the collar of his shirt, and often wedged a finger between the collar and his neck, twisting his head back and forth as if to relieve tightness. The tips of the collar were curled up; occasionally he would push them down, but inevitably they would curl back. He looked up again from his papers and commented, "I wish people'd get here so we can get the meeting going. We've got a lot to accomplish tonight."

Several other members had entered the room, but it was not until 7:40 P.M. that the necessary quorum was present. The TOEO Director had assessed the attendance and advised the president, "We're ready to do business now." The president formally called the meeting to order, and in a loud voice asked for the minutes of the last meeting to be read. The secretary read the minutes, which were approved as read.

The meetings never started at 7:30 P.M. Since the Board Bylaws specified that a majority of the voting members be present to constitute a quorum, no business could officially be conducted until that quorum was attained.

Prior to the formal beginning of the meeting, much last-minute agenda-setting and report-organizing occurred. If a division of opinion on a particular issue was expected, enclaves of voters formed in the hall, the men's room, or the conference room to crystallize positions and order arguments and strategies.

Minutes: The treasurer presented his report. He reported the expenditures and balance of this year for each of the OEO projects. The total balance at the present time is $79,667.26. Along with a Target Neighborhood Officer, several other members of the Board requested that the treasurer's report be printed and issued to the Board members regularly. The treasurer agreed to distribute these reports each month.

Reconstruction: The president called for the treasurer's report, which included a complete tally of the money awarded for specific projects and the amount that had been expended on those projects thus far. Two agency representatives discovered some minor errors in the budget, and corrected the treasurer. A Target Neighborhood Officer asked that a printed record of the budget be distributed to all the Board members on a regular basis. The president interjected, "I'm sure the treasurer will cooperate with that." An agency representative raised a "point of information" and indicated that although $68,000 had been awarded to a delegate agency for the Extension Worker Program, the treasurer's report showed that the $68,000 still remained unexpended in the budget after months of program operation. The treasurer looked at the figures and commented, "I guess I copied the figures wrong." Amid murmurs and some laughter, a citizen at large then made a formal motion that the budget figures regularly be written up and distributed to all members of the Board. It was seconded by a Target Neighborhood Officer and passed unanimously.

The question of the distribution of funds was always central to the Board meetings. There seemed to be a suspicion, on the part of at least some members, that funds were being "wasted" or "misappropriated." Those suspicions were heightened when, as in this meeting, inadvertent errors or inconsistencies were found in the financial records.

Minutes: An agency representative informed us that programs are now coming up for review and refunding. The Budget Review Committee will be meeting with the contracting agencies and Neighborhood representatives for the purpose of reviewing the programs, and will be making recommendations to the Board. The reporting agency representative requested that a representative from each Neighborhood Committee join the Budget Review Committee as a member. The president of the Board would make the appointment on the recommendation of the Neighborhood Committee. A Target Neighborhood Officer requested that the Neighborhood Committees be informed about the meetings of the Budget Review Committee so that they might participate more actively in the review process of the committee. The TOEO Director said that notices about meetings of this committee will be sent to both the chairman and the delegate of each Neighborhood Committee.

Reconstruction: The president called upon an agency representative to make a report about the Budget Review Committee. The agency representative apologized for asking to be taken out of turn on the agenda, but explained that he had another appointment. He told the group that this was now a funding and re-evaluation phase for those delegate agencies to whom the Board had delegated funding and responsibility for specific local poverty programs. He suggested that "one person from every Target Neighborhood Committee be placed on the Budget Review Committee, so that they can consider the financial issues for such projects as the Extension Worker Program and the Day Care Center." The TNOs vocally demonstrated approval of the suggestion.

An agency representative asked, "How will the Pre-School Study Committee fit with the Budget Review Committee for the Day Care Center?" The chairman of the Budget Review Committee answered that he did not know, and referred the question to the Director, who explained the interaction between the two groups to the satisfaction of all.

An agency representative asked about the present composition of the membership of the Budget Review Committee. The chairman responded that he didn't know for sure, but began enumerating the names of those whom he knew. The Director and another agency representative added a few more names. The chairman responded, "The committee has not met in some time, and several of the members named are no longer on the Board, so there will be need for replacements. There was not adequate representation from the Target Neighborhoods at the time the Budget Review Committee was formed because the Target Neighborhoods had not yet been fully established. This should be changed now, and there should be representation on the Budget Review Committee from the Target Neighborhoods." The Board members felt there was no need for a direct vote or action on the issue, and the chairman of the Budget Review Committee left the meeting as he had indicated he had to do.

The meeting came to a halt while the president determined how to get representatives from each of the Target Neighborhood Committees to serve on the Budget Review Committee. An agency representative suggested that TNOs recommend to the TOEO the individuals who would represent their committees. The president commented about the importance of "getting more people involved." He was interrupted by an agency representative who said, "Mr. President, it is in your power to appoint the committee, and there is no further need for discussion, so let's move on." A citizen at large took issue with the agency representative, exclaiming, "The democratic process in general may slow things down. Autocratic process is faster, but we know which one has the real advantages, so let's not rush things." The Director then explained to the president that each TNO could recommend a member from his Neighborhood to serve on the Budget Review Committee. The president was satisfied and discussion continued.

A TNO asked, "Since this concerns the performance of delegate agencies, can you get notification to all the Neighborhood Officers about when the Budget Review Committee will meet?" An agency representative answered, "That will be taken care of when the Neighborhood Officers make recommendations about who from their groups would sit in on the Budget Review Committee." There was some discussion, and it was agreed that notifications would be sent out to both the Neighborhood chairmen and the delegates they had selected whenever a meeting of the Budget Review Committee was to be held.

The report from the chairman of the Budget Review Committee was out of sequence with the agenda prepared prior to the meeting. No meeting of the Economic Opportunity Board ever fully followed its predetermined agenda. Often modifications to the agenda were made minutes before the meeting was to begin, or the exigencies of discussion during the meeting necessitated modification or shortening of the agenda. Agency representatives often complained about the "ignoring of the agenda." Target Neighborhood Officers seldom complained when the agenda items were not strictly followed. Similarly, agency representatives often became disturbed when standard parliamentary procedure was violated; Target Neighborhood Officers were far more tolerant of "irregularities" in procedure.

The suggestion to place representatives from the Target Neighborhood Committees on the Budget Review Committee reflected the TNOs' increasing demands for more participation at decision-making levels. It also reflected the awareness of most of the Board's not-poor members that opportunities for increased responsibility should be made available to the TNOs. Virtually every meeting of the Board contained a significant amount of discussion concerning the kind and amount of participation of the TNOs.

The impatient agency representative, and his argument with the citizen at large concerning efficiency *versus* democracy, was also quite typical of other Board meetings. Invariably some participant, particularly as the hour grew late, would complain about the length of discussion on a specific topic. Inevitably he would be answered by another participant who would urge the importance of the time-consuming processes of democracy. More often than not, those who pleaded the importance of democracy were those who were not happy with the way group opinion appeared to be running, and who wanted further discussion in the hope that the tide would turn in favor of their own position.

The agency representative who inquired about the way that the Pre-School Study Committee would articulate with the Budget Review Committee in an assessment of the Day Care Center was raising a process issue that continually reappeared during Board meetings. The Day Care Center was a poverty program, the responsibility for which had been assigned to a delegate agency in the community. The Pre-School Study Committee was composed of representatives from that delegate agency. What the agency representative was really asking was, to what degree would her Pre-School Study Committee maintain autonomy for its own evaluation and its own budgeting. Would the Budget Review Committee of the Economic Opportunity Board arrogate to itself the power of the Pre-School Study Committee to determine the operations of the Day Care Center? Delegate agencies, and their spokesmen on the Board, continually raised questions, and were questioned by other Board members, concerning the balance of power for program administration.

Minutes: The TOEO Director introduced a representative of the Bar Association and Legal Aid Society. The representative spoke of the desire of these groups to co-operate more closely with the OEO, and he explained the function of the Legal Aid Committee of the Bar Association, the Legal Aid Society, and the Lawyers Referral Group. Members of the Bar Association have been meeting with various Neighborhood Committees to discuss the various functions of these legal groups, and to discuss how to be of further help to the Neighborhood Committees and their members. Presently there is a panel of 30 lawyers who will take turns at being present at the meetings of the Neighborhood Committees to answer questions. They will continue to be present at the meetings as long as they are "fulfilling a purpose."

Reconstruction: The TOEO Director, through the president, called upon a Legal Aid representative, who proceeded to explain the services available through the Legal Aid Committee. He told the Board members that several lawyers had been attending Neighborhood Committee meetings and discussing the services. The representative mentioned, in passing, "When you folks really get your Neighborhoods organized, then we can send representatives to all the Neighborhood meetings."

"What does he mean *when* we get our Neighborhoods organized?" commented a TNO to those around him. "What does he think we've been doing for the past year!"

A citizen at large wanted to know how many lawyers had attended the Target Neighborhood Committee meetings. The representative answered, "Eight or nine."

The appearance of the Legal Aid representative had not been on the agenda. His presentation, however, was purely informational and demanded no action by the Board. The TOEO staff often arranged for such informational presentations, and inserted them into the agenda.

The Legal Aid staff had come to the conclusion that the best entry to the low-income population was through the Target Neighborhood Committees. Generally the lawyers were well received at the Neighborhood meetings, but occasionally TNOs would feel uncomfortable with such speakers, since they had been sent rather than invited.

The TNO who reacted to the Legal Aid representative's offhand comment concerning the extent of Neighborhood organization reflected a recurring conflict. Professional persons who visited Target Neighborhood Committee meetings sometimes were not favorably impressed with the way the meetings were conducted, perhaps judging them by their own standards. TNOs, on the other hand, were aware that where there was once no such gathering, now there was a meeting, and they were further aware of the effort it had taken to get the committee started. Thus they were angered by comments which indicated a lack of understanding of, or appreciation for, their leadership efforts.

Minutes: A Target Neighborhood Officer asked the Board to ratify the hiring of the director, Neighborhood aide, and secretary of the Neighborhood House. He also asked for ratification of the lease of the house in the Neighborhood, which rents for $100 per month. A citizen at large questioned whether the rental price was in keeping with the level of rents in that area. After some discussion, a Target Neighborhood Officer made the motion that leasing of the house be ratified. The motion was seconded by another Target Neighborhood Officer and passed. A Target Neighborhood Officer made the motion that the Board ratify the hiring of the personnel mentioned above. An agency representative seconded the motion and it was passed.

Reconstruction: The president called upon a Target Neighborhood Officer to present to the Board, for its ratification, the matter of hiring a staff and renting a building, at $100 per month, for the Neighborhood House.

A citizen at large (a businessman) asked, "Is that house worth $100 per month?" The TNO reporting responded, "It is, and the amount's in keeping with other rents in the neighborhood." Another TNO seemed to become angry, and said loudly, "We wouldn't pay it if it wasn't all right!"

Another citizen at large asked again, "Is that $100 a month in keeping with neighborhood rents? I can't believe it should be that much." The TNO reporting answered angrily, "You don't know that area very well, then!"

Another TNO quickly commented, "I rent property out in that area, and I know what the rents are. I rent a house that isn't quite as good as the one for the Neighborhood House and I pay $90 a month. The building for the Neighborhood House is going to get a lot of wear and tear, and I think $100 a month is a fair deal. Besides, they have some nice new facilities in there." A Target Neighborhood Officer made a motion to approve the rental. It was seconded by another TNO.

A citizen at large demanded, "Mr. President, shouldn't we discuss the issue now since this is really the proper time to discuss it according to parliamentary procedure?" The same citizen at large then wanted to know who drew up the lease. The TNO making the report answered that the lease had been drawn up by a lawyer, and had already been signed. A citizen at large exclaimed, "Already signed! I want to be sure that the money was spent wisely!"

Another citizen at large asked, "Who did we rent this from?" The TNO reporting said that it had been rented from a resident of the area, and the TOEO Director added, "There was no conflict of interest there."

A citizen at large then called for the question, and the president sought advice from the Director about how to put the question to a vote. The motion passed, with one dissenting vote from a citizen at large (the businessman).

The next issue for vote was the selection of personnel for the Neighborhood House. A TNO moved that the selection be ratified, and the motion was second by an agency representative. The president carried off the parliamentary move in perfect order, and the floor was open for discussion.

A Target Neighborhood Officer wanted to know how many applicants there were for the jobs. The TOEO Director responded that there were "five for the director's, eight or nine for the secretary's, and twelve for the Neighborhood aide's." A citizen at large inquired about the person who had been chosen as director, asking, "Wasn't he employed already?" The TOEO Director replied that he had been employed before as an Extension Worker.

The same citizen at large asked, "Was anyone picked for the job who lived in the area?" The TOEO Director responded, "All three of the people who were hired for jobs in the Neighborhood House lived in that Neighborhood." The citizen at large then wanted to know who took the new director's place in the Extension Worker job he left. The TOEO Director indicated that the replacement was "pending business until the Board decides whether or not the delegate agency will be continued as such."

The president asked whether they were ready for the question, and it was called for. The motion passed unanimously.

Some of the Target Neighborhood Officers resented that some other Board members would feel they were being "taken" by paying $100 a month rent for a Neighborhood House in an area which they knew and lived in. Often professionals on the Board, feeling it their duty to share their particular expertise with other members, inadvertently interfered with the antonomy or integrity of a TNO. This kind of conflict was true of the earlier meetings particularly.

That the lease for the Neighborhood House had already been signed prior to the Board's ratification was not unusual. Often arbitrary deadlines on the availability of funds for a specific community-action program were such that action had to be taken by TOEO staff before a Board meeting could be called. This problem was later averted by the decision of the Board to hold bimonthly, rather than quarterly, meetings, and by more efficient use of the Board's Executive Committee.

The president of the Board, newly elected and a former TNO, was having difficulty conducting the meeting according to parliamentary procedure. Ofter during this meeting he was corrected by agency officials or citizens at large. His lack of expertise, its causes and consequences, are important enough to Board dynamics to be discussed separately in this chapter.

The selection of personnel for the various community-action programs was, like the allocation of funds, an issue that recurred at every Board meeting. Considerable effort was made by the Board as a whole to guarantee that the available jobs would go to low-income persons who lived in the Target Neighborhoods. Agency representatives and citizens at large, however, were prone to argue that the qualifications of the person to be selected should equal or exceed those called for in the job description. The Target Neighborhood Officers were prone to disregard the job description, sometimes labeling the qualification requirements as "discriminatory."

Factionalism often showed up in connection with the choice of persons for jobs. A Target Neighborhood Officer might argue for a candidate from his Neighborhood. A minister citizen at large might argue for a candidate from his church group. An agency representative might argue for a person whom he considered to be "safe" and "not a rebel." Other participants might attempt to be influential in the choosing of personnel simply because they felt too distant from the decision-making processes of the Board. Such persons often would not care who was hired, so long as they felt they were instrumental in the hiring.

Minutes: A Target Neighborhood Officer presented the report of the Personnel Committee. He made the motion that the Board accept the creation of the positions of full-time bookkeeper and full-time clerk-typist for the TOEO. The motion was seconded by a Target Neighborhood Officer and was passed. It was reported that a person had been chosen for the job of full-time bookkeeper. The point was also made that the creation of the full-time position of clerk-typist is still pending business at the regional office.

Reconstruction: The president called upon the TNO who was chairman of the Personnel Committee. The TNO explained the hiring of a full-time TOEO bookkeeper, and the need to establish another part-time TOEO secretarial position. As he spoke, he displayed a chart showing the distribution of Neighborhood people who had been hired in various TOEO jobs. A Target Neighborhood Officer made a motion for acceptance of the personnel action, and it was seconded by another Target Neighborhood Officer. An agency representative asked about the salaries and the criteria for selection. The salary of the bookkeeper was said to be $4,200 a year, and that of the clerk between $250–$315 per month. The criteria for selection were interpreted to everyone's satisfaction. A TNO called for the question and the motion passed unanimously.

The chairman of the Personnel Committee, a very important committee of the Economic Opportunity Board, was a Target Neighborhood Officer. His report and his request for approval for personnel action met with relatively little resistance from the Board. His request was moved by a Target Neighborhood Officer, seconded by another Target Neighborhood Officer, and after some discussion the question was called for by a third Target Neighborhood Officer. Generally, the TNOs supported each other's efforts in this fashion.

Minutes: A citizen at large spoke for the Employment Committee. He said that presently in the Beautification Project 29 employees are working for the County and 15 for the City. Only three employees have lost their jobs with the County, but there has been more of a turnover in the City. An attempt is being made now to stabilize the work force in the City before men will be hired. There are still many applicants awaiting openings on this project.

Reconstruction: The president called for a report on the Beautification Projects from the Employment Study Committee. The chairman of that committee, a citizen at large, explained that there were twenty-nine employees left in the County program (three lost) and fifteen in the City program (seven lost). A Target Neighborhood Officer questioned the turnover, and the chairman stated that he felt "all things considered, the program is holding up real well." A citizen at large wanted to know whether any of the men were on welfare. The chairman replied, "Fifteen or sixteen of them were, but they are now off welfare." There was a noticeable murmur of approval from the group. Another citizen at large asked about the age range of the employees, and this was reported. The TOEO Director added that "OEO considered these men previously to be chronically unemployable."

A citizen at large wanted to know what the pay scale was, and the Director answered that question to his satisfaction. An agency representative asked about the trucks that were purchased by the county to be used by the Beautification Project workers, and another agency representative, who was responsible for purchasing the trucks, explained the number and kind purchased. The inquiring citizen at large, a political opponent of the agency representative, laughingly commented that he was afraid that the agency representative would "buy a fleet of trucks with county funds." The agency representative, also with a laugh, replied, "County funds are being protected." A citizen at large, quite impressed that fifteen or sixteen persons previously on welfare were now off the welfare rolls because of the Beautification Project, commented, "You mean those fellows are off welfare and drawing pay checks now?" Informed that that was "indeed the case," he responded, "Well, that's all right, by gosh! That's all right! Maybe this program *is* working!" Several of the Board members nodded or commented in approval. There being no further discussion or action, the president closed the discussion of the Beautification Project report.

Agency representatives and citizens at large were particularly pleased whenever any of the community-action programs succeeded in removing persons from the welfare rolls. This transition was taken to indicate the "rehabilitation" of the person, and offered the clearest kind of evidence that the poverty program was really working.

The exchanges between the citizen at large and the agency representative who were political opponents was not uncommon during Board meetings, especially if those meetings were near to election time. Several of the citizens at large and agency representatives were themselves politicians, or politically involved, and did not overlook the opportunity to impress a constituency or to put down an opponent if the occasion arose. On a few occasions during meetings the rhetoric of politically inspired debate temporarily submerged the substantive issues of poverty programing. Occasionally, a politically oriented TNO would become involved in that rhetoric.

Minutes: It was reported that $55,367 was left over from the previous Head Start Follow-through Program and from the summer Head Start Program. The motion was made by an agency representative that the action of the Executive Committee, which was approved by the Regional Office, and which stated that the $55,367 left over from the Head Start Follow-through

Program and summer Head Start Program be used for the 1966–1967 Head Start Follow-through Program, now be accepted. The motion was seconded by an agency representative and passed.

Reconstruction: The president called upon the TOEO Director to explain a proposed vote to merge $39,000 that was left over from previous Head Start Programs into the Head Start Follow-through Program for 1966–1967.

A citizen at large immediately asked, "I thought it was $62,000—isn't that what we said in the Executive Committee meeting? Now all of a sudden it's $39,000. We lost all that money in less than a week's time! Where did it go?" The Director called upon the treasurer to check the figures, and they were discovered to be inaccurate. Amid mumbles and laughter, the treasurer settled down to add the expenses, and then to subtract the total expenditures from the original financial award for the program.

During the interval, an agency representative asked, "When will the program start, when will the personnel be selected, and how will they be selected?" The Director answered the questions to the agency representative's satisfaction. The treasurer arrived at a corrected figure of $55,367, which upon review seeemed to be satisfactory to the membership. An agency representative called for a vote on the motion that the action of the Executive Committee be accepted. It was seconded by another agency representative. The question was called for by a third agency representative, and the motion was voted upon and passed, with four negative votes.

A budget figure that had been calculated by the Executive Committee, and introduced to the full meeting of the Board, was found to be inaccurate. This reflected a problem of co-ordination that Board members were never quite able to solve. The Executive Committee of the Board, consisting of the Board officers and the chairman of each Neighborhood Committee and standing committee, was intended to hash out substantive issues and strategies concerning poverty programs, and to present recommendations based upon their vote to the members at full Board meetings. It was hoped that the action of the Executive Committee would reduce the need for extensive and detailed discussion of program specifics during Board meetings. The members could consider the Executive Committee's recommendations, debate them if necessary, but come to a vote with relative speed.

Although the Executive Committee's determinations did have some effect toward "streamlining" Board discussion, and although the process became increasingly "efficient" over time, two major factors hampered the co-ordination between the Board and the Executive Committee. First was the factor of "maximum feasible participation." Not all the Board members, of course, were on the Executive Committee, and when it made recommendations about poverty programs, hiring, budgeting, etc., at full Board meetings, the many who were not members of the committee felt they should then have a chance to express their opinions. The participants— TNOs, agency representatives, and citizens at large included—often would demand exhausting detail concerning each and every item of each and every action recommended by the committee. Consequently, Executive Committee members would become frustrated at having to "go through the whole thing again," and would become defensive about their recommendations. Second, the Executive Committee meetings were often held several days, or even weeks, before the full Board meeting. Regulations, funding opportunities, deadlines for action, potentials for new programs, any or all could literally change from one day to the next for the TOEO. As a result, actions taken or recommendations made by the Executive Committee on many occasions were inconsistent, obsolete, or incorrect by the time they were presented at the meeting of the Economic Opportunity Board.

Minutes: The TOEO Assistant Director reported that the Indian group and the North-Topeka-East Neighborhood Committee are considering a joint venture of having a Neighborhood House in the North-Topeka-East area, and for the members of the

Indian community throughout Topeka. An agency representative, as well as other members of the Board, pointed out the
fact that the Neighborhood Extension Workers are working
in those areas and requested that consideration be given to
evaluation of the activities of the Extension Workers, and the
prospect of a Neighborhood House in that same area. He suggested that the consideration of these two projects be co-ordinated and integrated. The TOEO Director stated that the Budget
Review Committee will have the job of beginning to review
these projects, and that these questions will be raised at that
time. Two Target Neighborhood Officers pointed out the fact
that the Extension workers cannot do all the work required in
those neighborhoods and that Neighborhood Houses are
needed.

The TOEO Assistant Director also reported on the discussion
presently going on in a potential delegate agency regarding the
formation of an Out-of-School Neighborhood Youth Corps Program. The Program would cover youths between the ages of
16 and 21. While offering these youths part-time employment,
the main thrust of the program would be to help them get back
to school. The emphasis would be on remedial education. Once
in school the youths could be employed in the Neighborhood
Youth Corps Program for those in school. A citizen at large
asked about the length of existence of the delegate agency and
the number of its membership. The TOEO Assistant Director replied that the group has been in existence about six to eight
months and has about 45 to 50 dues-paying members. The
citizen at large asked whether this program would be a duplication of existing programs, and both an agency representative
and the TOEO Assistant Director replied that no such program
existed in the City. The citizen at large asked how these drop-
outs would be located, and whether there would be any limi-
tation of the youths in the program according to neighborhood
or ethnic group. The reply was that all the youths in the County
would be eligible, and an agency representative also said that
the school can easily identify those who have dropped out.

Reconstruction: The president called upon the Assistant Director of the TOEO, who introduced a newly elected Target Neighborhood Officer and reported the rekindling of interest in OEO within that area (North-Topeka-East). He then reported the Indians' interest in a Neighborhood House, and said that the North-Topeka-East Target Neighborhood and the Indians wanted to co-operate in such a venture. The Assistant Director commented, "The Indians wanted to set up a Neighborhood House for Indians only, but that's not in line with OEO policy."

The Assistant Director then moved on to explain another program for discussion. He told the group about a delegate agency "wanting to set up a program for high-school drop-outs. It would be called the Out-of-School Neighborhood Youth Corps, and would handle between fifty and sixty participants."

After explaining more of the program's details, the Assistant Director asked for discussion. A citizen-at-large asked, "What is the delegate agency like that's going to handle this?" The Assistant Director detailed the characteristics of the delegate agency, which was a nationally affiliated local chapter of a Mexican-American veterans' association. The citizen at large asked, "How would we work the program?" The Assistant Director explained the salary structure, and the various procedures for application and implementation, adding, "This isn't too specifically spelled out yet, because it's still in the idea stage." An agency representative wanted to know "if the delegate agency qualifies under OEO regulations as a delegate agency." Both the TOEO Director and Assistant Director replied that it did.

Returning to the first item reported on by the Assistant Director—the proposed Neighborhood House—a citizen at large commented, "I can't understand why you'd want to have this Neighborhood House over in *that* part of town. There's nothing over there in that part of town!" The Target Neighborhood Officers from "*that* part of town" whirled around in their seats, faced the citizen at large, and glowered at him. The Assistant Director immediately took issue with the citizen at large, and said, "There're lots of things over there, and lots of people who need help and who're interested in this program!" A number of the Target Neighborhood Officers rumbled agreement, and the citizen at large withdrew his comment.

About fifteen seconds later, however, he again exclaimed, "No, I'm still not satisfied! Why is it necessary to put a Neighborhood House in that area, when the Indians are living all over town?" The TOEO Director answered, "The Indians have special problems of their own that are related to being members of a minority group. They also have a common bond of heritage, and a common interest in certain kinds of arts and crafts and things like that. They feel very close to one another, but they don't have any place, besides the Reservation, where they can all get together. The Topeka Indians don't have a place they feel they can call their own here. They could do this in co-operation with the North-Topeka-East Neighborhood Committee." An agency representative added, "What the Indians want is to maintain some sense of identity. You can't blame them for that!" The questioning citizen at large agreed, and sat down.

Continuing with the discussion of the Neighborhood House, an agency representative who had come late rose and said, "You know, we have a $76,000 Extension Worker Program trying to operate here in Topeka. I think you ought to slow down and find out what effect the Extension Worker Program has before you start building Neighborhood Houses. You obviously have no clear goals for the Neighborhood Houses, you aren't quite sure what you're going to do, and none of this was talked about with the delegate agency of the Extension Worker Program beforehand. Besides that, this proposal didn't go through your own committee structure here."

Many of the participants seemed disturbed by the agency representative's comments, and there were several exclamations such as: "What's that?" "What're you talking about!" "No! No!" The TOEO Director challenged the agency representative, "That's not true! The Neighborhood House in Highland Park–Pierce went through all the committee structures that we have here, and as a matter of fact, I talked to you about it at length on a number of occasions. The plans for this new Neighborhood House now also are going through all of our committees. You're telling us now that the TOEO is supposed to tell the Neighborhood people to slow down. We can't do that. We can't sit on their ideas! This program is built on their ideas, and the purpose of this program is to give them a chance to express them, not for us to sit on them."

A Target Neighborhood Officer asked for the floor, and commented, "Well, I don't know about the Extension Worker Program. I get a feeling that some of their workers and aides are giving us an evaluation of that program by leaving it!" Another TNO added, "You can't expect one program to do all the work in this city. The problem of poverty is just too big."

A citizen at large agreed with the protesting agency representative, "The Neighborhood House looks to me like a duplication of the services of the Extension Worker Program. You know, it's too easy to spend this money that's coming in to us, and we should be more careful."

A Target Neighborhood Officer rebutted, "Don't stymie our ideas! Nobody can tell us what to do! We've been pushed around enough now! We're trying to do something constructive here, through the proper channels, and we don't want to be put down by people who don't really understand our problems."

Another TNO rose and said, in a very slow and measured voice, "I have just one thing to say: Let's be careful we don't *contribute to poverty*." He then sat down. A citizen at large asked him to elaborate on his statement. The TNO stood again and said, "All right. I mean adding to poverty by *slow action*. Why should we be arguing about legal procedure and so on, when we know that the Highland Park–Pierce Target Neighborhood had to wait almost a year to get its House? And all the while the poor kept suffering while we kept arguing!" Several of the Target Neighborhood Officers in the group were nodding approval, and there were several comments of agreement.

The president of the Board took the floor and underscored the importance of Neighborhood participation, and of working quickly so that the poor could be helped and could help themselves (as stated above, he was a former Target Neighborhood Officer).

A citizen at large commented, "Well, if it took that long to get Highland Park–Pierce Neighborhood House going, I don't see what the agency representative is worried about concerning this Indian–North-Topeka proposed Neighborhood House. If we move that slowly, I don't see any objection to our getting this other Neighborhood House going, because it's going to take some time to get it funded in Washington, anyway."

An agency representative rose and said, "It seems to me it's our duty to help these people out in any way we can. We should do it in as quick and efficient a manner as we can." A Target Neighborhood Officer, without recognition from the chair, proclaimed, "All we ever do is talk, talk, talk! Let's get things going!"

A citizen at large returned to the previously discussed topic of the Out-of-School Neighborhood Youth Corps Program, and asked, "Who selects the drop-outs?" An agency representative associated with education answered the question, assuring the citizen at large that there would be no duplication between the In-School Neighborhood Youth Corps Program and the Out-of-School Neighborhood Youth Corps Program.

A Target Neighborhood Officer leaped to his feet and said, rather heatedly, "We talk about human rights and human equality! Why, then, are some of you trying to kill our ideas here? Why should any ideas be killed? This is our chance to express our ideas, and we haven't been able to do it before. Some people here seem to like the old way of doing things, where they have all the ideas and they do all the talking, and it's their ideas that go into practice, and we just sat back and took it, saying nothing!"

An agency representative rose to say that he was "stupefied by the discussion of two separate proposals at once—the proposed Neighborhood House, and the proposed Out-of-School Neighborhood Youth Corps Program." He suggested that the TOEO send out, prior to Board meetings, more information about items that would be on the agenda, so that "we'll have more time to read these things over and consider these questions, and then we can talk about them more sensibly when we get to the Board meeting. I agree we should have free thinking going on here, and have plenty of time to express ourselves, and we can do more of that if we have a better idea of the proposals involved. "These ideas are developing, and interval progress reports should be made to the Board about them, and any other ideas too, so we can have a chance to review them."

Another agency representative stated, "We should always be careful about checking on the services that existing agencies have to offer before we start something new." One of the Target Neighborhood Officers retorted, "Some of them just don't get the message, do they? There's no duplication here! Both programs are needed! Can't you see that?"

The agency representative who had considerably earlier raised the issue about the duplication of services between the proposed Neighborhood House and the existing Extension Worker Program commented, "I was afraid that what I said would be misconstrued. I'm not opposed to the Neighborhood House. I think it's a good idea. All I'm asking is that you please evaluate the existing services first." A citizen at large agreed with the agency representative and said, "The purpose of this meeting is for us all to express our opinions. There's no need for 'yes men' here, so we should be able to say whatever we want, even if it's unpopular." A Target Neighborhood Officer challenged the citizen at large, "There're no 'yes men' here! What do you mean? We express what we think's best, and we have our say, and that's the way it's going to be!"

A citizen at large suggested that "we table the motion." The TOEO Director made haste to explain that there was no need to table a motion, since no motion had been made. "In fact," he continued, "this is just a discussion of ideas and nothing more than that." The discussion then summarily came to a halt, and the president moved on to other business.

This exchange among the Board participants is particularly revealing of the kind of confusion that can result when more than one agenda item, further confounded by "hidden agenda," are introduced concurrently for discussion. In the same report to the members the Assistant Director dealt with two discrete proposals: (1) The Neighborhood House under the joint sponsorship of the Indian Neighborhood Committee and the North-Topeka-East Neighborhood Committee, and (2) The Out-of-School Neighborhood Youth Corps Program, under the sponsorship of a Mexican-American veterans' organization.

As is apparent in the reconstruction of the discussion surrounding this agenda item, the participants shifted back and forth, inconsistently and almost without pattern, from one proposal to the other. At times it was difficult to determine which proposal a participant was addressing himself to when he had the floor. Furthermore, each of the two proposals had opponents and proponents who were arguing for one side or the other of a hidden agenda. The Out-of-School Neighborhood Youth Corps Program was being proposed by a schismatic faction of the Mexican-American veterans' organization, which had several months earlier broken from the local parent chapter and formed and chartered a chapter of its own. Most of the probing questions concerning the Out-of-School Neighborhood Youth Corps proposal came, consequently, from Board members who were supporters of the parent faction and opponents of the schismatic faction. Questions from the floor about the legitimacy of the sponsoring organization under OEO regulations were actually, according to the hidden agenda, questions about the legitimacy of that factional group to be chartered at all. Essentially, their internal organizational fight had found another battlefield—the Board meeting.

The agency representative calling for "evaluation of existing services" before the Board considered the proposed Neighborhood House was a representative of the delegate agency for the Extension Worker Program. He was concerned that the establishment of Neighborhood Houses by the Board would duplicate and dilute his agency's efforts with the Extension Worker Program in the Target Neighborhoods. His challenges to the proposed Neighborhood House might be interpreted as reflecting a hidden agenda for protection of his agency.

Other questions, particularly those about having the Neighborhood House "in *that* part of town," came from participants, themselves Negro-American, who felt that predominantly Negro Target Neighborhoods were more in need of the services of a Neighborhood House than were the Indians. Since funds were available at this time for only one new Neighborhood House, the hidden agenda of competition was inevitable.

Another and very important hidden-agenda item existed for the Target Neighborhood Officers as a group. For the TNOs, the Neighborhood House proposal was in no way a duplication of the existing Extension Worker Program—from the point of view of participation in the decision-making process. They felt they would have more say in the conduct and administration of a Neighborhood House than they ultimately had had in the Extension Worker Program. Thus some of the agency representatives and citizens at large, arguing objectively that there appeared to be duplication in the service *content* of Neighborhood Houses and the Extension Worker Program, essentially ignored *process* distinctions for the participants. The TNOs, on the other hand, perceived no duplication in the *process experiences* available to them under the two programs, but they essentially ignored the service *content*. When an agency representative or citizen at large pointed out a specific duplication, a Target Neighborhood Officer might accuse him of trying to "kill our ideas." When a Target Neighborhood Officer made a suggestion about expanding participation of the poor, he consequently might be admonished to "evaluate the existing services first."

The concurrent discussion of the two proposals and the hidden agenda finally ground to a halt, with very little having been accomplished beyond catharsis. At other Board meetings, a similar fate befell proposals confusingly segmented, presented multiply, or heavily laden with hidden agenda.

Minutes: The TOEO Director reported on the Work-Study Program. He stated that the delegate agency would not lower its requests for 20% local share in the program from participating agencies. The TOEO Director, following the approval given him by the Executive Committee to negotiate with the delegate agency, obtained approval from the Regional Office for the 16% which OEO can provide. He said that we will have to obtain the remaining 4% from donation. A contract has been signed with the delegate agency on the basis of 20%. A motion for the ratification of this action was made by an agency representative and was seconded by an agency representative. The motion was passed.

Reconstruction: The president called upon the Director to explain to the group about a contract being currently negotiated between the TOEO and the delegate agency for the Work-Study Program.

An agency representative inquired, "Pardon me if I'm ignorant, but what is the Work-Study Program?" The Director explained it to the agency representative's satisfaction.

The Director informed the group that the contract with the delegate agency for the Work-Study Program needed to be ratified. An agency representative asked, "Mr. Director, haven't you already signed the contract?" The Director answered, "Yes, but it still needs to be ratified." The agency representative laughingly commented, "That's just to keep you honest, right?" The group laughed, and after the motion had been made by an agency representative and seconded by an agency representative, it unanimously passed.

The president then asked if there was any further business, and there being none, adjourned the meeting. It was 10:00 P.M. The meeting had lasted for approximately two hours and fifteen minutes. After adjournment the conference room emptied quickly, except for a small nucleus of senior Target Neighborhood Officers and the Board officers, who talked briefly about the meeting before leaving. While the room was emptying, the Board president commented to people in general about the importance of "working together, and trying to beat poverty." The president then remarked, to no one specifically, "That was *some* meeting. I hope I did all right up here. I'm new to this, you know."

Board meetings typically lasted for over two hours, occasionally continuing beyond three hours. After about the first ninety minutes, members became restless, and obvious clock-watching began. Furthermore, it seemed as though the meetings became more disjointed and emotional as fatigue set in. Motions made toward the end of the evening would be debated heatedly, then suddenly passed, often unanimously, in order to "get the damned thing over with."

Clearly, poverty-board meetings, with their complex interpersonal interactions and sensitive agenda, should be limited to ninety minutes so as not to be further complicated by the fatigue of the members.

SOME COMMENTS ABOUT THE MEETING

The sample meeting reveals glimpses of the kinds of dialogues which rather consistently took place among agency representatives, Target Neighborhood Officers, citizens at large, and the TOEO staff in Board meetings. Furthermore, the reconstruction manifests conflicts stemming from some of the differences in values and orientations reported in Chapter 5.

For any given proposed program, agency representatives usually were concerned about the prerogatives of already established agencies, TNOs about the issues of participation and control, and citizens at large about cost and fiscal responsibility. Although the division of labor often broke down (more so as longevity of the Board increased), the task of the TOEO staff seemed primarily to be to provide program and proposal expertise. The primary task of the TNOs seemed to be to safeguard "maximum feasible participation." The other Board members seemed to emerge with responsibility for the pacing, economizing, and evaluation of programs. The process was complicated, of course, by members who had their own axes to grind concerning specific programs or individuals.

During the early Board meetings, TNOs seldom spoke, except to second a motion or ask a question. Generally they were nonplussed by parliamentary procedure, and not certain of the program language. The other members, agency representatives and citizens at large, dominated the meetings. As TNOs became more familiar with Board procedure and more comfortable in their own roles as indigenous leaders, however, their participation in discussion increased. Figure 2 shows a steady increase of Target Neighborhood Officers' statements (other than making motions or asking questions) about substantial issues during the meetings. The increase cannot be accounted for by TNO attendance, as Figure 2 indicates.

The curve for TNO statements expressed as the percentage of total Board statements peaks in June, 1966, and January, 1967. The June meeting was primarily concerned with the election of Board officers, in which a TNO was elected president. The January meeting was dominated by discussion pertinent to the hiring of a new TOEO director. TNOs always actively participated in discussions about hiring personnel. The two curve valleys, in December, 1966, and February, 1967, both indicate meetings primarily concerned with *long-range* budgetary planning. TNOs typically were relatively restrained during such discussions.

By the time of the sample meeting, Target Neighborhood Officers had shown a willingness to vote against majority opinion if they felt it necessary. (There had been none other than unanimous votes for the first ten months of the Board's operation.) Although Target Neighborhood Officers had the potential of voting as a block on a specific issue, they realized that their total strength was slightly over one-third of the Board's votes. The TNOs thus had become aware of the need to swing agency and citizen-at-large votes in their direction, and had begun lobbying when the situation called for it.

Several of the Target Neighborhood Officers felt the Board to be the most exciting part of their program participation, and were influenced accordingly. One commented:

FIGURE 2. Board Statements* of Target Neighborhood Officers, November, 1965–March, 1967

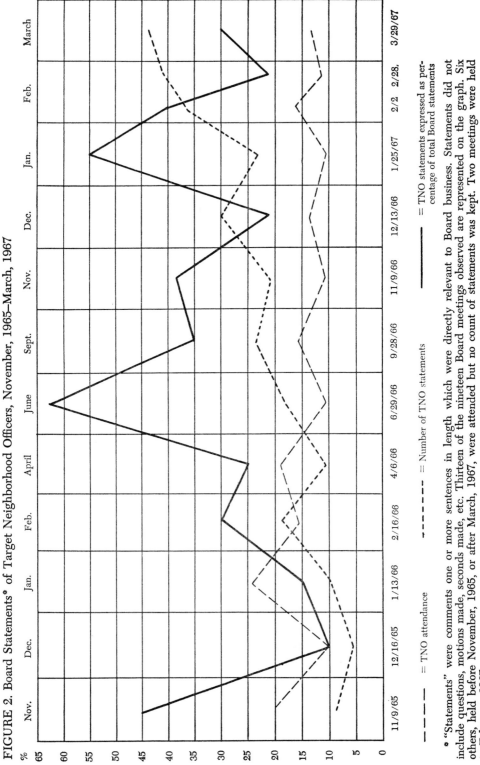

- - - - = TNO attendance

----- = Number of TNO statements

━━━ = TNO statements expressed as percentage of total Board statements

* "Statements" were comments one or more sentences in length which were directly relevant to Board business. Statements did not include questions, motions made, seconds made, etc. Thirteen of the nineteen Board meetings observed are represented on the graph. Six others, held before November, 1965, or after March, 1967, were attended but no count of statements was kept. Two meetings were held in February, 1967.

"Here my vote really means as much as anyone else's, even as much as the President of the University, who has all those sheepskins."

Another stated:

"It was great to hear the agency people make mistakes in grammar, and be mixed up, just like we are sometimes. They're people, just like anybody else, some of them are good and some of them are not so good. That makes me feel like we really can work together."

"I got up in front of that group and my knees shook," reflected another; "I never talked before a bunch of people like that before in my life. My knees still shake a little, but hell, man, so what—so do everybody's. Besides, what you're going to say is more important than how you say it—and we got important work here."

"Some of the other Board members might think we're just being stubborn," explained a man who had been a TNO from the beginning of the Topeka poverty program. "But it's not that at all. When we argue for five cents an hour more for a Neighborhood aide, or something like that, it's not the five cents alone that's important. It's the fact that it's one of us from a Target Neighborhood that's making the suggestion, and for the first time somebody's listening to us! That's what makes these meetings something special!"

Some of the other, not-poor Board members were also affected by the process experience of participation. An agency representative commented:

"I thought I was going to do a service for the poor by teaching things to the Target Neighborhood Officers. Now I find out that they have as much to teach me as I do them, and that they're very eager to play the role of teachers for a change."

A citizen at large stated:

"During the Board meetings sometimes we argue and argue and seem to go around in circles, but I don't think it's ever a waste of time. You can see changes in the Target Neighborhood Officers as they become more experienced. Some of the agency people get upset when Target Neighborhood Officers ask simple questions, or get bogged down in something that appears obvious. But the agency people have been on the program road for years. The Target Neighborhood Officers are just getting on that road, and are trying it out."

That the *process* experience of Board participation was to the Target Neighborhood Officers at least as important as, and probably more important than, their coming to terms with program *content* should be clear. The tendency, however, is for poverty boards and the staffs of poverty-intervention organizations to emphasize program content, and take the process experience of the participants, particularly the poor, for granted. In the Topeka poverty program, though much time was spent appraising Board members of program content, no formal training programs were conducted for members which would prepare them for the kinds of process experiences they would themselves have and would observe in others.

Training programs which emphasize those process experiences would seem to be of singular importance if the boards are to accomplish the goals of implementing poverty programing and providing meaningful participation for the poor.

On Being a Board President

The first president of the Economic Opportunity Board had been a professional man, who concurrently held the chairmanships of at least three other community voluntary social-welfare organizations. He was an expert at running meetings according to parliamentary procedure, and was fully acquainted with the goals, structure, and operating procedures of the Topeka poverty program. During his year as president, he was able to fulfill the duties of the office without instruction. Although he worked closely with the TOEO Director when necessary, he assumed that the day-to-day responsibility for the program was the Director's, and he left the task to him.

The first president was able to grasp immediately the components and ramifications of Board agenda, even if he did not see that agenda until minutes before the meeting was scheduled to begin. As the Director commented, "The President and I think alike, and have instant communication. We can cut a lot of red tape for efficiency and get right to the point."

So far as the first president was concerned, he was just a "traffic cop" at the Board meetings. He would abide by the Board's decisions on substantive matters and consider the Board to be responsible for those decisions.

At the completion of his term of office, he was praised by the Board but, though asked by the members to do so, chose not to run for re-election. Formally, he told the Board he felt "the opportunity to have been president of this fine Board was both a pleasure and an honor." Informally, he added that it had been "the toughest chairmanship I've ever held.'"

The Board members felt it was time for a Target Neighborhood Officer, a representative of the poor, to be president of the Board. Without contest, a Target Neighborhood Officer, an Anglo-American man who had been a participant in the program almost from its beginning, was elected.

From the onset it was apparent that the second president was quite different from the first. He was nervous about his role as president, was unversed in parliamentary procedure, and repeatedly admitted, "I'm going to have to learn a lot if I'm going to do a good job." He told the members, "This is the biggest job I've ever had, and I'm going to give it a lot of attention. You can believe that!" His having recently received a legal settlement for a serious injury he had sustained did, in fact, free him to concentrate on the president's job, which he considered to be "full-time, and a great responsibility."

The second president, as a former TNO, had been schooled in the "maximum feasible participation" mandate of the Economic Opportunity Act. He interpreted the mandate to mean that, as president, he should be involved in all major day-to-day decisions made by the TOEO staff. A number of conflicts between the president and the staff ensued, with the former feeling he was at times "being by-passed," and the staff feeling that he was "confused about his role and disruptive to the TOEO." The president felt that often he was "surprised by agenda items for the Board meetings," and that there were also times when he "wasn't informed about the real issues, and couldn't understand why there was so much heated discussion during a meeting, and didn't know what to do about it." Furthermore, he felt it his duty to comment, during a meeeting, on every motion made. This was quite in contrast to the first president's "traffic cop" role. In further contrast, the second president took personal responsibility for every Board decision, and on more than one occasion tried to reverse the Board's majority vote because he "felt they were wrong."

The first president met with the second, and advised him to play a more neutral role. The latter found it impossible to do so, felt "the people elected me to represent them," and took a personal interest in every phase of the Topeka poverty program, including its contacts with the regional and national Office of Economic Opportunity.

When a few months after the president's taking office the TOEO Director announced his resignation to take a job on the staff of the newly elected governor, the president took an even keener view of his personal responsibilities for the program, particularly for the participation of the poor.

In an interview with me, he particularized his views of the role he was playing:

"As president of the Board, I feel I have to be concerned with the Target Neighborhood Officers and the rest of the citizenry on the Board. If I can't do that successfully, then I should resign.

"Sometimes people think I'm a busybody because I speak up on so many things. I think that's my duty. Maybe I do talk too much sometimes, but somebody's got to do it, and that's what they elected me for. Not enough of the Target Neighborhood Officers say what they think or feel at those Board meeetings, but then they let me know afterwards how they think or feel. I wish they would speak up more at the Board. It's getting a lot better than it was when we first began, but they still could express themselves more often. The way it is now they either blow off too much steam, or they say nothing. They go from one extreme to the other. They'll learn, just like I'm trying to learn.

"At most boards, I understand, the presidents just sit back and don't do anything. Well, I'm not that kind of a person. As long as I continue to be president—and that may be a very short time, I don't know— I'm going to do it the way I think I should. I get lots of phone calls —you'd be surprised how many phone calls I get—every day from Target Neighborhood Officers and from agency people too. Some- times I get caught right in the middle of their opinions, which don't agree with each other. Then I'm not sure what's best.

"Sometimes I get confused. I don't want to scare anybody away from the Board, but I find out that I do. I feel I have to say things, but when I say them, some people get mad at me. Well, maybe that's the way it's got to be. Maybe some people always have to be mad. Maybe that's just how it works.

"Sometimes I think it takes a fully accredited idiot to take the job of president of the Board. But, I gave my word of honor when I took the job, and I can't quit in the middle just because it gets tough."

The president further commented about the need for training specific to that office, especially for those for whom middle-class meetings were not a way of life:

"I remember when I was younger, I told a fellow that I wanted a certain job and I could do the job because I could operate any wood- working machine around. The fellow said, 'Okay, you've got the job.' Then he took me into his shop, and there were machines there that I'd never seen before! I found I had to learn about those strange machines on my own, although he helped me a little bit, but I sure had to learn fast and learn a lot.

"That's kind of like the job of being president here. I came into the job and found out there're all kinds of things I didn't know about, but I couldn't find out about how to do the things, or find out about what things were from anybody. There were some times I see where I made decisions on only a little information. But what else could I do? Nobody ever gave me any information. I had to take what I could get. I wanted to do the best job I could, but what could I do if I didn't know all the things that were going on? Sometimes some of the things at the Board meeetings dropped on me like a big bomb, and I was caught flat-footed. I had to do the best I could with the information I had, and lots of times my information was just partial. I guess I've made a few mistakes, all right."

He concluded, somewhat sadly:

"Some of the people on the Board have so much skill in speaking, and know all about the rules and regulations of the meetings. They knew all about what was going to happen at the meeting before it happened, and knew how to handle those things. I wonder why those people wouldn't share any of their skills with me?"

In point of fact, the second president *was* disruptive to the accustomed division of labor in the Topeka poverty program. In point of fact, the TOEO staff *was* "by-passing" him and not keeping him informed about program details. Neither the president's nor the staff's actions were malicious or intended to disrupt or offend. They simply had entirely different views of the presidential role. The TOEO staff perceived the role in accordance with the example of the first president. The second president evolved his own view of the office because no one had, early enough, taught him differently. Subsequently, relations between him and the TOEO staff became quite strained, personalities became involved, and his term was indeed quite rocky until, his year completed, a new president was elected.

It would seem that plans for the training of board members should include a special training component for board officers, particularly if they are representatives of the poor. Furthermore, the staff of a poverty-intervention organization should expect and encourage a deeper concern for participation in decision-making from the low-income officers of the board than from the more affluent ones.

CHAPTER 7

Evaluation by Agency Representatives and Citizens at Large

WHAT DID THE agency representatives and citizens at large think about the local poverty program after they had experienced participation as members of the Economic Opportunity Board? To assess their opinions, they were formally interviewed in May, 1967. By that date the Board had been incorporated for twenty months, and members had attended nineteen regular and seventeen executive meetings of the Board. Thirty-two agency representatives and citizens at large were interviewed individually in their homes or offices. In this chapter, a percentage breakdown of non-TNO responses to the major interview questions is presented. Response categories are illustrated with sample quotes, and the distribution of responses is discussed.

QUESTIONS, RESPONSES, AND INTERPRETATIONS

Do you plan to continue as a member of the Economic Opportunity Board?

YES: 53 per cent

 WHY? Civic responsibility: 41 per cent

  "I'll continue to be a Board member if I have the opportunity, because I think the whole concept of OEO is going to continue to grow, and I think it's the responsibility of any civic-minded person to take part."

  Communication function: 29 per cent

  "In my job, we need help from the whole community, including the OEO. We've all got to work together on this program, and talk about it so we can know what each of us is doing."

  Humanitarian reasons: 18 per cent

  "I'm going to stay on the Board because I've been interested in people all my life, and these people need help, and I'd like to help them in any way I can."

  Other: 12 per cent

  "Well, I work for a service organization, and OEO programs have some relation to our programs, so we should be represented."

  "I feel I have a responsibility as a liberal, especially in terms of social change. It would be a real shame if this program was dominated by conservative thinkers, so I'm staying on the Board."

NO: 47 per cent

 WHY: Eliminated by legislation (Quie Amendment): 47 per cent

  "No, I'm not going to be a member of the Board anymore. I'm going to be thrown off by the new amendment, and I'm not happy about that, either!"

  Too much conflict during the meetings: 27 per cent

  "The damned Board is intolerable as far as I'm concerned. It's just a damned waste of time. I'm a professional person, and things are either black or white. Maybe this isn't the way it should be. It may have some gray in it; I just don't know. When everybody starts arguing among themselves, I just don't have the time for that kind of stuff. There's nothing being gained. I'm not critical of the objectives of the program, just all that damned fighting."

Overcommitted: 13 per cent

"I can't stay on the Board because I just have too many other things to do. I can't keep going to all the meetings that I have."

Other: 13 per cent

"I won't be working for the agency anymore, so I won't be representing them at the Board meetings."

A majority (53 per cent) of the agency representatives and citizens at large planned to continue as members of the Economic Opportunity Board. Their motivation for continuing to participate apparently was a sense of responsibility, either civic or humanitarian. In a few of the members that sense of responsibility reflected a *noblesse oblige* attitude toward participation. That "caretakers of the poor" view often squarely conflicted with the "maximum feasible participation" view of the Target Neighborhood Officers, particularly as they attempted to achieve increased autonomy and responsibility for themselves as Board members. A sense of civic or humanitarian responses among agency representatives and citizens at large, as was the case with many of those members, was functional if it was accompanied by a perception of the TNOs as having equal status on the Board.

A majority (47 per cent) of the agency representatives and citizens at large who were not continuing as Board members had been eliminated by the Quie Amendment to the Economic Opportunity Act. That amendment, implemented during 1967, detailed specifically the qualifications for membership on poverty boards. It was intended to guarantee that low-income representatives on a poverty board would constitute a minimum proportion of one-third of the voting membership. The Economic Opportunity Board had, from its onset, operated with qualification requirements for membership that gave the poor slightly better than one-third of the total votes. As pointed out in Chapters 2 and 3, the TOEO staff had with difficulty, but nonetheless successfully, recruited for Board participation a cross section of community citizens. Those citizens had for many months been attending Board meetings, serving on other poverty-program committees, and in general had been considerably involved in the program. They were not occupying Board positions which, under the new amendment, would go to representatives of the poor. Nonetheless, because their particular agency or group was not included in the new member qualifications, they had to be replaced with representatives from organizations and groups which were so qualified. Consequently, most of the non-TNO representatives who were eliminated by the amendment were angered by what appeared to them to be the "arbitrariness of Washington," and although they generally remained favorable toward the local poverty program, many of them expressed bitterness toward the national Office of Economic Opportunity.

A few of the non-TNOs chose not to continue Board participation because they were disturbed by the "conflict" and "fighting" that took place during meetings. Disturbance with conflict was also expressed by some non-TNOs who were eliminated by legislation, and by some who still had decided to continue participation. In general, the non-TNO Board members were not prepared for the kind of strenuous personal interactions that would take place during the Board meetings. They were not really aware of the differences in the view of the world that existed between TNOs and themselves, and were not prepared for the consequences of these differences. Very few of the non-TNOs saw themselves as being involved in processes that would foster social change or were aware of the kinds of individual and interpersonal conflict that could accompany such change. For most of them, the agency or club meeting was the model for participant conduct—a model that the Economic Opportunity Board meetings seldom, if ever, followed.

The non-TNOs on the Economic Opportunity Board often were startled by the contrast between what they expected Board dynamics to be and what they really were. No steps were taken to prepare them for the significant ways in which Board meetings might differ from the meetings of more typical organizations. Those differences, including the potential for conflict, the apparent "aggressiveness" of the TNOs as they increased their participation and tested their skills, and the importance of process experience for the participants, should be outlined in a board training-program. Many of the non-TNOs were not certain what their role was as a voting member of the Economic Opportunity Board. Some indicated that they expected their task to be educating the poor. Others thought their primary job was simply to represent their agency. Still others felt their particular professional expertise was needed for the formulation of program proposals. Only rarely did they conceive of their role as being a change agent, and consider the kinds of responses that might be associated with change. The "role" of the not-poor board member, consequently, would be a fruitful topic for discussion in board training-sessions.

What is your opinion of "maximum feasible participation" of the poor now, and has your opinion changed by virtue of your own participation?

FAVORABLE OPINION: 34 per cent

"I feel that 'maximum feasible participation' is the strongest aspect of the program. The way OEO has proved itself to me as a worthwhile program is the fact that it has involved the people at the grass-roots level in deciding policies."

MIXED OPINION: 38 per cent

"Well, my opinion's better now than it was when I first started. I had real apprehensions about 'maximum feasible participation' when the program started. It takes a lot more patience than the professional approach takes, but in the long pull, I think it's probably the best way to go. There seems to be a pattern. The first few meetings seem to be bitching sessions. After a while, they settle down to constructive ideas. These people release their frustrations at first. It really is the first chance for many of them to speak out. It's a real risk in the 'maximum feasible participation' aspect, though, because some people are too aggressive and some aren't aggressive enough. I suppose it balances out, though, and we've had some real good leaders in many of the Neighborhoods. It seems to me to be the best approach. I don't know; it has strong points and weak points."

"I like the idea, but I see the need for tremendous education or indoctrination to get the TNOs to a point where they can handle the job and handle decisions. It's feasible for them to run their programs, but with certain limits. To do this kind of job you need a certain amount of education and experience that you just don't get by being poor."

UNFAVORABLE OPINION: 28 per cent

"I'm against 'maximum feasible participation.' The blind can't lead the blind. One of the weaknesses is that everyone thinks participatory democracy is fine. It's just like it is in a home; children don't have the same voice as their parents, and they become more equal as they grow older and gain more knowledge. The poor are just not yet ready to be in a position of leadership."

"At first, it really sounded good to me. It sounded logical. You might have to pick and choose the best people to participate, and you might not be able to get them involved right away, but over-all it sounded real solid. Now I've seen it in action, and I feel disappointed in the involvement of the TNOs. Things have happened that I didn't expect. I accept part of the responsibility for not being wise enough to anticipate how they would react. The poor seemed to abandon concrete organizational functioning; they start breaking off on how it will affect them individually. Often, the poor won't go along with the majority rule."

The reader is reminded that this interview was conducted with Board members shortly before the second Board president, who had been a Target Neighborhood Officer, ended his term of office. The controversy surrounding his presidency clearly influenced some of the non-TNO Board members to take a negative view of "maximum feasible participation" of the TNOs.

Those non-TNO Board members who remained favorably impressed with "maximum feasible participation" of the TNOs were able to put the "aggressiveness" and the "lack of skills" of the Target Neighborhood Officers into the perspective that participation is an educational and/or socializing experience. Generally, these non-TNOs took the long view of TNO participation, and saw the "disruptive" concomitance of TNO inexperience as being temporary—to be overcome by sustained and increasing participation. Furthermore, some of those who supported "maximum feasible participation" saw their own roles as Board members being temporary, particularly as associated with leadership positions, and thought that eventually the skilled TNOs would dominate the direction of the program.

Many of the agency representatives and citizens at large were ambivalent about "maximum feasible participation." They liked the idea of the participation of the TNOs, but were not sure whether the disruptions to Board and program efficiency engendered by the participatory explorations of the TNOs were worth the rather intangible results. A further source of ambivalence concerning TNO participation resulted from uncertainty concerning the level to which that participation should aspire. There was no disagreement that TNOs should have votes on the Board, and participate in the discussions leading to decisions concerning poverty programing. But some non-TNOs wondered whether the TNOs were ready, or would ever be ready, for major policy-making roles.

Those agency representatives and citizens at large who had become opposed to "maximum feasible participation" usually proposed a circular argument, a self-fulfilling prophecy. TNOs should not be given positions of responsibility until they have the skills to enact such roles successfully. But the TNOs could not gain such skills unless they had the opportunity to experience positions of responsibility. A few of the non-TNOs never overcame the basic attitude that people are poor because they want to be, and those same negative characteristics made "maximum feasible participation" impractical.

The non-TNOs generally did not have a clear view of what "maximum feasible participation" of the poor meant, or what that participation might be expected to engender. Few individuals associated with the poverty program seemed to realize that "maximum feasible participation" would ultimately mean the acquisition and application of *power*—in the Economic Opportunity Board, in the TOEO, in all components of the poverty program. It would be crucial to include in board training-sessions discussions of what participation is likely to mean to all members.

What do you think of the Economic Opportunity Board in terms of its productivity and interpersonal interactions?

FAVORABLE OPINION: 3 per cent

"I think the Board is more productive now than it was before, mainly because there're more people involved in the discussions, and that's the most important production we can have."

MIXED OPINION: 25 per cent

"Productivity is pretty good, if you don't consider efficiency at the same time. It takes a long time to get things done, but we do get it done. There's much conflict on the Board, but this could be expected with the wide-spectrum background that the members come from."

"The Board has grown up tremendously in the past several months. It's taken the responsibility of keeping an inexperienced president in line. The major trouble has been that we've had a change over in TOEO directors, with such a long delay before hiring a new director. So many things hit us at once: the inexperienced president, the legislation demanding change in our Board, and the change-over in directors. That just rocked us for several months and made us unproductive. But we'll come out of it."

UNFAVORABLE OPINION: 63 per cent

"The Board's too big as a governing body. We just sit, sit, and sit. Everyone is carrying their own torch to the Board instead of trying to be fair about things. Things that we take hours to discuss, we could do in four or five minutes, and increase our efficiency."

"In the last year, the Board has been nothing but chaos and confusion. I don't know whose fault it is; I guess we should have tried to lead the president more. We've accomplished nothing, nothing constructive at all."

NO OPINION: 9 per cent

Those agency representatives and citizens at large who continued to see the Board as being productive defined productivity at least as much in terms of the processes of TNO participation as they did in terms of over-all Board efficiency. They tended to consider the relative inefficiency of the Board as a phase which would eventually be "outgrown." The inexperienced president, the membership legislation, and the change in TOEO directors were felt to be disruptive, but challenges with which the Board could cope.

Most of the non-TNOs who held unfavorable opinions of the Economic Opportunity Board centered their complaints on the inexperience of the second president. A few of them interpreted his difficulties as being proof that the TNOs should not be allowed to hold positions of responsibility in the poverty program. The president had been elected *unanimously* by the Board members, most of whom at the time of the election expressed a belief in the importance of having a TNO serve as president. Yet, though several members expressed dismay with the results of the president's "inexperience," not one of them, nor any member of the TOEO staff, recommended the support of formal training for him.

The production goals of the Economic Opportunity Board, and the characteristics of the interpersonal interactions that might be expected, were unclear to the non-TNO participants. Their expectations, then, would be determined by their previous experiences with community meetings. "Productivity" was assessed in terms of the number of proposals formulated and implemented, and the content of those proposals in dollars and services. "Interpersonal interactions" were expected to parallel the relatively abstract and affectively neutral-role relations in formally structured meetings. The productivity of participation for TNOs, however, since it was concerned with socialization and training, was as much related to the process experience of discussion and decision-making as it was to the outcome of those dynamics. Since the TNOs were not schooled in formal meetings, their interpersonal interactions were not abstract, but concrete, not affectively neutral, but highly affective. To discuss these phenomena with the not-poor could yield a deeper understanding of the incidence of "meaningless squabbles" and "unproductiveness" in poverty boards.

Do you feel that the poverty program has brought about any change in Topeka?

YES: 75 per cent

"There's been some change, mostly in the way that people who never came together before now view one another; it's an attitude change, really. We didn't have much luck with our second president, and that may influence the way some people look at all the participating poor. Most of us who are not poor, though, consider the case of the president to be a special case, and we've seen tremendous changes in the Target Neighborhood Officers themselves. I know I consider them to be quite different from what I thought they would be before."

"Topeka is a better city for having OEO. First of all, we're more aware of our poverty problems, and the welfare of hundreds of people has been improved, despite all the wrangling on the Board. There've been people who've been helped by finding jobs through OEO; we've been able to give jobs to over two hundred people. That's a pretty good start, and it's going to change their lives, that's for sure."

"Some specific things have changed. For example, Head Start has changed the education programs in low-income areas, the Neighborhood House has changed the poor area in which it was set up, and things like that. But maybe more important, there's a change in the awareness in the city of a need to do something about poverty. We haven't wiped out poverty, that's for sure. But we've taken a step in that direction."

NO: 22 per cent

"I don't believe that the power structure, if there is a power structure, has changed. They've shown a lack of interest or desire to participate in OEO. In fact, they're quite ignorant of OEO."

"I'd say there was no change from OEO. If they get 2 per cent value here in the city from OEO they're doing well."

UNCERTAIN: 3 per cent

Most of the non-TNOs felt that at the very least the poverty program had brought about specific changes in areas of the community as a result of specific programs such as Head Start, the Neighborhood House, the Beautification Program, Adult Basic Education, etc. Many of them also perceived broader, and perhaps more important, changes in the community at large—an increased insight into the problems and urgencies of poverty, and changes in attitudes of representatives of the TNOs and non-TNOs toward each other. Most of those who thought there had been no community change added that perhaps it was too early to see the benefits of the program, although a few were convinced that the only change would be that additional federal money would be spent in the city. Only a few of the agency representatives and citizens at large, at least at the beginning, actually thought about broad social or physical changes that might take place in Topeka as a result of the poverty program. Many of them, including some of the TOEO staff, thought the primary goal of the poverty program to be the extension of already existing services to greater numbers of the poor. The opportunities for participation seized by the TNOs gave the non-TNOs their first indication that something indeed may be changing. It would be profitable to encourage the not-poor to reflect about the potential for social and individual change among the poor, among themselves and within the community, and the role that they might play in introducing such change.

What are your opinions of the Target Neighborhood Officers in terms of their co-operation and capabilities?

FAVORABLE: 28 per cent

"I've been delighted by their enthusiasm. They've handled the job well and they show a great deal of pride, and they've shown the true spirit of identifying with their Neighborhoods."

"I've been rather impressed. You can see that they see it as a program for them, and they're trying to make the best use of it. At first they were rather timid, and they didn't contribute much. In the last year they've become more vocal and they've made some contribution."

MIXED: 47 per cent

"They're a good cross section of the economically deprived. Some are better than others. They're individuals—that's just the way people are."

"We do have some very capable Target Neighborhood Officers who have really grown. Some others have shown some real inabilities, but I'd like to think they were the exceptions."

UNFAVORABLE: 6 per cent

"I don't think the Target Neighborhood Officers know that they're really slowing things down for everybody."

NO OPINION: 19 per cent

The agency representatives and citizens at large who held favorable opinions of the TNOs were particularly impressed with their ability to enact or "grow into" leadership roles in their own Neighborhoods and on the Board. Those members generally tended to understand and value the "maximum feasible participation" mandate of the Economic Opportunity Act.

All the non-TNOs who expressed mixed opinions about the co-operation and capabilities of TNOs divided the TNOs into what amounted to "good" and "bad" categories. Criteria for the good-bad dichotomy included: manifestation of autonomy, dedication to representing Target Neighborhoods, and ability to perform effectively during Board meetings. The latter criterion was most often the basis for evaluation. Thus, more often than not, the "good" TNO, the one who was co-operative and capable, was the one who most effectively enacted the "meeting" role familiar to the non-TNOs.

Agency representatives and citizens at large who reported an unfavorable opinion of TNOs invariably did so in terms of the "inefficiency" that their participation on the Economic Opportunity Board brought about.

The agency representatives and citizens at large had, prior to their Board participation, preconceived notions about what representatives of the poor would be like. By these criteria, however they may have varied among individual members, the TNOs' performance was judged either favorably or unfavorably. It would be profitable for the not-poor of poverty boards to explore the stereotypes they may hold for the participating poor, and to discuss the ways whereby these stereotypes may be made flexible enough to accommodate reality.

Do you feel that the structure of the program has made it easier to reach the poor?

YES: 28 per cent

"Yes, the program has made it easier to reach the poor, because it's getting the agency people out of their offices and off their tails and into the Neighborhoods where they can get to the people who need help, rather than forcing people who need help to come to them."

"As the Target Neighborhood Officers have gotten more confident, and started acting on their own, they've become a very effective force for reaching the poor that couldn't be reached in any other way. People in the low-income Neighborhoods don't operate on an organizational basis, but on a person-to-person basis, and that's where the Target Neighborhood Officers are really effective."

NO: 28 per cent

"We're providing a very expensive education for a few representatives of the poor, but I just don't think we're reaching the hard-core poor who really need help."

UNCERTAIN: 44 per cent

"I just don't know, because it's too early to tell. How can you tell about the impact of something like Head Start upon those children, until years from now? How can you really evaluate the Neighborhood House until at least months from now? It's just too early to tell. We're just really beginning now."

The increased ability of helping agencies to reach the poor, the TNOs as expedients for making contact with needy persons who might otherwise not be reached, and the impact of particular poverty programs such as Head Start upon a Target group were the three main ways non-TNOs thought the poverty-program structure had made it easier for the poor to be reached. Most of the respondents were uncertain, however, about the efficacy of the program because not enough time had passed since it began. It was "too early" to tell whether or not the poor were really being affected. Several agency representatives and citizens at large felt that the program was not reaching the "hard-core" or disorganized poor, who were the real targets of the poverty program. Rather, they felt, the program was helping the "top layer" of the poor—the Target Neighborhood Officers—who needed help less than the "hard-core" impoverished.

There were varying definitions among the agency representatives and citizens at large about just who the "poor" were. To some of the non-TNOs the TNOs clearly were the "poor." To others, the TNOs were the "cream of the crop," and Neighborhood residents who were not at the meetings were the "hard-core poor." Just who the "poor" are that the program is trying to reach, and the degree of heterogeneity or homogeneity among them, are worthy topics for discussion by the not-poor.

Has your Board experience changed your view of the "poor"?

YES: 48 per cent

POSITIVE CHANGE: 80 per cent

"It's shown me that some Target Neighborhood Officers can take real advantage of the program, and have really blossomed out. Also, it's shown me that leaders among the poor can help the poor in many ways better than even us agency people can. We've picked up some new allies in this attempt to get at social problems."

NEGATIVE CHANGE: 20 per cent

"When all this began, I believed that people are poor for a reason, and that is that they just aren't motivated. Now I'm even more convinced of that."

NO: 52 per cent

"I had the utmost confidence in the Target Neighborhood Officers from the very first, and that confidence has proven correct."

"I still don't think they're capable of running a program that involves such a big budget."

Those non-TNOs who reported a change in opinion about the poor generally indicated an increased positive evaluation of the performance of the TNOs. Those whose opinions of the poor worsened seemed to be reinforcing a previously held "motivational" stereotype about the poor.

A majority (52 per cent) of the non-TNOs had not changed their opinions about the poor—citing their original favorable opinions of the TNOs as having been maintained by Board experience. A few whose initial opinions of the poor had been negative retained that evaluation. With this question, as with the previous question, there was apparent variation among non-TNOs concerning who the "poor" were. Some non-TNOs generalized the "poor" from the behavior of the TNOs. Others separately evaluated the TNOs and the "hard-core poor." Still others, especially some of those who maintained stereotypical negative views, generalized the "poor" from the behavior of persons involved in riots in other cities.

Has your Board experience changed your view of what can be done about poverty?

YES: 16 per cent

"Yes, my view has changed. Now I can see that poverty isn't like other things. It didn't start just today. It's developed over a period of years, and it'll take a period of years to try and eliminate it. It's rough going in the early stages, much rougher than I thought it would ever be, but the understanding of that makes me want to keep trying."

NO: 84 per cent

"No, my opinion hasn't changed. My experience on the Board has only reaffirmed what I believed in the beginning. That is, the only way to do something about poverty is to involve leaders of the poor in the program, and when they get involved they, like anybody else, will become increasingly capable and responsible."

"The poor will always be with us, and that's that."

There were few agency representatives and citizens at large who thought that their views of what could be done about poverty had changed. Those who did report a change indicated surprise with the capabilities of the TNOs, or a new awareness of the complexities of poverty intervention. Most of the non-TNOs who did not feel that their opinion concerning what could be done about poverty had changed, had "hope" for the OEO program at the onset and, despite some disillusionment with the Board and its "squabbling," generally still felt there was "hope." Similarly, those few who had been opposed to the local program from its beginning maintained that perspective.

The initial views of the non-TNOs concerning what to do about poverty were, however, vague. Do you concentrate upon the individual who is poor, and try to change him? Do you concentrate upon his environment, and try to change it? Do you increase the outreach of the present helping organizations, or do you try to restructure those organizations, and implement new strategies? Such questions need to be debated by the not-poor so that they may understand more clearly what efforts can be made.

Has your Board participation brought about any change in the organization that you represent?

YES: 34 per cent

"There's been a change in that we're now more aware of individual needs of low-income people. Also, we have, through the Board in particular, improved our communications with other agencies that are concerned with problems of poverty. We've always operated on the principle of people coming to us, and I think now we're switching somewhat and taking our services to the people. This is at least partly traceable to the feedback we've received from OEO.'"

"We're more sensitive to hiring low-income people now than we were before. By that, I mean we're willing to make some exceptions in qualifications in order to hire them, and give them a chance. Also, we were able to put activities into some areas where we had no programs at all before."

"Our training programs for staff now include sessions on problems of poverty, and various kinds of poverty programs. In particular we're stressing the importance of our employees' being sensitive to how clients can help themselves."

NO: 66 per cent

"There've been no changes in our organization because of OEO. After all, OEO is only going to be around a short time, and we're going to be around a long time, so it isn't too wise to change just because of something that'll influence you only for a little while."

"I can't think of any official agency changes. Poverty-program experience has changed certain individuals in the agency, particularly those who have been expected to deal directly with the poor. But this hasn't reached broad policy changes yet, and I doubt that it ever will."

Most of those agency representatives and citizens at large who reported changes were associated with organizations that had been contracted by the TOEO as delegate agencies, or were large contributors of services-in-kind, for specific anti-poverty programs in the community (e.g., Head Start, Extension Worker Program, Neighborhood House). Thus their organizations were closely linked with the activities of the Economic Opportunity Board. The changes noted included: increased outreach to low-income applicants; establishment of new facilities and/or programs; increased hiring of residents of low-income areas; more understanding attitudes toward low-income applicants; poverty-oriented components in staff training-programs; improved communication with other agencies; and greater awareness of needs, problems, and areas that needed attention. Being a delegate agency generally seemed to foster changes in that agency which enhanced its efforts toward the amelioration of poverty.

On the other hand, the creation of delegate agencies as an expedient for program management raised significant problems for both the TOEO and the delegate agency itself. Who actually was controlling the delegated program? The TOEO? The delegate agency? To what extent could the Economic Opportunity Board dictate to delegate agencies such specifics as the hiring of personnel, employees' salaries, and program implementation? Unless the division of labor is made lucidly clear at the time the contract is negotiated, arguments concerning the prerogatives of program management subsequently can interfere with the intended benefits of that program for the poor.

The "no change" responses came primarily from agency representatives and citizens at large whose organizations were not directly associated with the TOEO. Among those who indicated no organizational change, however, several mentioned specifically that their own role in the organization had changed somewhat. They had become the organizations' "experts" on poverty or their "liaison" with the poverty program.

If you could, would you change the Economic Opportunity Board?

YES: 87 per cent

"We need more of the detail work done by the subcommittees, especially the Executive Committee, so that the Board meetings wouldn't be so hectic and be concerned with such minute detail. Also, the agenda should be prepared more carefully, and sent out to us before the meetings."

"The present size of the Board is too large and unwieldy and unmanageable, and you just can't get a cohesive spirit. We ought to cut the Board's size in half, with the same proportions of representation."

"I'd drastically reduce the size of the Board. The Board needs to be comprised of people who appreciate the needs of people who need help. They don't necessarily have to be poor. We may wind up with all affluent people. If you have that kind of Board, you won't have any worries about procedures."

"The number of agency representatives and citizens at large on the Board should be reduced, so that the poor's position on the Board will be as great as the others' or greater, because it's their program."

"Get some young agency officials on the Board, instead of the older ones who have such preconceived ideas. The same with representatives of the poor. In general, the whole age level of the Board should be brought down. There're too many people on that Board who're too set in their ways because they lived them too long."

NO: 13 per cent

"I think the existing Board is as good as you can get. Right now, we're in a growing stage, and we really haven't tested out the structure as it exists. I'd want to see that tested fully before I made any recommendations about changing it."

"Some say you need a small Board to get things done; others say you need a large Board to get involvement. I believe in the large Board, just as it is, and I'm willing to accept the problems that go along with it."

The agency representatives and citizens at large suggested some major changes in the Economic Opportunity Board: reduce the size of the Board; increase the proportion of TNOs; decrease the proportion of TNOs; and restaff the Board with "younger" representatives. The respondents also suggested some changes associated with procedures and practices of the Board as it was then constituted: prepare and follow more adequate agenda; make more extensive use of subcommittees for the discussion and resolution of details; establish procedures for punishing chronic absentees by expulsion; replace the present Board president; lower the quorum required to call a regular session of the Board; refuse to implement the Quie Amendment for member qualifications; convene the Board more often; have the members wear badges to provide identification and stimulate interaction. The four changes most often suggested included: reduction of Board size, stronger agenda, a new president (specifically, a professional), and better use of the subcommittees. All four of these suggestions argued for formalization of the Board toward greater "efficiency."

Poverty-program planners face a dilemma when structuring their board. Smaller, formalized meetings may yield greater efficiency, but possibly at the expense of participation of the poor. Larger boards may provide opportunity for participation, but that participation may reduce or slow down the board's program output. Adequate training programs for boards, however, may help balance the advantages of participation and efficiency, thus making larger boards, with their wider representation, as desirable practicably as they are theoretically.

Are there individuals among the poor, especially the Target Neighborhood Officers, that you can formally or informally contact for community, Neighborhood, or personal issues that you didn't or couldn't contact before your own involvement in the poverty program?

YES: 63 per cent

"There're several TNOs that I can contact now, and other people in the low-income areas, that I couldn't contact before. I can give you their names, where they live, and even some of their phone numbers, since I interact with them that much. Frankly, that's the greatest strength of this program. I mean, the informal contacts we can make now. I can't even possibly estimate the number of people I contact now that I didn't before I was involved in OEO. People actually stop me on the street and ask me how they can participate in the program.'"

"I can contact low-income people now more on an individual-to-individual basis than on an official-to-"client" basis. They slap me on the back, and so forth, which they never would've done before. A few of them have phoned me, just to talk things over. That would never have happened before. Sometimes when I get a special problem that I think a TNO can help me with, I give him a call, too."

NO: 37 per cent

"I don't think I'm able to contact any more of the TNOs than I was able to before I got involved in the Board. I don't think that's happened. I feel this is unfortunate. I thought that it was starting, but then they seemed to feel that we were moving in, so we backed off. They cried for help at first, and once they got started they kind of said, 'Shoot, we can handle this by ourselves!' Once they feel more secure, then they'll know that we aren't trying to take over, and maybe we can have some useful interplay."

"No, I knew some of them before in my business, and they're fine people. Some of the others on the Board I haven't gotten to know, and frankly, I don't want to get to know them."

Most of the agency representatives and citizens at large reported increased formal and informal contacts with Target Neighborhood Officers, other individuals in the low-income Target areas, and other agency representatives and citizens at large as a result of participation in the poverty program. The potential for increased informal contact was particularly important, since it engendered a shift in role relations—from official-"client" to colleague-colleague. The importance of informal interaction, and the climate such an interaction provides for program innovation and TNO self-enhancement, cannot be overestimated. It would be important to stress to board members the benefits of such interaction.

A few non-TNOs complained that TNOs seemed to get "standoffish" as they became more experienced in Board activities. Generally, that "standoffishness" was a manifestation of a change in role relations between the poor and the not-poor. Many TNOs began to perceive themselves as initiators and not just passive recipients of social contact with the not-poor. That perception included the prerogative *not* to interact, if deemed appropriate. Non-TNOs occasionally would interpret the shift in role relations negatively, and would label the TNO accordingly. Poverty-intervention organizations are well advised to expect and discuss role strain among participants as process experiences increasingly have their impact.

Do you feel that OEO has a future in Topeka?

YES: 66 per cent

"It has a future in Topeka, and across the United States. I see it as an absolute necessity. It will become more stable, more institutionalized, and more effective, and it will start more action programs. The success will depend on organizing the Neighborhood Committees and upon the leadership of the Board and the TOEO."

"If you ask me, all that OEO has is a future, because it hasn't had much of a past. It's only scratched the surface, and hasn't touched enough lives yet."

NO: 3 per cent

"I never thought it would have a future, and I don't think it has a future now. It's a waste of time.

UNCERTAIN: 31 per cent

"The future depends on how aggressive the program remains. It needs to keep a certain revolutionary spirit. It'll be no more effective than traditional methods if it doesn't settle down, though, to a specific strategy."

"I've got to see what the new TOEO staff is going to be like. I may decide that I don't think the future is bright for community-action programs. On the other hand, I do feel that the future is bright in the field of education and in employment training under the poverty program. I do see a need for some kind of program where all the people sit down together and talk over the needs, but I'm not sure it has to be OEO. Besides, OEO is liable to be short on funds pretty soon, and die a natural death."

Although most of the agency representatives and citizens at large felt that OEO has a future in Topeka, they were not at all clear about what that future might be. There were many rumors circulating which painted a dim picture concerning the national future of OEO, particularly the community-action programs. The Economic Opportunity Board had yet to find a replacement for its director, had yet to reconstitute its Board according to the Quie Amendment, and had yet to solve the problem of its inexperienced Board president.

There were simply too many unknowns to be specific about the future of Topeka's poverty program, although most of the non-TNOs felt that there would continue to be a place for that program in the community.

As discussed in Chapter 3, uncertainty is endemic to poverty-intervention organizations—uncertainty about funding, uncertainty about the appropriate strategies for intervention, and uncertainty about the outcomes of that intervention. Some of that uncertainty could be avoided, or at least more adequately tolerated, if board members were encouraged to discuss the unknowns of poverty programing as well as the knowns. That is, board training-sessions should include examining alternative outcomes to intended planning, and exploring substitute strategies and/or funding should expectations not be realized.

THE PRESS AS AN EVALUATOR

The press provided a continuing non-TNO evaluation of the Topeka poverty program. An editorial run by the *Topeka Daily Capital* represents that supportive evaluation, which was indispensable for acquiring and sustaining community co-operation. The editorial, with identifying names removed, reads:

OEO PROGRAM ON MOVE

Six months ago when the Director of the Topeka Office of Economic Opportunity stood in a little church in North Topeka and explained the poverty program he envisioned for Topeka, the few residents of the neighborhood who were there were skeptical and reluctant to become part of it.

But three women were elected that evening as Neighborhood Officers, and other areas were subsequently organized in a grass roots self-help movement.

Those same neighbors, reluctant six months ago, have become active, concerned advocates of the OEO program. They are investigating area problems, discussing solutions provided by the Economic Opportunity Act and making progress in determining goals.

At a meeting of the City neighborhood officers, a sociologist was to speak about cities, their growth and problems. At 7:45 P.M. the Director prefaced the meeting by calling for discussions of any questions on two proposals—Day Care Centers for North Topeka and an Extension Worker Program in the neighborhoods—already approved for operation in Topeka.

At 9:30 P.M. the group of sixteen or so officers, white, Negro, American-Indian and Mexican-American residents, still were talking of the proposals, discussing details on contract and operation. The sociologist never got to speak. He said he would come back.

Before the meeting ended, officers were admonished by the Assistant Director to air their ideas and opinions more in a City-wide Board meeting, composed of Neighborhood Officers and community leaders.

"Sometimes Agency people will pull out a word about so long," the Assistant Director said, looking at the space between his hands. "I always tell them to slow down while I go out and get a sledge hammer and break that word down."

"I always felt," said one man, "that when I'm around those lawyers and doctors on the City Board that I couldn't keep up with them. But I'm going to say what I think next time. If I have an idea it doesn't hurt to express it."

The Director told each neighborhood group before it was organized into the OEO program that neither he nor his office would think up projects for Topeka. "You're on your own," he said. "We're here only to help you."

The Director has done as he promised. The only dissent entered against the record of the TOEO program was an anonymous charge of racial discrimination in hiring an assistant for the office. The charge was investigated by the Regional OEO office in Kansas City, and officials reported "insufficient evidence" to support such a charge.

When announcement of the investigation was made, neighborhood officers rallied around the Director and Assistant Director. At the Neighborhood Officers' meeting, they all nodded in agreement after discussion about the problem of charges.

"If something seems to be wrong," one man said, "bring it to the local Board. Let's not write any more letters."

While other cities in the Economic Opportunity program had been victimized by political appointees and subjected to national criticism for questionable usage of federal funds, Topeka's program has moved surely toward definite goals ordered by the persons for whom the poverty program was designed. The Director and Assistant Director are leading it.[1]

Members of the TOEO staff knew the importance of a good press to the success of the poverty program as they had interpreted it. They deliberately set out to cultivate rapport with concerned reporters from Topeka's major newspapers. The staff made certain that reporters were invited to all significant poverty-program meetings, and informed them of any newsworthy "break" in TOEO activities. That policy of co-operation with the press served the TOEO well during the entire period of our research, and should indicate to

[1] *Topeka Daily Capital*, Monday, January 31, 1966, p. 24.

other poverty-intervention organizations the importance of the press as a source of community evaluation of their efforts.

SUMMARY OF THE EVALUATION

A majority of the agency representatives and citizens at large planned to continue as Board members, most of them because they felt it was a responsibility. Most of those who did not plan to continue as members had been eliminated by legislation demanding Board restructuring, and they were not happy with having to leave.

The members generally were cautiously in favor of "maximum feasible participation" of the poor, as it had been structured for the Topeka poverty program. However, their opinions concerning the effects of the poor's participation to some extent reflected their negative perception of the leadership qualities of the current Board president, who had previously been a Target Neighborhood Officer. Similarly, members' perceptions of the Board's productivity and interpersonal interactions were largely negative, again probably influenced by the inexperience of the president, and also by the disturbing experience of seeing the directorship of the TOEO staff change hands at the same time the membership of the Board was being restructured.

A great majority of non-TNOs felt that the poverty program had brought about significant change in Topeka, particularly in attitudes toward representatives from among the poor and toward the poor themselves. Despite their generally unfavorable opinions of the Board president's methods, apparently most non-TNOs did not stereotype TNOs, but rather judged them individually and felt that the program had affected many positively. This view was reflected again in their opinions of the Target Neighborhood Officers in terms of their co-operation and capabilities.

The non-TNOs were somewhat ambivalent about the effectiveness of the poverty program, as structured, in accomplishing its goals of reaching the poor. Much of that uncertainty stemmed from the opinion that the program had not yet been working long enough to warrant a determination.

Several of the non-TNOs had changed their views of the capabilities of the poor, mostly in a positive direction. The majority of those whose opinions remained unchanged held positive views of the poor at the onset.

The members had not changed, to any significant extent, their views of what could be done about problems of poverty. Most of them continued to feel that there was potential among the poor to help themselves, and that the approach being taken by the local poverty program was probably a good one, but yet to be thoroughly tested.

Some of the agencies and organizations represented by non-TNOs had made policy changes to accommodate the goals of the local poverty program. Equally important, members of the agencies and organizations reported increased awareness of the needs and problems of low-income persons, and of the existence and complexity of poverty as a social ill.

Most of the respondents felt that the Board should be changed in one way or another—to reduce the size, to redistribute the voting balance, to set up and follow more specific agenda, to make better use of subcommittees, or to acquire officers with greater leadership skill.

A majority of these reported that they now formally or informally could contact Target Neighborhood Officers and other low-income persons for various community, Neighborhood, or individual problems. Bruyn has pointed out that whether community-action programs succeed or fail in terms of projects is perhaps less important than the interpersonal contacts made among individuals who otherwise may not have interacted.[2]

Despite the fact that many non-TNOs complained about conflict over specific issues during Board meetings, manifested concern about the leadership of the current Board president, and had some misgivings about the general structure of the Board, a majority felt that the poverty program had a promising future in Topeka, so long as things didn't "get out of hand."

The press can have a significant role in both presenting and influ-

[2] Severyn T. Bruyn, *Communities in Action: Pattern and Process*, pp. 112–113.

encing the community's evaluation of a local poverty program. It would profit a poverty-intervention organization to establish rapport, as did the TOEO, with reporters from major local newspapers.

A formal training program for the not-poor is essential. Included in such a program should be discussions of the following *process experience* determinants: the role of the individual as a board member and a change agent; the probability of, and the function of, interpersonal conflict during board meetings; the meaning, significance, and consequences of "maximum feasible participation" of the poor; the definitions of board productivity, goals, and strategies, including an examination of "process experience" as a board product; the potential benefits and problems of assigning poverty programs to delegate agencies; the characteristics of the poor, as compared with those of the not-poor; the views or stereotypes that the not-poor have of the participating poor, and the reality of the expectations they have for them; the functions of maintaining informal relations among board members; the relative advantages and disadvantages of a large poverty board *versus* a small poverty board; the role of the officers of a poverty board; and the foreseen and unforeseen consequences of poverty intervention.

CHAPTER 8

Evaluation by Target Neighborhood Officers

THE OPINIONS OF agency representative and citizen at large (non-TNOs) Economic Opportunity Board members have been presented and discussed in Chapter 7. What did the other Board members—the Target Neighborhood Officers (TNOs)—think of the poverty program after experiencing participation?

As were the non-TNOs, the TNOs were formally interviewed in May, 1967, after the Board had been incorporated for twenty months and had met for nineteen regular and seventeen executive sessions. A set of questions similar to those asked of non-TNOs was asked of TNOs, individually and in their homes. Twenty-three members were interviewed. A percentage breakdown of their responses to the ma-

jor interview questions is presented in this chapter. Response categories are illustrated with sample quotes, and the distribution of responses is discussed and contrasted with the responses of non-TNO
Board members.

QUESTIONS, RESPONSES, AND INTERPRETATIONS

*Do you plan to continue as a member of the Economic Opportunity
Board?*

YES: 65 per cent

WHY? Humanitarian reasons: 73 per cent

"Yes, I'm going to continue as a member. I guess it's because
of my dedication to the community and my interest in it, and I
guess part of it is because I'm just plain stupid, too! Well, really,
I think the Lord has put us here for some purpose, and that
purpose is to help our brothers, so I'm going to keep doing that."

Personal enjoyment: 27 per cent

"I'm really involved in the Board now, and I really enjoy it.
It's a whole new world for me. I didn't spend all those months
on the Board learning all those rules and things just to quit now.
I'm at a point now where I can get up and say things, and be
understood, and get my ideas across."

NO: 26 per cent

WHY? Job conflict: 25 per cent

"I dropped out because OEO helped me get a job that conflicted with my being a Board member. How about that!"

"I just can't keep working at two jobs and coming to all these
meetings at the same time."

Was not re-elected as a TNO: 25 per cent

"I got beat out in the election by a guy who campaigned
better than I did, I guess."

Programs inappropriate: 25 per cent

"No, I won't. I won't continue as a Board member. It's just a waste of time to us, and we never get a penny out of it. It doesn't meet the problems of my group. We need jobs, we need money for rent, we need money for food. I don't know what OEO was set up for. It doesn't meet our problems."

Resigned as a TNO: 25 per cent
"I tried and tried to get the Target Neighborhood organized, and never seemed to get anywhere, so I'm just tossing it in."

"I quit because I had another baby."

UNCERTAIN: 9 per cent
"I don't know if I'll continue as a Board member or not. It depends on the people as to whether I stay on as a Neighborhood Officer, and as a Board member or not. I may not run again as chairman, but I'll keep working with the program in some other way. If no one else takes the chairmanship, though, I will."

The majority of the TNOs planned to continue as Board members, most of them for humanitarian reasons, but several for reasons of personal enjoyment. More of the TNOs than non-TNOs indicated that they planned to continue Board membership, but this difference was influenced by the impact of the legislative amendment ordering Board restructuring. Several of the non-TNOs, but none of the TNOs, were to be eliminated from membership by the amendment. The TNOs more frequently gave humanitarian reasons for continuing Board participation than did the non-TNOs. TNOs' humanitarian reasons often included direct references to religious obligations; non-TNO humanitarian responses seldom did. Non-TNOs cited civic responsibilities as reasons for continuing Board membership; only a few TNOs cited this reason. Several TNOs stated that they wanted to remain as Board members because they found the meetings enjoyable and personally profitable; none of the non-TNOs cited enjoyment or personal profit as reasons for continuing.

It is not surprising that TNOs indicated more humanitarian-religious and fewer civic-responsibility reasons for program participation. TNOs were affiliated more with fundamentalist religions than were non-TNOs, and many of their discussions concerning the poverty program reflected a central "good neighbor," and occasionally a "missionary," orientation. Many non-TNOs were deeply enmeshed in community and complex organization activities, and consequently had developed a clear and pressing sense of community responsibility. In a sense, they were more secularized than the TNOs—their reasons for continuing participation were filtered largely through statements of obligation to country, state, community, organization, or political ideology. For TNOs, there had previously been little opportunity to experience the kinds of secondary associations which would instill the more secular kinds of orientations. In most cases, the only secondary association within the community opened to TNOs for active participation was the fundamentalist church. The fact that participation in the poverty program, including the Economic Opportunity Board, gave them experience with other kinds of secondary associations and other kinds of social roles may account for the fact that some of them cited personal enjoyment as a reason for continuing that participation.

Many of the non-TNOs complained about the amount of conflict that took place during Board meetings; some of them decided to resign from the Board because of it. A few of the TNOs commented about arguments among Board members during the meetings, but none of them gave conflict as a reason for withdrawing from participation. Interpersonal conflict during meetings discouraged TNOs from participation far less than did their experiences of program inappropriateness or inconsistency, role ambiguity, and difficulties with organizing their own Target Neighborhoods.

Occasionally, a TNO would be disqualified from Board membership because a job he had obtained in the poverty program created a "conflict of interest" between his job and that membership—a phenomenon that TNOs considered strangely incongruous, and definitely unjust. Non-TNOs took as a fact of organizational life that anyone in a situation of conflict of interest should resign one or the other position. TNOs, on the other hand, viewed having to choose between one or the other position, since both were in the poverty program, as being a not-so-subtle way of limiting increasing participation of the poor.

A few TNOs had to resign from Board participation because they could not afford the expense of that participation—their jobs included evening hours from which they would have to be excused for meetings, or the transportation costs to and from meetings overtaxed their budgets. The problem of dollar costs for program participation was a frequent complaint among them, even among those who chose to remain as participants. They felt that the agency representatives who attended the meetings were just doing their jobs, and were therefore being paid for participation. The citizens at large, they appreciated, were giving up some hours of their leisure time, but were not making a financial sacrifice. The TNOs, however, not only had to give up leisure (and in some cases, working) hours to attend meetings of the Board, Target Neighborhood Committees, and assorted other meetings in the poverty program, but had to stretch their meager resources to cover additional transportation costs. Many felt they should, at minimum, be reimbursed for those costs, and wondered why they should have to pay a price to participate in a program that was supposed to be financially beneficial to them.

In order to sustain active participation of the poor on poverty boards, training programs should include thorough discussions of their role in the poverty program, and should equip indigenous leaders with the kinds of skills which would maximize the possibility of successful neighborhood organization. Furthermore, there seems to be no logical reason why they could not be reimbursed for travel costs to and from meetings, or, perhaps better, paid a basic salary for what amounts to difficult and challenging work. Making the programs more "appropriate" in their view is, of course, of crucial importance for maintaining their active participation. The types and processes of program "appropriateness" are discussed at length in Chapters 12, 13, and 14.

What is your opinion of "maximum feasible participation" of the poor now, and has your opinion changed by virtue of your own participation?

FAVORABLE OPINION: 87 per cent

"All I can say about participation is, 'more!' We should be involved all the way to the top. That's the way it should be, and that's the kind of hope I have for participation."

"I thought this 'feasible maximum participation' thing was just a bunch of shit at first. But it's not. Our participation is the guts of the program. It should go as far as it's able to go. How the hell else are we going to let people know what our problems really are, and show them ways that we can solve them without everybody getting all screwed up?"

MIXED OPINION: 9 per cent

"It depends on the person's qualifications. The poor should participate as much as we can, but I think that we should have a lot more training sessions. You know, if we just go in there cold, then we're not going to do very well, and the people who're opposed to our getting any power can point at us and say, 'Look at them, they don't know what they're doing; they're all alike,' and so on. We need training sessions, and ones that we can help prepare, too."

UNFAVORABLE OPINION: 4 per cent

"I think people in the poor bracket lack understanding of participation, and what it means. We feel we should head up the whole program. We've got to have professionals heading it up, so that we can keep things in sound financial condition."

The overwhelming majority of TNOs favored "maximum feasible participation," and with participation had grown increasingly convinced that it was an important concept in the poverty program. Many of them, however, called for additional training, particularly for skills relevant to Neighborhood organization and parliamentary and strategic conduct during meetings. Most of them also felt that more opportunities for participation at higher levels of decision-making should be provided, and that methods should be worked out whereby increasing numbers of Target Neighborhood residents could have active participation in the poverty program. Some of the TNOs, though not disagreeing with the necessity for participation of the poor, did feel that the concept "maximum feasible participation" was too vague, and could too easily be manipulated by non-TNOs who held the majority of votes on the Board. Very few TNOs were uncertain about, or opposed to, active participation of the poor in the program. Those who did speak negatively about participation seemed to be willing to accept a traditional passive role vis-à-vis the active and directing role of the middle-class professional.

As discussed in Chapter 3, the question "how much power" or "how much participation" is a recurring dilemma for the poverty-intervention organization. Ideally, participation in the poverty program should be limited only by the skills and ambitions of the participants, and training which develops those skills and inculcates those ambitions should be readily available. If a poverty-intervention organization places an inflexible ceiling upon the kind and degree of participation of the poor, or if it unrealistically defines the skills and ambitions prerequisite to participation and attaining increased levels of responsibility, or if it offers opportunity for participation without providing training that allows successful role enactment, then the organization will be more oriented toward social control than toward social change. Furthermore, since that kind of social control intensifies the frustration of participants by publicizing possibilities without providing opportunities, the poverty-intervention organization probably will intensify the problems it attempts to solve.

Not surprisingly, the non-TNOs were less favorably disposed to "maximum feasible participation" than the TNOs. The uncertainty or disapproval of some of the non-TNOs no doubt was influenced by their negative perceptions of the former TNO who was the Board president at the time of the interview. However, the negative or mixed evaluations of many of them could be traced to misunderstandings of what "maximum feasible participation" means, and what its impact would be. In the absence of a clear definition of the term from the TOEO (or for that matter, from the national Office of Economic Opportunity), each Board member was at liberty to postulate his own definition. For the TNOs, that definition typically was in terms of power, and "all the way to the top." To the non-TNOs, the definition meant participation that did not "disrupt" a varied array of individual expectations for TNO performance.

What do you think of the Economic Opportunity Board in terms of its productivity and interpersonal interactions?

FAVORABLE OPINION: 22 per cent

"I was amazed by the co-operation from people who, when they were in their offices, weren't co-operative at all, or who didn't seem to be. Maybe it's because they are in a new place, and they have to sit with us as equals."

"The way I look at it, the Board is a classroom for me."

MIXED OPINION: 22 per cent

"I don't know how to answer that. At times I felt that people on the Board saw their positions as a feather in their bonnet. Some used it as a steppingstone to something else. If they want a job, and want to get involved in something else, they want to have it on their record that they were involved in a poverty board. I think the majority of the people wanted to help, but there's too much delay and red tape. There seems to be so many committees and subcommittees that nothing gets done. I go to the Board meetings, and sometimes the talk makes no sense, and then they kick the matter back to a Study Committee, and then they'd have a Study Committee study that Study Committee, and finally the thing would just seem to disappear."

"I don't think everyone understands what community action is. It took me a long time to learn it. It means involving all, from the very poor to the very rich. I don't remember any time that any community action was explained to the Board as a whole. I don't know if the Target Neighborhood Officers have the same view of the program that the agency and citizens-at-large people do. The whole Board needs training, so we can have the same kind of over-all view of things. The Board has brought together all different kinds of groups, and is trying to get us to work together and this has never been done before, so naturally you'd have a two- or three-year growing period."

UNFAVORABLE OPINION: 38 per cent

"I don't see where the Board has any say-so. Everything's done in the Executive Committee; everything seems to be settled before it ever gets to the Board. I think we ought to talk more about things at the Board than we do."

"We have too many people on the Board who use theory but not practice. We need their advice, but we don't need them to run the program. Every Target Neighborhood Officer should give a report of what's going on in his Neighborhood at each meeting."

NO OPINION: 18 per cent

The Target Neighborhood Officers who expressed favorable opinions about the Economic Opportunity Board were impressed primarily by the benefits of their own participation, and by what they perceived to be unexpected co-operation from non-TNOs. Those TNOs who gave unfavorable or mixed evaluations included in their complaints: the Board mechanisms were not getting enough money to the poor; the agency representatives tended to be self-centered; the meetings were boring; there was too much talk at the meetings; there was not enough talk at the meetings; the committee network was too complex; and there were too many abstract discussions which did not result in concrete action. The "too much talk" *versus* "not enough talk" opinions do not appear contradictory when "who's doing the talking" is considered—"not enough talk" referred to TNO participation; "too much talk" referred to non-TNO participation. The apparent inconsistency in evaluation of agency representatives as being "self-centered" and "co-operative" primarily reflects differing individual assessments of specific agency representatives; secondarily, it reflects both an ambivalence toward agency representatives and challenges to a negative stereotype from evidence of individual differences.

TNOs were more favorable in their evaluation of the Economic Opportunity Board than non-TNOs. This difference can largely be explained by the variance of members' assessment of the Board president. The non-TNOs were quite severe in their criticism of the president, and some of them tended to generalize about the Board in general by that evaluation. The TNOs, on the other hand, seldom criticized the president, who had formerly been a colleague Target Neighborhood Officer. They did not, however, favorably evaluate his performance, but rather seemed to empathize with him, and felt sorry that he was "falling on his face." Several of them thought that the president "needed help," and themselves took steps to offer him at least moral support whenever they could. Thus, TNO evaluation of the Board was less in terms of the assessment of the capabilities of the president, and more in terms of their own experiences and functions as Board members. They were impressed that they sat as "equals" with the "haves," and that participation taught them something. Nonetheless, their expectations for their own Board performance, the ultimate purposes of the Board, and the workings of various committees remained more or less unclear to them. Those ambiguities could have been resolved if the poverty-intervention organization had encouraged more formal and informal discussions about Board goals, structures, roles, and processes.

Do you feel that the poverty program has brought about any change in Topeka?

YES: 87 per cent

"There has been a change. Topeka's been a town with its head in the sand. We feel better now because we can express our needs, and the power structure is more aware of our needs."

"There definitely have been some changes. You can really see the results of community action. Well, right out here, you can see that we got street lights when we didn't have them before. Also, some people have gotten jobs because of the program."

"Yes, there's been some change in a way. More low-income people have become interested in social change. It's a hard program for people to understand. In the first place we often look for jobs or handouts. We can't accept the services or understand them unless it's in money terms. Maybe it's a change in the way we look at things, that there may be some hope. Maybe that's the change."

NO: 13 per cent

"No, I can't see where the program has done anything. There's not much more money getting to the poor. Nothing's really happening fast enough. Nothing's really changed except the words."

Target Neighborhood Officers saw some specific and concrete changes in their Neighborhoods, such as street lights, Day Care Centers, a Neighborhood House, and jobs, as a result of the poverty program. They felt that other citizens had become more aware of the existence of poverty in Topeka, and a number of those citizens, in influential positions, were willing to help do something about it. Some TNOs also perceived a shift in attitudes among the participating poor, a shift toward a sense of "hope." "Hope," as expressed by some of them in informal discussion, not only meant the possibility of improving one's financial condition, though of course that was extremely important to them; the concept also included an increasing sense of competence, of self-direction, of perhaps being able to improve one's financial condition and style of life by one's own choice. The TNOs who did not see change in Topeka as a result of the poverty program tended to evaluate that program by the criterion of immediate results. The impact was not dramatic or sweeping enough for them.

The TNOs saw more change in Topeka induced by the poverty program than did the non-TNOs. TNOs had clearer criteria for assessing change than did non-TNOs. TNOs lived in the areas directly affected by various activities of the poverty program, and when there were tangible results they could see them more readily. Several TNOs and non-TNOs agreed that elements of the "power structure" were now more aware of poverty in Topeka, and seemed to be more interested in its amelioration. Several TNOs and non-TNOs also agreed that their opinions of each other had shifted, favorably, as a result of their mutual participation in the program.

The assessments of change by Board members were made more difficult by the vagueness concerning exactly what the poverty program was supposed to change. Nevertheless, physical, informational, and attitudinal changes apparently were being made noticeably enough to be reported by large percentages of both TNOs and non-TNOs.

What are your opinions of the citizens at large, agency representatives, and other Target Neighborhood Officers in terms of their cooperation and capabilities?

CITIZENS AT LARGE:

FAVORABLE OPINION: 52 per cent
"I especially admire the citizens at large, because they're working for nothing, and they were always present at the Board meetings. I was mad as hell when some of them had to leave the Board because of that stupid amendment."

MIXED OPINION: 35 per cent
"I thought the citizens at large were always pretty good. But I really can't put my finger on what they've contributed."

UNFAVORABLE OPINION: 4 per cent
"I don't think the citizens at large will ever really understand our problems because you can't understand poverty unless you live in poverty. Most of them are in it to hold something over us or to gain prestige."

NO OPINION: 9 per cent

AGENCY REPRESENTATIVES:

FAVORABLE OPINION: 26 per cent
"They've come out of their offices and come to our meetings, and that wasn't easy for them, and I think they're doing a great job!"

MIXED OPINION: 44 per cent
"The agency representatives who are here understand the problems we have real well, but sometimes their own boards

control them and are slow in acting. I think they do their best, though."

UNFAVORABLE OPINION: 22 per cent

"You shouldn't have asked me that. I'm hot on that! I don't think the agency representatives are worth a damn! They're all here for selfish reasons. If you look at what's happening you can see that some of them are interested in shaping their own careers. I'm afraid some of them are more concerned about their own welfare than they are about the welfare of the people."

NO OPINION: 8 per cent

OTHER TARGET NEIGHBORHOOD OFFICERS:

FAVORABLE OPINION: 53 per cent

"We have a good set of Target Neighborhood Officers, and I don't know how we could get a better one. You know, when an agency representative leaves the Board meeting, he leaves the problem behind him. But us Target Neighborhood Officers still have it, and we have to live with it every day of our lives. I admire the Target Neighborhood Officers for that!"

"The only people who know the Neighborhoods and the problems are the Target Neighborhood Officers. Nobody else can really know about it!"

MIXED OPINION: 43 per cent

"Some Target Neighborhood Officers are better than others. All of us, though, can learn."

"I was a little disappointed by the Target Neighborhood Officers, because some of them seemed to have their own ax to grind. But most of us are doing pretty good."

UNFAVORABLE OPINION: 4 per cent

"The Target Neighborhood Officers are hoggish, and try to get everything for their own Neighborhoods."

Favorable evaluations saw the citizens at large as flexible, co-operative, and giving their time for no apparent benefit. Unfavorable evaluations of them included comments concerning their lack of understanding of the problems of the poor, dominating the meetings, and having always to go to them, since they would never come to the Target Neighborhoods. Agency representatives were favorably evaluated by some TNOs simply because they showed up at the Board meetings and seemed to take an interest. Agency representatives were seen by other TNOs to be "human," and actually interested in the problems of the poor. Unfavorable evaluations criticized agency representatives for not really being interested in or understanding the problems of the poor, for being self-centered and dominating the meetings, for not visiting the Target Neighborhoods, and for being more interested in their careers and the interests of their organizations than they were in helping the poor.

Citizens at large were evaluated more favorably than agency representatives primarily because their motives for participation were less often called into question. Since citizens at large were not employed by helping agencies, but were volunteers, the Target Neighborhood Officers were more convinced that they were "sincere" and wanted to work with the poor. TNOs often reported that it was easier to "get to know" citizens at large than agency representatives. At least part of this difference in evaluation can be accounted for by the fact that several of the TNOs had been, at one time or another, "clients" of the organizations for which the agency representatives worked. Consequently, it became difficult for TNOs to overcome the social distance created by the symbolism of the agency representative's formal title. Not a few TNOs considered their previous associations with community helping organizations to have been unsatisfactory or self-demeaning. The psychological contract (bad me–good you), to which they felt they had temporarily agreed in order to get help from an agency, complicated some TNOs' ability to relate to agency representatives, and vice versa.

Other TNOs were "buddies," "fellow sufferers," and generally favorably perceived. By the time the interview was held, however, some TNOs were in competition with others for limited poverty funds. Thus some of them evaluated others as being "hoggish" or "grabby" for their particular Target Neighborhoods. Those Target Neighborhood Officers who had resigned were also usually negatively evaluated by those who chose to remain as participants. The quitters were criticized for having "given up too easily." On the other hand, non-TNOs typically evaluated Target Neighborhood Officers favorably when they "identified" and "were aggressive" for programing for their Neighborhoods, and when they adhered to the middle-class model for expected behavior at a meeting. Those who negatively evaluated TNOs tended to do so by criticizing the "inefficiency" TNO participation caused the Board. TNOs evaluated other TNOs, however, primarily in terms of their "co-operativeness" and "friendliness." But the Target Neighborhood Officer who was assessed as pushing too hard for programing in his Neighborhood, at the expense of other Neighborhoods, was considered to be "hoggish." In no case was one TNO negatively evaluated by another TNO for interfering with the "efficiency" of the Board. They sometimes felt there was too much "red tape" during Board meetings, but blamed the system, not other TNOs, for that problem.

The only occasion when TNOs, agency representatives, and citizens at large got together in a group was during Board meetings conducting official business. Additional full sessions of the Board, scheduled not to conduct official business but to explore Board goals and processes, and to allow personal familiarization among the members, probably would have facilitated the breaking down, in many cases, of mutually held stereotypes. Furthermore, in such sessions, those individuals whose actions tended to suggest the stereotypes might have been encouraged, by group pressures, to modify their negatively evaluated behaviors.

Do you feel that the structure of the program has made it easier to reach the agencies and the poor?

AGENCIES:

YES: 62 per cent

"Definitely. Among my group, you don't really feel that you can reach the higher ups, but you're a spokesman for your people and you can talk to OEO, and OEO will carry your message almost anywhere. It's kind of like lobbying. To me a lobbyist can't do anything himself, but he can talk to one person, and that one talks to another, until somebody who can do something about it does it."

"It sure is easier to reach the agencies now, because we've gotten to know them and they've gotten to know us as persons, and we can get in touch with them by phone, or just by dropping in, almost anytime. I've gotten to agency representatives now, bringing with me somebody who needed help, several times, and it works out very good."

NO: 22 per cent

"I don't think so. There just aren't enough poor on the Board to make the agencies feel pressured. Their particular group can set up as a power structure."

UNCERTAIN: 16 per cent

"We've gotten more action out of some of the agency heads who're sitting on the Board, but we'll have to wait and see if that lasts."

THE POOR:

YES: 36 per cent

"Yes, the program has made it easier to reach the poor, especially through programs like the Neighborhood House, the Extension Worker Program, and the Day Care Centers."

NO: 44 per cent

"We haven't been able to reach enough of the people in the Target Neighborhoods yet because our Neighborhood Committees aren't well enough organized. Maybe in time we can do that better. When we want to make contact with an agency head, it's just one of us to one of them. But when we try to reach the residents of our Neighborhood, it's one of us to thousands of them, and we just haven't got time to get around to all that. We need some better form of organization to get everybody together."

"This amendment's going to cause us to lose what we've gained in getting to people in the Target Neighborhoods. The Board's going to be disorganized for quite a while, and we'd all been together for almost two years, and had gotten to know one another, and were beginning to find ways to reach people in the Target Neighborhoods better. Now that's all changed."

UNCERTAIN: 20 per cent

"It's too early to tell just yet if we're going to be able to reach many of the residents in our Target Neighborhoods. We're just beginning to get our committees going, and they'll be the best way to reach the poor. But I'm not sure if we ever can get our committees that organized."

The Target Neighborhood Officers clearly felt that the structure of the program had made it easer to reach the agencies than it had to reach the poor. Their formal and informal contact with agency representatives during Board and other meetings familiarized them with persons and procedures that facilitated access to the agencies. On the other hand, their Board experience contributed little to skills and strategies for reaching the poor or for organizing their Neighborhoods toward community action. Some TNOs also felt that the restructuring of the Economic Opportunity Board ordered by the Quie Amendment would eliminate several citizens at large who had worthwhile experiences to share with them concerning ways of reaching more Target Neighborhood residents. Those TNOs who felt the program structure had facilitated reaching the poor spoke, as did some of the non-TNOs, in terms of specific activities, such as the Neighborhood House, Day Care Center, etc.

The TNOs and non-TNOs who were uncertain in their evaluation virtually all thought it was too early to assess to what degree the poor, and to a lesser degree the agencies, would be reached by the poverty program. Some non-TNOs who gave a positive evaluation credited the Target Neighborhood Officers, and their person-to-person relations with residents, as being the key factor in the program's capability to reach the poor. TNOs were less willing to attribute that success to themselves, feeling they had not yet solved the problem of numbers. Some TNOs and non-TNOs agreed that the program was not yet reaching enough of the "hard-core" poor, non-TNOs indicating that TNOs should be more active in that endeavor. If the burden of reaching and/or organizing the poor is to be placed upon the indigenous leaders, then it is imperative that they receive training which would prepare them for the tasks.

Has your Board experience changed your view of the "middle class"?

YES: 52 per cent

POSITIVE CHANGE: 92 per cent

"I never had much dealing with that kind of people. I had a feeling that some of them just sat back and pulled strings, but had no compassion for other people. Now I know that some of them do care."

"Yes, the experience has made me understand *their* problems more."

"I think the agencies have changed their point of view about us, and when I saw that, I had to change my opinion of them, too. If they can see me as a human being, then I can see them as a human being, too."

"I don't feel they're so tough anymore. I feel that I can talk to them. I feel like they're just people."

NEGATIVE CHANGE: 8 per cent

"Before I went to the Board meetings, I thought some of the agency bosses were S.O.B.s. Now I *know* some of them are!"

NO: 48 per cent

"My views are still the same. They still don't give a damn about anybody but themselves."

"No. They're still 'haves' and I'm still a 'have-not.'"

"Like at first, I still think there are good ones and bad ones."

A majority of the TNOs changed their view of the "middle class" in a positive direction. In speaking of the "middle class," however, almost all of them referred directly to the agency representatives and citizens at large with whom they served on the Economic Opportunity Board. As a result of mutual participation, several TNOs came to perceive non-TNOs as approachable, interested, and human, giving and deserving respect. The positive changes were selective, and TNOs usually were careful to specify that "some" non-TNOs had become deserving of more favorable opinions. The negative opinion changes, or those negative opinions which were maintained, tended to be all-inclusive stereotypes held by a few TNOs. Most of the no-change indications came from TNOs who had maintained a "some good, some not so good" view of agency representatives and citizens at large. In the responses to this question, TNO evaluations of citizens at large tended to be more favorable than their evaluations of agency representatives.

Both TNOs and non-TNOs reported considerable favorable change in their views of one another's competencies, co-operation, and "human-ness." Some TNOs and non-TNOs, however, retained stereotypical "all bad" reciprocal views. Generally, those Board members who maintained those views were less active in the poverty program than those whose assessments of participants were based on individual performances. The more active members had opportunity for greater interaction, formally and informally, with other Board members, and consequently had greater opportunity to challenge whatever stereotypes they might initially have held. Poverty-intervention organizations should arrange continuing interactions among board members, in large and small, structured and unstructured, formal and informal group settings, in order to provide opportunities for members to challenge each other's stereotypical beliefs.

Has your Board experience changed your view of what can be done about poverty?

YES: 57 per cent

"We ourselves are really going to have to push to the front with good leadership. We have to keep at it, so there'll be changes. I know now that we aren't going to get everything we ask for, but if we keep pushing we can get some changes, anyway."

"The biggest change has been for me personally, and what I think I can do about poverty. I wouldn't be afraid to talk to people in charge of different programs now. Whether I could get anything done is another story, but now at least I know I can try."

"Yes. Now I think some programs are better than others. I think family planning, Head Start, the Neighborhood House, the Day Care Centers, and getting people jobs are the winners. I don't see much profit in the Job Corps, the Neighborhood Youth Corps, or in some of the job-training programs that get people ready for jobs that don't exist."

NO: 43 per cent

"My opinion hasn't changed yet, because I don't think the OEO has had that big an impact just yet. I'm not sure that I've seen enough of it to come to a conclusion about what can be done about poverty. Maybe OEO can do it, maybe not."

"I still am worried that we won't ever eliminate poverty completely but I still think that we can slow down the growing of poverty. We can do that by seeing that everybody has food, a place to live, and clothing."

Most of the Target Neighborhood Officers expressed changes in their opinions of what could be done about poverty. All the changes expressed were positive, indicating a growing confidence that perhaps something "really could be done." The increased positive evaluation included several references to specific programs which they had observed to be effective, and which had convinced them that the poverty program had potential. A few of them had thoughts about the need for their own number to "push harder" during Board meetings for the implementation of poverty programs. Those same few occasionally discussed alternative approaches to ameliorating poverty, such as guaranteed family income or negative income tax. It appeared to the research observers that there was more discussion among TNOs than non-TNOs concerning other poverty-intervention strategies as alternatives to the Office of Economic Opportunity. The Neighborhood House, which was primarily under the direction of some TNOs, did in fact experiment with a few "outside OEO" tactics for the amelioration of poverty (a case study of the Neighborhood House, and the involvement of TNOs, is presented in Chapter 14).

The initial opinions of the TNOs concerning what to do about poverty were, though sometimes inconsistent, considerably less vague than those of the non-TNOs. The non-TNOs generally had somewhat unrefined ideas about "changing," somehow, the physical and psychological conditions of the rather unclearly defined "poor." The TNOs' definition of the "poor" was more specific. The poor were themselves, the people next door, and the people who lived in their Target Neighborhoods. "Poverty intervention" meant jobs or better jobs, better housing, better education, and more self-determination for those residents. Most TNOs hoped that those improvements could be accomplished through the Topeka Office of Economic Opportunity, with their involvement.

Has your Board participation brought about any change in your own personal life?

YES: 83 per cent
  POSITIVE CHANGE: 68 per cent
    "I feel dedicated to the program, and I've never felt that way about anything before. It makes me feel like I want to help. It's made me more conscious of others around me. I know I've had tough times, but I didn't realize there were others who were also having tough times, and we could work together for things.

    "What do you mean, did it change my life! It got me the best-paying job I've ever had! Do you know what that means to me and my family?"

    "It's brightened my outlook on people. I've found that different people can work together, and they aren't that much different. I think it's made me more sincere about things; I mean, I take some things more seriously now than I used to."

"Well, it's changed my view toward myself. I feel more like a person now than I did before."

NEGATIVE CHANGE: 34 per cent

"My participation has made a lot of people mad at me because I didn't get them jobs, or didn't get the things they expected. Some people think I was just a complete flop, because I couldn't get the program to deliver for them what they wanted right now."

"Yes. My participation has made me realize that the poverty program is bull shit."

"It's changed my life, all right. My husband gives me hell for going to all those meetings. He thinks I'm wasting my time. I don't, but he makes it rough on me."

"It's been a bad experience for me. I felt inadequate, and it didn't puff me up at all."

NO: 17 per cent

"I'm still the same person I was before I joined the Board. Oh, maybe I know a little more, but I'm still the same person."

"The pluses and minuses have balanced out to not much change in my personal life. Because I was a Target Neighborhood Officer I lost the confidence of some people who had confidence in me before, and got confidence from some people who didn't place any in me before. I guess you could say I made some good friends because of OEO, and lost a few because of OEO."

Those Target Neighborhood Officers who expressed positive changes in their personal lives as a result of participation specified that it had improved their employment situation, changed their view of themselves or others, or given them opportunity to learn new social roles. The negative changes reported included: having Neighborhood residents become angry because the TNO did not "deliver" results quickly or completely enough; concern that to participate cost money (transportation); complaints that to attend all the meetings resulted in neglect of family and, consequently, family resentment; and some feelings of inadequacy when attempting to enact the role of Board member.

Several of them had procured employment in the poverty program, though only a few of the jobs were full-time and permanent. Most of the TNOs needed increases in income, and hoped that eventually their participation in the poverty program would provide them with opportunities to improve their employment situation. During the period of research, they had not been able to accomplish much in the way of raising their own incomes. Yet most of them continued to participate, and were content with the more intangible profits of opportunity for meaningful participation, the enactment of new social roles, and the enhancement of status as a Target Neighborhood Officer. As pointed out earlier, it seems incongruous that TNOs should have to make financial sacrifices in order to participate in the poverty program. Undeniably they had increased transportation and clothing costs, in some cases lost "working" hours, and in several cases were obliged to spend many hours a week away from their families (during more active periods, TNOs would spend three or more nights a week at various poverty-program meetings). One wonders whether the poverty program, consistent with the traditional American welfare ideology, wasn't expecting the poor to pay a "price" to get out of poverty.

Certainly the kinds of process experiences accumulated by Target Neighborhood Officers engendered valuable changes in self-concept and self-confidence. But it is hard to understand why the program could not have provided these poverty warriors with direct material rewards as well. It is one thing to request volunteer "community service" from relatively affluent agency representatives and citizens at large; it is quite another matter to expect such a donation from persons who are struggling to maintain bare subsistence for themselves and their families. Not all, but most of the Target Neighborhood Officers were classified, by OEO definition, as impoverished.

If you could, would you change the Economic Opportunity Board?

YES: 56 per cent

"Its size is too big. I'd cut it down, and give the poor more representation. Cut down the number of agency representatives, leave the citizens at large as they are, and increase the number of Neighborhood people."

"The Target Neighborhoods should be represented proportionally by size, rather than just two officers from each Neighborhood. Some of the Neighborhoods are bigger than others, you know. Although I think the smallest ones should still have two persons representing them, the big ones should have as many as five, and the agency representatives should be trimmed accordingly."

"We've got too damned many preachers on the Board just because they are preachers. We ought to get more people on there who can help us get jobs."

NO: 44 per cent

"For God's sake, let's leave the Board alone! There're too many people screwing around with it as it is! It's been hard enough to learn how it worked the way it is, without somebody coming along and changing it all around now. I'm just now getting used to it! That damned amendment's going to make it tough enough as it is."

"I guess I'd leave it as it is. Things run pretty good. Oh, we fight sometimes, but that's all part of the game. I wouldn't want to see it any smaller. It may be a little hard to handle, but that's the best way to let the others—I mean those that aren't in the Target Neighborhoods—know what's going on."

"I don't think we ought to change the Board any, but I never have understood who was supposed to be in charge of the Board meetings or in charge of the other meetings that are held in the TOEO office. I wish somebody would explain the whole picture to me. I know other Neighborhood Officers who're confused, too."

Several Target Neighborhood Officers wanted to modify the Board, in particular to increase the proportion of representation from among the poor. Those who argued against changing its structure liked its large size, and didn't want the Board changed when they were beginning to become accustomed to it. Several TNOs called for additional formal training in the structure and functions of the Board, as then constituted, but did not want the Board itself changed in any way. Along with a few of the non-TNOs, some of the TNOs argued that the Board had not yet really been given a full test of its capabilities as it was originally formed, and changes should be deferred until that test could be accomplished.

More non-TNOs than TNOs called for change in the Economic Opportunity Board. Many non-TNOs wanted to reduce its size—some wanting to increase, and some to decrease, the proportion of TNOs. The suggestions of the non-TNOs for modification were aimed toward shaping the Board into a more "efficient" operation. The suggestions for modifications put forth by the TNOs, on the other hand, were primarily aimed at increasing their participation and the relative number of their votes.

What is the ideal size for a poverty board? What are the ideal voting proportions? The answers to these questions depend a great deal upon the community setting, and the general climate for poverty intervention. Such questions, however, should be discussed by representatives from the poor and not-poor segments of the community, and an appropriate size and balance determined. Furthermore, in many cases it may be advantageous to consider the size and proportion of the board to be flexible, subject to change with changes in the community and emerging indigenous leadership.

No matter what its size or the proportion of representation, board proceedings will be greatly facilitated if all the members have the opportunity to participate in training programs which include discussions of board structure, program goals, parliamentary conduct and administration of a meeting, and discussions of member roles, perceptions, and interactions. The processes of planned social change, and the conflicts and stresses endemic to such change, should also be considered. Training sessions should be continuing, not simply one brief session soon after the board's inception. Often there is a high rate of member turnover in poverty boards, and new members need training. Furthermore, as the board brings about social and personal change, it encounters new and different problems which should be objectified for all the members. The scheduling for board sessions is a matter best left to local planners, but the sessions should be frequent and recurring. One strategy might be to have a major training session, focusing on process experiences rather than program content, during a full board session every quarter. In addition, perhaps the last fifteen minutes of every regularly scheduled board meeting, after the conducting of business, could be set aside for reflecting upon the evening's process experiences, and how they facilitated or impeded the productivity of the meetings. In the case of some poverty-intervention organizations, it may be advisable first to hold separate, and then joint, training sessions for representatives of the poor and the not-poor. Whatever the form or schedule of training chosen by local poverty-intervention organizations, those organizations should readily implement some procedure, whether it is called "training" or not, which would allow participants to reflect upon their expectations for, and experiencing of, program involvement. If opportunity is not provided for the expression of those expectations and experiences, then they will, inevitably, contribute to the hidden agenda of regular board meetings.

Are there individuals among the agency representatives, the citizens at large, and other Target Neighborhood Officers whom you can formally or informally contact for community, Neighborhood, or personal issues that you didn't or couldn't contact before your involvement in the poverty program?

AGENCY REPRESENTATIVES AND CITIZENS AT LARGE:

 YES: 74 per cent

"I guess I really could have contacted agency representatives before, because they probably were available, but I just didn't feel like it. I mean I didn't feel good doing it. Now, I see they're just people, and I go to talk to them just like I would anybody else, when I need something or want to know something. It seems to make a difference when you go to an office and say, 'I'm the chairman of a Target Neighborhood Committee.' It seems to make a difference to the way they listen to you. Maybe it's because they realize you've got a vote on the Board just like they do."

"Personally, I always felt that if I wanted to get something done for me and my family or friends, I should go see the top dog and not go through some jerk. The difference is that OEO taught me better ways to get to the top dog than just to make noise at the front door. One guy whose secretary threw me out of his office a couple of years ago, welcomes me right in now. Before, I couldn't even get by that secretary."

"I see citizens at large and agency representatives on the street sometimes, and we stop and talk, just casually, you know. If I need something for the Neighborhood I go and see them in their offices, and sometimes they even call me or come and see me if they want advice about some Neighborhood problem."

NO: 26 per cent

"I don't think there're any agency people who I could contact, especially informally. I don't even know if they'd know me or recognize me. They still live in their own world."

OTHER TARGET NEIGHBORHOOD OFFICERS:

YES: 100 per cent

"I made several good friends among the Target Neighborhood Officers, people who live in our Neighborhoods, who I'd never seen before. What's especially interesting is that their problems were like mine, and we had much in common, and realized there were others just like us. It makes you feel stronger, knowing that."

"Yeah. It's a nice feeling to be able to share problems with other Neighborhood Officers. Sometimes I get stumped at one of my meetings by some question or by somebody. When the meeting's over, or the next day, I call up another Target

Neighborhood Officer and tell him my problem, and usually I can get some help. Now that I've been around awhile, I find I can do the same thing for other new Neighborhood Officers. I don't feel so all alone facing all of this."

"We have a great bunch of Target Neighborhood Officers. Sometimes some of us get together at each other's houses just for the fun of it, and hardly even talk about OEO."

NO: Zero per cent

As indicated in responses to this and previous questions, Target Neighborhood Officers significantly increased, as a result of program participation, their formal and informal access to agency representatives and citizens at large (more so with regard to the latter). Several of the TNOs were especially impressed that occasionally agency representatives would contact them for their advice concerning Neighborhood problems. Agency representatives were encouraged to seek TNO advice not so much because they were considering the positive impact which that action would have upon the TNO, but primarily because TNO advice was valuable for increasing agency outreach. The majority of agency representatives and citizens at large, in their responses to the same question, agreed that formal and informal contact with TNOs had increased, and was most useful.

Every Target Neighborhood Officer reported that he had, as a result of the poverty program, met other TNOs with whom he now could interact for community, Neighborhood, or personal problems. Those who had been with the Topeka program from its beginning were an extremely cohesive group, often acting as a block regarding Board issues. Occasionally TNOs would be divided on a specific issue, but the division usually did not disrupt the clique of "old-timers." One "old-timer" only rarely would openly compete with another for control of an antipoverty activity. Rather, the competition was most often seen between or among newer TNOs or between new and old TNOs.

Those Target Neighborhood Officers who have had considerable process experience in the program can have quite different views of self, and self-in-society, than they had at the beginning of their involvement (a measure of that difference is presented in Chapter 9). Furthermore, they can be quite different from TNOs who are just joining the program. In order to minimize conflict among senior and novice representatives of the poor, and effectively to utilize the skills and knowledges of the experienced members, poverty-intervention organizations should use the latter as instructors or counselors in the continuing program of training for board members. No one can be more effective in expressing the "hang-ups" associated with being the person officially charged with representing a specific segment of the poor than a man who himself has experienced that role. An ideal combination might be experienced indigenous leaders who could "tell it like it is," and professionals who could objectify, in understandable terms, the dynamics of process experiences.

Do you feel that the OEO has a future in Topeka?

YES: 83 per cent

"We're having a bit of a rough time now, but we'll weather it okay. The important thing is that the poor have a future in Topeka now, whether OEO is around or not. We've got enough of a start so that at least some of us can keep at it, and co-operate with some of the agency people to get things going. OEO has just been a starter as far as I'm concerned. We don't have to lean on them, you know. Not as much anymore, anyway. So the idea of OEO definitely has a future, although I think the program will be around for quite a while, too."

"I think OEO has a future in Topeka, yes. We're getting programs going now that are going to get people more jobs. That's what we've needed all along, something tangible to show the people, like jobs and the Neighborhood House. We couldn't see tangible results before, so it seemed like there was nothing to the program."

NO: Zero per cent

UNCERTAIN: 17 per cent

"I think it has a future if it fulfills some of the programs it has now. It was dying rather fast there for a while. We were losing

people because they spent time and money, and didn't get anything out of it. The thing that really is going to work is that
Neighborhood House. We need more of them. If oeo can get
more Neighborhood Houses, then it'll have a good future in
Topeka."

"The future's pretty much up to Congress, isn't it?"

Most of the Target Neighborhood Officers felt that oeo has a
future in Topeka. Several of those who saw continuing promise for
oeo and those who were uncertain qualified their statements with
conditions that the future of the local program depended upon
demonstrating concrete results to the Target Neighborhood residents, sustained co-operation among Board members, and steady
federal funding. TNOs were more sanguine than non-TNOs about
oeo's future. Non-TNOs seemed to have a greater fear, perhaps born
of their understanding of governmental fiscal and administrative
policy, that the Office of Economic Opportunity might be cut back
in funding, or split up organizationally and distributed to other "old-
line" agencies. TNOs tended, on the other hand, to evaluate the
future of oeo less in terms of organizational structure than upon
their own experiences of the relations of their changed role and
participative opportunities. Several commented that as far as they
personally were concerned, the intentions of "maximum feasible
participation" would continue, regardless of changes in the name,
structure, or funding of a poverty-intervention organization. Again,
the importance of the process experience for indigenous leaders
was manifested to be at least as important as, if not more important
than, the specifics of program content.

SUMMARY OF THE EVALUATION

The majority of Target Neighborhood Officers planned to continue
as Board members, most of them because they felt it was a humanitarian responsibility. They looked much more favorably upon "maximum feasible participation" of the poor than did most of the
agency representatives and citizens at large. Furthermore, the Target
Neighborhood Officers called for increasing participation of the

poor, and wider representation of the Target Neighborhoods on the Economic Opportunity Board. Many of them tempered this view with an expression of the need for increased training programs for Target Neighborhood Officers—training which they thought would make them more capable of assuming the "top" positions not only on the Board but also in the TOEO. In general the TNOs were more favorable toward the workings of the Board, despite the current conflicts. It was a new experience for them, from which most felt they had profited. The TNOs thought there had been considerable change brought to the community by the poverty program, more change than was perceived by the citizens at large and the agency representatives. This may have been because the TNOs were living in the areas where the poverty program had its major impact, had been responsible for getting people jobs or services, and could see program impact more directly. The TNOs were more sanguine than other Board members about the potential for poverty intervention in Topeka, apparently because they viewed themselves as increasingly instrumental toward that goal.

Many of them seemed to feel more comfortable than formerly in approaching agency representatives with various kinds of problems, and felt that they now possessed better methods for getting answers to their questions and solutions to their problems. They were particularly impressed with the citizens at large on the Board, and often consulted them for advice. Although some of the Target Neighborhood Officers maintained reservations about the aloofness of some agency representatives, almost all of them had evolved a view of the usability of agencies and helping organizations. There was a rather widespread *esprit de corps* among Target Neighborhood Officers, and most of them frequently interacted in numerous official and unofficial settings. They agreed with the other Board members, however, that not enough of the hard-core poor were really being reached by the program, and several of them thought that the Neighborhood House approach was the most apparent solution to that problem. Many of the TNOs clearly expressed that they felt more confident as a result of their participation in Board activities, and were able to inaugurate actions toward the amelioration of poverty that they would have been uncomfortable with before. They agreed with other Board members that the poverty program had a future in Topeka, but several thought that the degree of its success in the future was contingent upon the capability of the program to demonstrate more concretely its worth to residents of the Target Neighborhoods. The problem of conflict on the Board seemed less disturbing to the TNOs than to the other Board members. As one TNO put it, "Hell, man, we've known conflict all our life. This is nothing new. You just ride with conflict, until you're able to pull something good out of it." The Target Neighborhood Officers, like citizens at large and agency representatives, felt that participation on the Board had enabled them to make an increasing number of formal and informal contacts with other persons who could help in action toward ameliorating poverty. Most striking and singularly important was the feeling of some of the Target Neighborhood Officers that those contacts, and the spirit of co-operation attending them, would enable poverty intervention to continue, as a community effort, even if OEO were no longer to exist.

A formal training program for indigenous leaders would seem mandatory for the success of a poverty program. Such a program should be similar to that offered to other participants, and should include discussions of the following *process-experience* determinants: the role of the representative of the poor as a board member and a change agent; the probability and function of interpersonal conflict during board meetings; the meaning, significance, and consequences of "maximum feasible participation" for indigenous leaders and the residents whom they represent; the definitions of board goals, strategies, and criteria for productivity, including an examination of "process experience" as a board product; strategies for neighborhood organization; discussions of the problems of indigenous leadership, and how that leadership can serve as a bridge between the poor and not-poor; parliamentary procedure and personal conduct during a meeting; recruiting and maintaining membership on neighborhood committees; the characteristics of the indigenous leader as compared with those of other participants; the stereotypes that the poor have of the not-poors, and vice versa; the expectations that indigenous leaders have for their participation in the poverty program; the expectations that residents of target neighborhoods have for the poverty program; the functions of maintaining informal relations among board members; the role of the officers of a poverty board; and the foreseen and unforeseen consequences of poverty intervention.

CHAPTER 9

Products of Participation

WHAT WAS THE IMPACT of participation in the poverty program upon members of the Economic Opportunity Board—in terms of the social-psychological characteristics presented and discussed in Chapter 5 (activism, anomie, integration with relatives, achievement orientation, future orientation, isolation, normlessness, powerlessness, alienation, and particularism)?

A number of experimental small-group studies, not directly concerned with the poor or poverty intervention, have demonstrated in general that a member's experience of meaningful influence in group decision tends to strengthen his satisfaction with membership, enhance his self-image, and facilitate changes in his attitudes.[1] A paper by Gottesfeld and Dozier reports an empirical measurement of social-psychological change among a cohort of poor as a function of their active participation in an OEO community-action program. The authors found a statistically significant decrease in feelings of powerlessness as measured by Rotter's I-E Scale,[2] showed an association of that decrease with length of service as an indigenous community organizer, and interpreted their over-all findings to indicate that "the aims of community action programs in making the poor more hopeful and ambitious about what they can do in their own behalf are being realized."[3]

[1] See, for example: L. Coch and J. R. P. French, "Overcoming Resistance to Change," *Human Relations*, 1, 4 (1948), 512–532; J. Levine and J. Butler, "Lecture vs. Group Discussion in Changing Behavior," *Journal of Applied Psychology*, 36, 1 (February, 1952), 29–33; Kurt Lewin, *Field Theory in Social Science*; Kurt Lewin, "Group Decision and Social Change," in T. H. Newcomb and E. L. Hartley (eds.), *Readings in Social Psychology*, pp. 330–344; N. R. F. Maier, "The Quality of Group Decisions as Influenced by the Discussion Leader," *Human Relations*, 3, 2 (June, 1950), 155–174; and M. G. Preston and R. K. Heintz, "Effects of Participatory vs. Supervisory Leadership on Group Judgment," *Journal of Abnormal and Social Psychology*, 44, 3 (July, 1949), 345–355.

[2] J. B. Rotter, "Generalized Expectancies of Internal vs. External Control of Reinforcement," *Psychological Monographs*, 80 (1966), No. 609.

[3] Harry Gottesfeld and Gerterlyn Dozier, "Changes in Feelings of Powerlessness in a Community Action Program," *Psychological Reports*, 19 (December, 1966), 978. See also: George Brager, "New Concepts in Patterns of Service: The Mobilization for Youth Programs," in Frank Riessman, Jerome Cohen, and Arthur Pearl, *Mental Health of the Poor*, pp. 412–421; Jacob R. Fishman and Frederic Solomon, "Youth and Social Action: Perspectives on the Student Sit-In Movement," *American Journal of Orthopsychiatry*, 33, 5 (October, 1963), 872–882; Ralph M. Kramer, *Participation of the Poor*; Alexander H. Leighton, "Poverty and Social Change," *Scientific American*, 212 (1965), 21–27; Robert Perlman and David Jones, *Neighborhood Service Centers*, pp. 59–60; Frances Piven, "Participation of Residents in Neighborhood Community Action Programs," *Social Work*, 11, 1 (January, 1966), 73–80; Frank Riessman, "New Approaches to Mental Health Treatment of Low-Income People," in *Social Work Practice*, pp. 174–187; Frank Riessman, "New Possibilities: Services, Representation in Careers," presentation to Planning Session for the White House Conference "To Fulfill These Rights," November, 1965, mimeograph; Hans B. C. Spiegel, *Citi-*

Based upon our interpretation of the Overlap Model and its implementation by the TOEO, it was hypothesized that, for Target Neighborhood Officers, participation in the poverty program would be associated with significant *increases* in activism, achievement orientation, and future orientation, and with significant *decreases* in anomie, integration with relatives, isolation, normlessness, powerlessness, alienation, and particularism. No significant changes were hypothesized for the participating Board members who were citizens at large or agency representatives.

It was further hypothesized that for TNOs the degree of change on the variables to be measured would be related to the quality of their participation, the length of their participation, and their willingness to continue participation.

To test these hypotheses, we readministered to Economic Opportunity Board members in May, 1967, the same set of scales we had administered in November, 1966, the results of which are described in Chapter 5. I shall refer to the May, 1967, administration as Admin II, and the November, 1966, administration as Admin I.

INDICES OF CHANGE

Forty-three Admin I respondents completed the questionnaires for Admin II—eighteen TNOs and twenty-one non-TNOs. Of the TNOs, seven were male, eleven female; three were Anglo-American, ten were Negro-American, three were Mexican-American, and two were American Indian. Of the non-TNOs (agency representatives and citizens at large), twenty-one were male, four female; twenty-three were Anglo-American and two were Mexican-American. TNO and non-TNO differences in annual family income, level of formal education, membership in voluntary associations, age, and length of Topeka residency were virtually identical to those differences found in Admin I. Non-TNOs again were significantly higher than TNOs in

---

zen Participation in Urban Development, Vol. 1, *Concepts and Issues*; Rudolph M. Wittenberg, "Personality Adjustment Through Social Action," *American Journal of Orthopsychiatry*, 18, 2 (April, 1948), 207–221.

income, education, and voluntary-association membership. The medians for Board attendance (TNO: ten meetings; non-TNO: eleven meetings) and tenure as Board members (TNO: seventeen months; non-TNO: twenty months) of course increased, but still without significant differences between the two groups.

The Board, particularly its non-TNO representation, had begun to be restructured by March, 1967, as required in the amendment to the Economic Opportunity Act. The restructuring at least in part explained the decrease in respondents from among the non-TNO group. Among the forty-three Admin II respondents were eight TNOs and thirteen non-TNOs who had terminated Board membership at some time subsequent to their having completed Admin I.

Admin II was conducted to provide indices of change and, unlike Admin I (which included all but three of the Board members), cannot be considered a "portrait" of the poverty Board. Admin II did not include new Board members for whom Admin I data were missing, and thus did not include all the then current Board members.

During the seven months between Admin I and Admin II, twelve Board meetings were held, supported by ten meetings of the Board's Executive Committee. Each Target Neighborhood Committee had met at least monthly, and several of the Study Committees held three or more meetings. Many Board members, particularly TNOs, had formally and informally discussed and formulated poverty projects with various local officials. The Board's agenda had included such issues as Head Start, Neighborhood Youth Corps, Day Care Centers, a Beautification Project, an Extension Worker Program, and a Neighborhood House. Considerable debate and member interaction had focused around the development, implementation, or maintenance of those and other programs. During the seven months between Admin I and Admin II, therefore, TNOs and non-TNOs were continually and often deeply involved in Board and related activities. Twice as many Board meetings were held during that period as in the previous thirteen months of the Board's corporate status.

Table 3 presents and compares TNO and non-TNO median scale scores on Admin II with median scale scores for the same respondents on Admin I.

TABLE 3. Comparison of TNO and Non-TNO Administration I Median Scale Score with Administration II Median Scale Scores for the Same Respondents (N = 43)

Scale[a]	TNO (N = 18)			Non-TNO (N = 25)		
	Admin I	Admin II	Significance of Difference[b]	Admin I	Admin II	Significan of Differen
Activism	16.0	18.0	p < .05	19.0	19.0	NS
Anomie	6.0	5.0	NS	3.0	4.0	NS
Integration with relatives	3.0	2.5	NS	2.0	2.0	NS
Achievement orientation	14.5	16.0	p < .05	17.0	17.0	NS
Future orientation	9.0	9.0	NS	10.0	10.0	NS
Isolation	16.0	15.5	NS	15.0	14.0	NS
Normlessness	10.0	9.0	NS	6.0	6.0	NS
Powerlessness	15.0	16.0	NS	12.0	12.0	NS
Alienation	41.5	41.0	NS	32.0	31.0	NS
Particularism	2.0	0.0	p < .05	0.0	0.0	NS

[a] Not used as Guttman Scales.
[b] Wilcoxon Rank Sum Test, one-tailed.
[c] Wilcoxon Rank Sum Test, two-tailed.

As hypothesized, no significant changes among non-TNOs in social-psychological variables were measured. On the other hand, the directional changes hypothesized for TNOs seem, with some exceptions, to have been supported. As indicated in Table 3, activism and achievement orientation increased, and particularism decreased significantly. Anomie, integration with relatives, isolation, normlessness, and alienation decreased, though not significantly. Future orientation remained unchanged. Powerlessness, running counter to the trend of results, increased, though not significantly. This last finding seems to conflict with Gottesfeld and Dozier's report of decreased powerlessness among indigenous community organizers, but it must be emphasized that neither the participant experience nor the powerlessness measures used in Gottesfeld's work and the present study are necessarily comparable. Dean, author of the alienation scale of which powerlessness is a component, reminds his reader that alienation may be influenced by situation.[4] At the time of Admin II, TNOs were generally favorably disposed toward the Board and its related activities. They had seen some accomplishments, recognized program potentials, and generally felt very much a part of the Board. Such experiences certainly influenced their hypothesis-supporting responses in Admin II. However, they were not content with the newly hired second Director of the TOEO, who they felt was "making too many decisions without us having our say." Several of them were actively attempting to influence or replace the Director, without much success and with accompanying feelings of frustration. That experience, since it was current with Admin II, might account for the increased powerlessness score. It might further be speculated that TNO increases in kinds of knowledge, competence, and confidence, which moved scale scores in the hypothesized directions, developed more quickly than the poverty program's capacity to accommodate them. The disparity between gaining increased skills and motivations, and the opportunity to use them as fully as desired, could have generated an increased sense of powerlessness. If that speculation is even partially accurate, the message for poverty-intervention organizations is clear: to stimulate aspirations and increase skills without providing an outlet for their use can compound frustration.

When TNOs were arbitrarily divided (by consensus of the research staff) into "Active" and "Inactive" categories (on the basis of meetings attended, offices held, observed performance, etc.), the changes in scale scores became more apparent. As shown in Table 4, Active TNO's followed the same pattern of change as TNOs in general (Table 3), but with increases in activism and achievement orientation, and decreases in normlessness, alienation, and particu-

---

[4] Dwight G. Dean "Alienation: Its Meaning and Measurement," *American Sociological Review*, 26 (October, 1961), 757.

TABLE 4. Comparison of Administration I Median Scale Scores with Administration II Median Scale Scores for TNO Categories: Actives, Inactives, Stayers, and Leavers

Scale[a]	Actives (N = 13)			Inactives (N = 5)			Stayers (N = 10)			Leavers (N = 8)		
	I	II	p[b]	I	II	p	I	II	p	I	II	p
Activism	16.0	18.0	<.05	17.0	16.0	NS	17.0	18.5	<.05	16.5	17.0	NS
Anomie	6.0	5.0	NS	5.0	6.0	NS	6.0	5.0	NS	6.0	5.5	NS
Integration with relatives	2.0	2.0	NS	1.0	3.0	<.05	2.5	2.0	NS	3.0	3.0	NS
Achievement orientation	14.0	16.0	<.05	15.0	15.0	NS	14.5	16.0	<.05	14.0	15.0	NS
Future orientation	9.0	9.0	NS	9.0	9.0	NS	9.0	10.0	NS	9.0	9.0	NS
Isolation	15.5	15.5	NS	16.0	19.0	<.05	15.0	15.5	NS	16.5	16.0	NS
Normlessness	10.0	8.0	<.05	8.0	8.0	NS	9.0	9.0	NS	11.5	8.0	<.05
Powerlessness	15.0	16.0	NS	15.0	19.0	<.05	18.0	16.0	<.05	15.0	16.5	<.05
Alienation	43.0	38.0	<.05	39.0	45.0	<.05	41.5	41.0	NS	40.5	40.0	NS
Particularism	2.0	0.0	<.05	2.0	0.0	<.05	1.5	0.0	<.05	2.5	0.5	<.05

[a] Not used as Guttman Scales.
[b] Wilcoxon Rank Sum Test, one-tailed.

larism attaining statistical significance. As did TNOs in general, Active TNOs showed a not-significant increase in powerlessness and no change in future orientation.

The pattern of changes for Inactive TNOs varied considerably from those of Actives and TNOs in general. Inactives, as indicated in Table 4, showed significant increases in integration with relatives, isolation, powerlessness, and alienation, and a significant decrease in particularism. Achievement orientation, future orientation, and normlessness remained unchanged, while activism decreased and anomie increased not significantly. These results may be interpreted to indicate that the quality of participation in poverty programs is related to the consequent social-psychological impact upon participants. The experience apparently was not neutral for the TNO— either he found opportunity for active participation and subsequently manifested changes in the hypothesized directions, or he for some reason was an inactive participant and manifested changes in directions opposite to those hypothesized. Participation can, therefore, have an impact upon some individuals that is the reverse of poverty-program expectations.

A comparison of Actives and Inactives on Admin I (see Table 4) yields no consistent initial differences which could explain the variations in change. It may be that the opportunity for active participation is limited for some TNOs, with the consequent development of increased personal frustration. Observational data at least partially support that interpretation—three of the Inactive TNOs felt they did not have the "skills" to become effective participants, and thus hesitated to make themselves "look stupid." To the degree that these findings are valid and can be generalized, they underscore the obligation of the poverty-intervention organization to eliminate, by flexibility and continuous training programs, factors which may prevent representatives of the poor from experiencing active participation.

Analysis of Active and Inactive non-TNO categories produced only one notable change. Non-TNO Actives ($N = 18$) showed a significant ($p < .05$) increase in particularism. This result, buttressed by observational data, may indicate that Active non-TNOs tended to shift to a more personalistic view of events and individuals, possibly as a result of their Board experience and interaction with the TNOs. TNOs, as indicated in Tables 3 and 4, tended to become less particularistic. One might speculate that TNO/non-TNO influence, at least on this variable, was mutual.

Eight TNOs terminated their participation in the poverty program in the interval between Admin I and Admin II. Some of those "Leavers" quit after becoming disillusioned, some "no longer had time" for participation, and some were not re-elected to TNO positions. As indicated in Table 4, those who remained—the "Stayers"— revealed a change pattern quite similar to that of TNOs in general (Table 3), with one striking exception—a significant decrease in powerlessness. By contrast, Leavers showed significant decreases in normlessness and particularism, a significant increase in powerlessness, and no significant changes in the remaining variables. These findings again highlight the fact that participation is not a neutral experience for the TNO, and indicate that to a considerable extent the powerlessness increase for TNOs in general was concentrated among the Leavers. One wonders what course of behavior TNO Leavers might take now, since their perception of norms is clearer but their sense of powerlessness more acute. At least two of the Leavers became outspoken and somewhat militant opponents of the poverty program.

Tenure as a TNO and the number of attendances at Board meetings (Admin II) showed low and not-significant negative correlations with anomie, isolation, normlessness, and particularism, and positive correlations with activism and achievement orientation. These relations are consistent with indices of over-all TNO change in the variables measured. There was a slight increase in the number of TNO voluntary-association memberships, and a slight increase in mean (but not median) level of income—neither change approaching significance.

The patterns of change for male TNOs ($N = 7$) were similar to those of female TNOs ($N = 11$). Males did, however, show a greater decrease than females in normlessness (Admin II, median = 9; Admin I, median = 12; $p < .03$).

Patterns of TNO changes were observed to vary for different ethnic groups, though the validity of interpretations is tempered by the small number of respondents distributed among the ethnic categories. Anglo-Americans (N = 3) showed increases in activism, integration with relatives, achievement orientation, isolation, powerlessness, and alienation; a decrease in particularism; and no changes in anomie, future orientation, and normlessness. Negro-Americans (N = 10) showed an increase in achievement orientation; decreases in integration with relatives, isolation, normlessness, and particularism; and no changes in activism, anomie, future orientation, powerlessness, and alienation. Mexican-Americans (N = 3) showed increases in anomie, isolation, powerlessness, and alienation, decreases in activism, integration with relatives, achievement orientation, isolation, normlessness, and particularism. American Indians (N = 2) showed increases in activism, achievement orientation, future orientation, powerlessness, and particularism; and decreases in anomie, integration with relatives, isolation, normlessness, and alienation. It might appear that the Negro-Americans and American Indians manifested changes more in line with the hypotheses than did the Anglo-Americans and Mexican-Americans. However, this is not clearly a cultural phenomenon, since nine Negro-Americans and both American Indians were among the Active TNOs, and all but one Anglo-American and one Mexican-American were Inactives. The key variable for changes in the direction of the hypotheses thus may be the quality of participation rather than ethnicity. This interpretation is supported by the fact that eight Negro-American TNOs, but only one Anglo-American and one Mexican-American TNO, were among the Stayers. On the other hand, neither American Indian TNO was a Stayer, and yet their changes tended to fit those hypothesized. These tenuous findings call for further research on cultural predispositions toward participation in poverty programs, and the impact of different kinds of participative experiences upon representatives from different ethnic groups.

Comparisons of Admin II with Admin I scale scores for those respondents who completed both administrations generally supported the hypotheses for directional, participation-related TNO change among the scaled social-psychological variables. Correlations among the variables, tenure as a TNO, and the number of attendances at Board meetings were congruent with the change data. One might conclude, therefore, that program participation generally had the impact upon representatives of the poor anticipated nationally by the Office of Economic Opportunity, and locally by the TOEO in accordance with the Overlap Model. If, as assumed, the social-psychological variables measured do reflect a view of self-in-society, then that view, for some TNOs, was modified toward increased confidence, trust, and feelings of control.

The impact of participation upon TNOs, indeed the directions of change in variables, appeared to be related importantly to the quality of the participation, and to the TNO's perception of his experience with the program. That finding, and the indication that participation is not in any case a neutral experience for TNOs, suggest to poverty-intervention organizations that at least as much attention should be given to careful planning concerning the *kinds* of participation representatives of the poor will experience as is typically given to determining their proportional representation. Similarly, the data suggest that attention be given to the possibility that opportunities for participation might be more accessible to, or differentially responded to, by males and females, and by members of different ethnic groups.

PART III
The Target Neighborhood Committees

▚▚

Part III focuses upon the structure and processes of the Target Neighborhood Committees, and the stages of committee development. It further focuses upon the indigenous officers of the committees—the Target Neighborhood Officers—including their attitudes underlying their perceptions of specific poverty-program functions; their perceptions of the leadership role; their struggles to enact the leadership role; their efforts to organize the committees and implement program goals; their shifting perceptions of the leadership role after they had participated in the program.

Chapter 10 presents a selection of quotes from Target Neighborhood Officers which give an indication of their attitudes toward important aspects of social life. The quotes, gathered during group discussions of discrete topics by Target Neighborhood Officers and the research observers, include references to family and youth, self-esteem, work and welfare, religion, and mental health. Analyses and interpretation of the quotes are offered, and discussed is the influence of the attitudes reflected by the quotes upon Target Neighborhood Officers' views of poverty-program activities.

In Chapter 11, the role of an indigenous leader in a poverty-intervention organization that operationalizes the Overlap Model by

Functional Marginality is described. The perceptions of the role of the "ideal" indigenous leader as reported by the staff of the Topeka Office of Economic Opportunity are contrasted with those of the indigenous leaders, the Target Neighborhood Officers themselves. Discrepancies among the views are discussed. The stresses and conflicts experienced by Target Neighborhood Officers as they attempt to enact the indigenous-leader role—here reported to center around being a bridge between the poor and the not-poor—are described, as are the methods by which Target Neighborhood Officers attempt to resolve those stresses and conflicts.

The stages of development of the Target Neighborhood Committee are detailed in Chapter 12. Seven stages of development are conceptualized (I. Orientation, II. Catharsis, III. Focus, IV. Action, V. Limbo, VI. Testing, and VII. Purposive), and modal individual and group behaviors bracketed by each stage are described. Special attention is given to the role of the Target Neighborhood Officer in each of the stages. The stages are discussed, with the practitioner in mind, as they relate to the dynamics of a poverty-intervention organization and the "maximum feasible participation" of the poor. Those Topeka Office of Economic Opportunity practices which stimulated, thwarted, or reversed the sequential progress of neighborhood-action committees through the stages of development are discussed. The stages are discussed, with the theorist in mind, as they relate to the relatively few studies and typologies of developmental sequence in small groups. It is suggested that "action" or "social-change" groups be considered entities for intensive theoretical and empirical inquiry.

Chapter 13 presents a case study of indigenous leadership in the Indian Target Neighborhood Committee, a committee which was never able to make the transition from Stage III (Focus) to Stage IV (Action). The establishment, development, group dynamics, and deactivation of the committee are described. The emergence, election, experiences, and exit of the chairman of that Target Neighborhood Committee are detailed, with emphasis upon his socialization and the frustrations and stresses inherent in his marginality between indigenous followers and the Topeka Office of Economic Opportunity. Differential views of, and expectations for, the leader's behavior, the committee's functions, and the poverty-intervention organization's operations are interpreted in terms of subcultural and socio-economic influences. Some suggestions are made to planners of poverty-intervention organization concerning the dynamics of indigenous leadership and the training programs for the indigenous leader.

A contrasting case study of a Target Neighborhood Committee that did reach and maintain the Purposive Stage (VII) is presented in Chapter 14. As in Chapter 13, the establishment, development, and group dynamics of the committee, and the emergence, election, and experiences of the Target Neighborhood Officer who was chairman are detailed and discussed. The sponsoring of a "Neighborhood House" by the Target Neighborhood Committee is reported as central to the committee's progression through the stages, and the circumstances surrounding that sponsorship are described. The Neighborhood House is reported here as having been a training ground for the participating poor, in which they developed organizational skills, new and more complex roles, and a sense of identity with peers, Neighborhood, and the broader community.

In Chapter 15, shifts in the Target Neighborhood Officers' perceptions of the indigenous-leader role, after considerable participation in the program, are reported. The shifts in perceptions are discussed as they relate to kind and degree of participation, and to sex and ethnic membership of the indigenous leader. The viability of the "bridge" expectation for indigenous leaders is also discussed.

CHAPTER 10

A Potpourri of TNO Attitudes

W ITHOUT THE PARTICIPATION of the Target Neighborhood Officers the Topeka poverty program, under the requirements of the Economic Opportunity Act, would not have been legally possible. Furthermore, TNO participation made possible the implementation of the Overlap Model and the Functional Marginality of the TOEO.

Under the Economic Opportunity Act, a wide variety of anti-poverty programs could be federally funded in local communities—Head Start, Neighborhood Youth Corps, Day Care Centers, Neighborhood Houses, the Job Corps, etc. Target Neighborhood Officers sometimes were initially ambivalent toward and occasionally resistant to, specific antipoverty proposals introduced for their approval by the TOEO. Part of that early ambivalence or resistance, which often manifested itself as a hidden agenda during meetings of the Board and Target Neighborhood Committees, seemed to have been influenced by TNO attitudes toward important aspects of social life —attitudes and aspects which had direct relevance for antipoverty activities. Some of those attitudes, which made good sense when considered as reflecting adaptation to an impoverished environment, were revealed by Target Neighborhood Officers in informal group discussions with the research observers.

Those informal discussions were conducted in the conference room of the research field station at least once, but usually twice, monthly, from November, 1965, until May, 1967 (for a detailed description of the meeting setting, the involvement of the research observers, and the role of the meetings in the poverty program, see Appendix A).

It became standard procedure for the Target Neighborhood Officers to suggest a general topic for each session. Five of those sessions, each concerned with a topic revealing attitudes important for determining perceptions of antipoverty activities, are reconstructed and presented in condensed form. The topics in order of presentation are: family and youth, self-esteem, work and welfare, religion, and mental health.

ON FAMILY AND YOUTH

Mrs. B, a Negro-American, opened the discussion on family and youth by complaining, "There just don't seem to be any family togetherness now. I remember when my brothers and sisters and me used to do things together. You can't find that now, too much."

The other TNOs agreed, and began tracing the sources for the lack of family "togetherness." Some of them felt that the problem was "kids growing away from their parents." Others agreed that the major causes of disruption were the broken home and the home in which both parents had to work. A Negro-American, Mrs. C, sardonically told the group:

"I got to laugh when I see on TV those people sitting down at a dinner table all together, and eating all at once. How am I going to do something like that, when one kid's off to work, another one's coming back from school, a couple more are over on the other side of town at the playground, and I got no time to fix a big meal because I got to go to work that night? Sure, I'd like to be able to do that, and have a big table and everything. Who wouldn't?"

Mrs. D, a Mexican-American, agreeing with Mrs. C, commented:

"My husband has to work at two different jobs, six days a week, and on Sunday he's so tired he sleeps all day. When a man has to do all that just to keep bread on the table, he hasn't time to be a proper father, and it's not his fault that he can't."

Mr. E, a Negro-American, talked about the prevalence of fatherless homes among the poor, and the impact in that situation of the family burden upon the mother:

"I'm not sure what they mean by 'Negro matriarchy,' but I know that any man in my Mamma's house sure knew his place, and if he got out of line, Mamma'd lay one up side his head! She had to raise us all alone, most of the time, so I guess she had to be tough."

Three antipoverty programs directly related to family and youth were currently being co-ordinated by the TOEO. In addition, a Job Corps Center was operating in a nearby town. The TNOs generally approved of those programs, but during group discussions expressed ambivalence about sending their own children into them. Mrs. B, for example, thought it would be all right for her teen-aged boy to enroll in the Neighborhood Youth Corps but not in the Job Corps, because "that'd take him away from home." She continued to explain what a "big help" he was to her, since he was the "oldest man in the family." Mrs. D had misgivings about both Head Start and Day Care Centers because "when kids are that small, they need their mammas." She appreciated that for some families it may be desirable for the wife to work, but argued that "even if it takes some sacrifice, the mamma should be with her babies."

Fatherless homes, according to Mr. F, a Negro-American, are caused by the pressures placed on a father as head of the household:

"He can't make out no way he goes. He got five, six kids when he's still a young man, he got no education, and no one gives him a break because he's black. How can he face the family every morning when he wakes up? He just leaves, that's all—maybe with a little drink, maybe with women, maybe by just drifting."

The discussion shifted to the various programs available for helping low-income women with homemaking skills. The female TNOs were in favor of counseling for diet and meal planning so long as the counselor didn't, as Mrs. B put it, "talk down to you, like you never cooked nothing before."

The issue of family planning brought brief but animated discussion from the Target Neighborhood Officers. Most of them felt that family planning is central to the amelioration of poverty. Mr. G, an Anglo-American, thought that it should be "a law." Mrs. D disagreed, stating that "God has a way of working those things out." Mrs. H, a Negro-American, didn't like the idea that family planning might be "pushed on Negroes without their really having anything to say about it."

The TNOs turned to a discussion of adult education as a means by which parents could improve themselves for their own benefit and for the benefit of their children. All of them thought that adult education in programs such as the one locally offered was very useful. However, Mrs. I, an Anglo-American, though she supported the idea of adult education, thought it more important for people to get jobs than to prepare for them:

"When you're hungry and you don't know where your next meal's coming from because you don't have a job, you aren't interested in big things like improving your mind, or getting an education, or maybe sending your kids to Head Start so they'll grow up better."

The conversations shifted back to the relative importance of education for children of the poor. Mr. G stated:

"If kids're going to get justice and equality for themselves, they've got to be armed with information. That's the thing that does it— information. I don't care what anybody says, if you've got the information, you can make it."

Mr. J, a Negro-American, frowned, and answered:

"Most of the people in the Neighborhood want their kids to go to school, and get all the education they can. But I don't think we push the kids as hard to get things like grades, and like that. We hear stories, and of course kids do too, about Negro kids who get good grades and still can't get jobs. So I guess we can't believe in the worth of education that much. You hear some people saying, 'Why train kids, anyway? They aren't going to get any jobs.'"

Mrs. B agreed, "That's right. Why get a good education, when you're going to end up in Miss Anne's kitchen anyway, scrubbing pots and pans, or doing day work?" Mrs. K, a Negro-American, added, "All my kids want to do is get out of Topeka and get to the big city. I know when they get up there, since they're drop-outs and all, they're going to find nothing but trouble. But they still want to go, and I guess I can't stop them."

Mr. H. concurred:

"Well, the kids don't want to wait, and I can't really blame them. They want to make money now, because they see money'll give them some place in the world, or at least they think it will. They see how important it is to have nice things, and a car, and they want to get a job now, and not wait for a long period of education until they get it. They don't want to take the time to get a lot of school."

Mr. E asked the group how one could encourage children to continue their education. He complained about the "generation gap" and said that it is "tough to get kids to see eye to eye with you." As an example, he told the members, "My oldest kids and I had a big argument about the riots. I kept telling them that that wasn't the way, and they kept saying, 'There isn't any other way.' One of my kids even said I was an 'Uncle Tom.'"

Returning the conversation more directly to education, Mr. J wasn't at all sure that attitudes toward education were any better now than they were when he was a boy. Leaning back in his chair, he mused:

"Sometimes we learn not to ask questions, when we're poor kids. I can remember situations myself, and situations my friends were in, where you just didn't dare ask your parents why something was so, because if you did, you'd find yourself slung across the room. If you kept asking questions, your parents'd say, 'What are you, a smart aleck?' I guess they thought when you asked questions like that, you're trying to show them up because they haven't had much of a chance to learn about things, because of discrimination and poverty. After a while you begin to be scared of asking your parents 'why,' because you might get your mouth slapped, and also you really don't want to hurt their feelings because they sometimes look like they feel bad because they can't answer you, or because they don't know the answer. Well, if that's the way it is with your parents, and you're afraid to ask 'why,' then you learn not to ask 'why' at all. So when you get in school, you don't ask anybody 'why' either, because the same thing might happen."

Mrs. D nodded her head in assent, and added:

"I remember bringing a book home one time, and my Grandma said, 'What good's that gonna do ya? That's just gonna get you in trouble.' I suppose times have changed, but I wonder how many people in the Neighborhoods still feel that way?"

Mr. G munched on a cookie, gulped some coffee, and changed the direction of the discussion:

"I've been trying to understand why so many kids are juvenile delinquents. They may be crazy, but maybe they're just trying to become good at something. They haven't had a chance to become good at anything else, so they become good thieves, or good dope pushers. Hell, they aren't stupid. Anybody who can drop a transmission from a car in five minutes, and run off with it, isn't stupid.

He knows how to work. The sad thing is that the kid who can drop a transmission in five minutes, and steal it, can't get a job as an apprentice machinist. It doesn't make any sense. I'll say this, though. That kid does get a chance for some training. They send him to reform school, and he learns how to be a first-rate thief. In there, he gets the best education in the world—even like a college education— on how to be a thief."

The rest of the TNOs agreed that many of the poor youth have little opportunity to be successful in "vocations" other than delinquency.

The program proposals for Day Care Centers, the Neighborhood Youth Corps, Adult Basic Education, and Head Start were considered by members of the Economic Opportunity Board, including the TNOs, in regular session. Those proposals always were approved unanimously by the Board. However, often there was extensive discussion about the details of the program prior to formal voting. During the discussion, TNOs would ask questions which reflected the sometimes overlooked fact that antipoverty programs aimed at the poor *family* as a unit, though having potential to ameliorate poverty, were nonetheless intervention. That is, the programs wedged into a balance of family social roles, no matter how precarious the balance may have been perceived to be by the middle-class observer.

The realities of, and reactions to, intervention were most clearly expressed by TNOs concerning proposals that included references to family counseling and/or family planning. They were not generally opposed to the counseling and planning, but some would become quite defensive if it appeared as though the intervention was unilateral. As with virtually all aspects of the poverty program, though the content of specific programing was of course important and potentially beneficial, essential also were the way the program was introduced, and the opportunity for TNOs to have a feeling of control and to acquire meaningful process experience. Though occasionally they had no choice, TNOs consistently attempted to circumvent the necessity of having to agree to the psychological contract "bad me—good you" in order to gain the benefits of anti-poverty programs for themselves and those they represented.

On Self-esteem

For one evening's topic of discussion, the research staff introduced the concept "self-esteem" as "the picture you have of yourself in terms of good or bad, valuable or worthless, and how that picture comes to be." Mr. H began the discussion with some introspective comments about the impact of prejudice and discrimination upon self-esteem:

"I don't like to be made small, and many times when you're poor, or when you're black, you're made small in lots of ways. I mean, suppose like in a shoe store a clerk sees a poor black person. He doesn't pay much attention to him, and then he tries to sell him some second-rate shoes at a high price, and things like that. Or you'll go into a restaurant, and other people get served before you. It's ways like that that make you wonder about yourself. That's especially true of kids. They wonder what's wrong with them when people look funny at their old clothes, or at their faces because they're a different color."

The TNOs all agreed, and began discussing the kinds of discrimination experienced by minority-group members and low-income persons in Topeka. Mrs. E exclaimed:

"Sometimes it seems like prejudice and discrimination here in Topeka is worse than it was in the South. It's harder to figure here. Here it's like a snake in the Garden of Eden—it tells you all kinds of nice things, but really can't stand you. In the South you know most white folks can't stand you, and you wonder why. Up here, they're nice to you, but you still can't get the job you want or live where you want, and you still wonder why, but it's even more confusing."

Mr. L, a Negro-American, concurred, but felt that in Topeka, and in the North in general, it wasn't just "whites that discriminate against Negroes, but Negroes are discriminating against Negroes." He continued:

"Poor Negroes come up here from the South, and they can't write, and they don't have education, and they find out that they're prejudiced against by the opposite race here. That's not too different, because they've come to look for that. But they find out something else that shakes them up and makes them feel no-good. They find out they're prejudiced against by the middle-class Negro too. By their own people! Their own people won't have anything to do with them if they've got a little money, and they say, 'Why don't you make it like we did?' Now this puts people in a real bind, because where're they going to go? They've got nobody to be with. Nobody wants them!"

The TNOs continued to discuss status and discrimination levels within the local Negro-American population, and considered the fact that the minority-group Board members who were TNOs seemed to be "different" in their orientations than the minority-group members who were non-TNOs. Mr. E complained, "Sometimes the Negro big wheels on the Board are so busy making it, they forget about their own people." Mr. G, an Anglo-American, interrupted to observe:

"You know, poor whites have quite a problem too, and maybe even more of a problem now. All the attention seems to be going to the poor Negro. Now, I know Negroes've had a rough deal, and I'm not against the help they're getting, or anything like that. You all know that. But middle-class people look at the poor Negro, now, and say, 'He hasn't had a chance, because he's Negro and people've been prejudiced against him,' and they look more kindly on him now, and are more willing to give him a chance. But the poor white person's still looked at with a hard eye. The middle class say, 'He's just white trash. He's got no excuse. He's white. Why hasn't he made it? He must be no-good. Nobody's been prejudiced against him.' I think now the poor white person has even a greater likelihood of feeling that he's a no-good."

Mrs. D chuckled, and added, "Yeah, and the Negro better look out for the white who thinks he's a no-good, because he's going to be looking for somebody who he can make worse off than he is!"

The research staff asked the TNOs what they thought being a Target Neighborhood Officer did for one's self-esteem. Mr. L responded:

"Like we were talking about prejudice. I have to be honest, and say that when I was younger there were times when I wished I was white. Right now, I have hopes—and I'm going to do something about it—that this program can make it easier for a man to be proud of being what he is."

Mrs. C agreed:

"A person gets self-respect from the kind of things she can accomplish. I feel respect for myself when I can bring up my kids proper and when I help my friends. Maybe that's why I work so hard at being a leader in the poverty program, because that way I can help my kids and my friends. At the same time, I get self-respect for myself, too."

Mrs. K. concurred:

"The way I see it, the poverty program's giving us residents a chance to broaden pictures of ourselves. It will, that is, if the kind of participation we have is more than just 'You can come up here and sit on the Board because we need some poor people just to get government money.'"

The TNOs stirred in their seats, and the conversation became more animated. Mrs. M, an Anglo-American, suggested that the poverty program "has to be careful. People from the Target Neighborhoods have to be looked at as individuals, not just part of some group to be 'lifted up into the middle class.' Each individual should have a chance to develop his talents and abilities as he chooses." Mrs. C excitedly reflected:

"You know, it's funny. One day I was just poor. Then all of a sudden I became a 'Target Neighborhood Officer.' I think the idea's okay, but sometimes I wonder if I and all of us aren't just being pushed around again, in another way. Is somebody using us as a cat's-paw again? Are we being used by other people who have their own fights, and they want us to fight for them? Are we just whipping boys for somebody else? All kinds of programs are being experimented with, you know. And it looks like we're the guinea pigs again. This time, though, maybe there's a chance for the guinea pigs to bite back, to have a real say in the program. That makes a difference in how I feel."

"How important are we really to this program?" inquired Mrs. N, an Anglo-American. "Are we just being used for propaganda? Does somebody really think our opinions are important, or is all this just so much crap?"

The TNOs were not agreed about the degree to which the poverty program was a form of manipulation of, or experimentation upon, poor people. However, they were all agreed that, no matter what the implicit rationale for the poverty program, the "door has been left open" for TNO participation, and there is a chance "for us to make the most of it." Mr. O, an Indian-American, summarized the TNO feelings:

"All I know is, if I haven't got a say in something, I don't really give a damn about it. I know others feel the same way. If you're just being used, and think somebody's just talking and not listening to you, you don't listen, either. You just smile and nod and leave, or you just leave, or sometimes you hit out in some way. If you can hit out, you can have your say in a way, and that can make you feel good, too."

Being associated with the poverty program, especially as a Target Neighborhood Officer, brought with it some challenges to, as well as reinforcers of, self-esteem. Mr. A, an Indian-American, told the group about a time when a Neighborhood resident approached him and said, "You should really feel proud of yourself, because you're one of the saviors of the poor." Mr. A responded, "God, I'm no 'savior of the poor!' That didn't make me feel proud of myself. I can't work any miracles! What would make me proud of myself is if I could just be a citizen, I mean a first-class citizen, like other people." Mrs. F, pouring coffee for herself and for some of the others from the large urn on a table in the corner of the conference room, reflected:

"Nobody likes to be called poor. I know some people who don't even want to become part of the poverty program because it means they have to take on the name 'poor.' You know 'poor' means more than just not having money. This may be one of the troubles with the Neighborhood elections in the poverty program. People just don't want to vote in one of those elections for poverty officers, because it means when they put their choice on that ballot, at the same time they have to say 'I'm poor, so now I can vote.'"

Mrs. I, vigorously nodding in agreement, added:

"The same thing's been happening whenever children've been asking my children at school what this oeo is all about, and why their father and I are involved in it. My children have a hard time explaining what it's all about, and a couple of times they've been teased, 'Your ma and pa are in a poverty program, your ma and pa are in a poverty program, ha, ha, ha!'"

Extending the idea of self-esteem to users of poverty-program facilities, Mrs. P, a Mexican-American, said, "I know for a fact they're some kids who're ashamed to go to school because they don't think their clothes are good enough. The other kids in school tease them because they wear patches." Mrs. Q, an Anglo-American, concurred:

"That's true! And a lot of mothers won't go to the clothing bank to get clothes they need for their kids because they're afraid they're going to have their pictures taken while they're standing in line. They don't want to be seen waiting in line, because that means they're poor, they need help, and it means all the other bad things that go along with being poor in people's minds."

The discussion returned to the stratagems for gaining self-esteem. Mr. L said:

"A man's got to have a way of expressing himself, and feeling he's worth something. This may sound bad, but I can understand why some of the men in Watts throw bricks through windows, and set fires. That may be their only way of saying, 'I'm a man, I'm somebody, listen to me!'"

"I can't figure out the best way Negro poor people can learn to think better of themselves. Is it better for them to organize in all-black groups, like this black-power approach? Or is it better to try to work with people in the white community who're interested in civil rights? I can't make up my mind. I don't know which one would give me, or the others, more self-respect."

The Target Neighborhood Officers discussed the two alternatives for awhile, and generally agreed that what I have called the Overlap Model—the concerted effort by representatives from various community components—was at least "worth a try," a view qualified by Mr. E, with, "as long as we have some real say-so."

The Target Neighborhood Officers began discussing the difficulties they were having in getting more residents to attend Target Neighborhood Committee meetings. (Chapter 12 presents those difficulties in detail.) Mr. E shared with the group his plan to get more people involved:

"We've been told, one way or another, for so long that we aren't worth anything that we get afraid to open our mouths, because we're afraid we're going to prove it. I've been thinking about writing a letter to the people in my Neighborhood. You know, one of those 'open' letters. I'd say things in there that would get them mad at me, and then they'd say, 'Who does that guy think he is, saying things like that about us?' If they got mad, then maybe they'd come to the meetings and find out who I am and tell me what they think. Sometimes people have to get mad to get confidence in themselves."

The TNOs discussed whether or not it was necessary to be "mad" in order to mobilize toward the amelioration of poverty. Most of them agreed that it was necessary to be angry, or at least to be "very dissatisfied." Mr. O laughed, and told the group:

"I know what makes me mad, and probably makes other people mad, is those bumper stickers on cars that say 'I fight poverty, I work.' What that says to poor people is, 'You worthless animal, why don't you get out and work, and drive a big car, so you can put a bumper sticker on your car, too?' I look at those stickers, and the cars, and the people who're driving them, and I say to myself, 'That's the enemy.' "

Mr. O wryly suggested to the other TNOs that if they were to put those stickers on their own cars, and mail others out to Target Neighborhood residents, it might triple the attendance at committee meetings.

For the poor to participate in a poverty program, whether as an indigenous leader or only as a recipient of goods and services, apparently involved a decision based upon a rate of exchange. To be a Target Neighborhood Officer brought with it role strain, identification with the poverty bureaucracy, and an official label which said "I am poor." However, most Target Neighborhood Officers were willing to accept those negative aspects of participation if that participation brought with it the opportunity for meaningful process experience, self-direction, and a genuinely important and controlling part in the over-all poverty program. Similarly, the individuals who participated as "clients" of the poverty program were willing to do so if the "bad me–good you" psychological contract was not too demeaning.

Target Neighborhood Officers in particular seemed acutely aware of the balance of their "psychological contract" with the poverty program. The obligations of that contract were a continuing hidden agenda during meetings of the Economic Opportunity Board. If a specific antipoverty proposal being considered by the Board was perceived by TNOs to reduce their active participation and degree of control, they could be expected to oppose, directly or indirectly, its implementation. As Mr. L had commented to the research observer after one of the Board meetings, "Take away our participation, and this whole deal becomes just another welfare program, and I won't have anything to do with that."

Not surprisingly, prejudice and discrimination were considered by TNOs to be most detrimental to self-esteem. Most remarkable was the fact that they perceived such discrimination to exist *within* minority-group socio-economic strata.

TNOs were very sensitive concerning who was being hired to work in various antipoverty activities. Some of them suspected discrimination if a substantial number of the employees, particularly those in responsible positions, were not members of minority groups and residents of the Target Neighborhoods. "How else can we know," asked Mr. E in an interview, "that this program isn't just more of the same old stuff?"

The discussion about the plight of "poor whites," who have no opportunity to justify their "failure" by blaming it on prejudice and discrimination, revealed a further complication of being an Anglo-American TNO. Not only did Anglo-American TNOs accept the label of being "poor" when they enacted their roles as indigenous leaders, but in some cases they had to endure abuse from Anglo-American relatives and followers for closely associating with TNOs who belonged to minority ethnic groups. Furthermore, Anglo-American poor apparently are not able to identify with the civil-rights movement, and draw support from that association. Though not a very pronounced tendency among TNOs in the Topeka poverty program, Anglo-American indigenous leaders might become resentful of minority-group indigenous leaders who can achieve cohesion and status through a civil-rights orientation.

Some of the TNOs had a suspicion that the poverty program might be just another way of "experimenting" with the "guinea pig" poor. That suspicion, if pervasive, could influence indigenous leaders' perceptions of what agency representatives or citizens at large would believe were "innovative" programs. Those TNOs who were convinced that they had meaningful "say" in poverty programing did not have suspicions about being "guinea pigs."

Do Target Neighborhood Officers need an "enemy" in order to mobilize themselves and their followers? The TNOs themselves were not certain, nor were they sure who that "enemy" might or should be. The Overlap Model, particularly as manifested in meet-

ings of the Economic Opportunity Board, provided TNOs with a
wide range of individuals and organizations that could arbitrarily
be labeled, permanently or temporarily, as "enemies."

ON WORK AND WELFARE

"Jobs, that's the heart of the problem," commented Mr. E as he
led off the evening's discussion:

"It's important the way a man gets a job, whether or not it's handed
to him by charity, and the attitude the people have who get a job
for the man who needs it. If he gets the idea they're looking down on
him and saying, 'Here, you take this job and do it because we're
doing you a big favor,' well, I don't know, but some people get resentful about that! Some people, including me, would rather not
work than have a job handed to them like that."

Mr. L strongly agreed:

"When I take a job, I've got to be able to say to myself 'I'm working like a man,' and there aren't many jobs around where you can
still be a man. I mean, there aren't many jobs around where you can
have something to say about what's going on, where you can give
your opinion, and have people listen to it. Having a job that lets you
be a man is one where you have some respect for yourself. It's one
where there's a chance for you to show what you've got. There just
aren't many jobs around like that for Negro men."

"Sometimes the poor man who's looking for a job is treated like a
puppy dog. You know what I mean?" asked Mr. O. He explained:

"Like us Indians. We're treated like little doggies who're thrown
a bone now and then and we're expected to wag our tails all over the
place. When you get a job that way, when you really need one bad
and you feel that someone's doing you a favor by getting it for you,
or if the boss knows you've had a couple of jobs before or that you've
been on welfare before, then you know you're being watched closer
than other employees are. I know I've thought sometimes that the
bosses're on my back more because they really don't expect me to
make it, anyway. It seems right that a person'd rather not work at

all than have to work when he's going to be watched all the time, and when people're waiting for him to make mistakes because they expect him to, anyway. They think 'After all, he's just another welfare type!'"

Mr. G said to the group, all of whom were excitedly involved in the discussion:

"If you get into a job you don't like, a job you don't think you can get ahead in, that's really not a job. What it is, is just an existence. And you have to suffer all the way along. It leaves no room for you to go up the ladder and get ahead, then there really isn't much sense in doing the same thing day in and day out. If you can't take any pride in your work, you can't take any pride in yourself. Like we talked about self-esteem before. A man's work is his self-esteem. Take the carpenter, for example. They know how it is to be able to put something together with their hands and look at it and say 'I built that.' I've seen some cabinetmakers working on things, and they take hours and hours, and weeks and weeks and weeks to do it. But when they're finished, they've got something they can be proud of. If you took those cabinetmakers and put them to work, without them having any say in it, on building some cheap stuff, they wouldn't be proud of what they're doing. They wouldn't like it even though they might make more money working on the cheap stuff. So it's something else besides money. It's pride!"

Mr. E agreed, pounding his fist on the table for emphasis:

"My brother's got a little two-bit farm out here, and there's no chance he's ever going to make much money on that farm. In fact, he lives from day to day. He has to scratch just to get along. He's a talented man. He could get a job somewhere else—he's got some education—but he won't do it because on the farm, that's *his* farm, and he does what he wants and he plants what he wants, and he's happy with it."

"Nobody likes to be manipulated, on a job or anywhere else," stated Mrs. M. She continued, "One way a person can escape manipulation is to not work at all. If they choose not to work, they're able to say that they at least did that! At least they can say that they've stayed away from work on their own!"

Mr. E became visibly angry, and pounding his fist in his hand, bitterly complained:

"Many of the jobs that Negroes who don't have educations can get are jobs where they've got to take racial slurs. I'm talking now about jobs like being a waiter or being a bus boy, where you get all kinds of comments from people who you wait on. I can only speak for myself, but I just couldn't take that, and I'd always end up punching somebody. You know, like when people call you 'boy,' and snap their fingers."

"What kind of a job can someone get who's had to be on welfare before, anyway?" asked Mrs. H rhetorically and answered, "He gets some kind of a low-prestige job; some kind of a job where he's mopping floors or stacking things, or other jobs that don't have much real satisfaction in them. But it's kind of a big thing to be able to say, 'Who needs to work? I can get along without working,' and then laugh about how you're getting money from welfare, and how you're beating the system. So you see, there's really not as much satisfaction in taking most of the jobs we can get, as there is in not working at all, because at least our friends and others who aren't working, and who are on welfare, can all get together and laugh about how we're not doing badly without having to work at all!"

"Yeah," agreed Mrs. C, adding, "sometimes when someone hasn't had a chance to get a job before, and she goes on welfare and later gets a job, her friends, who might be on welfare too, get jealous of her and tease her about getting a job. They ask her, 'What're you taking that job for? Are you trying to make a million dollars?' It's funny that that should happen, but it does. Other people are jealous of you if you try to get ahead. They think you're trying to show them you think you're better than they are."

The Target Neighborhood Officers began arguing among themselves about the relative merits of welfare *versus* work. They gener-

ally agreed that work was preferable, but that there were many miti-
gating circumstances which may make welfare the better choice.
The rate of pay, the character of the work, the dignity of the job, all
were important factors. Mr. O pointed out the importance of opportunity for promotion:

"Even though people may not have much education or much experience, they still have families and they have pride. They'd like
to know if they take a job, there's going to be a chance for promotion as they get better in it. But maybe they've learned from before
in other jobs they've worked in that they just aren't going to get
their promotion. They learn that other guys're going to get them,
and they just aren't going to get ahead. What's the sense in working
if you can't feel that you're going to improve yourself by working,
or that if you're going to get good at your job, you're going to get
some kind of reward from it?"

Mr. R, an Anglo-American, elaborated Mr. O's point:

"Some employers really take advantage of you if they know you
need the job, too. They figure they can give you less money, and
less promotions, than they can give somebody else who has choices
for a bunch of jobs. There are cases where men're being taken advantage of like that. Why should they want to take a job like that? Why
should anyone want to take a job if at the same time they're sure
they're going to be treated lousy?"

Mr. G stood up and, leaning on the table, told the group:

"I worked for a man once who liked to give breaks to fellows
who've been on welfare, or who hadn't been able to get a job in a
long time, and I remember talking to him about it. He said he hired
people like us because many times we turned out to be good employees. And he said he learned something when he first hired some
men who'd been on welfare. He said you've got to let people who're
working for you feel that they're on their own, and give them room
to feel they can make decisions about things. Sometimes those fellows had been away from a job for a long time, and also they

haven't had real good training, so they'll make mistakes. But he thought if you gave them room to make those mistakes, and helped them when they made them instead of chewing them out or firing them, then he'd find that those mistakes were really a drop in the bucket and in the long run, things work out. He also said that he'd give a fellow who didn't seem to be producing enough the toughest job he could find. He'd say to him, 'Here's the job, here's how to do it,' and then he'd go away and leave him alone. And darn, if he doesn't turn out to be a good man for the job, just because he'd been given responsibility for it on his own. He had the right idea."

Mrs. D asked Mr. G why he wasn't working for the man anymore. Mr. G responded, "I quit him because he didn't pay enough money." All the TNOs laughed, Mr. G along with them. "That man had all those good-sounding ideas, but he was still putting you on, wasn't he?" teased Mrs. C.

After further discussion, the Target Neighborhood Officers came to the conclusion that "a good job" incorporates both a decent wage and opportunities for self-esteem. To have a job in which you felt great, but didn't make enough money to feed your family, was not satisfactory. On the other hand, to be making enough money to feed your family but having to "lick somebody's boots" to do it was considered to be very difficult, and perhaps "welfare is better."

Mr. O suggested to the group that there are ways to increase the hourly wage one might be getting. He explained: "Here's the way I do it. If I'm getting just a lousy dollar an hour, I figure that I work two hours on an eight-hour workday, and that way, I'm getting four dollars an hour, which I think's about what I should be getting for my work."

"You can do that kind of thing with promotions too," sanctioned Mr. E. "People get criticized for going from job to job, and not staying with one job very long. I've done that myself. But hell, man, if you can't go up in a company, at least you can go from company to company. If you can't move up, you can at least move sideways. You know what I mean?"

The discussion then turned specifically to welfare, and Mrs. Q asked Mr. E why, "with all those kids," he didn't go on welfare rather than working at a low-paying job. Mr. E answered, very seriously:

"The way I figure it, with all my kids, if I went on welfare, I could get almost seven hundred dollars a month. My job sure doesn't pay me seven hundred a month, but there's a reason why I want the job rather than getting that seven hundred dollars on welfare. It's because I like my work, and I have some say in what I'm doing. I'd rather do work than get the seven hundred."

Mrs. C abruptly interrupted, "Who says being on welfare's not work! You've got to learn how to act just right when you go down for an interview for welfare." She stood up, unbuttoned her coat and rebuttoned it, skipping one buttonhole so that the material bunched up, and the hem hung unevenly. She hunched over, lowered her head, and raised her eyes to make eye contact with the rest of the group, and with a dramatically forlorn expression explained, "You've got to make sure to keep your head down low, and look sad, and not speak up, and all that." The group laughed, and Mrs. C began to laugh with them. She added:

"It takes real training to be on welfare. I don't mean to fake, that's not what I mean. I mean when you need welfare, you still can't go in there and look too proud, because you're liable to get a bad time. You know, the people who have you fill out the forms expect you to look a certain way. Well, sometimes it takes work to look that way."

The female TNOs, many of whom had had experience with welfare, laughed and nodded agreement. Mrs. P continued the discussion:

"I agree that being on welfare's work. But the hardest part of it is getting up the nerve to go up to somebody and say, 'I'm poor, and I need help.' That's very hard to say, and it's real work to say it, because no matter how you try to say it, it still seems to come out 'I'm a no-good.'"

Mrs. I introduced another facet of the welfare-work question to the group:

"I know of some cases, too, that might show another problem why people who're on welfare don't want to work. Some of them can only get part-time jobs, and then that amount is deducted from their welfare check. In some cases they end up with less money than they'd get by just staying on welfare. This happened to us one time, when my husband got hurt. We had to go on welfare for a while. Well, he isn't the kind of man who likes to keep quiet, even though he was hurt, and so he went out and did a little work just so he could keep himself occupied. He made forty dollars. The welfare people called me and asked me if he was working, and I couldn't tell a lie. I told them that, yes, he made forty dollars, and two weeks later they called us and said we couldn't get a welfare check that month. That hurt us very much, and we were in trouble for food and it made it tough on us. It'd have been better, I guess, if I had lied, but I couldn't do that. It'd have been better if my husband hadn't worked that little bit, but he can't do that. Maybe next time I'll just lie."

"Does anybody really like to be on welfare, though, even though it may be better than taking a rotten job?" inquired Mrs. N. She continued: "I know a family that's been getting financial help for twenty years, and then something went wrong with one of the checks they were supposed to get, and the woman went to the agency and cursed everybody out with really foul language. I couldn't figure that out at first, but then I thought about it and it came to me. Nobody likes to be that dependent on anyone else. They may know they need the money, but they're bitter about it because they can't get the money for themselves. They're kind of trapped in the situation. They can't get out of it, and it really isn't comfortable for them to take that money. It's sort of like a big child being fed milk except that these are big people who are being kept in the same position as little children, and they don't want to be treated like little children!"

"Some people think that OEO is a welfare program, and they won't come near it because of that," interjected Mrs. B. "I was in a department store the other day and a lady came up to me and said, 'I understand you're involved in this OEO program. It sounds interesting, but is OEO another one of those give-away programs? If that's the case, I don't want to have anything to do with it.' I told her about OEO and that it isn't a give-away program, and then she seemed to be a little bit more interested in it. Well, that woman has four kids, and her husband's gone. She's on welfare herself, I know she is, and yet she says she doesn't like the idea of give-away programs even though she's receiving some of it. It's more than just the money, isn't it?"

The conversation returned to the importance of pride, and what one "had to do to get the money." As the evening's discussion came to an end, Mrs. K offhandedly commented, "Well, at least somebody profits from welfare—that's the social workers." The group laughed, but then quickly evolved the position that there are "some good and some bad" social workers. The major criterion for the judgment "good" or "bad" was the relative degree of discomfort the social worker imposed upon the applicant. Mrs. M, as the TNOs began leaving the conference room, suggested:

"I think we're too hard on the welfare officials. Those people have to fill out so many forms, and have so many regulations to follow, that they never really get a chance to see that they're working with people. I don't really blame them. I blame the system. I feel kind of sorry for them. I think some of them feel just as trapped as we do."

Several antipoverty programs directly relevant to jobs and employment were implemented in the Topeka poverty program. Those programs, including a Beautification Program, a Manpower Training and Development Program, and the On-the-Job Training Program, were discussed by TNOs in their Target Neighborhood Committee meetings and in meetings of the Economic Opportunity Board. Not surprisingly, TNOs were quite concerned about the "quality" of the jobs which would be available to Neighborhood residents, or the kinds of jobs for which training programs would prepare them. Some of the non-TNO's felt that "any job is better than no job at all" for people who are impoverished. As indicated by their discussion in the meeting with the research observers, many of the TNOs, and perhaps many of those whom they represented, were not of that opinion. Under some conditions, being on welfare, though certainly not considered to be a comfortable situation, might be preferable to degrading or unrewarding employment.

Target Neighborhood Officers discussed the various strategems by which an individual, in a demeaning job situation, could nonetheless enhance his self-esteem—strategems such as lateral mobility (hopping from job to job) in the place of upward mobility, and working only a few hours of an eight-hour shift in order effectively to increase one's hourly income. Even in work conditions that were perceived to be oppressive, there were ways, as the TNOs revealed, by which an individual could neutralize manipulation and gain some control over the work experience. The exploited or frustrated individual could create for himself an *ad hoc* process experience, in which he became the entrepreneur of at least his own time and effort. Furthermore, TNOs indicated that the act of not working could, in itself, in at least a limited way, contribute to one's self-esteem— in the sense that not working was an *active* withdrawal from a job in which one would have to be painfully passive. Target Neighborhood Officers, then, were more or less influenced by this perception of work and nonwork—a perception which seemed to differ generally from that of non-TNOs. One might assume that to the non-TNOs a deliberate choice to not work, unless the individual was independently wealthy or seriously ill, physically or mentally, would be considered somehow immoral. One might further assume it would be very difficult for non-TNOs to understand how the choice to not work could, relative to other options, contribute to self-esteem. Commented, for example, one non-TNO, "I don't understand why some of these people won't take the jobs around that are available. I know for a fact they need dishwashers down at the hotel, but they just can't get people to take the job. What's wrong with being a dishwasher? It's a good, clean, honest work. I worked as a dishwasher myself while I was going through college." Needless to say, the person who worked as a dishwasher while going through college may have quite a different perception of that task from the person for whom it is the unchosen zenith of occupational mobility. Antipoverty opportunities that offered such "good, clean, honest work" might easily be perceived differentially during program discussions by the poor and the not-poor.

Similarly, one would be hard pressed to find a non-TNO who would conceive of welfare as a form of work. Some of the Target Neighborhood Officers, on the contrary, discussed welfare as precisely that—as a form of physical and psychological work surrounding a role enactment and a set of operating procedures. Playing the welfare role apparently could, for some individuals, be as demanding as engaging in gainful employment, although no TNO felt that welfare was anything more than in some cases the lesser of two evils.

Target Neighborhood Officers felt that, with the exception of peers who had experienced poverty, other people judge harshly those who were "on the welfare rolls." Even some persons who themselves were on welfare would hide or deny the fact that they were. To the degree, therefore, that the poverty program was identified with welfare, it was eschewed by some persons who otherwise might have participated as indigenous leaders or as beneficiaries. Target Neighborhood Officers themselves were extremely sensitive about any comparison made between the welfare system and the Office of Economic Opportunity. To a man, they did not want to be identified with a welfare program. The major distinguishing factor between welfare and the poverty program was, as they often stated, the opportunity to participate in decisions concerning the programing. If that opportunity was challenged, then the poverty program became more welfare-like, and this meant that their identification with the program became threatened.

ON RELIGION

The topic for the evening's discussion—religion—had been decided by the Target Neighborhood Officers at an earlier session. All the Target Neighborhood Officers in attendance except Mr. E had seated themselves around the large table, and were passing around cookies to eat with their coffee. He had not yet sat down. He stretched out his hands, and in pontifical tones began the discussion:

"America has slid back from God. We will not solve our poverty problems until we return to God. We as Neighborhood leaders should get down on our knees and pray to God for guidance. The same thing destroyed the Romans and it will destroy us. They allowed their morals to go down and they were destroyed from within, not just from without. We're going to have to get down on our knees or we're all lost. We talk about changing things ourselves and saving ourselves, but we can't do it; nobody can but God. We must pray, pray, pray."

The other TNOs quietly listened to Mr. E, two of them murmuring an occasional "Amen!" Mr. A, an Indian, smiled and wryly commented, "Who the heck has time to pray? I have to work at two jobs." Mr. L quickly agreed with Mr. A, exclaiming, "God doesn't pass antipoverty laws, the legislature does! We've got to get out and work and get the legislature to pass more laws to help us. Right now they're more interested in voting for cows and oil wells, not people, and nothing except us voting for better people's going to change that."

The differences in opinion among the TNOs—one view perhaps more "sacred," the other more "secular"—were quickly established in the evening's discussion. The Target Neighborhood Officers continued their conversation, becoming more specific about the functions of religion for the poor. Mrs. F reminded the group, "Remember, blessed are the poor. Religion helps us make it through this tough world. If we remember that, Christ'll do right by us, we can have faith in the mercy of God, and he'll let us exist in peace."

"That's right," agreed Mrs. B. "There's a difference between being poor in spirit and poor in material things. You can be poor in material things, and still be very rich in spirit. It's not possible for a rich person to be Christlike. Only a poor person can be Christlike. Well, maybe a rich person can be Christlike, but it's tougher for him."

Mr. E added, "We need both rich and poor to be saved. I mean, we need someone we can help in order to be saved. Jesus said, 'The poor you have with you always.' We need the poor for fulfillment."

Mr. A asked, "Don't you think that fear of the unknown is what really makes people become churchgoers?" Mrs. F shook her head negatively and argued, "Religion means help for the poor, I don't care what anybody says. It helps us, because we realize there's going to be a better life somewhere else. It gives us something to cling to. If we didn't have religion for that, we'd be in worse shape."

Mr. L cleared his throat, and quietly stated:

"People who don't work, don't eat. That's a fact of life. You've got to have a living faith, one which is part of your everyday life. One which fits in with the world as it is, not the world as you'd like it to be. I think that the truly religious man cannot be quiet. He has to be active. He has to try to change things. He has to realize that he has certain things he has to do, and that's really what God's will is."

The discussion ceased for about a minute, as if the Target Neighborhood Officers were absorbing what Mr. L had just said. Finally, Mrs. J said contemplatively:

"My mother thought church was real important. My kids, I don't know if they even think about it. Sometimes people say that's what's wrong with things today. I don't know. I go to church mainly because I like to talk with other people who're there. But I don't see where going to church helped my mother give us anything she didn't have. It didn't give us better food or get us more money. I don't know. Maybe my kids will find something to believe in that'll fix things better."

"Sometimes you've got to do things that aren't very churchlike," commented Mr. A. "I stole a loaf of bread when I was a kid. Actually, I stole more than one. I didn't feel guilty at all, because my stomach was filled after I ate it. I thought then, and I think I still think that way, that the ends justify the means that you take to get there."

The Target Neighborhood Officers shifted the emphasis of their conversation to the ministers of churches in the Target Neighborhoods. Mr. H complained:

"The church should give to the poor, but sometimes they have difficulty telling who's poor and who's not. Sometimes what they give falls into the hands of a Judas. Sometimes ministers are very free to give the 'word' to the poor, but are not willing to give their actions to the poor! Ministers should do more to change things than just bringing a basket of can goods around at Christmas time."

Mrs. D nodded approval and said, "There might even be some ministers who're opposed to the poverty program, because if we all get educated we'll move out of the Neighborhood and they won't have a congregation anymore!" Again smiling, Mr. A added, "Let's not forget that after the sermon, the minister passes around the collection plate. He needs money. I need money. We all need money."

The remainder of the meeting was taken up by the research staff's report, at the previous request of the Target Neighborhood Officers, concerning the general progress of the study.

The Target Neighborhood Officers' discussion of religion revealed two divergent points of view. The first, the more secular view, was also perhaps more closely related to the "Get off your knees and hustle" mandate sometimes referred to as the Protestant Ethic. The other, perhaps more sacred, view of "God will provide" or "Blessed are the poor" is interesting as it relates to social change—or more correctly, resistance to social change. The sanctification of the state of being poor, the promise of life hereafter to those who endure the deprivations of this world, and the belief that the poor are somehow more Christlike might have significant impact upon the degree to which a Target Neighborhood Officer chooses to become involved in social action. If some of the extrinsic or dogmatic aspects of a religion have been embraced by indigenous leaders as a defense system in the face of deprivation, then to enact a more active "secular" social role might, at least temporarily, be unsettling.

Given their attitude toward religion at that time, Target Neighborhood Officers can be expected to have more than simply a content perception of antipoverty activities proposed with a church as the delegate agency. A hidden agenda may evolve in which some of them are arguing more for, or against, a particular form of religion, an orientation to religion, or the worth of religion than they are arguing for, or against, the program itself.

As in the Topeka poverty program, ministers often emerge, at least early in the program's development, as representatives of the poor. One might expect that, with increased process experience in the program, indigenous leaders would reassess the competence or qualifications of such ministers to be their representatives. In the Topeka program, the role of most of the ministers became less and less central as indigenous leaders themselves became more and more experienced.

On Mental Health

The Target Neighborhood Officers asked the research staff, at the beginning of the evening's session, to discuss briefly what mental illness is as juxtaposed with mental health. After a few definitions and some general discussion about categories of mental health and illness, the Target Neighborhood Officers, as was their custom, directed the conversation. Mrs. D suggested, "When a person's said to be 'mentally ill' people think the worst. It's sort of like being called 'poor.' The word brings with it all kinds of other things. You know, like the person became sick in the head on purpose. Or it's because he hasn't got any will power, or he's sinful, or something like that."

Mrs. F, agreeing with Mrs. D, added:

"Neighborhood residents hide mentally ill persons because they're ashamed of the fact that a family person might be mentally ill. This might be because of ignorance, but it exists. There's also a problem of having a large family, like most of us do, and then there's no time for really considering people who're mentally ill. You just don't have that much time to pay attention to any one person."

"Families like to take care of their own people who're sick," remarked Mrs. P, "no matter what kind of sick they are." "That's right," concurred Mr. H; "we all know people who've been put into an insane asylum because other people wanted to get rid of them. If a family loves a person, they'll want to keep him around." "Besides," Mrs. B added, "the poor are more scared about being involved in treatment for mental illness. It's not fashionable for us like it is for the rich class. We believe we should be able to pull ourselves together if we're mentally sick." "Hell," exclaimed Mr. R, "therapy's for rich people! We go to jail."

The Target Neighborhood Officers then turned their discussion from therapy to the therapist. Mrs. Q complained:

"Psychiatrists leave a bad taste in my mouth. It does that to people in my Neighborhood too. They're a bunch of rich people trying to tell us what to do. I had to take my daughter to one one time, and we were scared stiff to go up there. In fact, I was petrified. They have such fancy offices. I walked in and this fancy doctor scared the life out of me because he was so formal. I didn't like sitting around in that waiting room, either, with all those other people who were all dressed up. I don't know, but it was just hard to feel at home there."

Mrs. J inquired, "I've heard those therapists have all had therapy themselves. Doesn't that mean that they were all crazy, too?" The research staff explained that undergoing therapy is part of some training programs for psychotherapists.

Mrs. N proclaimed, "I don't know if I want to tell everything to anybody, like you do in a therapy session. I don't know if I'd want to depend upon someone to make my decisions for me." "Make your decisions for you," exploded Mr. H. "I heard about a fellow who had to pay a psychiatrist a dollar a minute just to *talk to him.* Man, I'd like to have a racket like that. Ministers and bartenders do the same thing, but they don't get a dollar a minute." The group laughed, and Mrs. I, amid the laughter, declared, "I don't think you should tell a psychiatrist anything! It's none of his business! People think when you go to a mental-health place you're completely crazy and have to be locked up. There doesn't seem to be any half-way point. People think you're either completely crazy, or you're not crazy at all."

"Trust is the big problem," Mr. L suggested. "A neighborhood person feels he can trust his minister, but I don't think he feels yet that he can trust a psychiatrist or a psychologist. He just hasn't seen enough of them around, in places where he can understand."

Mrs. F exclaimed excitedly:

"What can people expect! Here you have a twenty-one-year-old well-dressed social worker telling a woman with ten kids what to do, how to live her life, and how to clean up her mind! Of course people are going to resent that! The same goes for the psychiatrist. There's a man who's making six thousand dollars a month telling someone how to be mentally healthy on sixty dollars a month!"

Mr. E shared a story with the group about one of his own experiences:

"I had some trouble one time when I was in the Army with paralysis in my leg. A white psychiatrist came to me, and I didn't tell him a thing. Then they sent me a Negro psychiatrist, and he was a fellow who seemed to know the score. I put my confidence in him, when I just couldn't put my confidence in a white psychiatrist. My leg got better."

Mrs. C laughed and said, "That's because your leg's a black leg!" The group laughed loudly, and then began seriously to discuss the factor of "trust" as it contributed to seeking help for mental problems. Mr. L suggested, "Somehow we, as Target Neighborhood Officers, should try to help bridge the gap between people who can make people well and the people who're sick. Someone's got to bridge the gap between the poor and the psychiatrist."

"I wish mental-health people would put more time on prevention than they do on treatment," Mrs. K said. "They ought to get out in the Neighborhoods more, and let people get to know them as persons, instead of being in those big offices. Then they ought to work more with ways to keep people from getting sick. Maybe they'd make less money that way, but they'd do a lot more good."

Mr. A, nodding his head, agreed:

"I like the idea of having community mental-health centers right in the Neighborhoods, because then we can all see what the psychiatrists are really trying to do, and learn how to use their services to the best of our own advantages. There's talk that a program for community mental-health centers is available, and we may be talking about that at the Board meetings. We ought to give that some good consideration."

The meeting with the research staff was cut short on the evening of discussing mental health because the Target Neighborhood Officers had to attend a "leadership session" conducted by the Topeka Office of Economic Opportunity. However, even in the relatively brief period that the TNOs discussed the topic, indications of some relevant attitudes emerged. Again, it was obvious that the Target Neighborhood Officers were quite sensitive to arbitrary "labels"— such as "poor" or, in this discussion, "mentally ill" or "insane." The social distance between the therapists and the low-income patient could be seen, from comments of TNOs, potentially to interfere with the seeking of therapy or with the therapeutic process itself. The Target Neighborhood Officers felt it would be beneficial to all concerned if mental-health practitioners spent more time in their Neighborhoods, and became "familiar" to them and with their problems.

It seems clear that the attitudes of TNOs and their followers toward mental-health programs (such as community mental-health centers) may be influenced by stereotypes derived from, and maintained through, social distance. Discussions of such programs during training sessions of poverty boards could reflect those attitudes and stereotypes.

The quotes presented and interpreted throughout this chapter are taken to reflect some Target Neighborhood Officers' attitudes which were likely to influence, at least initially, their perceptions of poverty-program activities. Homogeneity of those attitudes, in kind or degree, among all TNOs is not meant to be implied. The quotes themselves, in fact, testify to heterogeneity. The quotes and interpretations are offered to let the reader catch additional glimpses of the expressed views of individual TNOs, and to set the stage for the chapters to follow which describe the TNOs in action within their own Target Neighborhood Committees.

CHAPTER 11

Indigenous Leadership: Perception of a Role

THE STRUCTURAL AND FUNCTIONAL DE-
SIGN of the Topeka poverty program included the expectation that
the Target Neighborhood Officers, as indigenous leaders, would
serve as a bridge between the poor and the not-poor members of the
community. That was to be their contribution to the implementation
of the Overlap Model.

The participation of "indigenous nonprofessionals" in OEO and other local helping programs and projects has been one of the main tactics of the "War on Poverty."[1] Residents of low-income areas have

[1] See, for example: George Brager, "The Indigenous Worker: A New Approach to the Social Work Technician," *Social Work*, 10 (April, 1965), 33–40;
Arthur Pearl and Frank Riessman, *New Careers for the Poor*; and Robert Reiff

been serving as supporting staff in, for example, neighborhood service centers, manpower training, Head Start, day-care facilities, poverty-intervention organizations such as the TOEO, and various health, education, or welfare agencies. Through the efforts and neighborhood contacts of indigenous workers, agency and program "outreach" to the isolated poor often has been extended. The workers themselves, it has been assumed, have benefited from their experiences in indigenous-worker roles.[2]

Riessman argues convincingly for the widespread utilization of indigenous workers. However, he carefully makes clear that the impact of inclusion upon workers, and their efficiency as change agents, will in large part be determined by the training they receive in preparation for the work role. "One of the greatest problems experienced by the non-professional," Reissman writes, "is role ambiguity or lack of role identity. That is, he doesn't know who he is or who he is becoming. He is no longer a simple member of the community if he ever was one, nor is he a professional. Actually, he is a highly marginal person . . ."[3] Levinson and Schiller support Riessman's observations in their study of indigenous nonprofessionals in a social-welfare agency. The nonprofessionals found themselves in discrepant roles vis-à-vis both higher-status professionals and the client community, and could not comfortably relate to either.[4]

---

and Frank Riessman, "The Indigenous Non-Professional: A Strategy of Change in Community Action," *Community Mental Health Journal*, Monograph No. 1, 1965.

[2] Frank Riessman, "The 'Helper' Therapy Principle," *Social Work*, 10 (April, 1965), 27–32.

[3] Frank Riessman, "Strategies and Suggestions for Training Non-Professionals," Albert Einstein College of Medicine, Department of Psychiatry, New York, 1968, mimeograph.

[4] Perry Levinson and Jeffry Schiller, "Role Analysis of the Indigenous Nonprofessional," *Social Work*, 11 (July, 1966), 95–101. For other accounts of role conflicts experienced by indigenous personnel, see: Charles F. Grosser, "Local Residents as Mediators Between Middle-class Professional Workers and Lower-class Clients," *Social Service Review*, 40, 1 (March, 1966), 56–63; and D. C. Dubey and Willis Sutton, "A Rural 'Middle Man in the Middle': The Indian Village Level Worker in Community Development," *Human Organization*, 24 (Summer, 1965), 148–151. The role conflicts experienced by indigenous per-

We are here concerned with the Target Neighborhood Officers, the volunteer indigenous leaders associated with the TOEO. The volunteer indigenous leader, as a representative of his neighborhood and a voting member on a poverty board, has nationally become one of the major exponents of the indigenous worker.

In our research we became concerned with the degree to which indigenous leaders were willing to assume the expected marginal position between TOEO and the target-area poor. What was the structure of the role to be enacted? What were some individual characteristics of the leaders, and how did those characteristics relate to the degree of role enactment? What was the impact upon the TNOs of their assuming the Overlap Model bridge relation between the poor and the not-poor? What styles of role enactment were associated with "success" as a TNO? How did leaders perceive their marginal roles, and how did this perception relate to other personal characteristics?

To approach answers to those questions, and to complement our observation data, we constructed an *ad hoc* Role Perception Scale which was included as part of the questionnaire administered to Economic Opportunity Board members in November, 1966 (Admin I).

In the Role Perception Scale, each TNO was asked to assess the relative importance of two juxtaposed TNO role tasks—one specifying a responsibility to the TOEO, the other specifying a responsibility to Target Neighborhood residents. The scale's option of "seesaw" responses allowed each respondent to choose the TOEO responsibility as exclusively important, the Target Neighborhood resident responsibility as exclusively important, the two tasks as equally important, or to assign some balance of relative importance on a nine-point continuum between the juxtaposed tasks. Ten pairs of tasks were pre-

---

sonnel parallel those described for the foreman in industry. See, for example: Burleigh B. Gardner and William Foote Whyte, "The Man in the Middle: Position and Problems of the Foreman," *Applied Anthropology*, 4, 1 (1945), pp. 1–28; Fritz J. Roethlisberger, "The Foreman: Master and Victim of Double Talk," *Harvard Business Review*, 20, 3 (Spring, 1945), 285–294; and Donald E. Wray, "Marginal Man of Industry: The Foreman," *American Journal of Sociology*, 54 (January, 1948), 298–301.

sented for TNO evaluation. An eleventh item asked TNOs to place themselves on a nine-point continuum from "rich" to "poor." (The Role Perception Scale is presented in Appendix E.)

TNO responses were scored in two ways, thus yielding two interpretations of the Role Perception Scale. The first scoring procedure assigned a value of 1 to the "TOEO is exclusively important" end of the continuum, and increased by 1 each response position up to a maximum of 9 at the "Target Neighborhood resident is exclusively important" end of the continuum. The higher the summated scale score for the eleven items, the more the TNO was taken to be oriented toward the Target Neighborhood residents; the lower the score, the more the TNO was taken to be oriented toward the TOEO. That interpretation was called the Orientation Scale.

The second scoring procedure assigned a value of 5 to the center— "equally important"—point on the continuum between juxtaposed TOEO and Target Neighborhood resident responsibilities. A value of 1 was then subtracted for each continuum point of distance the respondent's marked choice was from center. The closer the summated score was to 5, the more the TNO was taken to assign to his role a marginal position between the TOEO and the Target Neighbor-Marginality Scale.

Scores for the Orientation and Marginality Scales were analyzed for relations to TNO demographic data, reasons for becoming a TNO, tenure in the program, and other scale variables.

The TOEO Director and Assistant Director were asked to respond to the Role Perception Scale, and to key their answers to what they thought would represent the "ideal" TNO. The intention was to determine the expectation that the TOEO staff had for the TNO role, and whether that expectation actually represented the Overlap Model specifications for TOEO organizational design.

In order to acquire at least some indication of scale validity, six members of the research staff predicted, on the basis of their field observations, the Orientation and Marginality scores for each TNO prior to the administration of the scale. As a means of assessing internal consistency, an item analysis was performed on the Orientation Scale.

THE PERCEPTIONS

The TOEO Director's assessment of the "ideal" TNO role yielded an Orientation score of 5.00 and a Marginality score of 5.00. Thus he expected the TNO to be oriented equally to the TOEO and the Target Neighborhood residents, and assumed the TNO role to be exactly marginal. The Assistant Director's assessment yielded an Orientation score of 4.91 and a Marginality score of 4.73. He expected the ideal TNO to be oriented slightly toward the TOEO, and perceived the TNO role to be not exactly but still quite marginal. It is safe to conclude that both Director and Assistant Director held the "bridge" expectation for TNO's, as expected by the Overlap Model.

Research-staff predictions for TNO Orientation responses correlated .39 with actual scores; predictions for Marginality responses correlated .49 with actual scores. Orientation Scale item analysis yielded the following correlations between total scale score and items one through eleven, respectively: .57, .45, .41, .59, .56, .35, .62, .59, .74, .71, and .29. Although not intended to obscure the fact that the Role Perception Scale was an *ad hoc* instrument, these findings suggest modest validity and internal consistency for the scale.

Table 5 presents correlations of Orientation and Marginality scores with TNO demographic data and other questionnaire scale scores.

Orientation Scale: The median Orientation Scale score for TNOs was 5.45, with a range of 3.18 to 7.55. As a group, therefore, TNOs appeared to be slightly oriented toward the poor, and clearly more oriented in that direction than expected by TOEO staff. As indicated in Table 5, TNO age was significantly related to Orientation score, the younger TNOs showing a greater degree of orientation toward the poor. Higher Orientation scores, also as indicated in Table 5, were related negatively to income, education, activism, achievement orientation, and future orientation, and positively to anomie, integration with relatives, isolation, normlessness, powerlessness, alienation, and particularism. Although most of the correlations are low and account for little of the variance, the pattern of results indicates that orientation toward the poor was generally associated with character-

TABLE 5. Correlations of Orientation and Marginality Scale Scores with TNO Demographic Data and Other Questionnaire Scale Scores[a] (N=23)

	Orientation Scale	Marginality Scale
Age	−.43[b]	.06
Income	−.05	.39
Education	−.03	.05
Tenure as TNO	.35	−.02
Activism	−.38	.44[b]
Anomie	.26	−.26
Integration with relatives	.04	−.14
Achievement orientation	−.23	.18
Future orientation	−.29	.51[b]
Isolation	.05	−.10
Normlessness	.08	−.14
Powerlessness	.15	−.22
Alienation	.12	−.20
Particularism	.18	−.21

[a] Pearson r.
[b] $P < .05$; df = 21.

istics taken to be influenced by poverty.[5] In other words, it might be concluded that those TNOs who tended to perceive their roles as oriented toward the poor were themselves more like the poor.

There were no statistically significant differences in Orientation scores between males and females or among ethnic groups. Orientation scores were not consistently related to types of reasons for becoming a TNO, or to drop-out rate.

The positive correlation between tenure as a TNO and Orientation Scale scores can not itself be considered an index of change, but may have presaged the increase in Orientation scores which were revealed by the readministration of the questionnaire, and which will be discussed further when we consider change data in Chapter 15.

Marginality Scale: The median Marginality Scale score for TNOs was 3.91, with a range of 1.73 to 4.64. Therefore, as a group TNOs did not perceive their roles to be especially marginal, and were markedly less oriented toward marginality than expected by TOEO

[5] See Chap. 5, n. 13.

staff. As indicated in Table 5, TNO Marginality scores were positively related to age, income, education, activism, achievement orientation, and future orientation, and negatively related to anomie, integration with relatives, isolation, normlessness, powerlessness, alienation, and particularism. Although again most of the correlations are low and account for little of the variance, the pattern of results indicates that higher Marginality scores are generally associated with characteristics taken to be influenced by membership in the middle socio-economic class.[6] This interpretation is supported by the negative .32 correlation found between Marginality and Orientation Scale scores. The more the TNO perceives his role to be marginal, in accordance with TOEO expectations, the less he tends to be oriented toward the poor. It is tempting to suggest that, to the degree that the TNO enacts the marginal role expected by the TOEO, he becomes divorced from the Target Neighborhood residents he is supposed to represent.[7] However, considering the size of the sample and the low correlations among the variables, such a suggestion could at best serve as a stimulus for further research.

Of ten major local poverty-program offices held by TNOs, seven were held by TNOs with the highest eight Marginality scores (offices including, for example, president and vice-president of the Economic Opportunity Board; chairman and vice-chairman of the TNO Leadership Committee; chairman of the Personnel Committee; and members of the Board Executive Committee). Higher Marginality scores consequently appeared to be related to deeper involvement in the formal TOEO organization.

Types of reasons for being a TNO also seemed related to Marginality scores. Of the highest ten TNO Marginality scorers, seven gave humanitarian reasons for assuming leadership (e.g., "I felt it was a

---

[6] *Ibid.*

[7] Some observers have commented upon the potential "co-optation" of indigenous leaders by established agencies. See, for example: Charles F. Grosser, "Community Development Programs Serving the Urban Poor," *Social Work*, 10 (July, 1965), 15–21; Martin Rein and Frank Riessman, "A Strategy for Anti-Poverty Community Action Programs," *Social Work*, 11 (April, 1966), 1–5; Philip Selznick, *TVA and the Grass Roots*; Hans B. C. Spiegel, *Citizen Participation in Urban Development*, Vol. 1, *Concepts and Issues.*

good way to help my fellow man"). Of the lowest ten Marginality scorers, six gave "default" explanations for their leadership role (e.g., "I stopped by to pick up my wife at the meeting and they elected me chairman, because nobody else would take it"). TNOs with higher Marginality scores tended, therefore, to have comparatively elaborate and abstract explanations for enacting a leadership role which they tended to perceive as marginal.

There were no statistically significant differences in Marginality scores between males and females or among ethnic groups. Of the highest ten Marginality scorers, only three remained with the program throughout the period of this study. Of the lowest ten Marginality scorers, five remained. That finding, and the very low but negative relation between the Marginality score and tenure as a TNO, may indicate the stresses of maintaining the marginal TNO position —stresses which now, and in subsequent chapters, will be discussed in detail.

SOME CONFLICTS IN EXPECTATIONS

Field observation of, and interviews with, Target Neighborhood Committee members and TOEO staff suggested some important differences in their expectations for the Target Neighborhood Officers —differences which contributed to the stresses of the TNO "bridge" position. The TOEO staff generally expected of TNOs: (1) immediately to play an active rather than a passive role vis-à-vis an agency-like organization; (2) to have faith in the development of specific community-action programs over a long period of time—thus to manifest considerable future orientation; (3) quickly to become comfortable with, and rather expert in, the impersonal techniques of bureaucracy; (4) to be tolerant and understanding of delays in the implementation of community-action programs while they were being processed through the machinery of bureaucracy; (5) from the beginning, to be firm and confident leaders, able to make decisions and cast votes for programs which affected their followers, and to be able to interpret to their Target Neighborhood Committee membership reasons for those decisions and votes; and (6) to keep their memberships informed about, interested in, and trusting of, a governmental organization, and thus to be representatives of that organization to committee members.

Members of the Target Neighborhood Committees, on the other hand, generally tended toward and assessed their TNOs in accordance with: (1) a traditionally passive rather than active mode of interaction with formal organizations; (2) an emphasis upon present, rather than future, orientation; (3) an evaluation of experiences on a personalistic, or particularistic, rather than an impersonal, or universalistic, basis; (4) little tolerance for delay of results concerning programs; (5) a rather marked ambivalence toward authority, including the authority represented by their own indigenous leaders; and (6) a skepticism about, and suspicion of, agencies, and thus almost a guilt-by-association indictment of their leaders' participation as representatives of an agency.

TNOs who attempted to enact the marginal role expected of them, and whose Marginality Scale scores were comparatively high, often complained to the research interviewers about the stresses endemic to being bridges. A Negro TNO grumbled, "I can't understand it. You do everything you can to help your people in the committees and it turns out later they resent it. I don't understand why that is. I can't understand why they don't seem to understand what I'm trying to do!" An Anglo TNO commented, "It seems the minute you become a leader, you make enemies among the people you're trying to help!" A second Negro TNO exclaimed, "It's almost as if the better job you do as chairman, the more the people give you a bad time about being 'OEO's man!'"

Another Anglo, still commenting about the attitudes of followers, reported:

"Well, this is the way it happens to me. I go into the group, and if I don't do anything they think I'm a bad leader. On the other hand, if I start telling them ideas, they say, 'Who do you think you are?' When you try to get something done, when you try to get a meeting organized, they think you're ramroding."

A Negro chairman commented, "One of our problems is, at this time anyway, I think we offer a picture of words to the people rather than something they can see and feel."

A Mexican-American agreed: "Sometimes I think we let our meetings get boring. We seem to talk and talk, and offer promises, programs, and procedures. There's nothing wrong with that, because poverty's something that's not going to be overcome overnight—it's going to take a long time, even generations, before the whole problem's whipped. But most of the members don't feel that way. They don't believe anything's ever going to be done, and they're not going to believe it unless I can show them something right away!" "I guess," summed up one Negro TNO, "that I would almost rather be an interested follower than a leader."

Alternatives for Indigenous Leaders

The degree to which the various expectations held by the TOEO for TNOs conflicted with the values and expectations of the officers' followers determined, in large part, the kinds of adjustments the leader made to that conflict. Important also were the TNOs' motivations for wanting to be leaders within the TOEO complex. If, for example, the leader primarily participated because he hoped to improve his social standing, and was not particularly concerned about the responses and reactions of his people to his behavior as an agency representative, then his experience of conflict seemed minimal. As one TNO put it, "A guy who just wants to climb an organizational ladder has no problem being a leader. If any of his members give him a bad time, he just points to them and says, 'If you had any stuff you'd pull yourself up by your bootstraps too!'" It may well be that in some cases the membership, showing antipathy toward the leader, encouraged him to "turn his back on his people," and "look out for himself."

A second alternative, one for the leader who was interested in representing and helping his people but who negatively experienced differences in TOEO and resident expectations for his indigenous-leadership role, was simply to resign the position of leadership. One leader who did resign put the problem in focus:

"It's not the OEO that's the whole problem and it's not the Target Neighborhood residents who're the whole problem. It's the business of the Neighborhood residents and the OEO getting together that's the tough nut to crack, and a serious leader who wants to bring them together is right in the middle of the nut cracker."

A third alternative was represented by the leader who chose to remain marginal—to remain of and for his members, yet an active participant in the OEO structure. He generally was a high Marginality scorer, and often was motivated by religious, humanitarian, or sense-of-duty considerations. He was willing to endure, for some length of time, the conflicts in value and role expectations that existed between the members of his committee and the TOEO. Such leaders were, therefore, the most effective in operationalizing the Overlap Model. But to maintain such marginality, to act as a bridge over which rode the chargers for social change, was a difficult and taxing task.

The poverty-intervention organization that calls for such indigenous leadership would be well served by providing extensive training for the incumbents of such a role. The curriculum for "marginality training" might include discussions of: active *versus* passive interaction with formal organizations; the dynamics underlying differential attitudes toward authority; the incidence of role conflicts and value conflicts illustrated by examples that can be drawn from the leaders' own experience; the process of delegating authority; and, in understandable terms, the social psychology of groups. This is not to say that the Overlap Model and its components are the most effective method to ameliorate poverty and bring about social change, nor to say that indigenous leaders who assume a bridge position between the poor and the not-poor are the most effective agents for social change. Rather, it is to say that if a poverty-intervention organization expects its indigenous leaders to enact such roles, some provision should be made for their adequate training. The staff of the poverty-intervention organization also should be aware that there may be considerable variation among its staff, the indigenous leaders, and the poor whom they represent in perceptions of, and expectations for, indigenous leadership.

CHAPTER 12

Target Neighborhood Committees:
Stages of Development

As STRUCTURED during the planning phase of the Topeka poverty program, the twelve Target Neighborhood Committees (TNCs) were intended to be key components of the intervention process, and a primary source of indigenous involvement. Each TNC was organized by the TOEO Assistant Director, who sought out friends and informal leaders in the Neighborhood, publicized and arranged the first meetings, explained OEO possibilities, encouraged the election of officers, and then attempted to retreat to an off-stage and consultant role during subsequent meetings. Once thus organized, the TNCs were to be responsible for their own Neighborhood surveys, proselyting, publicizing, and program development. Five TNCs had held preliminary meetings by July, 1965, three by October, 1965, three by March, 1966, and the last in October, 1966. Of those twelve, ten continued to function with varying enthusiasm and participation up to the completion of this research project.

After the TNCs had been established, they were scheduled to meet every two weeks—until June, 1966, when monthly meetings were scheduled. Each TNC had three Target Neighborhood Officers (chairman, vice-chairman, and secretary) elected by the membership. Meetings usually were convened in the evenings at 7:30 and adjourned at about 9:30, although 10:30 adjournments were not uncommon. The meeting places were church halls, schoolrooms, public-shelter houses, and on a few occasions private homes. Attendance ranged from five to ninety members and averaged about fifteen.

During the course of this study, the research staff observed and documented a total of 174 TNC meetings. This chapter will present the TNC stages of development, and the associated behavior of the members, observed by the research staff during that time.

The proposition that discrete stages of development might be discernible was a working hypothesis in the over-all research design. Though identical in organization, purpose, and socio-economic status of members, TNCs differed in Neighborhood geography and demography, distribution of ethnic groups, leadership styles, and opportunities for committee autonomy—factors causing the observers initially to be less than sanguine about the identifiability of general stages of development. However, the opportunity to attend a large number of meetings over a sustained period of time enabled us to report, and readily agree upon, TNC developmental characteristics representing seven distinct stages: (I) Orientation, (II) Catharsis, (III) Focus, (IV) Action, (V) Limbo, (VI) Testing, and (VII) Purposive. We further concluded that differences among the TNCs determined in part the pace with which a given committee moved through the stages, the stage ultimately reached, and reversions to earlier stages, but did not significantly alter the sequential order of the stages. As illustrated in Figure 3, each stage was conceptualized to merge with, or phase into, the next. Some of the be-

FIGURE 3. Target Neighborhood Committee Stages of Development

I. Orientation	✿✿✿✿✿✿✿✿✿✿_____
II. Catharsis	✿✿✿✿✿✿✿✿✿✿_____
III. Focus	✿✿✿✿✿✿✿✿✿✿_____
IV. Action	✿✿✿✿✿✿✿✿✿✿_____
V. Limbo	✿✿✿✿✿✿✿✿✿✿_____
VI. Testing	✿✿✿✿✿✿✿✿✿✿_____
VII. Purposive	✿✿✿✿✿✿✿✿✿✿

Asterisks indicate duration of stage (modal dynamics).
Broken lines indicate continuation of some behaviors typical of a given stage.

haviors attributed to earlier stages were seen to continue throughout the entire period of group development, and no generality in the number of meetings was observed for a specific stage (some TNCs progressed through two stages in a single meeting). Nevertheless, each stage clearly bracketed a set of modal group dynamics and was labeled accordingly.

During the course of the study, one TNC was observed to reach the Purposive stage; one Testing; four through Action to Limbo; three Focus; two Catharsis; and one Orientation. The stages of TNC development, as typologized and presented, serve as a showcase for the processes of individual and group participation. The interactions among indigenous leaders, committee members, TOEO staff and agency representatives can, in the framework of TNC developmental stages, be described as they relate to social and personal change, and impediments to such change.

STAGES OF DEVELOPMENT

Each of the TNC stages of development, and the associated modal group dynamics, will be presented in order, followed by a discussion of the functional role of the TOEO in relation to that stage. The Target Neighborhood Committees, attempting to provide an omnibus milieu to generate an understanding of self, self-other, and self-environment, were thus most fragile human groups. A poverty-intervention organization such as the TOEO, choosing to establish such groups as the Target Neighborhood Committees, can do much, advertently or inadvertently, by commission or omission, to determine the efficacy of these groups for individual and social change. This will be illustrated by pointing to actions of the TOEO which encouraged or discouraged progress through the stages of development, or engendered reversions to earlier stages.

I. *Orientation Stage*:

During the Orientation stage, the attendance at Target Neighborhood meetings was the result of the TOEO Assistant Director's field work. The time, the place, and the agenda of the meeting were decided by him. He functioned in the role of chairman, directed the proceedings, and did most of the talking.

The participants generally were skeptical, and were motivated to attend the meetings primarily out of curiosity. They had little intention of continuing to attend the meetings. Several of the participants were there only because a friend had asked them to come. Many introductions were made before and during the meeting, and there was much "getting to know you" interaction.

The Assistant Director explained to the group the structure, functions, and rationale of the Topeka Office of Economic Opportunity, and the Topeka poverty program. He stressed the "maximum feasible participation" mandate of the Economic Opportunity Act. He reiterated to the group, "This is *your* program," and assured them that OEO was not a "give-away" organization but a "self-help" opportunity. He outlined the various programs that could be funded, and the national and local procedures for formulating, submitting, and implementing community-action proposals, punctuating his comments with examples from already established TNCs.

The participants tended to be passive, though attentive. The Assistant Director called for questions about the poverty program. The first queries were polite and somewhat dutiful, and were concerned with the TOEO's structure and procedures. Further pressing by the Assistant Director yielded questions from the participants centering on "What can this do *for* me?" He encouraged the participants to discuss their "do *for*" assumption *versus* the Office of Economic Opportunity's "do *yourself*" expectations.

The Assistant Director's informal and offhand approach to the group, and his continuing emphasis on "*your* program" gradually created a more relaxed climate for the members. Spontaneity of expression increased, passivity decreased, and the members of the group began interacting more freely with one another. The questions they put to the Assistant Director became more intense, vital, and challenging, and reflected their skepticism about the poverty program's being different from any other welfare program and really "theirs."

The group did not yet perceive itself to be the "Neighborhood Committee," but with the urging of the Assistant Director, the members decided upon a permanent meeting place and a regularly scheduled meeting time. The Assistant Director suggested ways of increasing attendance and the importance of the members' thinking about electing Target Neighborhood Committee officers.

The members became more familiar with the Assistant Director, the TOEO, the meeting environment, and with fellow members. Role expectations and boundaries were explored, and the program was interpreted by each member according to his own needs and experiences. Decisions were made about further participation.

The Orientation stage (I) marked the first contact of the Topeka Office of Economic Opportunity, through its Assistant Director, with a group of low-income Neighborhood residents on their own "turf," and indicated whether or not bases for TNC development and member participation could be established. Both bases were in large part resultants of trust—not in an abstract organization or program, but in the staff members who represented the TOEO or explained the program. The Neighborhood residents tended first to assess and test the man; if satisfied, they then accepted what he said not because of the office he held but because of the person he was. If the staff member was rigidly formal, aloof, and unwilling or unable to speak concretely, he—and consequently his message—most likely was rejected out of hand. An informal, particularistic, and personalistic approach to low-income Neighborhood residents was most important. If the staff member lacked the sensitivity to understand that, the TNC never got beyond the Orientation stage. Worse, because stereotypes were reinforced, some TNCs burst into a fiery and terminal Catharsis stage (II) during which the staff member and the TOEO were thoroughly roasted for every real and imagined injustice experienced by the participants at the hands of "them."

Once acceptance of, and trust in, the staff member had been at least tentatively secured, the task for the TOEO was to make meaningful for the participants the purposes and potentials of the poverty program. Zealous to replace skepticism and suspiciousness with credibility and participation, the TOEO at times was tempted to "Madison Avenue" the program among the poor—to oversell it with glittering catch-words and thus to conjure up expectations for sudden and miraculous personal, social, and physical changes in the Neighborhoods. Sometimes in the beginning the huckstering increased TNC participation, but the "bandwagon" usually was all but deserted when the miracles were not forthcoming. On those occasions when the TOEO oversold the immediacy of poverty amelioration, it usually could look forward to later inheriting the critical legacies of "promises, promises," "another pie-in-the-sky deal," and "same old story." That criticism was compounded by anger at a violation of trust and by plummeting TNC attendance. Even when the TOEO presented a more realistic picture of community action through OEO, it often still was not able to keep pace with the member demands for action. But at least there was a less drastic difference between the ideal and the real, and there was a chance to maintain participation of the poor.

It was not easy for the TOEO staff to stimulate the kind of TNC climate that would encourage member participation and the emergence of indigenous leadership. The staff member necessarily dominated the Orientation stage (I) and, enjoying the limelight and gratified by the polite (and passive) attention of the audience, he sometimes forgot that an essential part of his job was to gadfly TNC autonomy. Furthermore, he knew from experience with other TNCs that an increase in the spontaneity of members brought with it the none-too-pleasant Catharsis stage (II). Hence he was at times hesitant to yield TNC control—a hesitancy which stopped the TNC at Stage I (with the possibility of a Stage II cathartic eruption) and ended the opportunity for process experience for the poor.

II. *Catharsis Stage*:

During the Target Neighborhood Committee meetings, the participants learned from interaction with the Assistant Director that the members of the TOEO staff generally were not, at least in the field, restrictive. The Assistant Director could be cross-examined, challenged, and criticized without fear of punishment. The participants felt they could assert themselves, but were not yet sure about what.

The participants began to sense the potential of "maximum feasible participation" and to consider that the program, as idealized to them, could not exist without their co-operation.

The climate of invitation, freedom, and status equality stimulated participants to go beyond just questioning and to make statements of opinion about the feasibility of the national OEO and TOEO philosophy, structure, and potential programs. Members took the floor and openly discussed and debated their opinions among themselves. The Assistant Director still chaired the meeting, but was far less the center of activity.

The poverty-program focus on the amelioration of social ills cued a few members to introduce personal or "I know a case" stories of suffering in poverty. Other members, often the majority of those present, added stories of their own, all of which were met with overt commiseration and empathy by the rest of the group.

The suffering relived in the stories generally was concerned with hunger, unemployment, housing, health, children, discrimination, and powerlessness. Blame began to be affixed for the suffering, first to a vague and disembodied "them" or "the system," then somewhat more specifically to people with money and various community agencies or local government offices. The blame fanned into anger, and the anger spiraled with raised voices, hearty agreement, and in some cases choruses of "Amen!"

The members excitedly gave examples of times when they had "beat the system" or by their efforts had turned a degrading situation into one-upsmanship. Many of the examples seemed to be "as if" or wish-fulfilling in nature, but nonetheless were rewarded by the group with laughter and enthusiasm.

Although the Assistant Director suggested various opportunities among the OEO programs for the amelioration of the members' expressed sufferings, the high-pitched emotion of the group was maintained for its own sake, and the members continued the cathartic process. Occasionally the liberated anger was turned upon the Assistant Director and the Topeka Office of Economic Opportunity. The Assistant Director, however, by his absence of defensiveness, prevented either himself or the TOEO from becoming the sole cathartic focus. The participants began to differentiate between the TOEO and a general "agency" stereotype.

During the cathartic process, the members developed an "us" *versus* "them" feeling, which fostered rudimentary group cohesion and identity. The potential indigenous leaders became apparent. Members still had doubts about the efficacy of the Topeka Office of Economic Opportunity, but their enthusiasm for participation increased, stimulated and reinforced by cathartic gratification and the opportunity to express themselves. The members did not yet have a clear understanding of what they might change, or of stratagems and tactics for change.

If during the Catharsis stage (II), the staff member argumentatively identified with the community agencies under attack, became personally defensive or self-righteous (e.g., accused the group of "ingratitude"), or in some other way made himself and the poverty program the focus of hostility, the TNC very likely would lock in the Catharsis stage and begin digesting itself in its own juices. For example, one of the TNCs almost foundered when the TOEO Director, who was quite adept at dealing with agency and city officials, became adamant and defensive while a speaker during a TNC's Catharsis stage. Consequently, he was grilled, chided, and systematically "put on" by virtually the entire membership, then flatly informed never to return to their meetings. Only the earlier personalistic ground work and emergency follow-up by the Assistant Director forestalled that TNC's immediate disbanding (a detailed description of this event is presented in Chapter 13). The TOEO staff members (or the staff members of other poverty-intervention organizations) would have been more ready and able to absorb their share of TNC cathartic fall-out had they realized that angry exhortations often are the beginnings of self-expression and group cohesion.

When the TOEO staff gained that perspective, it was able to continue urging the channeling of aggressive energy toward more constructive usage.

III. *Focus Stage*:

During this stage of TNC development, the Assistant Director urged the election of officers, and chaired the nominating and election processes. The TNC chairman, vice-chairman, and secretary—the Target Neighborhood Officers—were elected. The chairman would take over the proceedings, but leaned heavily upon the Assistant Director for program information, agenda, and help in conducting the meeting. The elected officers generally were those who had been most outspoken during the Orientation and Catharsis stages, or who were already informal leaders in the Neighborhood. The Assistant Director avoided retaking the chairman role, and attempted to reinforce the autonomy of the indigenous leaders.

At the chairman's request, the Assistant Director supplied detailed information concerning available OEO programs (e.g., day-care centers, adult basic education, Neighborhood Houses, manpower training, Head Start, housing rehabilitation, small-business loans, etc.). The Assistant Director suggested that the group conduct a survey of Neighborhood needs, and instructed the members on survey techniques.

A Neighborhood survey was supervised by the TNC chairman, and was conducted by the members. With the help of the Assistant Director, the results of the survey were tied in with specific potential OEO programs. The survey-taking itself stimulated the members' interest and heightened their awareness of Neighborhood problems. They were surprised that so many others were "in the same boat," and they began to see themselves as "representatives" of the poor.

The group discussion of needs and alternative solutions would begin to taper to consensus on one need. The appropriate OEO program was explored and debated.

Some of the officers met with TNOs of other Target Neighborhood Committees and discussed problems, needs, and programs. The group boundaries and points of interaction became clear, and the TNC began to perceive itself as the "X Neighborhood Committee" (X usually was a geographical location, or the name of a neighborhood). The Target Neighborhood Committee chairman and vice-chairman attended meetings of the Economic Opportunity Board, Executive Committee, and TOEO Leadership Training Sessions as voting members, and reported their proceedings to their own memberships. TNC members felt they were represented in, and part of, the larger poverty-intervention organization. Group cohesion grew, and attendance increased sharply.

Although interest was growing toward a specific community-action proposal, there was still little awareness of the complications or delays involved in its formulation and implementation.

The TNC chairman learned basic parliamentary procedure and struggled to inaugurate it. The secretary began to take minutes. The members learned to ask recognition from the chair before speaking. The meeting moved toward increased formality, though spontaneity and freedom of expression continued.

The most significant aspects of the Focus stage (III) were the election of an indigenous leader to the position of TNC chairman and, through him, the merging of a member-specified Neighborhood need with a member-specified OEO potential solution. The TOEO staff member had the delicate task of helping to focus needs and alternative OEO programs without usurping the rightful role of the fledgling chairman. The staff member was apt to advocate his pet project for what he perceived to be the outstanding Neighborhood problem. Although his overt directing sometimes resulted in a more quickly enacted Focus stage (III) and even precipitated the Action stage (IV), the members then missed the process experience, and the TNC did not advance beyond the Limbo stage (V).

The evolution of member consensus on needs and solutions further solidified the group, prevented entrenched, circular, and Catharsis-returning (II) debate, and could be properly stimulated and achieved by the chairman with the active participation and considered support of his TNC membership.

To encourage the emergence and subsequent TNC election of indigenous leaders, and then not to provide them an adequate leadership-training program, seriously could impair the efficacy of a TNC. The Target Neighborhood Officer's job, particularly the chairman's, was complicated, often controversial, and always time- and energy-consuming. He had to be able not only to understand, but to lead members through, the varieties of individual and group behavior reflected in the seven distinct stages of TNC development. He had to be a recruiter and orienter of new members, a catalyst for, and absorber of, catharsis, a focuser of needs and programs, a taskmaster and implementer of community-action proposals, an innovator of techniques for maintaining group cohesion during a production drought, a protector of member control in TNC-sponsored programs, and a philosopher-statesman in the community-aligned, future-oriented, autonomous TNC. The Target Neighborhood Officer had to publicize, prepare the agenda for, conduct, and record TNC meetings. He represented his TNC and Neighborhood to the TOEO staff and to agency and local government officials in various meetings of the Board, Executive Committee, Study Committee, and civic association. Conversely, he represented the TOEO, the poverty program, and the "not-poor" world to the residents in his Target Neighborhood. The TNO had to meet all those responsibilities in his "spare" time, as a volunteer without pay, and in the midst of almost continual role and value conflicts between his followers and the TOEO. He had to be a bridge between the "haves" and "have nots," and an agent for social change—neither role of which was easy to enact successfully or possible to enact painlessly.

In an attempt to help indigenous leaders, the TOEO inaugurated weekly "Leadership Training Sessions" for TNOs. The first few sessions were presentations by TOEO-arranged speakers—mostly agency officials discoursing on services available in Topeka. The remaining "training sessions," as a result of the TOEO's dedication to "firm up" organizational structure and to co-ordinate program planning, became little more than business meetings preliminary to Economic Opportunity Board functions. The TNOs thus had available no systematic training for such vital functions as Neighborhood organizing, conducting meetings, leadership, the delegation of authority, strategies and tactics for poverty amelioration, or dynamics of social change. What skills they employed in the TNCs they either brought with them from experiences prior to the TOEO, or learned on their own by watching the professional staff or other not-poor participants in action. The lack of TOEO commitment (during the period of this study) to training for TNOs was probably in large part responsible for the fact that only one TNC managed to reach the Purposive stage of development (VII)—and that only by fierce determination and the leadership of an exceptionally sensitive and dedicated chairman (see Chapter 14). The absence of adequate training made the difficult job of TNO much more difficult, and in some cases impossible, for the incumbent. TNCs naturally were influenced by the abilities, knowledge, and frustrations of their leaders.

IV. *The Action Stage*:

During the Action stage the TNC decided by vote upon a specific community-action proposal and requested more detailed information and application procedures (this often was the first major vote, besides the election, conducted by the TNC). The Assistant Director provided the requested information. The members began to obtain "services-in-kind" in the form of volunteered services pledged, materials or housing donated, etc. In some cases, a single community organization contributed the entire local share and became a "delegate agency." Target Neighborhood Committee members collected and assembled evidence of the need for, and support of, the proposed program from Target Neighborhood residents, relevant professionals, and agency officials. This evidence was included in the final proposal to the national or regional Office of Economic Opportunity.

TNC meetings sometimes were held more often than regularly scheduled. Subcommittees were appointed by the chairman to accommodate the gathering of proposal data. The members participated in Study Committee meetings, particularly those pertinent to the Target Neighborhood Committee's chosen proposal. The members sought advice from Study Committee members who were professionals in the areas concerned with the proposal. In the case of some proposals (such as a Neighborhood House, a Day Care Center), a special Advisory Council (approximately twelve members) was required by the TOEO. Target Neighborhood Committee members would compose about half of the Advisory Council membership, and interacted with citizen-at-large members (who often had provided major portions of the local share) concerning program details.

The TNC members spent many hours gathering proposal data. The meetings manifested a marked degree of excitement, enthusiasm, and euphoria. The members became caught up in the momentum of activity, and felt *"we"* are really *doing* something *now.* The TOEO staff continued to reinforce the Target Neighborhood Committee members' involvement, and repeatedly iterated the *"your* program" dictum. The attendance at meetings continued to increase.

The Target Neighborhood Committee's group cohesion was strong. The committee had worked up "a full head of steam" toward what was perceived to be a concrete goal. The members became more curious about accomplishments of other TNCs, and good-natured feelings of competition among TNCs emerged.

Some sense of the power of participation was gained by TNC members during the process of preparing the proposal. The members' interaction with professionals and agency officials began to develop a concept that community organizations are for everyone, that they are "usable" commodities, and they are not to be feared. The members' stereotypes of the "haves" were challenged through experience with them as fallible, approachable, and in most cases, reasonable. The Target Neighborhood Officers and the members of TNCs became more involved with other community activities and further defined the potential of their participative roles.

The Target Neighborhood Committee chairman became more comfortable with his leadership role. The Assistant Director still was an active participant, but in the role of called-upon consultant. Parliamentary procedure became more formal during this stage, though it still was by no means restrictive. The chairman began to delegate authority. More detailed minutes were taken by the secretary. As additional members participated, the TNC chairman met the first challenges to his authority. A loyal opposition developed, and "floor" leaders were occasionally apparent.

The TNC turned the proposal material they had developed over to the TOEO for preparation of a formal grant application. The TOEO staff returned the application, after it had been appropriately drawn up, to the TNC for its approval. After TNC approval, the application went to the Application Review Committee, the Exec-

utive Committee, and the Economic Opportunity Board for discussion and approval. Target Neighborhood Committee members
became impatient with the delays for review, and became angry
if opposition to the proposal was expressed by any of the review-
ers. After the community-action proposal had been cleared
through the local review machinery, it was, with great ceremony,
sent to the national or regional Office of Economic Opportunity.
The TNC members felt a sense of accomplishment, but eagerly
and impatiently awaited the results of their request.

During the Action stage (IV), a TNC would actively gather
Neighborhood data and resources for a chosen OEO proposal, and
would turn to the TOEO for expert advice. Affected by its enthusiasm
to get the proposal funded and on record, the TOEO sometimes was
predisposed to interpret TNC requests for consultation as waivers
of self-government or pleas for external management. But by that
stage the TNC members usually would have identified with the
proposal, felt a sense of control of it, and saw it as evidence for the
meaningfulness of their participation. TNC cohesion had crystal-
lized around the proposal, and the officers had invested their leadership reputations in its development and outcome. The proposal at
this point was more than X dollars or X services; it was, in itself, a
complex social process, easily disrupted by undue external intervention.

The local share of funding for a community-action proposal was
acquired during Stage IV. Misunderstandings between the TOEO and
delegate agencies or service-in-kind donators about the participation
of the poor sometimes relegated the TNC to a secondary or token
position in control of, and influence concerning, the proposal. It was
a mistake to assume that the not-poor, even though they were sym-
pathetic and co-operative, understood immediately the dynamics or
importance of process experience for participating poor.

The feeling of having submitted "our" proposal helped to sustain
the TNCs through the long wait for feedback, and encouraged TNC
evolution toward the Purposive stage of development (VII). Even
if the proposal was *not funded*, the accumulated process experience

and sense of control could stimulate TNCs to "profit from our mistakes" and "not miss next time." On the other hand, Catharsis (II)
and eventual group disintegration resulted if a TNC could not claim
the Action stage (IV) as its own—even if the proposal *was funded.*

V. *The Limbo Stage*:

The Topeka Office of Economic Opportunity expected a Target
Neighborhood Committee to continue regularly scheduled meetings during the time its community-action proposal was under
federal review (it would be at least several months before members knew the decision on their application). TNC members had
traversed Orientation, Catharsis, Focus, and Action stages, and
had built individual enthusiasm and group cohesion which culmi-
nated in a completed proposal. They had placed a moratorium on
skepticism, hazarded participation, and gambled faith in the TOEO
in the belief that *their* program could produce *results.* Members
were neither tolerant of, nor prepared for, long delays in feedback
concerning their efforts. An enthusiastic reliving of the preparation
experiences maintained the TNC "head of steam," but only briefly.

The TNC was encouraged by TOEO staff to develop a second
community-action proposal, but the TNC was hesitant until they
had a decision concerning the first. The members manifested the
need to reassure the credibility of the OEO. As time lengthened
from the date of application, their optimism faltered, and skepticism returned. Impatience was fed by rumors of legal, administrative, or fiscal problems in Washington or regional OEO head-
quarters. "I told you so" became a commonplace comment. The
members felt powerless about the fate of a proposal over which
they had assumed control, and in which they had invested themselves. Doubts grew about this really being *"our* program."

The frustration of the delay engendered some recurrence of the
modal behaviors seen in Stage II (Catharsis). The TOEO Assistant
Director, who had been reporting to the TNC on the progress of
the proposal's review, was at times blamed for not expediting the
proposal (though it was the Director who was the recipient of
most of the blame attributed to the TOEO staff). Other TNCs were
envied competitively if their proposals had been approved first.
Some non-TNO Economic Opportunity Board members and agen-

cy officials who explained or defended the slowly moving bureaucratic review machinery, and counseled patience, were recast by
TNC members according to the old stereotype.

The Target Neighborhood Committee chairman caught some
blame for, or frustration from, the delay, particularly if his explanations were perceived by the members to be a defense of "those
guys who're holding up our proposal." TNC attendance fell off.
Some TNC chairmen continued to hold meetings, not caring about
the attendance. Some canceled their meetings until feedback was
forthcoming. Others initiated or implemented expedients for at
least temporarily maintaining group cohesion. The following expedients were observed among the Target Neighborhood Committees:

1) The TOEO offered a series of invited speakers to address the
   TNC. The speakers usually were from community agencies
   dealing with social problems (e.g., Urban Renewal, Welfare, Employment, Public Health, Public Housing). Bringing agency officials onto TNC ground tended to increase the
   members' confidence in interacting with agencies. The presence of the agency officials often served to provide the
   group with a temporary "enemy" for additional catharsis, or
   to displace frustration due to the proposal delay. TNC group
   cohesion was stimulated by a juxtaposition of "us," the members, and "him," the speaker.

2) A few Target Neighborhood Officers placed emphasis on the
   social functions within the TNC. During the meetings, OEO
   business would be brief and secondary. The attendance at-
   traction was "socializing." For example, a seamstress or
   hat-making member would show her work and demonstrate
   techniques. A covered-dish supper might be held, or the
   members might share an ice-cream social. Some Target
   Neighborhood Committees gave large Halloween, Thanks-
   giving, or Easter parties for children, or sponsored such
   attractions as teen-age dances and wiener roasts.

3) To maintain group cohesion, a Target Neighborhood Committee chairman might place emphasis upon the ritual of
   formal organization within his committee. He would develop
   a sharp and sophisticated parliamentary procedure for the

meetings, and the group would enjoy the meeting as an educational game. Under those circumstances, the chairman would establish a plethora of subcommittees, and member delegates were sent to every Study Committee meeting. Most of the following TNC meetings would then be taken up by systematic reports from members who had attended the meetings of other committees. The Target Neighborhood Committee structure was supported for its own sake, and in turn maintained group cohesion.

4) A Target Neighborhood Committee might suggest a series of joint meetings with other TNCs, generally related to social functions. Group cohesion within the host TNC was stimulated by contrast and interaction with other Target Neighborhood Committees' members.

5) A Target Neighborhood Committee might launch a major proselyting campaign. The group looked inward, and raised questions about its own effectiveness and power in light of the proposal delay, and decided that more members meant more leverage. Recruitment was difficult, however, because of the feedback problem on the proposal. Those new members who were recruited stimulated some previous Stage I (Orientation) behavior, and provided group cohesion for older members, who had the opportunity to educate the initiates about the national and local poverty programs, and the place of the TNC in the over-all structure.

6) In a few cases, a TNC would follow the advice of the TOEO staff about formulating a second proposal. In this case, however, when the TNC was impatiently waiting for approval of its first proposal, no single new proposal ever got beyond general discussion. During the general discussion, another new proposal would be introduced. In effect, the TNC flooded itself with incipient proposals, and it was the variety and resulting discussion that helped to maintain group cohesion.

If the Limbo stage (V) was too protracted—if information concerning the proposal under review was too long forthcoming—the TNC chairman would find himself powerless to maintain group cohesion. In such case, the TOEO Assistant Director would be

254 Poverty Warriors

forced to take over the chairman role, because of the retreat or
resignation of the duly elected chairman. TNC members would
revert to their initial passivity, and attendance withered.

The significance and extent of the Limbo stage (V) revealed a
major organizational problem in the TOEO, which perhaps parallels
similar problems in other poverty-intervention organizations—the
delay in feedback to the poor concerning the efficacy of their participation.

The TOEO concentrated almost totally on the generating of community-action proposals fundable under the provisions of the Economic Opportunity Act. The Act provided an important source of
money and ideas for the TNC and, as discussed above, feelings of
responsibility for a proposal could be a beneficial process experience
for the low-income participants. However, the time span between
application and decision became crucial when TNC cohesion, member interest, and leadership effectiveness were riding with the
proposal.

Direct action for locally solvable problems was one strategem for
acquiring quick and visible knowledge of results. The TOEO was,
particularly during its formative year, unwilling to support TNC
moves toward *direct* action. It was committed to a marginal position between the poor and the not-poor, and wanted to make certain
that "everyone stayed on board." Potential TNC direct action usually meant demands for improved street lighting, police patrolling,
bus service, recreation facilities, garbage collections, etc. in the
Neighborhood—a tactic which might have indicated dissatisfaction
with, or protest to, city and agency officials. The TOEO Director expressed concern that those officials might withdraw from participation on the Economic Opportunity Board, or that local share might
become more difficult to obtain if he supported the TNCs' endeavors toward direct action. Consequently, the TOEO encouraged only
TNC action that centered around OEO proposals. The disruptive effects of the prolonged length of Limbo (V) for the TNCs were in
large part by-products, therefore, of the TOEO's forcing all TNC
social-process eggs into the formal-proposal basket.

The impact of delayed *versus* prompt knowledge of results was dramatized when the members of one TNC learned at one of their meetings that the community-action proposal they helped sponsor nine months before had finally been approved. They reacted impassively to the news. During the same meeting the TNC chairman announced that a mailbox had been placed in a requested location in their Neighborhood. The members applauded wildly, patted each other and the chairman on the back, and literally exploded their enthusiasm. They independently and directly had approached the Post Office for the mailbox less than one week earlier. Group solidarity, member satisfaction, and leader effectiveness were stimulated more that night by the quickly acquired mailbox than by the long-delayed sixty-thousand-dollar community-action proposal.

Community-action proposals were important and ultimately were rewarding to TNC members. But the TOEO, or any similar poverty-intervention organization, in order to be creative, needs also to help committees with other not necessarily OEO or program-specific activities which could yield immediate and concrete results and reinforcement.

VI. *The Testing Stage:*

During the Testing stage the community-action proposal was returned to the Topeka Office of Economic Opportunity and word was passed to the TNC chairman, who formally announced the proposal funding at the next TNC meeting. The participants, including the Target Neighborhood Officers, seemed less than enthusiastic about the approval. Some of the members commented, "It's about time!" Others inquired, "So? What now?" The chairman was asked to review what the proposal was "all about."

The TNC members struggled to again identify with the proposal which they hadn't seen or controlled for some months, and which had been "out of our hands" under review by federal, regional, state, and local officials, some of whom had altered the proposal to fit policy, fiscal, or statute requirements.

Implementation of the program funded by the approved proposal began, led by the TOEO, the Advisory Council for the program, or perhaps a delegate agency. The availability of funds

attracted other groups or organizations that now wished to participate in the program implementation, but had not been involved in
the proposal preparation.

The Target Neighborhood Committee members rekindled and
asserted TOEO's "This is *your* program" exhortations. They tested
the validity of "participation," and evaluated and examined the
reality of their opportunity for power and control.

The Target Neighborhood Officers and members attempted to
intensify their participation in decisions concerning implementing
the program, formulating operating policies, and hiring personnel.
Some conflicts arose between Target Neighborhood Committee
members and not-poor poverty-program participants, ostensibly
over various procedural issues. But the basis of their conflict actually was concerned with the distribution of program control. Target Neighborhood Committee members were asking, "How much
of this program is really *ours?*" "Will we continue to be influential
now that the money's here, or have we been used to do the leg
work, and are now going to be pushed into a corner and expected
to be quiet again?" This was a period of testing the viability of
new and tentatively enacted roles, the assertions of the TOEO, and
the trustworthiness of the community.

Group cohesion was tentatively sustained by the testing task.
The chairman's potency for accomplishment was under observation
by the members. The Assistant Director served primarily as liaison
among program participants while the Director supervised program implementation.

During the Testing stage (VI) the TNC members sought to validate the worth of their efforts, and the degree of their control of,
or influence in, a funded community-action proposal about to be
implemented. The TOEO again at times was inclined to "hurry" implementation at the expense of TNC member involvement. The TOEO
also again was in a position to re-emphasize the importance of the
poor's continuing participation, this time to the "local share" donators or the delegate agency—whose main concern was to bring their
own expertise to bear and get the money working. The Testing stage
indicated the TNC's tenacity, and also revealed the degree of sin-
cerity and understanding of the not-poor poverty-program partici-

pants. At the onset of the program, participation of TNC members was clearly needed in order to make a case for federal antipoverty funding. Once the proposal had been funded, however, TNC members sometimes inadvertently were considered less "useful," were limited only to token representation, and the TNC was forced to revert to earlier developmental stages—most likely to Catharsis (II). If the TNC was already strong enough it could recover from such a setback, but with much difficulty.

VII. *The Purposive Stage*:

During the Purposive stage, the Target Neighborhood Committee members' own efforts yielded satisfactory feedback, and they felt a sense of meaningful participation. The TOEO's "*your* program" assurances were seen to be dramatized and overstated, but the members had evolved a realistic view of their potential for power and accomplishment in a co-operative community program. The TOEO and other community organizations were seen as having utility for Neighborhood and self-improvement. The TNC members were not consumed by the importance of status *within* the TOEO structure, but were insistent only that services of the TOEO be available when needed and wanted.

The Assistant Director was *invited* to meetings, but was only a passive consultant. The Target Neighborhood Officers tended to obtain and read OEO announcements and regulations themselves, rather than to depend upon TOEO staff interpretations. With the help of the membership, the chairman set up his own TNC agenda, and freely deviated from the regular meeting schedule when necessary. Parliamentary procedure was functional, not ritual, did not squelch spontaneity, and was clearly secondary to the more important tasks of the meetings. Attendance was steady, and included teens and elder citizens. There was no compulsion to proselyte, but many contacts with Neighborhood residents were made by members as a result of program development.

The chairman was comfortable conducting the meetings, which were emotionally low-keyed, relaxed, and laced with humor. The group developed a working philosophy (e.g., "to develop ourselves and our Neighborhood, and to become part of the community"). TNC members, particularly officers, fully understood the psychological importance of the process experience of participation for the poor. The members participated in meetings fully and freely, with no fear of being "put down." The members were content with the chairman, and the loyal opposition functioned constructively. The chairman was not defensive, encouraged debate on issues, encouraged volunteers for functional subcommittees in order to widen participation, and maintained participative democracy in all decision-making. All relevant issues were put to a vote.

The TNC members manifested flexibility in adaptations to alternatives for meeting Neighborhood needs. They were more tolerant of delays. They were able to accept defeat, profit by it, and to philosophize, "Win some, lose some—but don't make the same mistake twice." The group decided upon programs and activities which had *attainable* goals, and in which they would have continuing participation and a share of control. The group occasionally reverted to modal behaviors of earlier developmental stages, but those reversions were accepted and understood in the perspective of group philosophy, purpose, cohesion, and identity.

The individual member tended to perceive himself to be an integral part of the TNC, but also to be an integral part of the Neighborhood and, to a growing degree, of the community. He tended to feel, "For the first time, I'm in the mainstream of community life." TNC members and officers participated as board members, delegates, etc. in civic organizations other than the TOEO. They felt more at ease in approaching city officials when necessary, and were quite able to argue cases or present requests effectively. They used voting, boycott, or public-protest sanctions if necessary. The TNC demonstrated its ability to get city action (e.g., street repairs, lighting, zoning) which benefited the entire Neighborhood.

The Target Neighborhood Committee established and maintained autonomy from the TOEO. It was not dependent on the TOEO for action, and independently inaugurated activities and programs that were not OEO-specified community-action proposals. The members felt that the TNC was an entity in itself. There was no antagonism toward the TOEO, but the members thought that the Neighborhood was their first concern, and the TOEO was considered one of several useful alternatives for Neighborhood and individual development. There was some conflict between the members and the TOEO Director about their "straying from the fold," but the TNC prevailed and co-operative interaction emerged.

By the time a Target Neighborhood Committee reached the Purposive stage of development (VII), the members viewed the TOEO as secondary to its own Neighborhood group and as a major source —among *other* sources—of funding, services, and consultation. The process experience of participation had worked as hypothesized, but the TOEO staff sometimes became concerned with the result. During their labors to develop and maintain the organization itself, members of the staff, in the midst of tremendous pressures to produce proposals, sometimes were inclined to forget that it was to be hoped that meaningful participation of the poor logically would result in TNC autonomy and the self-direction of its members. The staff occasionally perceived the growth of self-reliance to be "straying from the fold" and to be threatening to organizational integrity. More disastrously, in a few instances, the TOEO staff inadvertently challenged the autonomy of a TNC by limiting the dissemination of new program information to those TNCs which, still in earlier stages of development, were more dependent upon the TOEO. Whenever they had time to think about such matters, staff members avoided such hazards by reminding themselves that the TOEO was not intended to be an end in itself, and that its structure and function should be kept flexible and changeable so that it could accommodate the social and personal changes it purported to stimulate.

When Purposive (VII) autonomy for the TNC did not have a chance to develop, Catharsis (II) autonomy often resulted. The former was goal-oriented, nondefensive, flexible, predominantly rational, and co-operative. The latter was goal-less, hostile, rigid, predominantly emotional, and alienative. A brief discussion of two contrasting TNC cases and their interaction with the TOEO may clarify those differences in autonomy.

The only TNC to have reached the Purposive stage of development (VII) during this study had been deeply, vitally, and possessively involved with a community-action proposal subsequently funded by OEO and, to the chagrin of the TNC, virtually taken over by a delegate agency. The TNC was plunged into Catharsis (II), berating the delegate agency, the national poverty-program, and the TOEO. However, the process experience of developing the proposal had strengthened group cohesion, indigenous leadership, and member self-confidence sufficiently that the TNC was able to harness its anger, retool itself, and determinedly progress again through the Focus (III) and Action (IV) stages—with a new proposal. The second time, though, TNC members were aware of potential pitfalls. They chose to apply for a Neighborhood House, which would be established literally in their own backyards. The TNOs and members selected their own source of local financial support, and picked their own Advisory Council.

The proposal was submitted and the TNC was guided through Limbo (V) by the chairman, who meticulously followed and reported to his members every detail of their proposal's review. About two months later the proposal was approved, and the chairman quickly and resolutely assumed leadership in its implementation. He requested help from the TOEO staff, but firmly established that its role was to be consultative. The chairman, TNC members, and the Advisory Council named the Neighborhood House staff.

In the ensuing months, the TNC and the Neighborhood House staff as a team initiated direct action for Neighborhood improvements, sought program funding from other than OEO sources, and took public stands on issues concerning community social problems.[1] The Purposive stage (VII) TNC retained its view of the TOEO as a friendly and useful colleague that could, like TNC members, learn from mistakes.

By contrast, Catharsis (II) autonomy became apparent in a TNC that previously had never become involved with programs or activities which the members felt were theirs. The TOEO Director lived in that Neighborhood, and either he or a social-worker trainee attached to his office attended all the TNC's meetings. The incumbent chair-

---

[1] For further description of the evolution of the Neighborhood House, see Chapter 14, and Louis A. Zurcher, Jr., and Alvin E. Green, with Edward Johnson and Samuel Patton, *From Dependency to Dignity: Individual and Social Consequences of a Neighborhood House.*

man's election had been openly supported by the TOEO, and he was functionally secondary to the Director and the social worker in organizing and chairing the meetings. The Director and the social worker flooded the necessarily passive members with ideas for programs, but none of them seemed to "take hold" in the group. As time and inactivity went on, some of the members became dissatisfied with the chairman and with the fact that "we don't get a chance to run our own meetings." Two TNC members became outspokenly antagonistic toward the Director, the social worker, and the chairman. The regularly scheduled TNC annual election was due, and one of the outspoken members declared himself a candidate for chairman, running "against the power structure of the TOEO" and "for the Neighborhood people." After a hard campaign by both candidates, the incumbent was narrowly defeated by the "protest" candidate. The research observers covering the election noted that "the people who declared they were going to vote for the challenger all seemed *angry*, and often made statements such as 'Now we'll get them' or 'This will show them.'"

The new chairman immediately heightened his verbal attack upon, and declared TNC independence from, the TOEO. He boycotted other TOEO-organized or -sanctioned meetings, and held his own TNC meetings with little communication before or after with the TOEO.

The striking characteristic of the Catharsis (II) autonomy was that it did not in fact generate any Neighborhood action or mobilize the TNC. For a time the members reveled in creating new epithets with which to label the TOEO and its Director. Then, gradually, the group fell into factionalism, and members began arguing among themselves about "where we're going." The result was a quasi-revolutionary special election in which the "protest" chairman was ousted from office and replaced by a newly emerged indigenous leader, who wanted to see "less complaining and more action around here." That new chairman began to attend other poverty-program meetings, re-established diplomatic relations with the TOEO, and, before the completion of this study, had led the TNC up to the Limbo stage (V). Thus the TOEO through organizational inexperience lost a TNC to Catharsis (II) autonomy, but later regained its alliance. Other poverty-intervention organizations that underestimate the importance and advantage of maintaining the kind of TNC freedom which yields Purposive autonomy may be less fortunate.

SUMMARY

Based upon the research staff's systematic observations of modal individual and group behaviors in 174 meetings of twelve Target Neighborhood Committees over a period of nineteen months, seven possible TNC sequential stages of development were identified and labeled. The stages were: (I) Orientation, (II) Catharsis, (III) Focus, (IV) Action, (V) Limbo, (VI) Testing, and (VII) Purposive. The times spent in any stage by any given committee at any given meeting varied extensively and situationally among the TNCs, and therefore no universal time schedule is suggested. The role of the policies and practices of the poverty-intervention organization was seen to stimulate, arrest, or reverse TNC evolution through the stages of development.

None of the observations recorded during the course of the study called for conceptualization of a stage of development beyond the Purposive stage (VII). It is possible, however, that over time a Purposive stage group might on its own, or by linkage with another social structure (e.g., a Neighborhood House), evolve to an Institutionalized stage of development (VIII). One might speculate that the major characteristic of institutionalization would be the emergence and interaction, within the group itself, of subgroups which themselves might sequentially manifest the modal behaviors attributed to the other stages as outlined.

The developing TNC is a fragile social group, easily diverted from its course toward the amelioration of poverty. The poverty-intervention organization with which it is associated can help sustain the committee in its progress through the stages of development by, for example: using a *personalistic* approach to potential participants; *realistically* explaining the purposes, possibilities, and limitations of OEO; making available a wide range and free choice of attainable goals; guaranteeing meaningful and *powerful* participation; providing an understandable and usable *training* program for indigenous officers; maintaining freedom for the development of committee *autonomy* and program *control*; and offering support for not only future-oriented OEO community-action proposals, but for *immediately reinforceable* direct-action Neighborhood endeavors. It is apparent that TNCs must be considered, in themselves, to be vital social processes.

SOME REFLECTIONS ON THEORY

I shall now digress briefly to discuss the seven conceptualized TNC stages of development as a possible contribution toward further understanding of development sequence in *natural* groups—an area with which, according to Tuckman's review of the literature, "few studies or theoretical statements have concerned themselves."[2]

Tuckman's classification model for developmental sequence in small groups divides fifty pertinent studies into three *setting* categories: Therapy Groups, Training Groups, and Natural or Laboratory Groups.[3] In Therapy Groups, "The task is to help individuals better deal with their personal problems. The goal is individual adjustment. . . . Each [member] has some debilitating personal problem." In Training Groups (T-Groups, Human Relations Training Groups), "The task is to help individuals interact with one another in a more productive, less defensive manner, and to be aware of the dynamics underlying such interaction. The goal is interpersonal sensitivity." In Natural Groups, "The group exists to perform some social or professional function over which the researcher has no control. Members are not brought together for self improvement; rather they come to do a job. Such groups may be characterized by appointed or emergent leadership." Laboratory Groups—combined with Natural Groups in the classificatory scheme—are "groups brought together for the purpose of studying group phenomena . . . have a short life . . . may not have leaders . . . are given a task or tasks which they are to complete."[4]

2 Bruce W. Tuckman, "Developmental Sequence in Small Groups," *Psychological Bulletin*, 63, 6 (1965), 384–399.
3 *Ibid.*, p. 385.
4 *Ibid.*, pp. 384–385.

As the reader can see from the presentation of the TNC stages of development, the TNCs do not fit precisely into any single *setting* category. Rather, the TNCs manifest task, behavioral, and member characteristics, some of which seem appropriate to Therapy Groups, some to Training Groups, and some to Natural Groups as defined and illustrated by Tuckman (Laboratory Groups are not comparable to TNCs and will not be further considered in this discussion).

Both Therapy Groups and TNCs have members with debilitating personal problems—TNC members' difficulty being mostly traceable to the environmental and interpersonal restrictions imposed by poverty, deprivation, and discrimination. Therapy Groups and TNCs also both assume the efficacy of social therapy and utilize it to ameliorate personal malaise. "Maximum feasible participation," "your program," and other stimuli for free expression and decision-making operationalized in the TNCs reflect the TOEO's expectation that, by meaningful involvement, the poor will boost their self-esteem and self-confidence, increase their ability to control significant aspects of the environment, and liberate frozen capacities and potentials. Several of the Therapy Groups studies reviewed by Tuckman report characteristics which parallel TNC dynamics, e.g.: initial situation defining;[5] tendency for dependency;[6] hesitant participation;[7] derogation and negativity;[8] crisis period of conflict;[9] working through hostility;[10] we-consciousness;[11] freedom and friendliness;[12] awareness

[5] G. R. Bach, *Intensive Group Psychotherapy*, pp. 268–295.

[6] W. R. Bion, *Experience in Groups*.

[7] R. J. Corsini, *Methods of Group Psychotherapy*, pp. 119–120.

[8] A. Stoute, "Implementation of Group Interpersonal Relationships Through Psychotherapy," *Journal of Psychology*, 30 (July, 1950), 145–146.

[9] S. Parker, "Leadership Patterns in a Psychiatric Ward," *Human Relations*, 11, 4 (November, 1958), 287–301.

[10] J. Mann, "Group Therapy with Adults," *American Journal of Orthopsychiatry*, 23, 2 (April, 1953), 332–337.

[11] J. Abrahams, "Group Psychotherapy: Implications for Direction and Supervision of Mentally Ill Patients," in Theresa Muller (ed.), *Mental Health in Nursing*, pp. 77–83.

[12] A. Wolf, "The Psychoanalysis of Groups," *American Journal of Psychotherapy*, 3, 4 (October, 1949), 525–528.

of the group as an organism;[13] group becoming an integrative-creative-social instrument.[14]

Training Groups and TNCs both purport to foster interpersonal sensitivity and stimulate individuals to interact more productively and less defensively. TNC participation is intended to provide the poor with an opportunity to experience like-situated others, to disrupt alienation, and to partake of co-operative membership in an increasingly cohesive social group. Some reports of Training Groups studies reveal processes which are similar to TNC dynamics, e.g.: learning how to learn about others;[15] discovery of self-other relationship;[16] learning how to give help;[17] gaining openness to experience;[18] consensual validation;[19] growth of group security and autonomy;[20] development of new group culture by generating norms and values peculiar to the group as an entity.[21]

Lastly, both Natural Groups and TNCs perform specific work tasks under appointed or emergent leadership. TNCs are charged with developing community-action proposals, and generate the emergence of indigenous leaders. Some dynamics described in the few Natural Groups studies parallel TNC dynamics, e.g.: deliberation to commit

---

[13] E. A. Martin and W. F. Hill, "Toward a Theory of Group Development: Six Phases of Therapy Group Development," *International Journal of Group Psychotherapy*, 7, 1 (January, 1957), 20–30.

[14] *Ibid.*

[15] L. P. Bradford, "Membership and the Learning Process," in L. P. Bradford, J. R. Gibb, and K. D. Benne (eds.), *T-group Theory and Laboratory Method*, pp. 190–215.

[16] Eléonore L. Herbert and E. L. Trist, "The Institution of an Absent Leader by a Students' Discussion Group," *Human Relations*, 6, 3 (August, 1953), 215–248.

[17] Bradford, "Membership and the Learning Process," pp. 190–215.

[18] L. P. Bradford, "Trainer-Intervention: Case Episodes," in Bradford, Gibb, and Benne (eds.), *T-group Theory and Laboratory Method*, pp. 136–137.

[19] Warren G. Bennis and H. A. Sheppard, "A Theory of Group Development," *Human Relations*, 9, 4 (November, 1956), 415–437.

[20] R. T. Golembiewski, *The Small Group*, pp. 193–200.

[21] R. M. Whitman, "Psychodynamic Principles Underlying T-group Processes," in Bradford, Gibb, and Benne (eds.), *T-group Theory and Laboratory Method*, pp. 310–335.

one's self to the group or not;[22] increasing expression of opinions;[23] positive interdependence among members;[24] group philosophy becomes pragmatic, task-oriented;[25] member control is established.[26]

In summary, Therapy Groups are primarily characterized by patterns of individual adjustment; Training Groups by processes of interpersonal sensitivity; and Natural Groups by individual and group orientations to task performance. By design and in practice, however, TNCs complexly manifest significant aspects from among *all* those patterns, processes, and orientations.

The paucity of studies concerning developmental sequence in Natural Groups forces Tuckman to present a rather restricted view of that *setting.* He suggests Presidential advisory councils and industrial groups to be representative examples of Natural Groups and concludes that "the stage of emotional response to task demand is not delineated [in Natural Groups studies], presumably due to the impersonal and nonthreatening nature of the task in these settings."[27] Clearly there are Natural Groups in which the task is neither impersonal nor nonthreatening, and where emotional response is a delineable and vital part of the group dynamics. Though cautiously offered as specific cases in need of cross-validation, the TNCs might be considered Natural Groups and the parameters of that *setting* expanded accordingly. Perhaps a more heuristic alternative would be to establish and support with research a new *setting:* "Action Groups" or "Social-Change Groups."

[22] W. C. Schultz, *FIRO: A Three Dimensional Theory of Interpersonal Behavior,* pp. 168–188.

[23] R. F. Bales and F. L. Stodtbeck, "Phases in Group Problem Solving," *Journal of Abnormal and Social Psychology,* 46 (October, 1951), 485–495.

[24] H. M. Schroder and O. J. Harvey, "Conceptual Organization and Group Structure," in O. J. Harvey (ed.), *Motivation and Social Interaction,* pp. 134–166.

[25] H. C. Modlin and Mildred Faris, "Group Adaptation and Integration in Psychiatric Team Practice," *Psychiatry,* 19, 1 (February, 1956), 97–103.

[26] R. F. Bales, "The Equilibrium Problem in Small Groups," in Talcott Parsons, R. F. Bales, and E. S. Shils, *Working Papers in the Theory of Action,* pp. 111–161.

[27] Tuckman, *Psychological Bulletin,* 63 (1965), 394.

Tuckman further refines his classificatory scheme by conceptually separating the developmental sequence within each group *setting* according to *realm*, either Interpersonal or Task, and adds that the distinction is a fuzzy one in Therapy and Training Groups "since the task is a personal and interpersonal one in that the groups exist to help the individuals deal with themselves and others."[28] For the same reasons, the interpersonal-task distinction is no less fuzzy in TNCs, and the situation is further complicated by the presence of a specific task—to formulate community-action proposals.

Within the *setting* and *realm*, Tuckman presents his hypothesized developmental sequence, summarized as "Forming," "Storming," "Norming," and "Performing."[29] Those four general stages can be seen in substance and sequence within the TNC stages of development. The seven TNC stages could perhaps have been parsimoniously reduced to four by combining Focus (III), Action (IV), Limbo (V), and Testing (VI). The reduction might have contributed to the generality of group stages beyond the poverty program, but would have made them less useful to the poverty practitioner.

I do not mean to imply a sweeping generality of the dynamics in the seven TNC stages of development to other Natural Groups. Rather, the plea is for comparative studies of similar groups and detailed investigations of the relation of developmental sequence to specific independent variables.

[28] *Ibid.*, 385.
[29] *Ibid.*, 396.

CHAPTER 13

"Walking the Tightrope": An Example

CHAPTER 11 DISCUSSED Target Neighborhood Officers, TOEO staff, and Target Neighborhood resident perceptions of indigenous leadership, and how variations in those perceptions engendered TNO stress. Chapter 12 outlined the stages of development of Target Neighborhood Committees, and the individual and group behaviors associated with and contributing to those stages. In order further to illustrate TNC dynamics and the process experiences of indigenous leadership, I now present a detailed case history of one TNC and its leader.

I shall concentrate on describing and analyzing the life history of a Target Neighborhood Committee that was able to reach only the Focus Stage (III), and eventually deactivated. Since the formation of indigenous leadership is of such crucial concern to the success and continuance of a TNC, and since most significant among the reasons for the subject TNC's deactivation was the problem of role conflict in indigenous leadership, the dynamics of such leadership are presented as they were associated with socialization processes within the group, the group's interaction with agency and TOEO officials, and the dynamics of "followership." This presentation highlights the differences in role expectations and value orientations between the members of the committee and the TOEO. Those differences and expectations worked toward fractionization of rapport between the poverty-intervention organization and the Target Neighborhood Committee, and put the indigenous leader into a position in which he strained to maintain that rapport at the expense of disapproval from both sides.

THE INDIAN NEIGHBORHOOD COMMITTEE

The case history is that of the Indian Neighborhood Committee, one of the twelve originally structured for the Topeka poverty program. The Indian Committee was intended to represent that ethnic group city-wide rather than in one specific Neighborhood. Earlier discussions with Indians who resided in Topeka indicated that their subcultural ties, and the pressures resulting from being an ethnic minority, summated to give them a feeling of groupness that transcended neighborhood boundaries. It was this feeling, and an awareness of the physical and social ills among them, that prompted the formation of the committee.

That all the members of the TNC were Indian-Americans could be viewed as disadvantageously limiting the generality of interpretations to be drawn in this chapter. On the other hand, the life situation of the Indian generally includes his having been treated as a United States Government welfare problem, his manifesting marked ambivalence toward authority figures and organizational representations, and his expecting a leader, as a "chief," to solve insolvable problems. Those factors establish a set of conditions which made the interaction between the committee members and the TOEO, the development of indigenous leadership, and the incidence of socialization and "followership" more clearly discernible within the Indian group than any of the other TNCs, all of which had fewer significant influences. In other words, some of the proc- esses which were manifested in a minor key by the other committees seemed to be manifested in a major key by the Indian Committee. Historical and contemporary subjugation, and styles of life to cope with it, seem to be common factors among the poor. Since the Indians have had many generations of experiencing and reacting to subjugation, their striking responses to the sudden opportunity for "maximum feasible participation" proved valuable for understanding the reactions of others who were thrust into the same situation.[1]

THE INDIANS OF TOPEKA

Approximately 300 Indians, most of them Prairie Potawatomi, live in clusters of families in five different sections of Topeka. Thirty miles north of Topeka, at Mayetta, Kansas, is the eleven-square-mile Prairie Potawatomi Reservation. According to a 1963 census, another 503 Indians reside on, or immediately around, the Reservation.[2] There is considerable interaction between the Topekans and the Mayettans—frequent relative and friend visitations, clubs and re- ligious memberships in common, and traditional gatherings and ceremonies. Evidence has been presented for a growing sense of community among the Prairie Potawatomi, partly as a result of in- creasing acculturative stress from interaction with the white com- munity.[3]

[1] An important series of anthropological field studies of the Prairie Potawa- tomi, conducted by the Department of Anthropology at the University of Kan- sas, yielded insight pertinent to cultural influences upon the members of the Indian Committee. Relevant data from those studies, particularly those concern- ing value orientations, bases for role expectations, and traditional forms of inter- actions with white organizations, are quoted and referenced throughout this chapter.
[2] James A. Clifton and Barry Isaac, "The Kansas Prairie Potawatomi: On the Nature of a Contemporary Indian Community," *Transactions* of the Kansas Academy of Science, 67, 1 (1964), 1–24.
[3] *Ibid.* and James A. Clifton, "Culture Change, Structural Stability and Fac- tionalism in the Prairie Potawatomi Reservation Community," *Midcontinent American Studies Journal*, 6, 2 (1965), 101–122.

Virtually all the male Indians who are employed are blue-collar workers or laborers. The employed female Indians work primarily in jobs that do not require special skills or training, with the exception of a few who are registered or practical nurses.

The majority of the Topeka Indians would qualify as "poor" (less than $3,000 annual income for a family of four). This generally low income level is due to a number of factors: lack of education which keeps them from getting jobs requiring advanced skills or training; job discrimination against Indians; and the seasonal or temporary nature of the jobs which are open to them. In a number of cases, the human needs of the Indians are critical—adequate nutrition, housing, and health facilities. In short, the Indians living in Topeka number among those for whom the programs of the "War on Poverty" were intended.

FIRST ENCOUNTERS WITH THE TOEO

In June, 1965, the Assistant Director of the TOEO, contacted, as a normal part of his task to organize Target Neighborhood Committees, several ministers who had Indians in their congregations. Of the ministers who were asked to make announcements from their pulpits concerning the TOEO, one in particular, the minister of the Methodist Indian Mission, seemed especially interested. He volunteered his church as a meeting place, and on an evening in July, 1965, eight Indians joined him to hear the Assistant Director explain "what the TOEO is all about." According to the Assistant Director, the Indians who attended were "suspicious, very skeptical that such a program could work, and really asked only a few questions that indicated they were interested at all." The Assistant Director "left it up to them whether they wanted to know any more about the TOEO, and about forming a committee of their own." The Indians agreed to meet again, in the same place, two weeks later to see whether or not the Assistant Director would "tell the same story a second time."

The second meeting was held on schedule, but was not chaired by the Assistant Director, since he had to attend an emergency meeting in another part of town. Instead, the meeting was conducted by the Director of the TOEO. Fifteen Indians attended this meeting, and the

Director reported a response from the group quite similar to that of the first meeting. He indicated that, typical of the Orientation Stage (I) of TNC development, the Indians were "pretty quiet, seemed rather skeptical that the program could do them any good, and seemed only mildly interested." Nevertheless, the Indians agreed to schedule a third meeting, to be held again in the same place and again two weeks later. (At this time, the other established TNCs were meeting on a twice-monthly basis.)

In the interval between the second and third meeting, the local press—primarily because of the influence of the Director of TOEO—became interested in "what the Indians were starting to do for themselves," and decided to send a reporter and a photographer to the forthcoming meeting of the Indian Committee.

Thirty-five Indians attended the third meeting, which was presided over by the Assistant Director. As indicated by the account in the press and the report of the Assistant Director, the Indians were far more outspoken at this meeting than they had been at the previous two. Several of the statements recorded pointed to a feeling among them that "we should do something for ourselves, because nobody else really cares about Indians." One of the participants commented, "We're getting to be like the white man—we don't take care of our own anymore." A number of questions were raised by those attending concerning the organizational structure of the TOEO, its goals, and what it might mean to the Indian. According to the Assistant Director, most of the questions still were "suspicious and skeptical. They wanted to know how much the Director and I were getting paid for running the TOEO. They wanted to know about the Director's politics, and whether or not this was just a political organization. They asked a lot of questions at this meeting, but almost all of them seemed to challenge us to prove that we weren't there just to take advantage of the Indians, but rather to offer them ways that they could help themselves through OEO programs." At this meeting, the Assistant Director suggested to the group, as he had during the first meeting, that they should think about electing a chairman, a vice-chairman, and a secretary, thus establishing themselves as a bona fide TNC. The Assistant Director commented that "they seemed hesitant to elect leaders, almost as if nobody wanted to take that responsibility. Some of them even commented, 'You'll never get an Indian to be a leader!' " Though the Indians were still not "sold on this program" they agreed to get together for a fourth meeting, to be held two weeks later.

It was now September, and the Indians had not yet established direction from indigenous leadership. The fourth meeting of the committee found the Assistant Director again unable to attend, and the Director substituting for him. Of this meeting, the Director reported:

". . . all hell broke loose. They aggressively questioned me about my politics, my motivations for running the Topeka program, and about the worth of their becoming involved in such a program. Everytime I'd answer a question, they'd sharpshoot another one at me. I was just getting my feet on the ground in the OEO program, so some of their questions I couldn't answer directly, but I told the group that I'd try and find out for them as soon as I could. They seemed to take great delight in catching me with questions for which I didn't have ready answers. In general, I got the feeling that they were less interested in finding out about the TOEO than they were in giving me a bad time!

When the Indians were obviously harassing me, they very pointedly continued to call me 'Sir.' Almost every one of the questions they asked me was anteceded by 'Sir,' as if they were using that exaggerated politeness as another way of being hostile. Many of them seemed to be having fun trying to get my goat, or trying to embarrass me. When one of them would succeed in coming up with some question—for example, about the way the Bureau of Indian Affairs' policies overlapped with OEO policies—he'd be rewarded by laughter and encouragement from his friends."

The fourth meeting ended with no indication of whether or not any other meeting would ever be held by the Indians concerning the TOEO. The Director said that he was "discouraged about that group," and wondered whether or not it would be best to forget about trying to help them organize into a committee. The Assistant Director decided to make a final attempt to get the Indians together, and arranged with some of them to hold a fifth meeting within the next two weeks. During the time between the fourth and fifth meetings, the Assistant Director contacted a number of the Indians to "find out what happened at the fourth meeting." He discovered that during the previous meeting, many of the participants saw the Director as an "agency official," and therefore determined that he was "no more than another Indian agent," and his program was no more than "another one of those Government handouts like they have on the Reservation. It's another one of those deals where we're always told what to do, and told what we'll get."

An interesting discovery made by the Assistant Director, and through my own subsequent interviews with the Indians participants, was the fact that several of the Indians who attended that meeting seemed actually to enjoy themselves. One of them declared, "I haven't had such a good time giving an official a bad time for as long as I can remember." Another commented, "Boy! We really had him going! I'll bet he knows what old Custer felt like!" The zest with which the Indians baited the Director during the fourth meeting, and the apparent enjoyment that many of them seemed to gain from being harassers, points to behavior associated with the Catharsis Stage (II) of TNC development and to an interesting phenomenon among the Indians that was best described by an Indian respondent in an unstructured interview. He commented, in referring to the fourth meeting and also to other experiences that he and several of his friends have had with agency officials, that "the Indian has a way of 'putting on' people who're big-shot agency representatives." The respondent then, with great glee, told a story:

"One time the Government gave us a bunch of old cows they had left over from somewhere. They told us that all we had to do was to give back to the Government the first calf that any of these old cows might have. They told us we were supposed to use the cows to improve our livestock. Well, about a week or so after the Government official had left the Reservation, we started killing off those cows, and had some of the biggest feasts you'll ever see in your whole lifetime. After a while, the Government official came back again, looked around, and said, 'Say, where have those cows gone?'

"We all put on our most innocent faces and told him, 'You know, sir, those cows up and got sick, and just seemed to die off.' The Government man then sat us down and began to tell us all about the diseases that could kill off cows, and the ways we could prevent those diseases. We still kept our innocent faces on, and asked him all kinds of questions about the diseases and about how we could save our cows in the future. Inside we were all busting our guts to keep from laughing! When the Government man left, we rolled around on the ground, laughing until tears came to our eyes! We tell that story over and over, and every time we tell it, we laugh almost as hard as we did when it happened. Even now, just telling it to you, I can't keep from laughing out loud."

In a discussion about the Indians' participation in OEO programs, the supervisor of an eight-state Indian poverty-intervention organization reported that he had observed, time and time again, the Indians' ability to "play games with people." He described the Indian as "having a way of engaging in verbal repartee, almost like role playing, with representatives of agencies." In response to a question about the dynamics underlying the "putting on" behavior, the supervisor, himself an Indian, said, "I'm certain that the interaction of the Indians with Government officials has led them to adopt such a façade, behind which they can offer to agency officials what they expect, and yet can maintain some control over the situation. It's a chance for them to take the lead, aggressively, in a situation with a power-authority figure, in a situation where they usually never have the opportunity to take the lead."[4]

The Assistant Director, with the co-operation of the Methodist minister, managed to get together eight Indians for the fifth meeting, held in the same place as the previous ones, the Methodist Indian

[4] See also Robert L. Bee, "Patterns of Acceptance and Integration of Development Programs in an American Indian Community: An Interim Analysis," University of Connecticut, 1968, mimeograph; David Wellman, "The Wrong Way to Get Jobs for Negroes," *Trans-Action*, 5, 5 (May, 1968), 9–18.

Mission. This meeting focused primarily on what had happened during the meeting two weeks earlier. The participants told the Assistant Director not to let the Director "ever come out to talk to us again," and they said that the Director "was more confused than we were, and he reminded us of the Indian agents that our fore-fathers had to put up with on the Reservation." They stated flatly, "We want nothing to do with him in the future." Thus the Indians soundly rejected someone whom they perceived to be "just another agency official." Yet, they did not reject the Assistant Director, who, objectively, was as much an agency official as was the Director. The difference seemed to be that to the Indians the Assistant Director, because of his working-man background and his belonging to a minority ethnic group, was "someone just like us." Furthermore, the Assistant Director, having served a long apprenticeship in union organizing, approached at the onset a number of Indians directly and established personal rapport with them. They had a chance to get to know him as a person, rather than as an agency official, before any formal meeting had been held. This basis for understanding between the Indians and the Assistant Director established him as a "regular guy." One of the Indians summed up their view of him, saying, "Well, once in awhile, he's got to wear a suit and tie and sit behind a desk in that OEO office, but he's not the kind of guy who's going to forget that he used to roll his sleeves up and get his hands dirty like the rest of us. He talks our language."

The Director, therefore, as perceived by the Indians, was from the beginning, stereotyped as an "agency official," who should, if possible, be "put on." Any chance that he might have had to negotiate successfully with the Indians, for the purpose of their establishing a TNC, was severely impeded by the expectations that they had for him as a "big wheel from the Government." On the other hand, the Assistant Director was able to take a more personal approach to the Indians; as one of them put it, "A Mexican-American has a lot of the same kind of problems as an Indian." Because of his more direct manner and simple language in dealing with them, the Indians seemed willing to go along with him and "take a closer look at this white man's 'War on Poverty.'"

By the conclusion of this fifth meeting, the few Indians who were attending agreed that "maybe we ought to get some officers pretty soon," and scheduled elections for a meeting to be held two weeks from that night. They further agreed among themselves to "get the word back out to the people who said they wouldn't come to any more of these meetings, and tell them it might be worth another try."

Reports of the first five meetings between the Indians and staff members of the TOEO revealed several consistent and interesting patterns of interaction. It seemed quite clear that members of the staff of the TOEO took very seriously the goals of the "War on Poverty," and earnestly were attempting to afford the Indians an opportunity, with no strings attached, for full participation in the decision-making, formulating, and implementing basic to the program. Yet they, particularly the Director, were met with an immobilizing admixture of skepticism, suspicion, passiveness, verbal aggression, and ridicule. Apparently, only their evolving perception of the Assistant Director as a "regular guy who might be trusted" encouraged some of them to remain passingly interested. The nature of these interactions provokes analysis.

It is not surprising that the Indians' initial reaction to the presentation by the TOEO was one of skepticism and suspiciousness. With good historical reasons, such attitudes toward Government organizations and the people who officiate them are endemic to Indians—and the Potawatomi are no exception. Those who were curious enough to come to the first few meetings found it very difficult to perceive the TOEO as being anything different from the Bureau of Indian Affairs or county welfare-agencies. Thus, at the onset, the Indians enacted the passive-aggressive role noted by other social scientists observing their behavior vis-à-vis agencies. Leon, for example, describes Indians' interactions with the Bureau of Indian Affairs as "passive compliance with what is expected and a tendency to sulk and be stubborn. Aggression is rarely expressed openly."[5] Spindler and

5 Robert L. Leon, "Maladaptive Interaction Between Bureau of Indian Affairs Staff and Indian Clients," *American Journal of Orthopsychiatry*, 35, 4 (July, 1965), 723–728.

Spindler,[6] and MacGregor[7] also discuss the passiveness manifested by Indians toward agency authority, a passiveness born of a series of defeats and the failure of physical aggression, and agree with Leon that covert resistance and subtle and controlled expressions of hostility remain significant components of the passivity pattern. Writing specifically about the Potawatomi, Searcy reports that historical accounts of Potawatomi behavior, many of them recorded by acculturating agents, indicate a cultural theme of co-existing passivity and aggression.[8] Referring to Vogt,[9] she adds that the conflict between passivity or dependence and aggression is found in many American Indian groups, especially the more acculturated groups.[10] The Prairie Potawatomi, by virtue of the characteristics of their community, are a highly acculturated group.[11]

The first two meetings of the Indians with the TOEO followed, therefore, what might have been the expected and typical pattern— the Indians relatively quiet, passive, and covertly resistant through the mechanisms of suspiciousness and skepticism. The third meeting, however, and the intensified discussions, explanations, and publicity that preceded and followed it, demonstrated to the Indians that the TOEO, unlike the Bureau of Indian Affairs or county welfare-agencies, possessed no sanctions for, nor controls over, them. Here was a white man's agency—symbolic of all the historical, physical, social, and psychological torments imposed upon the Indian by the white man —and it could not hit back! By the fourth meeting, consequently,

[6] George Spindler and Louise Spindler, "American Indian Personality Types and Their Sociocultural Roots," *Annals* of the American Academy of Political and Social Science, 311 (1957), 147–157.

[7] H. MacGregor, "Task Force on Indian Affairs," *Human Organization*, 21, 2 (1962), 125–137.

[8] Ann Searcy, "The Value of Ethnohistorical Reconstructions of American Indian Typical Personality: The Case of the Potawatomi," *Transactions* of the Kansas Academy of Science, 68, 2 (1965), 274–282.

[9] E. Z. Vogt, "The Acculturation of American Indians," *Annals* of the American Academy of Political and Social Science, 311 (1957), 137–146.

[10] Searcy, *Transactions* of the Kansas Academy of Science, 68, 2 (1965), 274–282.

[11] Clifton and Isaac, *Transactions* of the Kansas Academy of Science, 67, 1 (1964), 1–24.

there was no longer a need to enact the traditional passive role, and covert resistance quickly and easily turned into active verbal aggression. The opportunity to express hostility doubled when the white Director rather than the Mexican-American Assistant Director appeared at the meeting and was systematically and vigorously "put on." The flames were fanned when the Director was perceived to express his authority defensively, and attempted to "put some order" into the meeting.

Concerning the Reservation-dwelling Potawatomi, who, as pointed out above, have close ties and frequent meetings with their relatives and friends in Topeka, Gossen writes:

[they] find themselves almost totally dependent on stable and satisfactory relations with white men and their institutions; i.e., county welfare agents, public health agents, local law enforcement agencies, the Bureau of Indian Affairs, tribal lawyers, loan agents, creditors and white farmers to whom they rent their allotted lands. It is definitely not in the Potawatomi's best interests to antagonize these individuals and agencies, but at the same time, these very persons and institutions may have consistently exploited, cheated and deprived him of the social and economic means to better his minority situation. Injustice will seek expression and resolution —even if the only available vent is a traditional animal fantasy.[12]

Gossen is reporting on Potawatomi folklore, and the function it serves as an escape valve for acculturative stress. In particular, he presents, in its modern context, an intensive study of one traditional tale—the Coon-Wolf cycle. The story is essentially a series of episodes in which the Coon (clearly identified as the Indian) dupes and destroys the Wolf (clearly identified as the white man). The pattern of the Coon's success and the Wolf's downfall is consistent from episode to episode. The Wolf attempts to take the Coon's food. The Coon, however, cleverly outwits the Wolf by lying to him about the source of the food, and about how much the Wolf can get if he goes directly to the source. The Wolf, motivated by his greed, inevitably rushes to follow the suggestions of the Coon, and just as

[12] Gary H. Gossen, "A Version of the Potawatomi Coon-Wolf Cycle: A Traditional Projection Screen for Acculturative Stress," *Search: Selected Studies by Undergraduate Honors Students at the University of Kansas*, No. 4 (1965), 14.

inevitably meets with disaster, usually at the hands of the farmer. Thus the Coon verbally and with much amusement, beguiles (or "puts on") the Wolf, who is safely and indirectly eliminated by a third party. In the same way, covert resistances and "putting on" are indirect ways of thwarting representatives of agencies perceived as powerful and oppressive. When, however, as in the case of the TOEO, the Wolf in effect has no teeth, the general level of overt aggression, including the vehemence of "putting on," can safely be heightened. Relevant to the nature of "putting on," Searcy reports, when discussing major "psychological traits" of the Potawatomi, that aggression typically tends "to be channeled into hostile and at times humorous verbalizations."[13]

The passive-aggressive mode of interaction with power figures has been reported as representative of other ethnic minorities having a history of subjugation and impoverishment. Pettigrew describes "aggressive meekness" and an "impervious mask of passive acquiescence" adopted by Negro-Americans individually interacting with white authority, and other writers have described a similar pattern within the subculture of Mexican-Americans.[14] Unwilling compliance with, and controlled hostility toward, components of society perceived to be responsible for their powerlessness and alienation seems also to be a significant pattern among impoverished whites.

A few of the Indians, in spite of the disaster and apparent finality of their fourth meeting, had agreed to meet again with the Assistant Director. Cardinal among the reasons for their continuing interest was the fact that the Assistant Director did his utmost to present himself informally, as a person rather than an official. As he explained:

---

[13] Ann Searcy, "Contemporary and Traditional Prairie Potawatomi Child Life," *K. U. Potawatomi Study Research Report Number Seven*, University of Kansas, Department of Anthropology, Lawrence, Kansas, September, 1965, mimeograph, p. 56.

[14] Thomas F. Pettigrew, *A Profile of the Negro-American*; Arnold Meadow and David Stoker, "A Comparison of Symptomatic Behavior of Mexican-American and Anglo-American Hospitalized Patients," *Archives of General Psychiatry*, 12, 3 (1965), 267–277; and Louis A. Zurcher, Jr., and Arnold Meadow, "On Bullfights and Baseball: An Example of the Interaction of Social Institutions," *International Journal of Comparative Sociology*, 8 (March, 1967), 99–117.

"I make personal contact with them, and talk to them plain, and straight from the shoulder. If I walk into their houses, sit down and have a cup of coffee or a beer with them and just be one human being to another, then they'll listen, and maybe believe what I say. But if I walk in there waving a bunch of papers around and using a bunch of big bureaucratic words, they'd throw me right out the door. How do I know that? I know it because if some guy came into my house with a bunch of double talk, I'd throw *him* out the door!

"The same thing goes for someone standing up in front of a group at a meeting. If the fellow uses big, fancy words and I don't know what he's talking about, I'll holler out, 'Wait a minute! Let me go get my sledge hammer and break up those big words so I know what you're talking about!' I try to remember that myself whenever I'm standing up in front of a group of people who haven't had a chance to get used to those college-degree words.

"It's the same thing with titles. You know, if you work for a big organization with a lot of other people who have worked for big organizations, they'll listen to you if they're impressed by the title you have. It doesn't make any difference whether they know you personally or not, the title's what counts. But with the people out here in the Target Neighborhoods, and it seems especially true with the Indians, just to announce yourself with a title doesn't do the trick. As a matter of fact, a lot of times a title makes them suspicious of you. It's the person that counts, and not what's before or after his name.

"Take the Indians, for example. What have titles and big words meant to them? All they've meant are reminders of a big Government organization far away that has, over the generations, taken away their land and in a lot of cases, their rights. I guess what I'm trying to say is that with low-income people in general, and with Indians in particular, you've got to get them to accept you as a person, and to trust you, before you can even begin to talk to them about an organization like the TOEO and what it can help them accomplish."

It is not remarkable that the Potawatomi accept individuals in terms of how they are as "people" rather than by what official status they have. Not only have they had generations of negative experiences with "officials," but theirs was, and to a large extent still is, a social system of extended families.[15] Cohen writes that "the world view" of individuals in the type of society which fosters extended kinship contains definitions of human relationships in terms of "propinquity, intimacy, and solidarity," and influences the perception of social situations in terms of close personal bonds.[16] Redfield describes behavior in the ideal type familial society as "personal, not impersonal. A 'person' may be defined as that social object which I feel to respond to situations as I do; a person is myself in another form, his qualities and values are inherent within him, and his significance for me is not merely one of utility."[17]

The Assistant Director clearly was sensitive to the Indians' value orientation for personal relationships and the influence of the value orientation upon perception, evaluation, and acceptance of unfamiliar individuals, things, or ideas. His own people—Mexican-Americans— have a history of, and in many cases still maintain, extended family or *compadre* systems, and have been reported to manifest a similar value orientation for personal rather than impersonal interpretations.[18]

Divesting himself as much as possible of his "officiality," and approaching the Indians as "just another guy looking at what OEO is all about," the Assistant Director campaigned to interest more of the Indians in the scheduled sixth meeting.

THE ELECTION OF THE "CHIEF"

It was at the sixth meeting of the Indians that I myself began observation within the group, and was introduced as "a good friend"

[15] Charles Callender, "Social Organization of the Central Algonkian Indians," *Milwaukee Public Museum Publications*, No. 7, 1962; Searcy, "Contemporary and Traditional Prairie Potawatomi Child Life."
[16] Yehudi A. Cohen, "Patterns of Friendship," in Yehudi A. Cohen (ed.), *Social Structure and Personality*, pp. 353–354.
[17] Robert Redfield, "The Folk Society," *American Journal of Sociology*, 52 (January, 1947), 301.
[18] Edward P. Dozier, "Folk Culture to Urbanity: The Case of Mexicans and Mexican-Americans," University of Arizona, 1964; Charles P. Loomis and J.

by the Assistant Director (the previous five meetings have been
reconstructed from interviews with Indian participants and TOEO
staff). It was now early October, and the Indian group was more
than ten weeks old. Yet it still had in no way identified itself with the
TOEO, nor had the members viewed themselves as a TNC. Those who
had participated in the previous meetings did so for a number of
reasons, no one of which seems to align itself with the goals of the
poverty program. Some came because they were "curious about what
this was all about." Others attended because "it was a nice opportunity to spend some time chatting with friends who live across
town." A few sat in on the meetings because "it was fun to needle
some Government man a little bit." The Assistant Director hoped that
tonight's meeting would be different from those held earlier. He had
a feeling that "the Indians are, I think, beginning to see the opportunities the program has to offer, and I think they may be about
ready to elect themselves some officers. Also, I think they're beginning to trust us, and to see that maybe we aren't like the bad picture
they have of Government officials." During the week prior to this
evening's meeting, the Assistant Director had made personal contact
with about twenty Indian families, felt that he had begun to establish
rapport with some of the Indians, and that they were beginning to
have confidence in him. Thus he had hopes that the meeting shortly
to start would reveal, more than had any of the meetings before, the
beginnings of an Indian TNC.

While we were waiting for the meeting to begin, a small group
of participants, including the Assistant Director, the minister, and
myself, stood in front of the Indian Mission, talking quietly. All the
Indian men were wearing work clothes but each had at least one
Indian accouterment on his person—a beaded belt, a silver-jade
buckle, an ornamental watch fob, etc. The men were talking about
how tough times were now, and how difficult it was to "get jobs that
pay a living wage, and don't seem to end just when you're beginning

Allan Beegle, *Rural Social Systems*; Louis A. Zurcher, Jr., Arnold Meadow, and
Susan Zurcher, "Value Orientation, Role Conflict, and Alienation from Work,"
American Sociological Review, 30, 4 (1965), 539–548.

to get your head above water." The general tone of the conversation was depressed until one of the men said excitedly, "Remember how it was right after the war?" The other Indians perked up, and one of them exclaimed, "Yeah, man! In '45 and '46 *anything* went!" These comments kicked off a lively and spirited conversation in which the men shared with each other "sea stories" of drinking, fighting, and seducing (the last was largely implied, sometimes with circumspect glances at the minister, who was standing nearby), and with several references to the "way we could go anywhere we wanted to because we were veterans just like anybody else." As the Indians continued to relive the time when society allowed them more status and more freedom than perhaps at any other time in their lives, other couples would approach the Mission. Invariably, the woman would go inside and sit with the other wives, while the male would join the growing circle of "braves."

The meeting was scheduled to begin at 7:30 P.M.; at 7:45, the Assistant Director suggested that we all go inside and "get the show on the road." The Indian Mission was an old, worn, two-story frame house, with one room set aside as the place for worship. The furnishings were mismatched and secondhand. On the peeling walls were a crucifix, a few faded religious pictures, a notice of the record highest Sunday donation ($35.00) and last Sunday's donation ($1.40), and a crayoned announcement of a forthcoming revival meeting. There were fifteen people in attendance, six of them women. All present besides the Assistant Director and myself were at least part Indian. One of the women had a small baby in her arms.

When all of us were seated and settled, the Assistant Director opened the meeting. After a very brief review, he came to the point, stating that "the purpose of the meeting tonight is to find out if you're interested in this program, and if you are, for you to elect officers." He re-emphasized to the group that the TOEO was not a welfare program, and anything that was to be accomplished would have to be started and supported by the people here. He asked if there were any questions.

During all of the Assistant Director's five-minute talk, the people sat and listened attentively. When he asked for questions, they continued to sit silently and face forward attentively. All that could be heard was the occasional gurgling of the baby. Finally, the baby belched loudly, and the group laughed. One Indian man commented for all to hear, "That's the way I feel about it, too!"

One of the men asked the Assistant Director, "Well, what're we supposed to do now?" The Assistant Director responded with the suggestion that they think about electing officers. Another of the men said, "Maybe we should think about this some more." He then asked if there was any literature on the program, and the Assistant Director, responding in the affirmative, went out to his car to get some. While he was gone, a man said, loudly, "I don't know what the hell this is all about. That Assistant Director guy is okay, but what are *we* supposed to do? It's *their* program!"

The Assistant Director returned and handed out some pamphlets, which contained pictures of poverty families and dwellings and outlined some of the programs available through the Office of Economic Opportunity. The Indians looked through them with interest, and as they did, they made a number of embarrassed, yet amused, self-references. "Where'd they get a picture of *my* house?" "Where, what page?" "Page 13." "Hell, that's *my* house, not *yours!*" (The picture was a broken-down shanty.) "Look, here's a picture of me and my family!" (Laughter) "I ought to charge them for this!" (More laughter.) "Well," voiced one disgruntled female, "at least they don't have any tepees in this book." One could immediately feel the sensitivity these people had to being labeled as "poverty" types. The comment about tepees especially seemed to highlight an aversion to being stereotyped or "pointed out" in an unfavorable light. It was quite reasonable to assume that these people—in fact, any people in poverty situations—did not necessarily view themselves as "problem" people. They had struggled to maintain an adjustment in a world restricted to them by poverty and prejudices, and in most cases they took some pride in having "made out in this lousy world." In a later interview, one Indian pointed out, "That's part of the reason why it's so hard to get a group of Indians together into a committee with the TOEO. No Indian's ashamed of not having a lot of money, but he doesn't like the other things that go along with being called 'poor.'

He knows that when most people use the word 'poor' they also mean worthless, lazy, shiftless, and just plain no-good."

The self-references stimulated by the pamphlets launched a number of questions from the Indians. They wanted to know more specifically what the "programs are that have been *started by your office*." The Assistant Director reminded the group that programs were not "started" by his office, but that his office only helped carry out the ideas of the TNCs. An Indian then asked, "Well, what're you going to do *for* us?" Again, the Assistant Director repeated that "this is not a welfare program. Whatever's going to done has to be started and supported by you." One of the men then straightforwardly suggested, "The Indians'd be interested in forming a committee if you guaranteed them that they would have food and clothing for the winter when they're out of work." A very clear difference could be seen between the expectations that the Indians had for the TOEO, and the expectations that the TOEO had for the Indians and other Target Neighborhood residents. The Indians, at this stage, still viewed the TOEO as a Government agency, and saw the Assistant Director as a "good guy who'll help us get what we've got coming from this 'War on Poverty' program." The Indians were judging the TOEO in accordance with their long-standing experience with the United States Government—an experience that is based firmly upon the principles of paternalism. On the other hand, the TOEO, reflecting the rationale and goals of the "War on Poverty," expected the Indians—as it expected other Target Neighborhood residents—to become actively involved as participants in the "War on Poverty"—to assess and voice their needs, to select feasible programs to meet these needs, and to use the TOEO as a service. The key component in this conflict of expectations was the process of active beneficiary participation in a social-amelioration organization, as opposed to traditional passivity to, and dependence upon, such organizations. As the Assistant Director continued to interpret the Economic Opportunity Act to the people, there were several objections raised that "this is not President Johnson's program!" "That's not what President Johnson wants to do for us!" The parallel could be seen, historically, with promises made by the "Great White Father" to the Indian, only to be exploited by some criminal Indian agents. In spite of the Assistant Director's closeness to the participants that evening, in spite of the fact that they were not attacking him personally, there were still some feelings of misgivings about the TOEO's being like a interfering Indian agent.

One of the men asked the Assistant Director, "Why don't we just write down on a piece of paper the programs we want, and then you send these back to Washington for us?" The Assistant Director explained that it wasn't quite that simple, and if they wanted a Day Care Center, a Neighborhood Aide Program, and so on, they would have to become active in demonstrating the need, planning, and carrying out of a number of the specifics for the program. The same man added, "Well, you know we've never had to do much planning for things like that. Usually, somebody else does all the planning for us. Where do we begin?" The Assistant Director suggested that they talk with their friends and neighbors and try to put together a list of specific needs that the Indians might have, such as employment, housing, education, and so on. "Why do we need this here TOEO, anyway? Why don't we just send this list of needs directly to Washington?" inquired a man. Another answered, "Washington's a long way from here. Maybe if we got together with this OEO thing here in Topeka, then anything we write down would carry a lot more weight." "Yeah," another commented, "maybe we'd better string along with this deal." "Say," asked a third, "you said there were some other committees already going great guns. What're they doing?" The Assistant Director explained about the Day Care Center, Neighborhood Aide Program, Neighborhood House Program, etc., fostered by other TNCs. "Those ideas came from them?" the man persisted. The group was visibly impressed with this, and it seemed that the program, at this instant, became more believable to them. "Those other committees that have gotten these different programs, you say they already have officers?" asked an Indian woman. The Assistant Director assured her this was true. A man then urged, "Well, let's get us some officers, too!" All the members agreed vocally to the suggestion, but then the action dramatically ceased.

Several dynamics worked to engender this silence. First, the participants were not familiar with the procedures for nomination and election. Clifton and Isaac[19] and Searcy[20] have reported that the Potawatomi have had relatively little experience with tribal self-government, hence with the procedures associated with such self-government. Second, as a later interview with a participant indicated, there was some feeling of inhibition about *electing* a leader—"You know, we just don't *elect* chiefs." Third, and again revealed in later interviews with the participants, there is a devaluation placed upon volunteering for leadership among the tribes from which the Topeka Indians come. One of the respondents explained that he had quite early learned the lesson of not "trying to be the big-shot leader." He amplified his reasoning with an example:

"My father told me that if you made it obvious you wanted to be a Number One man, then you'd give other people a feeling that you thought you were better than they were, and that would be the worst kind of bad manners there are."

Another respondent supported this view:

"Grandpa gave us good advice whenever we wanted to play sports in high school. He used to tell us, 'Don't be *too* good at football, or anything else. Don't make people think you're showing off. If you're playing in a game, stay far enough out in front so you can win the game, but don't make anybody else look bad! I suppose there's nothing wrong with winning, but don't forget that it might be one of your brothers who's going to lose.' We listened carefully when he told us things like that."

A third respondent concurred also:

"I can remember when I used to run in track meets, and I was fast as the wind. I remember usually being able to win easily, but lots of times staying a couple of feet ahead of the second man so that I'd just across the tape first. Then after the race was over, I'd turn to him and say, "Boy, you sure gave me a tough time!" and I could see that

---

[19] Clifton and Isaac, *Transactions* of the Kansas Academy of Science, 67, 1 (1964), 1–24.
[20] Searcy, "Contemporary and Traditional Prairie Potawatomi Child Life."

he'd feel good about it. I'd do this even though I knew I could have run away from him at any time."

There thus appears to be a rather complex and somewhat ambiva-. lent attitude toward leadership when that leadership may involve competition or active pursuit. It appears to be another matter, however, if leadership is thrust upon an individual by his peers. "If your people turn to you and *make you a leader,*" commented an Indian, "then you have no choice but to be a leader. To refuse, even though you may not want to be a leader and have done nothing purposely to get it, would be the same thing as telling your brothers that you think your opinion, the opinion of one man, is better than all of theirs." Apparently, the important element is, according to these respondents and our observations, that the individual should not appear *to want* *to be a leader,* and should not overtly compete with his brothers. (This attitude, as revealed by the respondents, is generally intra-mural in nature. There seems to be less such feeling when an Indian group is competing with an Anglo group in sports or other kinds of extracurricular activities.) This complex reaction to the leadership role was nicely illustrated during a Potawatomi Pow-Wow. A visiting chief was called upon to lead the group in prayer, and he responded, "The greatest honor that can be given to a man is to be asked to stand before his people and lead them. There're many others here tonight who're more worthy than I to have this honor. But, so that I will not embarrass them by naming them, I'll do what you wish."

A fourth factor fostering the hesitancy of the Indians to present themselves as candidates for election that evening, or even to nominate others, was the general ambivalence toward authority—including both having a hand in establishing authority or becoming authority. One of the participants, later interviewed, explained:

"You know, we Indians seem to be afraid of authority. We know from our past history that we can't break through the power of authority. We learned this from the Federal Government. We don't particularly like sitting back and giving in to authority all the time, and sometimes we'll take little digs at officials if we can get away with it, but usually we do what we've kind of learned the hard way— we sit back and let the authorities take care of us.

"You can see this among the Indians themselves, too. I saw a great example of this with our bowling league. The league was to be part of a Pow-Wow Club that we'd started. It took us a couple of months to get anyone to be officers of that Pow-Wow Club, because of the same kind of thing I was just talking about. Nobody wants to be a leader, and it seems like nobody even wants to set up officers over them. Anyway, we drew names out of a hat to see how to divide our league into four-man teams. Just by chance, three of the officers of the club were placed on one team. On another one of the teams in the league, the four best bowlers were members. But this wasn't by drawing out of a hat, it was by agreement, because this team was going to represent us in a bigger bowling league, and we thought they should have experience together.

"Well, a funny thing happened. The team with the officers on it bowled against the team with our top four bowlers several times. Now, on the record, the pin average of the officer team was many pins lower than that of the team of best bowlers. But the team with the best bowlers *never* defeated the team with the three officers on it during our league or even during practice games. They bowled together at least ten times that I can remember. We used to tease the team of best bowlers after they'd lose, and I remember them telling us, 'How can you beat a team that has all chiefs on it?'"[21]

None of these responses should be taken to indicate that the Indians participating in the meeting that evening, or any other Indians for that matter, inevitably cower in the face of authority or authority figures or totally avoid becoming a leader. Rather, these observations indicate rather clearly an ambivalence toward authority and leadership—an ambivalence that quite understandably could impede or delay the development of indigenous leadership within a proposed Indian Committee. This ambivalence was further complicated

---

[21] This is a fascinating parallel to Whyte's observations of the distribution of bowling scores according to status within the corner gang. See William Foote Whyte, *Street Corner Society.*

by the fact that anyone elected at the meeting that night would be a leader *within* the TOEO—itself identified as a Government agency. This would mean becoming a member of the very organization that the Indians had so recently lambasted, and toward which they were still quite skeptical. We return now to the meeting in progress.

After a rather lengthy and awkward silence, broken only by considerable foot shuffling, shifting in seats, and coughing, the Assistant Director explained briefly the standard procedure for nomination and election and called for elections, saying, "Don't any of you think you've got some leaders here?" There was another shorter pause, and then finally one of the older men present was nominated for chairman. He stood, and said very seriously, "I consider this a great compliment to be nominated as a leader, but I have to decline because my health is not good." He in turn nominated another man, who thanked the group but declined because he didn't "really have enough time."

A few minutes before, while the Assistant Director had been explaining to the group the procedures for nominating and electing officers, Mr. A, a forty-eight-year-old heavy-equipment operator, had gotten up from his chair and stepped outside the door "to have a cigarette." He stood quite near the entrance, well within earshot of what was going on inside. Mr. A had attended the fourth and fifth meetings of the Indian group and on both occasions had been the most outspoken, aggressive, and skeptical of the participants. He is an intelligent and articulate individual, with a quick and keen sense of humor, and had been a key figure in the process of "putting on" the Director of the TOEO a little more than a month before. Mr. A was one of the individuals with whom the Assistant Director had developed a personal friendship and a mutual respect.

After the first two men had declined nominations for chairman of what was now becoming the Indian Committee, and while Mr. A was still standing outside smoking his cigarette, a man suddenly said, "Wait a minute! I know who a good man for the job is! It's Mr. A. He's a fighter, he is, and he'll be a good representative for us. He knows what's going on, too! I put up Mr. A for the job!" Mr. A was called back into the church and told that he had been nominated. They asked him if he would accept the nomination and he replied, in a soft voice and with a shrug of the shoulders, "I guess so, if that's the way you want it." He was elected by acclamation, and seemed visibly pleased as his friends congratulated him. Mr. A later informed me that he had gone outside "because I had a feeling that I might be nominated by the people, and I didn't want to be around if I was." He also said later that he had thought, at the time of the nomination meeting, that "the job of chairman might be worth a try, but I'm not going to work very hard to get it." It was quite clear that he didn't actively pursue the nomination, and, in fact, left the room before the nominations began. In that way, perhaps, he was able successfully to resolve a conflict between wanting to "take a crack" at being the chairman, and whatever ambivalence he had toward actively pursuing or accepting a position of leadership and authority. There was little doubt that he was pleased that the people had elected him, even though, as he said in his brief acceptance speech, "I'm still not quite sure what the hell we're going to do, but if we hang on, maybe we'll find out."

The election of the vice-chairman was a far simpler matter. It seemed that once the chairman, the head man, was established, anything else was secondary. Only one man was nominated; he accepted and was elected by acclamation. For secretary, the group nominated Mr. A's wife. After looking to her husband for approval and receiving it, she accepted and was elected by acclamation.

The Indian Committee was within the Focus Stage (III) of development and was formally established as a TNC, with all the rights and privileges of representation and votes due any other TNC. The newly elected chairman discussed with the Assistant Director and the group a time for the next meeting, and the reconvening date was set for two weeks later. Mr. A then adjourned the meeting, and there was another round of handshaking, congratulations, and some strong indications of a "we feeling" within the group. As the participants filed out the door of the Indian Mission, one of the men turned to the newly elected chairman and said loudly, "Good night, Chief." Mr. A beamed.

THE COMMITTEE BEGINS TO FORMALIZE

The day after Mr. A had been elected chairman of the Indian Committee, he began, as he reported, "going around to the houses of Indians that I know personally and talking up this OEO program with them." He said that he chose to go to the homes personally because he "knew from working with my people before that sending memos or announcements about something was a waste of time. The fact of life is this—if I can get people to come out to these next couple of meetings, it's mostly because they're my friends, not because they believe that the program's going to do them any good." Describing what he referred to as "the Indian mind" and the responses he was getting to his efforts, he said:

"It's rough going! The first question they ask me is, 'What good will this do me *now?*' They want to know if the program can get them a better job *today,* not next month or next year. They want to know if the program can guarantee that they'll have enough to eat during the winter when they're out of a job. I try to explain to them that this is not that kind of program, it's not welfare or anything like that. I try to explain to them that it's maybe a chance to take a part in running some of this 'War on Poverty' themselves, but it's hard for them to understand that and it's hard for me to explain it— I don't know enough about all this OEO stuff yet. I know some of the other Target Neighborhoods are getting Day Care Centers, Neighborhood Aides, Neighborhood Houses, and things like that, but that doesn't answer the meat-and-potatoes questions the Indians ask me. For example, one of my friends asked me, 'What would this OEO do to help me get a job?' I told him the OEO would probably refer him to the employment people. He shrugged his shoulders and said, 'Well, that's just the same old thing. I've been sitting down at the employment office day after day anyway, and nothing happens. If I want to be referred, I'll just look in the Yellow Pages of the phone book!'

"Right now, the Indians aren't concerned with long-range programs that may help them in the future to get better jobs or better standards of living. As one of my friends put it, 'We aren't interested in some big feast next year—what we want is a loaf of bread on the table now!'

"There's another problem too, and that's the attitude we seem to have. A lot of the people I've been talking to tell me, 'What's the use? You know that program isn't going to change anything for us! You know we've been talked to by agency people until we're blue in the face, and then we find out that most of it is just talk and nothing more.' There's a feeling among us of not even wanting to try to change things, because we don't think we can. Look at all the opportunities we've had in the past. Indians can go to school, have all their tuition paid, their board and room, their clothes, their books— and not many of us take advantage of it. I remember when I was in school thinking, 'What the hell's the difference whether I get an education or not; that's not going to open doors to me closed by prejudice.' So, you kind of sit back, relax, and ride along with life, letting the Government take care of you, but not really liking it.

"Well, you can see what you've got against you when you try and talk to the Indians about taking an active part in this OEO program. First of all, they don't think it's going to work or that it's going to help them, and second, they don't want to take an *active* part in anything. I know how they feel about it, and they know I know how they feel and that I feel pretty much the same way myself at times. But I tell them that maybe we ought to give this a try and see what happens. I think some of them will show up at this meeting coming up, but none of us are really believers yet."

Questioned about his willingness to work as a leader of a TNC, even though he was still skeptical of the program and was encountering difficulties in getting others interested, Mr. A admitted frankly:

". . . at first I thought the whole idea was just so much stuff, and it was just another one of those agency games that we have to play. But then it occurred to me that the way the Indian has been in contact with the Government before was on the basis of a whole Reservation. Here in Topeka, we aren't on the Reservation and so maybe we don't have to be so quiet. I thought maybe if a bunch of us here in Topeka could get together, come up with some suggestions about ways to improve things that we're unhappy about, then the force of our group, through the TOEO, would give us a louder voice than we've been able to have before.

"There's a Mexican-American organization here in town that started because of problems like we have, and now they're organized in thirty states and when they speak, people listen! I thought also this might be a good chance to change the picture that people here in Topeka have of us Indians. If we got into the OEO like the Neighborhoods have, then maybe people'd get a chance to see that Indians really aren't like they've always believed.

"I don't know if any of this makes sense, or if I can do anything about it. I guess the thing that really sold me on taking the job of chairman is that the people asked me to. You just don't turn that down."

At 7:45 on the evening of October 5, 1965, Mr. A called to order the seventh meeting, held again in the Indian Mission and attended by thirty people. He told the group, "I'm not much of a talker, and I'm not quite sure how to go about this. As a matter of fact, my wife told me I'm like the bottom half of a double boiler—I make a lot of steam, but I don't know what's cooking up above." Mr. A then called upon the Assistant Director to explain again "what OEO is all about, and what the Indians can do about it."

Following the brief talk by the Assistant Director, Mr. A introduced one of the evening's speakers, an Indian who was the director of a program to stimulate Indian participation in OEO programs throughout eight Midwestern states (not including Kansas). The speaker outlined what the Indians were doing, particularly dwelling upon the victory of the United Council of Tribes in South Dakota in a recent land and civil-jurisdiction dispute. He impressed his hearers, stating, "You see what Indians can do if they get together—they can even beat the state." He described the difference between Indian participation in the OEO programs and their traditional interaction with the Government:

"In OEO the Indians have a chance to actively develop their own program. For a change, the Indian can be a decision-maker, not the Government; he just doesn't have to take what the Government hands out to him. There're some disadvantages to having things handed to you all the time. After awhile you get used to having things handed to you and you're not much good for anything else. The important thing is that you've got to get involved and take an active part, and you've got to get together into a group—because that way you have more power. You know, this reminds me of a story. There was once an Indian all by himself who was wandering across the plains, and he saw a large group of blue-coated soldiers. Being a brave, he wanted to attack them, but then he figured, 'I can't beat them by myself,' and he started to go away disappointed. But then he thought to himself, 'Maybe I should go back and get some other braves to join me.' So he went back to the village, gathered a large group of braves, and together they went out and attacked the Army. That, my friends, was how Custer lost his hair! See what you can do together!"

The speaker had a visible impact upon the group. Here was an Indian reporting to them that Indians *could* do something in the OEO program. After he had finished, Mr. A added:

"You see! There's power in numbers. If we can get together, and work through this OEO organization, maybe we really can get some things changed around here! Now I don't know a heck of a lot about organizing. When I'm down at the bar I can always get a pool game or a ball game organized, but that's a little different from this! That's why I've asked a couple of guys from this Mexican-American organization to talk to us about organizing, and how they did it."

Mr. A then introduced an officer from the local chapter of a national Mexican-American organization, who explained:

". . . the only way we Mexican-Americans could get first-class citizenship was by banding together and using the power of a group. Even lawyers, who know the law very well, joined together in an

organization because they know that if they stand alone as individuals, they wouldn't be heard. The problems of the Mexican-
American are very much like the problems of the Indians. The
Mexican-Americans and the Indians are at the bottom of the ladder
when it comes to prejudice and discrimination. Like the Mexican-
Americans, the Indians have a very strong heritage of which they
can be proud. This makes it easier to work together and to organize."

When the officer had finished, Mr. A commented, "There's another
example of how working together will get you somewhere. We owe
it to ourselves as *friends and tribesmen* to help one another out. It's
the only way we can get along and get ahead!" Mr. A was again
hammering at the friendship obligations of one Indian to another.
As shown above, intuitively he had assessed the personalistic value-
orientation among his people, and saw this as the first means of getting them together. He was aware that he could not immediately
start talking about specific problems without first building a base of
acceptance for the TOEO within his group: "You've got to offer the
Indians something more than just a bunch of program talk, at least
at first. You've got to offer them, when they attend the meeting,
something that's more important to them—like friendship. Then
gradually, maybe they'll start talking about the specific things in
the TOEO on their own—and it'll come from them, not be pushed
down on them from up above."

Mr. A's strategy, and the stimulation from the testimony of the invited speakers of the evening, had the hoped-for effect. One of the
participants asked, "Well, if we're going to get together, we might as
well see what this OEO operation has that we can use. Why don't we
write down all our needs and then take up these needs as subjects
in future meetings? Maybe that way we can develop our own programs." There was general agreement within the group about that,
and there was the first indication of the development of an agenda
for meetings to come. Mr. A followed up the suggestion by telling
the group he would accept those lists any time the people wanted to
give them to him. He said, "This'd be something quite a bit more

than getting a 'tough luck' slip to go see the chaplain and then getting nothing but a bunch of words in return. Here's a chance that maybe we can do something for ourselves."

The question came up about ways of getting more Indians involved in the meetings. One participant commented that "the only way you can get Indians together on a regular basis is to have a social or a pow-wow." Mr. A agreed, adding, "You know, sometimes you have to fight Indians to get them to accept ideas that are really good for them." A discussion opened among the members to the effect that "Indians don't really like to accept help from people, especially from people who aren't Indians. We like to prove we can make it ourselves, and that we can go it alone." These were fascinating remarks, seeming to contradict other comments that the Indians had made that same night about wanting the Government or the TOEO to "give them food, jobs, and clothing *now*, not tomorrow." The apparent contradiction again revealed the complexity of Indians' attitudes and ambivalences toward traditional Government paternalism. It also revealed one of the basic difficulties in getting the group of Indians together on a relatively permanent basis under the auspices of the TOEO.

Another question came from the floor, the man inquiring, "What about paying dues? Maybe we ought to pay fifty cents a year, or something." Mr. A responded that he didn't think this was necessary. He felt that "the purpose of this organization doesn't call for dues." The man began to argue with Mr. A and said, somewhat derogatorily, "Well, Mr. Chairman, sir, you can't expect people to be interested if they're not going to pay a little dues." Mr. A continued to disagree, saying, "We only want people here who're interested. We don't want their money. We don't want anything more from them than just their participation." The questioner smiled and said somewhat softly, "Okay, Mr. Chairman, okay." That was the first show of disagreement between a follower and the leader. For a moment the interaction had almost the undertone of Mr. A's own previous behavior with the Director of the TOEO—that of "putting him on." In a subsequent interview, Mr. A remembered this incident quite well and said, "Well, you know, that was the first time I felt uncomfortable being the chairman." The incident was to be a harbinger for later indigenous-leadership problems.

Mr. A suggested to the group that they get some of the coffee and cookies that had been provided. Then, looking a little bewildered, he blurted out, "I don't know how to end this thing!" He appealed to the Assistant Director, "What do I do now?" The Assistant Director explained to him the procedures for adjourning the meeting, and Mr. A began to do just that, until he was loudly interrupted by several members of the group: "Wait a minute! What about setting a time for the next meeting?" He apologized and the group agreed to hold another meeting two weeks hence. There appeared to be a genuine desire by the members of the committee to continue their meetings.

It was now after 10 P.M., and the meeting had run its course for two and a half hours. Many of the people went home, but about ten of the participants, all male, moved off to a side room in the Indian Mission. Here, Mr. A again began holding forth on "the Indian mind." He reflected with the group:

"The Indian's been kicked around so much and promised so much and faced with so many phonies that he's learned how to play the game with them, and how to lead them on. He knows how to get what he can out of them and then laugh it off after it's over with. That's what makes it so tough to get Indians interested in a program like this OEO. Any program like that, coming from the Government, is guilty until proved innocent. Well, this OEO program looks to me like it's a little bit different from the usual kind of stuff we get. I think we ought to give it a fair look, but trying to convince other people about it is really a tough job."

The group agreed with him, one participant commenting:

"Yeah, you know it may sometimes look to others like Indians always let themselves get pushed around, and never do anything about it. Well, there's not a hell of a lot we can do, because we never have had too much power and the other guys have usually always held the cards, but we have our own quiet kind of ways of letting the pushers know who's boss—like the way we ate up all those cows!"

The group laughed with relish at being reminded of the famous cow story. Again, the need was manifested by the Indians to demonstrate that they did, in fact, have definite ways of maintaining some control over the various elements that influence their daily lives.

The conversation shifted to "the way you get disgusted with programs and agencies and stuff like that because of all the red tape." Mr. A told the group about how well impressed he was with a juvenile officer who was now no longer in Topeka:

". . . he was a guy who could be respected. When any case came to him, he looked over the whole situation, what it meant to the people involved, and then he made a decision. He checked into the families, and you could approach him as a friend, and he talked to you that way. He didn't just go by some book or some rules and regulations that're written down like they had nothing to do with people. I tell you, that's the only way things can be done right—you've got to approach people as one human being to another. This is especially true of the Indians, and I'd guess it's true of other minority groups who're just damned sick and tired of being dealt with by agencies like they were things and not human beings."

Mr. A then commented on the Assistant Director's approach to the Indians:

"Now look at the Assistant Director here, for example. Suppose he'd come to see us the same way that Director did—with all that fancy talk, those titles, like he knew all the answers and he knew what was best for us. Well, if he'd done that, there wouldn't have been any meeting tonight, or any other meeting of the Indians as far as OEO is concerned. Instead, he met us eye to eye, and got to know us personally. That makes all the difference in the world, and if the OEO doesn't realize that, then they're in big trouble."

The personalistic value-orientation and its powerful influence were again sharply manifested.

At this point, the Indian who had earlier raised the question about dues came back to his argument. "I still think," he said to Mr. A, "that if we're going to have a group here, we ought to have dues." Mr. A tried to reason with him, "No, we don't want dues. We just want interest! We don't want to take anybody's money—except maybe the Government's!" (The group laughed.) The questioner argued some more, and finally said very heatedly, "Well, you know damn well that in any *white man's club* they charge dues!" Following that statement he remained silent. It was easy to sense the resistance that this man had to being labeled as a member of a "poverty" organization. He much preferred the committee to be one in which members paid at least token dues, like the clubs whose doors are always closed to the Indian. By paying some small amount, the member might also feel a sense of control in the organization—a sense of control which could extend to more active participation. One had the feeling that the questioner was really arguing that he couldn't believe active participation could be made available to the Indian unless he paid for it in one way or another. Mr. A conceded to the man that he "might have a point, and I'm going to give it a good deal more thought. Maybe we can talk more about it at the next meeting."

It was 11 P.M., and Mr. A suggested that "we all go home now, and then let's see what'll happen at the next meeting." With that, he went over to a small counter in the back room, reached under a shelf, and pulled out an old, battered brief case. He fumbled with the lock, and mumbled sheepishly, "I'm not used to working this damned thing yet." Finally he got it open, stuffed in a few papers and rearranged them, then snapped the brief case shut, and with no less *savoir faire* than a Madison Avenue executive, Mr. A left the Indian Mission.

THE COMMITTEE LOOKS FOR A PROJECT

Mr. A again spent considerable time prior to the eighth meeting of the Indian Committee making personal visits to the homes of Topeka Indians, attempting to get them to come to the next meeting. He and the vice-chairman had also attended, as voting delegates from the Indian Committee, the first meeting of the Economic Opportunity Board. Though he was silent throughout the meeting, he took several notes and commented afterwards, "I'm amazed at the scope of the organization, and the number of people and agencies that're involved in it. We may have something here!" He was a little concerned, though, about the pace of the meeting:

"All these motions and votes on different proposals and things go so fast you hardly have time to think about them. You just get finished being asked to vote on one proposal, and before you really understood what that vote was all about, another one comes along. I wish they'd slow down a bit! At first I thought it was just that I was stupid, but then I talked to some of the other committee officers and found they felt the same way, too.

"I hope the TOEO and the agency people don't forget that this is all kind of new to us. Another thing worried me, too. Every time there was a vote, everybody voted 'Yes'; nobody ever voted 'No.' I hope it wasn't because a lot of the people just didn't understand what was going on. I know that was the case with me. A couple of times I voted 'Yes' and didn't know what the hell I was voting about, but went along with the rest of the people."

Mr. A arrived at the Indian Mission for the eighth meeting of the Indian Committee several minutes before the scheduled starting time of 7:30 P.M. He was dressed pretty much as he had been at the previous meetings that he had attended—work clothes, heavy boots, and a sweater. Tonight, however, clutched in his left hand as he walked through the door to the meeting room, he held again that symbol of his authority and organization, the worn brief case, and instead of sticking it out of sight under a shelf, he plopped it down on the table at the front of the meeting room.

Nineteen people were in attendance—ten men and nine women. Raising his voice, Mr. A said, "Let's see if we can get the ball rolling. I reckon we're all here now, so this meeting comes to order. We *are* all in order, aren't we?" (The group laughed softly.) He then went to his brief case, fumbled again with the lock, and pulled out *typed* minutes of the last meeting. He briefly reviewed the proceedings and emphasized that the important lesson learned was "we

have to get together if we're going to get anything done." He asked
the members if they had written down the specific needs that they
felt the Indians had. Several of them said that they had talked about
these needs, but hadn't yet written them down, so Mr. A distributed
some paper and pencils and asked them to "put them in black and
white." He stopped for a second, laughed, and then said, "We've
done a lot of talking but we haven't had any concrete ideas. I've got
one concrete idea now—there's coffee up here, so come up and help
yourself." (The group laughed.)

Mr. A continued, "These meetings are going to be very informal,
so if anybody has anything to say, just say it, speak right up. You're
going to have to go along with me for awhile, because I really don't
know how to run a meeting." Several of the members discounted his
last remark, saying, "You do okay, 'Chief!'" "Yeah, you do fine."
"Keep up the good work, Mr. Chairman." Mr. A seemed pleased
with this response and said, "Well, this's a group affair, and we've
got to work together if we're going to get anywhere."

Members then orally offered some suggestions for programs that
the Indians could pursue, and Mr. A read a few others from the papers that he was collecting. Included were suggestions for ways of
providing jobs for high-school drop-outs, training programs for adult
Indians, a counseling program for Indian high-school students still
in school, legal aid, and a few others. The Assistant Director explained to the Indians, "All of the programs you've mentioned so far
are already going in Topeka, so there's not much need in setting up
new ones." Mr. A shook his head and said:

"Boy, getting these poverty programs going is going to be tough!
It looks like the Indian's too late again. You know, speaking of the
poverty program, I heard an interesting joke the other day that
probably tells us why the poverty program's so tough to get started.
This Government guy asked a down-and-outer what can be done to
get him out of poverty. The guy tells the Government man that he
can put him on one of those committees and pay him for it. The
Government man then asks the down-and-outer, 'What will you do

then?' 'I'll move out of the Neighborhood,' said the guy. 'Well, if you move out of the Neighborhood,' said the Government man, 'then you won't qualify for the poverty money anymore.' "

The group laughed appreciatively and Mr. A added, "You see, this is kind of a round-robin thing, and we have to figure out some way to stop it from going around in circles." One of the men then raised a question, "Say, is this poverty program here in Topeka going to be like that one in Kansas City? I've heard that in that Job Corps thing, only rich boys got the jobs." Mr. A quickly answered, stating vehemently:

"No, I don't think that's going to happen here. The guy who was the head of that Job Corps program here in Topeka talked to us at that Board meeting the other night, and he convinced me that they're being very careful about that here. Also, I don't think there're any guys here who're trying to latch onto the poverty program for high salaries. The biggest problem we're going to have here in Topeka is getting people interested and getting the programs to reach the people. I think TOEO may have trouble doing that."

At this point Mr. A was actually defending the TOEO whose Director he had "put on" and whose goals he had overtly questioned a few months before. There was not much doubt that he was still somewhat skeptical that the program would work the way it promised to work, but he thought it definitely was worth a try, and that it shouldn't be attacked until it had been given a fair chance. "I don't know," Mr. A added as an afterthought; "sometimes I get the urge just to go up to one of the agency officials like the employment people, grab them by the neck, and threaten to beat the hell out of them unless they get Indians better jobs. I remember once I had to jerk the principal of a school across his desk before I could get him to understand my problems and my kid's problems." He then smiled somewhat sheepishly, looked at the Assistant Director, and said, "But I guess that's not the way to do things. At least it hasn't worked very good in the past. Maybe with this OEO organization to help us, we can have a louder voice and get more done. I don't know."

An Indian man startled everyone by demanding in a loud voice, "Let's get some proposal going! All we do is talk!" Mr. A swallowed and said:

"Well, what about this one? An Indian who's not present at this meeting suggested that we think about forming an old-folks' home for Indians. We all know some very old Indians who can't care for themselves very well anymore, and maybe we could help them out. Those old-timers won't go into welfare homes, because they aren't used to the food and they aren't used to the people. But maybe if there was a little home for them run by Indians themselves, they'd be more willing to go there when they need help. What do you think about that idea?"

There were several assenting replies from the group. One man said, "This sounds like a good deal. If we could get a home for the aged Indians, then it'd be the same kind of environment they're used to. You know, it doesn't make any difference where we go— we're still Indians."[22] Another participant suggested that the members "talk to some aged Indians and see what kind of a place they'd like to have to go to." Another asked, "How'll we go about doing something like this? How could OEO help us?" The Assistant Director explained that perhaps such a program could be pursued under Title Five (the Migrant Section) of the Economic Opportunity Act. "If this was the case," he explained, "then the home for the aged would have to be on the Reservation." The Indians objected to this, and one of them said, "Oh, no! The Indian agent people on the Reservation usually give us the run-around when we try and get some program going through. We'd rather have this home right here in Topeka, not on the Reservation." The group all agreed with him. A woman added, "We want a program of our very own!" The Assist-

[22] Searcy reports that respect for the aged is traditional among the Potawatomi. See Searcy, "Contemporary and Traditional Prairie Potawatomi Child Life," pp. 274–282.

ant Director explained that if this was the case, then the home would probably be funded under Title Two of the Economic Opportunity Act (Community Action Proposal) and therefore 10 per cent local share would have to be provided. The Indians wanted to know what that meant, and the Assistant Director explained it to them, adding, "I don't think it would be difficult to get the 10 per cent local share for such a good project."

"Hey," interjected one of the participants, "what about Medicare? What about the Welfare people? Is there any way they could tie their payments in with this?" The Assistant Director suggested that it might be a good idea to get someone from the State Welfare Department to come to their next meeting and talk to them about that. Mr. A asked, somewhat incredulously, "Is that possible?" The Assistant Director said that indeed it was. Mr. A then commented, "I'm a heck of a chairman—I don't know anything. But give me time, and I'll know more in the future." The Assistant Director inquired, "Would you like me to arrange a speaker from Welfare for your next meeting?" Mr. A replied that they would, but added, "Let's make sure we all agree on this first." One of the members suggested that "we vote on this issue," and Mr. A turned to the Assistant Director for help on how to run the voting procedure. After a brief conference, Mr. A then called for a motion, called for a second, got both, and then called for the vote, which was unanimously affirmative. The members seemed pleased with this, and one of them remarked, "History's been made—that was the first vote we've ever had!"

The question about the Indian home for the aged came up again, and someone suggested that the proposal to investigate developing such a home be put into a motion. This time Mr. A carried off the procedure without the Assistant Director's advice. The motion passed unanimously, and the Indians' first community-action project was officially on the drawing board.

Mr. A began to adjourn the meeting without setting a date for the next meeting. Again, as at the last meeting, he met with objections from some of the participants who wanted to know when they would get together again. It was agreed that they should meet, as they seemed routinely to be doing now, every two weeks. The date for the next scheduled meeting was December 14, and one man laughingly commented, "That's a good time to have a meeting. In fact, we could even have a meeting on Christmas Eve, then, like those guys in the white shirts who work in the big office buildings, we could have that real 'organized' feeling!" (Everybody laughed.)

Mr. A adjourned the meeting and several of the members remained to make small talk and drink more coffee. He mentioned to the group that he was "getting hold of a little book about how to run meetings" because he "didn't know what the hell was happening." In a later interview, he reflected:

"Sometimes during those early meetings I felt kind of lost about what to do while standing up there. I wanted our meetings to be informal, because that's the way it's got to be with the Indians who come to the meetings. Sometimes I'd think that if we had a little more order in the meetings, and if I knew how to handle all those motions and things like that, things would go a lot smoother and maybe we'd get a lot more done. I don't mean that we should get real fancy, like they do at those Board meetings, but just so we'd have a little more order. When I'm standing up in front of that group, I like to think I know what I'm doing, and where the meeting's going."

After some experience Mr. A, in common with most of the indigenous leaders of TNCs, was inadvertently leaning toward increased formalization of his meetings.

About fifteen minutes after this eighth meeting had adjourned, all the remaining members began to leave. Mr. A picked up his brief case and started out the door. As he stepped into the cold night air, he shivered and said, "Man, it's cold out here! Or maybe," he added, with a jerk of his thumb back toward the Indian Mission, "it's because I get so sweated up about this chairman job."

"We're Shooting for the Moon"

About eight days after the Indian group had last met, the TOEO inaugurated weekly "Leadership Training Sessions" for the TNC officers. The Director called upon the officers to tell "what's happening with your committee." When Mr. A's turn came up, he quipped,

"You mean something's been happening?" (This was the first time Mr. A had come in contact with the Director since the "putting on" interaction. He later admitted in an interview, "I felt kind of funny being there after I'd given the Director such a hard time before. When he asked me what was happening, I just couldn't resist taking one more little shot at a big wheel, even though by that time I'd begun to understand how rough it is for him to get a program like that going.") The rest of the officers, who had from the onset found Mr. A to be "good-humored" and "willing to say what he's got on his mind," laughed with him. Mr. A then became quite serious, and said that they had had some meetings, "during which we've been talking about ourselves and pretty much enjoying ourselves. I think we're beginning to get the idea across that we can't do anything individually, but we can get something accomplished by joining together." He went on, "I don't know about the rest of you and your Target Neighborhoods, but the question asked most often of me is about employment, and about how the OEO can help get jobs for people who need them."

He picked up a small pamphlet on poverty and pointed to a picture. "Look at this picture and you'll see what I mean," he said, pointing to a photograph showing members of his group sitting around a table at their meetings. "It looks like a bunch of Indians sitting there waiting for their welfare checks!" The other officers again laughed with him. "Well, anyway," he continued, "it looks like we finally found something we can get together on, though. We want to try and get a home for aged Indians, and we think this idea shows a lot of promise. There's a saying, you know, that old Indians never die—they just fade away. Well, maybe we can help the old Indians fade away comfortably."

Mr. A had motivated twenty-two people, eleven men and eleven women, to come to the Indian Mission on a freezing December night for the ninth meeting of the Indian Committee. He opened his brief case and searched through the papers which had fallen out into a heap on the table. He apologized to the group for not being able to find the minutes and said, "There're so many things to do to keep this show on the road that sometimes I forget things." He then called the meeting to order, and introduced the guest speaker for the evening, the director of the State Welfare Department. The official began explaining what Medicare would mean to the Indians. He spoke directly, unpedantically, and left plenty of time for questions. The Indians made a number of pointed inquiries, all of which were straightforwardly answered. Several of the questions related directly to the relation between Medicare and the proposed Indian home for the aged. Mr. A, a number of times, contributed information about other homes for the aged in the Topeka community, and the way they were operating, indicating that he had, previous to tonight's meeting, done a considerable amount of spade work. Questioning came to an end, and Mr. A suggested to the group that they "write down questions on pieces of paper if you don't feel like asking them out loud." In an earlier interview he had mentioned that "I know a lot of Indians who just don't think it's right to sound off in public and a lot of others who're just scared to do so because they don't have the right words." He added, "If you have any other questions that come up after this meeting, then write them down and give them to me and I'll go down to this man's office and get the answers for you."

A woman asked the official, "Will you answer some questions about Welfare tonight?" The official responded that he would. Mr. A looked a bit concerned about this turn of events. (In the earlier interview he had stated, "I'm a little bit afraid the Indians're going to give that Welfare man a bad time at the meeting. You know what I mean, like the bad time we gave to the Director of the TOEO when he came to our get-together. In fact, a couple of the members have already said, 'It looks like we can have a little fun with the guy when he starts giving us the old Welfare double-talk.' I hope the fellow plays it straight with us, and doesn't try and give us the runaround, or he's not going to forget that night very quickly.") The Welfare official, however, answered the many questions asked of him with honesty and no defensiveness. In fact, he agreed with several of the legitimate criticisms that were made of welfare inequities, and suggested to the group, "Maybe you can help to change the laws that restrict us people who work for Welfare."

A man outlined for the official a specific case which he thought had been handled unjustly. The official agreed, "There seems to be a basis for a grievance there, and I'd suggest that you inaugurate a grievance procedure." Mr. A picked up the official's statement, asking, "Can we here in this committee represent the Indians in a grievance case or an appeal case to your office?" The official felt that would be a good idea. Mr. A looked at the group and, nodding approvingly, said, "You see, maybe we've got something here." Turning again to the official, he repeated, almost as if he wanted to make sure he had heard correctly, "So then, you'll recognize us if we represent our people?" "Yes, indeed! I'm convinced that if the poor represent themselves, they can get more done," the official reaffirmed. "By God," exclaimed Mr. A, "maybe working through this OEO organization *is* going to give us a bigger say in things!" He turned back to the official and said, "Well, it might not be very long before we have something on your desk!"

(Mr. A later indicated that this encounter had been one of the high points of his experience with the TOEO:

"I got the feeling that maybe some doors would open to us, so we wouldn't be pushed around all the time and we could have our real say about things. I think probably I had more faith in the OEO at that moment than I had at any other time. I figured that the OEO was going to give us a chance to get together with agency officials the same way we used to be able to get together with that juvenile judge—to be listened to as people, and not as numbers. I thought that with OEO with us, and us with OEO, we might have the stuff to get past the smart-aleck clerks by the front doors of the agencies, and get a chance to talk as equals with the men behind the big desks. Yeah, I guess I was really full of hope at that time.")

After the Welfare official had finished answering the questions, he was thanked and applauded, and he left. That he had not been "put on" by the Indians was owing to a number of reasons, some of which might have been: (1) He was the "top man" of the Welfare Department, and represented a very powerful source of control over many Indians' lives. (2) Comfortable with his own position as the top man, he was able to tolerate legitimate criticism of his organization, and thus did not, by becoming defensive, help to create the conditions for spiraling angered interactions. (3) He was introduced by Mr. A, the "Chief," and that gave him some basis for acceptance by the group. (4) The group had requested that he come to the meeting as a guest, thus he was not wished on them by higher authority. (5) The Indian Committee, struggling in the Focus Stage (III), had at least temporarily left behind the behaviors associated with Catharsis Stage (II).

Mr. A now began looking through the pile of papers that had fallen out of his brief case, and pulled out several newspaper clippings about OEO programs, local and national. As he passed them out to the members, he commented, "I cut these out because I think we ought to have an idea of just how big this program is. I think it's important that we see that although the OEO has been getting a lot of bad publicity around the nation, there're still good parts of the program that maybe we can latch on to." Mr. A, as further revealed by his newspaper-clipping searches for OEO information, was becoming quite deeply involved as a TNC leader. He had attended the Board meeting, the Leadership Training Sessions, had volunteered to serve on the Health Study Committee, and was recommended by the TOEO to serve on the community's Legal Aid Advisory Committee. He spent several hours a week of his off-the-job time consulting with the Assistant Director about the local program, and "talking it up with Indian families." He had asked the other indigenous leaders to "refer any problems that Indians in your Neighborhoods might have to me, so I can see what I can do about it for them," and he had, in fact, gone with one Indian who had been referred to him to the Veterans Administration in order to "help the guy get through the tangle of red tape for this Veterans Administration benefits."

It was with this hope and enthusiasm that Mr. A now brought the attention of the members to the business of the old-age home proposed at the last committee meeting. He called upon the Assistant Director to report "what the TOEO has discovered about ways that we might fund the old-age home." The Assistant Director told the group that he had written several letters to Government officials but hadn't received any definite answers yet. He suggested that the Indians set up a subcommittee and come to the OEO office for further discussion of the details of the proposal. Mr. A agreed, and thought that the "subcommittee should have among its members at least one older person who understands the problems of the aged, and one younger person who can see the long-range program."

He called for volunteers for the subcommittee, and got none. He asked one woman, who "didn't have time." He then asked a man, who responded, "This'd be a good deal, this old-age home. But how far would OEO go into it? How long is this OEO going to last? There seems to be a lot of conflict around the nation about OEO, and I wonder if it's going to be around next year? There're all kinds of things we ought to consider about an old-age home. We've got to worry about staff. It takes a lot of money, probably at least a hundred thousand dollars." Mr. A cut in somewhat impatiently, "That's true, but this is like any fight—you've got to hit first, even though you don't know what the outcome'll be." The Indian responded, "You know, this is a very long-range program, and we just can't get this going next week!" A couple of the other participants audibly agreed. Another asked, "Even if we were able to get this off the ground, who'd we get to go to the home for the aged?" Mr. A commented, "I know there're lots of problems with this proposal, and I know we really don't know too much about the direction we're going in. But we've got to plant the seed before we get the tree!"

A participant asked, "Would this be a segregated place?" Mr. A responded, "We don't mean it to be. What we talked about was providing a place where old Indians could go, especially those who probably wouldn't go anywhere else at all. Besides," he joshed, "I don't think anybody else could stand the tom-tom music!" The group laughed mildly, and a participant asked, "Where're you going to get the 10 per cent local share to fund this thing?" Mr. A responded, "Where do you get this *you* stuff? This is *us*, not just me. I don't know where we're going to get the 10 per cent yet, but OEO has got some feelers out for us." Mr. A called upon the Assistant Director to explain again to the group "the procedure that'll be necessary for applying for a program like an old-age home." After giving a careful and detailed explanation of the procedure, the Assistant Director commented, "It'd be at least a year before you'd be able to begin operation of such a home." The group reacted very negatively to this, and there were comments about the length of time involved. "Here we go again," muttered one man; "another one of those pie-in-the-sky deals."

A woman asked, "Is this going to be a rest home or an old-folks home?" Mr. A replied, now a bit nervously, "What do you keep asking me for? It's going to be whatever *we* decide it to be. Man," he sighed, "this sure gets complicated!" The Assistant Director again urged that the group "appoint a subcommittee to look further into the possibilities for the old-age home." Mr. A again called for volunteers, and again there was no response. A long pause followed, finally broken by Mr. A's saying, softly and with resignation, "Well, if we can't get anybody, we might as well forget this thing." He then quickly added, a little louder, "Well, we'll all let it hang until the next meeting. You know what I think's wrong? I think we're shooting for the moon here, and maybe that's one of the problems with some of these OEO projects. I wish there was something we could get done right away!"

Mr. A suggested that it might be time to adjourn (it was 9:40 P.M.). Since the other TNCs were going on a monthly-meeting schedule instead of twice monthly, the tenth gathering of the Indians was scheduled for late January. Mr. A commented, "It's a good idea we're going to once-a-month meetings. It looks like when we have meetings too often, all we do is talk." He looked around the group for a moment, then said, "I guess this meeting's adjourned."

Most of the participants left immediately after adjournment. Only six or seven members remained to have some coffee and socialize a bit. Mr. A seemed somewhat depressed and commented again about the "Indian mind" and the fact that "the group seems undecided about the possibility of the old-age home." He repeated his earlier statement about having "to throw the first punch in a fight, without knowing what the outcome'll be. I'm afraid when we get right down to talking about the specifics of a long-range program like this one, the people're going to show that old we-can't-win attitude and be afraid before they even get started." (In a later interview, he reflected:

"That was a very tough meeting for me. When the guy from Welfare was talking, and it looked like our committee might be able to represent Indians who needed help in dealing with that agency, I was very excited about being the chairman and what we could do for our people. Later on, in the very same damn meeting, when the people started getting so doubtful about even *trying* to get the old-age program going, I began to get disappointed. It's the same damn thing we always see—we quit before we even start. Then it seemed to me like the people during that meeting started giving me a bad time. The guy from Welfare has no trouble at all, but I start catching hell because the old-age-home idea's going to take so long and it's so complicated. For awhile there I began to get the feeling that some of my own buddies were 'putting me on.' Toward the end there I got the rotten feeling that I was losing touch with the group, that they saw me as being way across the room, just another agency official. I can tell you this—I don't like that feeling!")

After about ten minutes of conversation following this ninth meeting, Mr. A picked up his brief case and shoved it under his arm. He walked out of the Indian Mission over to his parked car, and as he got in, commented to his wife, "Damn it, I have to work harder at this than I do at my own job!"

The following day, an article appeared in one of the local newspapers, reporting the events of the meeting of the Indian Committee. In the article, mention was made of a point that had been discussed by the State Welfare Department official and Mr. A—the relative merits of providing cash *versus* grocery orders for needy persons. To Mr. A was attributed a comment that indicated it would be better for Indians to receive grocery orders rather than money, because the Indians have a tendency to spend all their money on beer and leave nothing for food. Mr. A felt that he had "been misquoted, and what I said was given the wrong slant. That article sure got me into a lot of trouble with the Indians! A couple of them said to me, 'Who the hell do you think you are—some big wheel now because you're an

OEO officer? You think you're better than us now, so you can say things about us!' When you take the job as a committee chairman, you're on the firing line, that's for sure!"

THE "CHIEF" IS ABSENT

During the month of January, Mr. A continued to attend the Leadership Training Sessions for committee officers. He began taking an active part in these meetings, asking questions, offering suggestions, making and seconding motions on various agenda items. He continued to be respected by the other indigenous leaders for his "outspokenness," and appreciated for his sense of humor. At one of these meetings, he became particularly interested in the proposed Neighborhood Aide Program, fostered by two other TNCs and sponsored by the TOEO. He saw the possibility of an Indian Neighborhood aide, working on a full-time basis, "doing a lot of good to help Indians meet their needs and approach the agencies." He emphasized the point that "the Neighborhood aide who works for the Indians has to be an Indian, someone they know and can get along with, or else none of them'll open their doors to him." Though he later changed his mind, Mr. A was seriously considering applying for that job himself. During this time, another Economic Opportunity Board meeting was held, and he attended, remaining silent throughout the meeting but taking notes, and showing interest. He again commented, following the meeting, "All the votes were 'Yes' votes, just like the last time. Doesn't anybody ever say 'No' around here? Maybe they're like me— they don't know enough to say 'No.' Sometimes I get the feeling," he added laughingly, "that they let us into OEO because they figure all we can say is 'Aye.' "

A few days before the scheduled January meeting of the Indian Committee, Mr. A had to leave town to attend the funeral of an out-of-state relative. Before he had left, he instructed the vice-chairman of the committee to conduct the meeting in his absence. By 8:00 o'clock of the meeting night, only four Indians had arrived, including the vice-chairman. The door to the Indian Mission was locked, and a telephone call had been made to get someone with a key. By the time the key arrived—at 8:30—no Indians remained but the vice-chairman himself, along with the Assistant Director and two non-Indians. The vice-chairman suggested that "we cancel this meeting, and get together again when Mr. A returns."

Upon his return, Mr. A reported that he had "contacted several Indian families before leaving, and told them to go ahead and have the meeting anyway. It's funny. It seems like Indians come to depend upon one leader, and although they might give him a bad time when he's standing up there in front of them, they won't get together without him." He immediately contacted the participants in the committee, and rescheduled a meeting for the end of February.

Mr. A attended two more meetings of the Leadership Training Sessions while preparing for his February meeting. At the first one, when the committee officers collectively decided that they should elect from among themselves a chairman, vice-chairman, and secretary and thus establish a Committee of Neighborhood Officers, Mr. A was nominated, along with three others, for the top position. In response to the nomination, he said, "I'm afraid I'm going to have an awful lot going in the future, and I'm probably going to have to miss a few meetings. I'm honored that you nominated me, and that you have confidence in me, but I'm going to have to decline." He reported later, "That's all I'd have had to do—become an officer of the officers —then my people would really have given me a bad time about becoming an organization man!"

At the second of the Leadership Training meetings, Mr. A became quite interested in a Medicare Alert Program that the TOEO was trying to get under way. He became angry at one point with "all this talking about the thing. Let's get it off the ground! Let's get it going in a hurry! Why do we always dilly-dally around so much? One of the biggest faults with this whole program is that there's too much talk and not enough action!" At the same meeting, when asked if he would serve on a panel of committee officers who would make themselves available to explain to various civic organizations what the TOEO was doing, he replied, "I'm still afraid to voice my own opinions when talking to some strange group. I'm afraid that my opinions won't say what the people I represent really think." (He nonetheless agreed to be on the panel and did actually have contact with some civic groups. He explained in a later interview, "I didn't get on the panel just because I wanted to sell OEO to people. I knew that most, if not all, of the Indians were still very skeptical about OEO, and if I was going to represent them it wouldn't be right for me to blow the OEO horn. I got on the panel because I thought it was a good chance to show other people in the community that Indians are interested in all kinds of things and maybe to help break down the rotten picture that they have of us.")

Toward the end of the Leadership Training meeting, all the officers began talking about the degree of interest within their committees. Mr. A, with some force, said, "When we first started our meetings, we discussed and cussed a lot. Now, interest seems to be falling off. Unless we can get something that develops in the quick future, we're not going to hold the interest of the members much longer." The other officers agreed that they were having the same kind of difficulty, and one of them suggested that "maybe we can get some social workers out to help us get more interest." Mr. A laughed and replied, "I'm afraid my people don't have a very good view of social workers. They've seen too many people come out to 'help' the Indians who think they're experts on Indian life because they've read a couple of Zane Grey novels! But this Neighborhood Aide Program, maybe that's different. If we can get an Indian Neighborhood aide, one who lives right out there with us, then maybe that'll be a different story." In a later interview, he said:

"I really believed that getting an Indian Neighborhood aide would make a lot of difference to the Indian Committee. I don't mean just because a full-time Indian Neighborhood aide who knew his way around could be a big help to the Indians, but also because it'd prove to them that the OEO really could accomplish something for the Indian, and I mean specifically for the Indian.

"I talked this Neighborhood aide idea up with an awful lot of people, and I pretty much put it on the line that this was going to show us all that OEO really had the stuff—that it was able to get something concrete for us. Quite a few of the people who I talked to said, 'Aw, come on, they'll never hire an Indian,' and I argued with them, and told them that they would. In a way I was giving my word to the people that an Indian would be hired and that I was willing to put my faith in the OEO that this would be accomplished. I wish to hell I'd kept my big mouth shut!"

At the Board meeting held during February, Mr. A had a supporting hand in running the meeting, since the president and vice-president of the Board were both unable to attend. He helped to set up the agenda for the meeting, worked with others in preparing the packets of information for each Board member, and made several motions concerning Board action. After the meeting had been adjourned, he commented, "Well, that was kind of fun, but damn it, I'm getting the feeling I'm a company man. What's worse, I think some of my committee members are getting the same feeling!"

MR. A's LAST COMMITTEE MEETING

At the February meeting, the eleventh of the Indian group, there were twenty-one women, ten men, and five children. Mr. A had said that he had "campaigned like hell" to get a good turn-out. He seemed quite a bit more nervous than he usually was before a meeting. Possibly it was because the Assistant Director of the TOEO was not able to attend, but more probably it was because he had been "getting a lot of guff" from the Indians he talked to about OEO. He searched hurriedly through his brief case for a list of the procedures for carrying out a meeting, but couldn't find it and decided to "fake it." He called the meeting to order and, after a short search for the minutes, instructed the secretary to read them.

He then turned to the business at hand, and said, "Many of you have come to the meeting wanting OEO to help you with problems. The Government won't duplicate programs already in effect. They can't do what's already being done by another agency, like the Welfare Department or the Indian Agency. OEO's prime target is to run interference between you and other agencies. At least that's the way I see our committee here. Then there may also be some other special programs that we can go into with OEO money. Actually, I guess the biggest benefit you get from OEO participation is what you learn by being a part of it . . ." A woman interrupted him, "I don't see no sense to it. Why call us here if there's nothing in it for us right away?" Another woman said, "It seems like we always have to go through a hundred steps and fill out a hundred forms before we can get help. Is this going to be another one of those deals?" One of the men spoke up, "Sometimes the kind of help an Indian can get through the Indian agencies isn't as much as other people get through other agencies. I think our problem is we don't know the right people. Maybe it'll help us to go through this oeo outfit." Mr. A agreed, "Now you're talking! That's what got me interested in oeo, and if it works, that's what's going to keep us all interested! And remember, this isn't like Welfare; they aren't going to give us anything. We've got to get it for ourselves! That's a big difference. By coming together into groups like this, by getting a voice for ourselves, and by having the force of oeo behind us, maybe we can get a lot more done!"

One of the participants asked Mr. A about the progress of the proposed old-folks home for Indians. He answered, disappointment in his voice, "I guess we were just shooting for the moon there. We have to get 10 per cent of the funding, and that's just out of reach for us. I guess everything fell through—there was too much complication." One man murmured, "I told you so," but otherwise the group remained silent. Mr. A continued to run through the reports on programs that he had observed or discovered through his participation in other oeo activities. He told the group about job placements for youths, the Head Start Program, Small Business Loans, and the Legal Aid Program. He paused for a moment and said, "I know we'd all like a program where all we'd have to do is turn in our names and have everything done for us, but that's not the way it's going to work here. We've got to decide what we need, and then go after some of the available programs." A woman remarked, "Yeah, that's okay! But all these programs take so long to get going. What can we get going now?" Mr. A then continued describing to the group the local oeo-sponsored Job Corps, Work-Study Program, Day Care Center, and the Neighborhood Aide Program. One of the men challenged him, "Those programs all sound very good, but will they put bread on the table?"

A woman angrily broke in, "This program sounds too good to be true. I don't believe it. I really don't think this oea [*sic*] would help me out the door. They wouldn't give me anything!" Mr. A answered, "Come to an Economic Opportunity Board meeting sometime and see how many people are interested in this program, and a lot of them are from the agencies, too—they all want to try and help us, or I should say, help us to help ourselves." He continued, apparently growing angry, "Why're you getting mad at me? This isn't my program, you know. If you don't like something, let's do something about it, but don't give me a bad time!" (Mr. A commented in a later interview:

"At that point in the meeting I began to feel like I was another person. By that I mean I knew exactly how the people who were giving me a bad time felt, and damn it, I agreed with them. I know and understand why they were interested in getting something done now, particularly with regard to jobs and the comforts of life. I could see now that they were beginning to sharpshoot me with questions, and I thought to myself, 'I should be out there with them, not standing up here.' But I kept trying to answer their questions, and I kept defending oeo. I did this even though I could understand the meaning of the questions they asked better than I could understand the meaning of the answers I gave them!"

Mr. A was beginning to feel sharply the disparity between his role as a TNO and his role as a member of an Indian subculture. For him, this was a difficult conflict to resolve, primarily because, as he subsequently reported, "The people seemed to be forcing me to make a choice. It seemed to me that they were saying, 'Either you're with us or you're against us—either you're an oeo officer or you're an Indian, you can't be both.' I wasn't sure what I was going to do.")

It was now 9:15 p.m., and Mr. A suggested that they show the film they had scheduled for this eleventh meeting. It was a documentary, dramatizing the victory that the South Dakota Indians had won concerning land rights. The moral of the film, according to Mr. A's introductory remarks, was "what Indians can do if they get together and really try." The film was started, and as it progressed, more than half the audience got up and left. After its completion, Mr. A commented, "I guess some of them left because the hour was late, but I'm sure a lot of them left because they don't like to see that Indians who got together and fought could do things for themselves. I think they'd rather have things given to them. They couldn't watch that and sympathize with those Indians without admitting they were wrong themselves."

Mr. A saw no reason for formally adjourning the meeting, and while the film was being put away and the projector boxed up, he talked with a few of the participants. "I'm wondering," he said thoughtfully, "if it wouldn't be better to form an Indian group outside the OEO, built around social and cultural interests—like the Pow-Wow Clubs. Maybe that'd work to get the Indians together, and then we could tie in with OEO. I'm not sure what to do; all I know is I'm getting tired of being a target!"

THE CHIEF RESIGNS

Since the TNCs had established a schedule of one meeting per month, each of them had a fixed and predetermined day for meetings. The Indian Committee had decided to meet on the fourth Tuesday of every month. The next gathering was scheduled for March 22, 1966.

Three meetings of the Leadership Training Sessions were conducted in March before the next committee meeting date, and Mr. A attended all of them. At the first of these he argued for a new approach in the Target Neighborhood Committees, stating:

"I don't think it's enough for the TOEO just to present itself as a service organization to be used by the Target Neighborhoods to implement programs. I'm not saying that that isn't helpful nor that it shouldn't be continued, but I've tried to get that 'service' idea across time and time again, and it just doesn't go across, not with the Indians at least.

"I'm wondering if there isn't some way the committees can organize to accomplish some quick, concrete goals. I'm not sure what I mean—maybe jobs would be a good example—but I just have a feeling that if we're going to get people to have confidence in the OEO, we're going to have to produce results fast, because most of us just aren't used to thinking in terms of long-range goals."

Mr. A clearly revealed in this session his sensitivity to the *action-* and *present-*orientations of those whom he represented, and to the conflicts these orientations had with the expectations of the TOEO. The other officers agreed with his analysis, since the same problem had been a recurrent and significant one for all the indigenous leaders.

Delegates from a small, incipient local "concern" group, called the Voice of the Common People, attended the second meeting of the March Leadership Training Sessions. Mr. A, who had attended one of their meetings as a member of an OEO panel, was at first attracted to the group and commented that he thought "maybe here was a different, more direct way of getting people involved in changing their way of life." He was later disillusioned by this group, however, considering them to be "more confused than I am."

Later in the same March session, Mr. A suggested to the other officers that "we have a leader-exchange program. You know, it can be a problem if the same man shows up meeting after meeting in the committees, and stands up there in front like a big wheel. I'd like some of the other leaders to come over to my group and talk to them, so they can see there really are other elected officers, too." The rest of the participants agreed with this, but no schedule was set up for exchange visits. It appeared as though Mr. A was looking for some way to get himself out of the limelight, and thus out of the heightening role conflict that he was experiencing.

The approaching elections for TNC officers was a topic of discussion at the third March Leadership Training Session. During the course of this meeting, Mr. A was cut off in the middle of his discussion of something because "there's a long agenda, and a lot of voting to do." He became quite angry at this and said testily, "I'm sorry if I interrupted your program!" In a subsequent interview he commented:

"I figured that that was a bad sign. It's hard to do much discussing at the Board meetings because the agenda's so loaded, and things have to get done in a hurry. But when I saw the Leadership sessions going the same way, I figured the TOEO was going to get itself in trouble because that old red tape was starting to get snarled. I think I was really getting kind of tired of it all at that time. I remember saying at that meeting when we were talking about a program that was to run three years, that I wondered whether or not OEO would even be around in three years. I guess I was beginning to get tired, all right!"

Shortly before the scheduled twelfth meeting of the Indian Committee, Mr. A informed the Assistant Director of the TOEO that he had "taken an evening construction job, which will make it difficult for me to continue serving as an OEO officer." The Assistant Director, in a later interview, commented, "Mr. A really doesn't want to work at an evening job, but he has to take what he can get right now. The job may not last too long, and maybe he'll be able to let the vice-chairman run the show until he gets a daytime job that he'll like better." This eventuality, however, did not materialize. At the meeting of the Indian Committee scheduled for March 22, no one showed up but the Assistant Director and a few agency representatives. No Indians, not even the vice-chairman, came to the Mission. The meeting was, of course, canceled by the Assistant Director.

Mr. A had still not officially resigned as chairman of the Indian Committee, nor did he intend to, until near the first of April he discovered that the delegate agency administering the Neighborhood Aide Program had hired not one of the Indians whom he had encouraged to apply, but a man whom he perceived to be "not an Indian, but an outsider." He became furious when he learned of it, and felt that the Indians had been "given a raw deal again." He felt that he had "given his word to the people" that an Indian would be

TOEO Assistant Director and was told that "the delegate agency has the primary responsibility for the hiring, and there's not much we can do about it." He went to see the supervisor of the Neighborhood aides, and ended up becoming even more angry because of what he perceived as a holier-than-thou attitude on the part of the supervisor. He then attempted to talk with the top official in the delegate agency but said he was told that "he is out of town." Mr. A said that he had "seen him go into his office just a little while before," and so far as he was concerned, "that was the last straw." By the time the Economy Opportunity Board met on the evening of April 6, the president of the Board had in hand Mr. A's letter of resignation. The Board accepted it, and instructed the secretary to send Mr. A a letter of commendation for his "diligent and sincere labors on our behalf."

COMMENTS OF AN EX-CHAIRMAN

Mr. A, getting together with me for a discussion of "why I quit," commented:

"Now that I'm apart from OEO, I can say a lot of things that maybe I should have said when I was inside it. But when you're inside of an organization, you feel some loyalty toward it, for the greater good, I guess. I don't mean to say that just the TOEO is why I quit. I think they're sincere in what they're trying to do, and probably have one of the best programs in the country. I think the Assistant Director is doing a hell of a fine job, and working with the other committee officers is an experience I'll never forget. But some of the ways the TOEO works, and I guess it has to work that way to get the job done, causes problems—especially for committee leaders. I found myself right in the middle of them. I suppose in some cases they're worse with the Indians. I just didn't like walking on the tightrope of problems, so I resigned."

In response to a question about what those problems were, he said:

"It's not that I had any trouble learning my way around in the OEO committees and all that stuff, although I do think there's too much time wasted in all that formal procedure and form filling-out. I think I learned a lot from that experience, though. What bothered me most was the way the other Indians acted at my being involved in the TOEO, and the fact that we couldn't find a program that seemed to be suited to us. We pick a program, like the home for old-aged Indians, and then when we get down to the specifics of the program, all we could come up with were objections and do-nothing comments. I think that's one of the things that bothered me, that we seemed to have a built-in feeling of defeat before we even started. We wouldn't take chances because we were afraid we'd be turned down. We kind of say to ourselves, 'Who's interested in the Indian, anyway?'

"A good part of this feeling of defeat and not wanting to get involved in the programs that we talked about was because all of the programs that we considered couldn't be put into operation for months, or even as long as a year. That kind of planning doesn't mean much to us, because we've got a long history of being disappointed about promises in the future. What we needed was something we could see, something we could get done now by our committee.

"I can give you an example of what I mean. We were trying to get together a group for a Pow-Wow Club and we were having trouble getting members. Well, one of the things we needed on the Pow-Wow grounds was a toilet. A few of us said we were going to build it ourselves, but a lot of the others said, 'Oh, no, you'll never be able to get the parts for that. You'll never be able to do it,' and all that same kind of talk. Well, by God, we got together the parts for it. We scrounged around and got used fixtures and we started putting it together. Finally, we got it finished, and it wasn't any outhouse, either, but a nice rest room, and it looked good. We'd done it ourselves, and those people who said we couldn't do it had to take back their words, and we got together an active Pow-Wow Club. Well, that's kind of a simple little example, but the point I want to make is that we needed something like that in our OEO committee, something we could get done quickly and that everybody could see. About the only programs that seemed to suit OEO were long-range programs.

"I don't mean to knock the programs that take time to develop. For example, I think programs like Head Start, and the Day Care Centers, and so on are great and very important. But what does that mean to the Indian who's attending the meetings, and how's that going to hold his interest? He needs and wants something he can dig his teeth into here and now. Remember the story about the cows? Well, that was an example of how we can jockey around agency officials, but it's also an example of how we're interested in things in the here and now. Rather than think about using the cows for breeding, so we could develop a good herd years in the future, we ate some of them during the next couple of weeks.

"What I'm saying is that I think the OEO should have some short-range programs the people can get involved with right away in their own front yard, so to speak, so that the accomplishment will stand up and bite them! Not being able to set up something like that bothered me quite a bit, because I knew how the people felt and yet we couldn't come up with anything that we could get going right away. We weren't used to doing things for ourselves, and I felt that I was letting them down by not being able to get the ball rolling faster."

Mr. A took out a cigarette, lit it, and took a long, thoughtful drag. As he exhaled the smoke he reflected:

"I guess I thought that hiring an Indian Neighborhood aide would do the trick. It seemed to me that that might be the kind of *now* result that would pull us together, and get us off and running. I pretty much put my reputation on the line with that one, and I talked it up all over the community, how we were going to get an Indian hired as a Neighborhood aide. Like they always do, some of the doubters told me it would never work, and they'd never hire an Indian. I argued and argued with them, and then when I found out who they had hired, I felt like I'd been sold out. It's not that I have anything against the guy they hired. He's a very nice guy, and he'll try to do a good job; but it's just that he's not a real Indian and he isn't even from this area."

Concomitant to the growing Prairie Potawatomi sense of identity (referred to earlier in this chapter) is apparently a growing sensitivity as to who is a Potawatomi and who is not. Mr. A, thinking that one of the people he had recommended would be hired as the Neighhood aide, had convinced his followers that they would therefore be represented by a local Potawatomi, or at least by a member of a closely related tribe or band. However, the delegate agency chose a man, on the basis of formal qualifications, who was only one-eighth Indian—and that one-eighth from a tribe not related to, and not particularly friendly with, the Potawatomi. In the view of many of his followers, therefore, not only had Mr. A failed to demonstrate that the TOEO "was really interested in the Indians," but also he was held responsible for violating a tradition of "looking out for one's tribal brothers."

Mr. A sighed and continued:

"You can imagine what happened to me when the other Indians found out who'd been hired. I'd spread it all around that this was going to be proof that this OEO program was really interested in the Indians, and it fell apart.

"Now, I know it really wasn't the TOEO's fault that they couldn't dictate who the delegate agency was going to hire, and I know the delegate agency hired that guy fair and square. But that didn't make any difference. I'd become interested in OEO because I thought it was going to be kind of a go-between between us and the agencies, and I felt let down that they couldn't do something about it. Besides that, how do you explain to your people about 'delegate agencies,' and all that stuff? The people didn't blame the delegate agency, they didn't blame the OEO, they blamed *me*! I was the leader and I was supposed to produce, and I didn't."

He took a gulp of coffee, and continued:

"It's been that way ever since I became chairman of the Indian Committee. The people aren't going to trust the OEO—it's just the opposite. They aren't going to trust it because it's an agency. Any belief they put in its programs comes about because someone they have faith in tells them it might be worth a chance.

"Well, I was the one they had faith in, and I told them it might be worth a chance. So then, when things didn't happen fast enough, or when they didn't work out the way we'd like them to, I was the one that caught hell. I'll give you an example. A while back, one of my people called the Assistant Director and told him she couldn't come to work because she wasn't feeling well. He asked her who she was, and she told him, 'I'm Mrs. V, and I was hired by Mr. A to work on the Medicare Program.' But I didn't hire her! Nobody had hired her! I did tell her to go down to the OEO office and fill out the application. But you see, she saw me as being the guy who was going to get her the job—just for the asking! So, she didn't fill out the forms and naturally she didn't get the job. Now she'll never trust me again.

"Whenever anything would go wrong with the program, the people would feel that I let them down. As I told you before, it's not organizations that count with us, it's people—and I'm people."

Asked to explain further what he thought was the Indians' view of his leadership, he answered:

"Some of the people give you a bad time, and they say to others, 'He thinks he's really something big now because he's rubbing shoulders with big people.' That's hard to take, and it's hard to hold together people who think you're running out on them. I know you aren't going to be liked by everybody in a group. I know that, but it's still tough to take when you're trying your best to keep a group together. The way I figure you can overcome that, is if you can quickly get something going—that is, to produce, to solve some kind of problem they may have. If you can do that once, just once, then the people'll give you room to make some mistakes. They'll say,

'Well, it's okay that he goofed this one, because he's done something else for us already.'

"I kept looking for that answer, for that one right-now solution, and I never found it. I thought the Neighborhood aide deal would work, but it didn't. So then what happens is that some of the people start figuring you're in it just for yourself, and they say you're a 'sell-out' who's turning his back on his own people.

"So there you are, the committee leader. On one side, you've got some people in the community who don't like it that an Indian is a leader and is kicking around town trying to do something for his people. On the other side, you've got your own people giving you a bad time because you're not working miracles for them overnight. *I just got tired of walking the tightrope!*

"As I said before, I don't want to sound like I'm criticizing the whole OEO program, because I'm not. They're a young outfit, and are still learning. But one of the things that I don't think they realize yet is just how tough it is to be a committee officer! By that I mean, a leader who really wants to represent his people."

Mr. A was asked what he thought of the organizational structure of the TOEO. He replied:

"I think it's okay, especially the part where the people who're from the Target Neighborhoods get a chance to be involved. But over the months that I was in OEO, I saw there might be a danger of it becoming more and more like an agency. Sometimes, for example, I got the feeling that the Assistant Director's hands were tied as he got more and more involved. It seemed like he had to spend more and more time in the office, and didn't have as much time as he'd like to have had to spend out in the Neighborhoods with us.

"I think they realize that problem in the office and I hope they watch it carefully. If they ever lose the person-to-person contacts they have in the Target Neighborhoods, then the program's going to completely fall apart. I think it's going to be a tough job to teach that lesson to some of the agency representatives who sit on the Economic Opportunity Board. Another thing, they better be careful about those big, long agendas they have for some of the meetings.

That doesn't give the people enough time to talk, and that makes it especially tough on the committee officers. We aren't used to all that meeting stuff, you know."

In summing up what he had gotten out of the experience with the TOEO, Mr. A repeated a number of opinions previously expressed:

"I learned a lot about how agencies work, and that there're lots of people besides Indians who're poor and don't know what to do about it. I think maybe I helped a little bit, especially through the panels, to change the picture some people have of Indians. A lot of people seem to be surprised that Indians were even thinking about taking an active part in something, that we weren't all just sitting around in front of our tepees and collecting welfare checks.

"I probably wouldn't have minded staying with OEO and getting more and more involved. I actually kind of enjoyed it. But the thing was that as I got more and more involved, I seemed less and less able to get my people what they wanted as fast as they wanted it. If I'd stayed with OEO, I'd have learned a lot more for myself, but I'd have had to leave my people behind. I guess I just couldn't bring myself to do that."

Although Mr. A resigned as chairman of the Indian Committee, he continued to be an informal leader in the community, and on occasion attended poverty-program meetings. In May, 1966, the Assistant Director of the TOEO attempted to reactivate the Indian Committee. Mr. A attended that meeting, and when called upon to explain to the group his experience as an indigenous leader, he complained of "how difficult it is to get the Indians to come together. Then when you do get them together, and try to lead them, they end up hating you. It's a tough job." He added, "The main accomplishment I think I had in my year of participation was to change the picture of the Indian a little bit around town. I'm afraid I didn't accomplish very much else." As the meeting progressed, and a new chairman reluctantly accepted the position, Mr. A commented, "Boy, it feels good to be back out here again, instead of up front! I feel like a human being again. The new chairman'll find out pretty soon how tough it is to be a leader. You know, there're some of my people who still won't talk to me. I actually got some people to hating me because they thought I was siding with the OEO sometimes. Every time my name would get into the paper, I'd get half a dozen more enemies. It's a tough job."

Mr. A had attempted to enact the bridge role expected by the TOEO staff in accordance with the Overlap Model (his Marginality Scale score had initially been comparatively high). Perhaps more than any other Target Neighborhood Officer, he manifested the kinds of stresses that can result when the leader is caught between the conflicting expectations of his followers and the poverty-intervention organization. Mr. A further demonstrated the responsibility that a poverty-intervention organization has to train its indigenous leaders for the process experiences they will encounter as well as for the program content they must know. The Indian Committee traversed the Orientation (I), Catharsis (II), and Focus (III) Stages of TNC development. Somewhere in the merging between the Focus (III) and Action (IV) phases, however, it bogged down. The members were able fairly clearly to specify their needs, but none of the OEO programs available seemed to be "real" enough, or reachable enough, to them. The alternative programs they saw as possible were all judged to be "shooting for the moon." Consequently, the dilemmas of indigenous leadership and the rejection of "distant" programs conspired to deactivate the Indian Committee and to discourage its members.

CHAPTER 14

"Action, Together!": A Contrasting Example

THE CASE HISTORY of the Indian Committee in Chapter 13 demonstrates some of the dynamics which engendered indigenous-leader stress and arrested that committee at an early stage. In Chapter 12 it was briefly mentioned that one TNC had, by contrast, attained the Purposive Stage of Development (VII). Presented now are elements from that committee's case history which seem to have contributed to its having reached and maintained the Purposive Stage.

FORMATION OF THE COMMITTEE

The Highland Park–Pierce (HPP) Target Neighborhood Committee held its first meeting in early June, 1965, in a Neighborhood church. That and the next meeting were organized and primarily conducted by the Assistant Director of the TOEO. The modal group dynamics of the early meeting, held twice monthly and attended by an average of sixteen members, followed closely those outlined in the TNC stages of development (Orientation [I] and Catharsis [II]). By the end of July the committee had elected a chairman, vice-chairman, and secretary and had moved its meeting place to a shelter house in the Neighborhood's small park. All three officers and all committee members were Negro-American. About half of those attending were female; age range for total membership extended from teenagers through elder citizens. All but a few of the participants were "poor" by OEO criteria. Highland Park-Pierce, an area of some 400 acres, houses about 1,200 persons, 85 per cent of them Negro-American. City surveys have termed it "blighted."

Each meeting was opened with a prayer offered by a chairman-designated member. A sample of the prayers, which usually followed the same theme, was: "Dear God, we give thanks for the opportunity to get together tonight, and we pray for peace and harmony among us, so we can help ourselves and help others who have less than we do. Give us the knowledge to learn about all these programs and the strength to use them in the way they will do some good. Help us find the answers to the problems of poverty and find ways to get more dignity for ourselves and the rest of our people."

As the meetings progressed, the TOEO Assistant Director phased himself out as an active organizer, and indigenous leadership took firm hold of the HPP Committee. The Assistant Director continued to attend meetings, but in a consultant capacity—speaking only when questioned by TNOs or members.

The chairman, Mr. L, was a forty-six-year-old male hospital worker who was actively religious and had been a resident in the HPP Neighborhood for thirty years. He had been one of the first residents in a Target Neighborhood to become interested in the Topeka poverty program. Later, he would be elected by the Target Neighborhood Officers of the other TNCs to be chairman of the Leadership Committee, and elected by members of the Economic Opportunity Board to be their vice-chairman. His comparatively high Marginality Scale score agreed with his expressed intention, at least at the onset, to implement the "bridge" expectation for indigenous leaders.

A FIRST PROPOSAL

Shortly after the election of their officers, the HPP Committee members, their TNC firmly in the Focus Stage (III), began working in earnest toward sponsorship of an OEO community-action proposal. The members' discussion focused primarily on needs for recreation within their own Neighborhood. Consideration of those problems yielded to consideration of the problems of Neighborhood youths in general, and then to a broader consideration of the general isolation of the Neighborhood population from knowledge about, and utilization of, available community services. Dialogues among representatives of the HPP Neighborhood Committee, members of various relevant Study Committees, representatives of the Topeka Recreation Commission, and TOEO staff brought a consensus on the need for, and possibility of, an Extension Worker Program. The Extension Workers would be hired from the various Target Neighborhoods in the city and would serve as ombudsmen between Neighborhood residents and community agencies or service organizations. The Recreation Commission agreed to be the "delegate agency," and to contribute the mandatory 10 per cent local share of over-all program funding. The HPP Neighborhood Committee agreed to be one of the proposal sponsors.

Now in the Action Stage (IV), members of the HPP Committee diligently conducted surveys and gathered the letters of support required for an OEO action proposal. The interactions stimulated during the proposal preparation were gratifying to all the participants. The not-poor, approached for advice and support, seemed surprised and educated by the "dedication" and "ability" of the participating poor. The Target Neighborhood residents seemed surprised and encouraged by the co-operation of the not-poor. The TOEO planners were pleased that the mixing of representatives from different socioeconomic levels in the pursuit of the community-action proposal seemed to be having the intended effect: breaking down stereotypes, enhancing communication, and developing new skills.

By mid-August, the Extension Worker community-action proposal, having been processed through the structure of the TOEO Review Committee, was enthusiastically forwarded to Washington through the Regional Office of Economic Opportunity.

"WE BLEW IT"

More than four months elapsed before the HPP Committee members were informed that the Extension Worker proposal had been approved by the Office of Economic Opportunity in Washington. During the interim of the Limbo Stage (V), several changes were made in the proposal at the suggestion of the regional OEO and the local delegate agency—changes made to accommodate the proposal to standing or recently established organizational policies and guidelines. The committee members began to perceive the Extension Worker proposal as becoming more and more distant from them. During those meetings in which they had discussed the preparation of the application, and during those times when they had actively gathered supporting documents and agency co-operation, they had referred to the Extension Worker planning as *"our* proposal." As the long review of the application wore on and as changes in the proposal were made—in the members' view, somewhat arbitrarily and beyond their control—they began to refer to *"that* proposal." Finally, by the time in late December when the TOEO staff announced the proposal's approval and the delegate agency had begun implementing the program, the reference became *"their* proposal." The members had lost their feelings of identification with the proposal they had so excitedly generated.

From August to December, 1965, attendance at the HPP Committee meetings had gradually declined, until Mr. L, faced with the quandaries of Limbo (V), canceled several meetings because he feared "the members would ask about the proposal, and I had no answers for them."

As the Extension Worker Program was implemented by the delegate agency, the HPP Committee members expressed their specific disappointments. They had expected that they would have more "say" in the launching of the program, particularly with regard to writing job descriptions and hiring personnel from among the Target Neighborhoods. They also had expected that the Extension Workers were to help the Target Neighborhood Officers organize their Neighborhoods and increase attendance at their meetings. The delegate agency, on the other hand, expected that the Extension Worker Program was to be its administrative and fiscal responsibility, and desired to fit that program into its superordinate organizational goals. That conflict in expectations was generated at least in part by the vagueness of the terms "maximum feasible participation" of the poor and "delegate agency"—concepts which the neophyte TOEO was not yet able clearly to define. As a result the participants, poor and not-poor, who were involved in preparing and implementing the Extension Worker Program came to their own conclusions about, and created their own definitions of, the issues of program power, control, and purpose. Those conclusions and definitions often conflicted operationally.

HPP Committee members attempted to register complaints concerning their frustrated expectations to the TOEO staff and at meetings of the Economic Opportunity Board. They were unable, however, at this time, to gain satisfaction of their expectations.

At their first meeting following the approval and implementation of the Extension Worker Program, the HPP Committee members, having entered the Testing Stage (VI), reflected upon the outcome of the proposal they had sponsored. They felt their own participation in its preparation had been "good experience" and had taught them how to "talk the agency language" and to see that "not all the agencies and agency people are alike. Some know what's happening and are willing to help us like we want to be helped; some don't know what's happening and can only help us in ways that tie us up." Many of the members were angry that they had "lost the Extension Worker Program." A few announced that they had "had enough of this OEO" and would "never come to another meeting." Most of them, though angry and disappointed, felt that they "just hadn't had enough experience to know any better" and had "let our say in the program get away from us." At the end of their discussion, Mr. L summarized member consensus:

"Maybe in a way this has been good for us. For all of us this was the first time trying to put together something like this. The delegate agency, and other agencies like it, have done this a thousand times. They know their way around. We don't *yet*. Let's face it: we blew it! But I think we learned some of the ropes, and I don't think it'll happen again. We're not going to quit. But we're not going to work hard on a program and then give it away again, either!"

"THIS TIME, WE KNOW BETTER"

The members of the HPP Committee, returning temporarily to behaviors associated with Focus and Action Stages (III and IV), reviewed Neighborhood and individual needs revealed by the survey they had conducted while preparing the Extension Worker proposal. They discussed possible alternative programs with TOEO staff and decided that those needs could best be met by establishing a "Neighborhood House" in Highland Park–Pierce. The officers and representatives of the HPP Committee met with Study Committees and TOEO staff, and agreed upon the following formal goals for the proposed Neighborhood House:

(1) To provide a point of contact between low-income persons and existing services and to provide bridges between the persons and the services; (2) to provide a rallying point and a home base for the people of the Neighborhood for the promotion of OEO and other related groups; (3) to provide a full range of counseling services for all age groups of the Neighborhood; (4) to provide a place for family education in food marketing and preparation, clothing, consumer education, and any other courses which would help to strengthen family life; (5) to provide a place for part-time care of preschool children; (6) to provide an outlet for leisure-time activities for the people of the Neighborhood; (7) to provide a place for the training of professionals and nonprofessionals in how to work with people in a low-income neighborhood.[1]

[1] Topeka Office of Economic Opportunity, *Annual Report for 1965–1966*, pp. 16–17.

For the Target Neighborhood residents there was another major, though unwritten, purpose for the Neighborhood House—"to give us the opportunity to run our own program." This goal was openly stated by the officers of the HPP Committee, and was quite apparent in their subsequent participation in the preparation of the Neighborhood House proposal. Mr. L carefully and consistently remained in a decision-making position through each step of the planning. The TOEO staff and Study Committee representatives clearly were established and maintained solely in a consultative position by the officers and members of the HPP Committee. The TOEO staff, aware of committee members' disappointment with their lack of participation in the implementation of the Extension Worker Program, accommodated, after resolving some conflicts concerning administrative responsibilities and functional roles, the committee's press for more autonomy. The Neighborhood Committee and the TOEO staff agreed that the Neighborhood House Program would not be handled by a single delegate agency. Rather, the local share of funding would be supplied by a number of nonrestricting organizations, and the Economic Opportunity Board would be the over-all sponsor—with immediate guidance to be provided by an Advisory Council, to consist of eight Neighborhood residents and seven representatives from community agencies. The Neighborhood Committee members insisted that they choose the community-agency representatives who were to serve on the Advisory Council. They chose those individuals by the criteria of demonstrated interest rather than organizational position. Furthermore, the Neighborhood Committee cautiously decided, with constant reference to "our continuing to have the say," which community organizations they would approach to help them accumulate local financial share. On the basis of the criterion for potential autonomy, the Neighborhood Committee requested and received most of its required local share from the Menninger Foundation. The balance of support was contributed by the Shawnee County Agricultural Extension Service, an agency which had for three months before made available, on an unconditional and invitational basis, homemaking, landscaping, cooking, sewing, and Youth Club advice to the residents of the Highland Park–Pierce Neighborhood. Letters of cognizance and promise of future co-operation were requested from, and supplied by, the Juvenile Court, the County Health Department, County Welfare, the YMCA and YWCA, and the local Board of Education.

The HPP Committee officers stayed close to the proposal through the procedure of TOEO application review, and presented the case for approval to the Economic Opportunity Board. The Board unanimously agreed to endorse the proposal. Mr. L, along with TOEO staff, took the completed proposal to the regional Office of Economic Opportunity in Kansas City. After two months' review by this office, during all of which time Mr. L remained in close touch with regional and TOEO staff, and combatted the effects of Limbo (V) by giving regular blow-by-blow reports to his TNC members, the Neighborhood House proposal was approved and funded. Mr. L excitedly announced the good news to committee members and, after sharing their exuberance, solemnly stated:

"Okay, we can be happy about this. But let's not get too excited, yet. Remember what happened last time. The real work's before us now. We've got to get the Neighborhood House going, the way we want to get it going! We made some mistakes with that Extension Worker Program before, and it ended up not being our program anymore. This time, we know better. Now, who's going to be on the leasing committee . . ."

From its beginning, the Neighborhood House was functionally *one* with the HPP Committee, and that committee moved quickly through the resolute Testing Stage (VI) into the Purposive Stage (VII) of TNC development.

IMPLEMENTATION OF THE NEIGHBORHOOD HOUSE

After considerable exploring and a few disappointments, the Advisory Council (of which the HPP Committee officers were members) located a building and property which they agreed was both within the budget and an appropriate setting for the development of the Neighborhood House. The building, situated on a corner lot with considerable yard space, was a relatively new two-bedroom, full basement, family residence. The property was centrally located in the Highland Park–Pierce Neighborhood, and the building, constructed on a small knoll, was visible and accessible from all sides. The Neighborhood residents, particularly those on the Advisory Council, were enthusiastic about the selection. Many of them excitedly discussed what classes would be held in what rooms, how the kitchen should be set up for homemaking activities, how the basement could be fixed for a recreation room, etc. The acquisition of a tangible structure served to convince those Neighborhood residents who had previously been somewhat skeptical that "maybe something *could* be done." One resident, thumping his fist against one of the walls, mused, "I've heard lots about all that poverty money, but this is the first time I've ever seen it do anything *real*." Several of the Neighborhood residents had observed with curiosity the Advisory Council's inspection of the house before the final choice had been made. After the lease had been signed, a not-poor member of the Advisory Council asked, "Ought we get the word to the Neighborhood residents right away?" A Neighborhood Committee officer laughingly replied, "The people knew all about it before the ink was dry. You can bet on that!"

Three staff members were to be hired for the Neighborhood House: a director, a Neighborhood aide, and a secretary. As outlined in the Neighborhood House proposal, the director was to have the following qualifications: (1) a high-school education plus experience; (2) a willingness to participate in continuous on-the-job training to improve his skills in carrying on the project; (3) a resident of a low-income Neighborhood; (4) a general familiarity with social agencies in Topeka; (5) experience with working in groups situations; (6) mature judgment and a sensitivity to people; (7) administrative abilities; (8) a minimum age of twenty-five. The Neighborhood aide was to have the following qualifications: (1) completion of at least the ninth grade; (2) a resident of a low-income Neighborhood; (3) mature judgment and a sensitivity to people; (4) minimum of eighteen years of age, age twenty-one desirable. The Advisory Council was to accept applications, interview candidates, and make recommendations to the Economic Opportunity Board for final approval. Candidates' "person orientation" was to be a key criterion.

The Advisory Council conducted its personnel search and selection in accordance with the qualifications specified in the proposal, with one exception—they agreed that, if possible, all staff members should be hired not from *a* low-income Neighborhood, but from the Highland Park–Pierce Neighborhood itself.

From among several candidates, the Advisory Council chose as director Mr. Y, a forty-year-old Negro male resident of the Highland Park–Pierce Neighborhood. He had been a charter member of the HPP Committee, and was employed as one of the workers in the Extension Worker Program. He helped the Advisory Council choose a Neighborhood aide (a Negro female) and a secretary (a Mexican-American female), both of whom were also Neighborhood residents. The selection of all three staff members and the selection of the site for the Neighborhood House were unanimously approved at a subsequent meeting of the Economic Opportunity Board.

As an employee of the Extension Worker Program for six months, and an active member of the HPP Committee, Mr. Y had accumulated considerable experience in the attempt to be a bridge between existing community agencies and their target populations. The low-income areas assigned to him by the delegate agency included Highland Park–Pierce. His hiring by the delegate agency had been influenced and applauded by HPP Committee members, as was his performance on the job, even though they had continued to feel frustrated with their participation in the implementation of the Extension Worker Program. However, Mr. Y had not been satisfied with his job as an Extension Worker. He didn't, he said, reject the whole Extension Worker Program:

"There're some parts of it that were good, especially those parts which gave us elbow room to bring agency services to people who needed them but who wouldn't try and get them, or who don't know anything about them at all. . . . The part that bothered me most was that the decisions for the program were being made by people in offices with lots of experience, and the people in the Neighborhoods with no experience weren't getting a chance to get some, the way the program was supposed to work. We had to bend the needs of the people to fit the policies of the delegate agency. The delegate agency wasn't able to bend its policies to fit what the people wanted in this case. I'm not sure how to go about getting the Neighborhood House going. But one thing's for sure—it's going to start with the people, and go from there, if it's going to go at all."

The Neighborhood House staff, the HPP Committee, and members of the Advisory Council met frequently to determine expenditures for furnishing and stocking the House. Lists were made for things needed: utensils, tables and chairs, cooking equipment, hardware, books, recreational equipment, musical instruments, office equipment, etc. Some of these items were budgeted for in funds awarded by the Office of Economic Opportunity. The other items, suggested some of the not-poor members of the Advisory Council, "could be donated from individuals or groups in the community at large." The resident members of the Advisory Council expressed a preference for acquiring donated materials from within the Neighborhood itself, however, so "the people will feel even more that the House belongs to them, and it won't be like getting charity." Occasionally during the first few Advisory Council meetings the not-poor members, long experienced in organizing agency and/or volunteer programs, found themselves dominating the discussion. However, the fact that specific not-poor members had been invited by the Neighborhood residents created a climate of give-and-take in which unintended domination by virtue of expertise did not last long. A Neighborhood member explained, "There were some times in our early meetings where the others wanted to walk when we wanted to run, and we wanted to walk when they wanted to run. But we all knew we wanted to go in the same direction, and had the same goals for the House. Sometimes we all did a lot of talking about not much important. But it didn't take us very long before we broke what was left of the sound barrier between us."

Three months after the proposal had been approved, the Neighborhood House was, in the opinion of the staff, ready for formal

"Open House." Committees of Neighborhood residents had, on weekends and during off hours, scrubbed, painted, and remodeled parts of the House to meet their needs and specifications. Some of the women had sewn and hung brightly colored curtains at the windows. A group of teenagers had cleaned and painted the basement. The kitchen was furnished with a stove and refrigerator, and stocked with supplies and utensils. The main room of the House served as a reception area, and had desks for the secretary and the Neighborhood aide. Its walls were decked with announcements and circulars of Neighborhood activities and opportunities. One of the bedrooms was set up, with desks and files, as Mr. Y's office. The second bedroom, considered to be the the most important room in the House, was the "meeting room." This room contained comfortable chairs and a coffee table holding several large ash trays. It was in this room that Mr. Y or his staff members would meet with Neighborhood residents who "wanted to talk things over." Mr. Y felt that a relaxed, "unofficial" atmosphere was the only way that many of the Neighborhood residents would willingly and easily talk about their needs and problems. "In this room," he commented, "people can ask for help without having to trade in their dignity." He added, "There's no desk in this room, as you can see. That's because desks are the same as fences to people who aren't used to them." Formal and impromptu HPP meetings were held in this room or, if more space was needed, in the basement.

Announcements of the forthcoming Open House were placed in the Topeka newspapers and distributed as circulars to the Neighborhood residents. Special invitations had been issued to agency and local-government officials. At an earlier planning meeting, one of the Neighborhood residents had expressed some concern about "who was going to be the speakers at the Open House." Mr. Y smiled and, with bemusement, replied, "Sometimes we may have trouble getting jobs or getting respect, but we never have any trouble getting speakers."

On the morning of October 16, 1966, the staff, the Advisory Council, and approximately twenty Neighborhood volunteers (all members of the HPP Committee) pinned on identification tags, arranged the Neighborhood House pamphlets that had been prepared, and put last-minute touches on decorations and refreshments. A little later in the morning, when the official proceedings were about to begin, the group had increased to about fifty people, not including newspaper reporters and television cameramen. Several telegrams of congratulations had arrived from state and local officials, and a number of local dignitaries had made their appearance. Brief speeches were given by Mr. L, as chairman of the HPP Committee, Mr. Y, as director of the House, two city commissioners, the Director of the TOEO, and the then acting-president of the Menninger Foundation. After the speeches, the principals gathered around a green ribbon that was scotch-taped across the entrance door of the House. Together, amid the flash of cameras, they cut the ribbon with a pair of elementary-school scissors. All present warmly applauded, and there was much sharing of congratulations.

Throughout the rest of the day, HPP Committee members conducted tours of the House, dispensed refreshments, and shared their enthusiasm with visitors. By the end of the Open House, nearly one hundred people had signed the guest book, and it was estimated that a total of approximately two hundred people had stopped by. That evening, both press and television reported the formal opening of the Neighborhood House.

Throughout the day Neighborhood residents displayed obvious pride in, and a keen sense of ownership of, the Neighborhood House. The members of the Advisory Council who did not live in the Target Neighborhood had, by agreement, played a relatively minor role in showing the House. The Neighborhood people felt that this was "Highland Park–Pierce's House" and "residents should do the presenting." The numerous references throughout the day to "our" and "we" attested to the depth of involvement of those residents who were sharing their pride with the visitors.

After all the visitors had left, and the Neighborhood House had been cleaned up, the staff and a few volunteers warmly reflected the day's success. Mr. Y nodded and then said, in a tired voice, "So much for window dressing. Now the job begins."

MAKING CONTACTS AND BUILDING PROGRAMS

The early phase of Neighborhood House operations reflected Mr. Y's Extension Worker experience and the general goals for the House as stated above. The Neighborhood House staff and the HPP Committee were, at this time, *content*-oriented. They were deeply dedicated to making available to needy Neighborhood residents those community services which were presently available. The staff viewed the Neighborhood House as a bridge between community organizations and Neighborhood residents. That staff view of the functions of the Neighborhood House coincided with the views held by the "clients" who came to the Neighborhood House for help of one kind or another. The first question asked by most of the Neighborhood residents who came in contact with the House, was, "What can it do *for* me?"

Very shortly after the House had opened its doors, the staff was averaging two hundred significant contacts with Neighborhood residents each month. HPP Committee members continually served as voluntary field workers and made referrals. Most of these contacts required one or more follow-up consultations. Individual problems confronted and solved were concerned with such life basics as: housing, food and clothing, mental and physical health, employment, bail bonds and legal help, loans and financing, education, family difficulties, and recreation. Working relations had been established with more than twenty community agencies and service organizations, including: County Welfare, Public Health Service, School Board, Family Service and Guidance, Agricultural Extension Service, YMCA, YWCA, Topeka State Hospital, the Menninger Foundation, Kansas Neurological Institute, Police Department, Juvenile and Probate Courts, Employment Service, Labor Department, city commissioners, Urban Renewal, Kansas Teachers Association, Washburn University, city library, local hospitals, Human Relations Commission, Small Business Loan Association, State Technical Assistance Office, United Fund, and local church groups. Those organizations were readily available, through the expediting of the Neighborhood

House staff, to residents for services, consultation, and in many cases employment opportunities. Through the operation of the Neighborhood House, residents were able to acquire services that they in some cases did not know existed; in other cases they were uncomfortable or unfamiliar with the required application procedures. Similarly, the agencies and organizations, through the efforts of the Neighborhood House, gained access to a segment of the community that had been, and probably would have continued to be, unavailable to them.

But something more was being offered by the House than a proliferation of available services. That "something more" was quite apparent to the beneficiaries who lived in the Neighborhood. They felt, for the first time, that they were initiating their contact with service organizations and therefore felt less embarrassed about asking for help. They were able to approach relatively impersonal agencies with the personal support of the Neighborhood House staff. Consequently, the agencies were perceived to be less fearsome and formidable.

The House staff provided unquestioning and unconditional, but realistic, support to Neighborhood residents. Very often they would accompany an individual on his first or on a difficult visit to a service organization. As a result, many Neighborhood residents "learned their way around" in complex organizations, and began to see them, as do members of middle and higher socio-economic classes, as usable societal components. They began to feel that the "system" was less constricting than their previous experience had led them to believe. They saw that once one knew the language and "which buttons to push," there was room for negotiation within the system. A Neighborhood resident summarized, "There's a lot more freedom around than I thought there was. I found that out as I learned the ropes." Successful experience in one encounter with a complex organization usually generated a self-confidence toward future encounters with such organizations. For example, the Neighborhood House staff was contacted by a resident who had received notification from his finance company that, since his payments were in arrears, his car was about to be repossessed. The man sincerely and unavoidably had been unable to maintain his payments as scheduled, yet he needed the car to continue his employment. However, he was certain that he had "had it," and there was "nothing I could do to keep my car." He said that he had called the Neighborhood House "as a last resort." The man thought he should personally contact the finance company, but frankly stated he was "afraid to talk to them. They can talk rings around me. Besides, I haven't got a chance." Mr. Y, in his capacity as Neighborhood House director, met with the man and discussed the nature of contracts, financial terms, refinancing possibilities, interest rates, etc. The resident was surprised that "this stuff is not as complicated as I thought." Armed with new information and alternatives, and supported by a telephone call to the company from Mr. Y, the resident confronted the finance-company officials and successfully accomplished a mutually agreed-upon resolution of the issue. Later, he happily reported to Mr. Y that he had "straightened the matter out." He added, "When I was in there talking those words and the finance people were listening to me, I was surprised that it was really me talking!"

The Neighborhood residents now looked upon those organizations making services available through the Neighborhood House as having been invited into the area by *them.* This perception increased agency acceptability within the Neighborhood, and increased the usability of their services. One community organization, for example, before the establishment of the House, had attempted to recruit resident attendance at a nutrition-and-cooking class to be conducted in the Neighborhood. Its efforts obtained little response, although it was known that there was considerable eagerness among the residents to add to their homemaking skills. Later, the House staff and the HPP Committee became concerned about this, and the Neighborhood aide was assigned to meet with fellow residents who were known to be interested in nutrition and cooking. At first, informal individual chats were initiated. These eventually led to gatherings of about twenty women, who would meet over coffee and discuss what their needs were, and how they would like to see them met. A few recipes were exchanged, and some of the women decided that each week they would take turns hostessing this informal group by preparing a snack. As the group evolved and developed, it formulated its own interests and, with the Neighborhood aide serving as a resource person, leadership emerged from among the group. After a few meetings, the women realized that their own sources of information were being exhausted. They discussed the possibility of looking outside the group for new information and counsel. Finally they decided to invite the agency representative whose program had failed earlier to be a participant in the class. She agreed, and with her expert advice the group, up to this writing, continues to thrive with striking member satisfaction. The content of class instruction now is no different from that offered in the instructor's first attempt to recruit Neighborhood attendance, but there is nonetheless an essential difference. The first time the agency representative had invited Neighborhood residents to attend *her* formally organized class —a class which the residents had no hand in preparing or formulating. This time, however, the residents had evolved, from informal discussion, their *own* class and were inviting the agency representatives, whose help they had decided they needed, to attend *their* gathering.

The staff of the Neighborhood House was particularly concerned with the relatively high unemployment rate in the Neighborhood. However, they wanted to do more than "just get jobs" for those in need of them. From his own experiences and from consultation with the HPP Committee and Neighborhood residents, Mr. Y concluded that some unemployed men had not taken available jobs because the work was degrading, or the conditions under which they had to accept employment were too distasteful. "A man's not going to take a job," he commented, "if it makes him less of a man." He shared with his staff what he thought was an important distinction—the distinction between "giving" a man a job and his "taking" a job. "A man *takes* a job when he thinks it's worth something, not just financially. He *takes* a job when he can be proud of it, and when he can be glad to say that it belongs to him. When a man is *given* a job, he belongs to the job; the job doesn't belong to him. He also belongs to the people who give it to him, and he's expected to be grateful for something he probably really didn't want." The House staff was committed to finding jobs for residents that were worth *taking*. Jobs that had no future, that did not pay a living wage, or that were undignified for the individual were discouraged or avoided. The staff established a list of residents who were unemployed, underemployed, or dissatisfied with their present employment. Anytime the staff or HPP Committee members came in contact with worthwhile jobs, they would distribute the information to those on their list. Opportunities for better jobs, or training which would make possible better jobs, were communicated on a Neighborhood-wide basis.

Members of the House staff had considerable success stimulating "chronically unemployable" residents to take worthwhile jobs. One of the reasons for their success was that they chose to ignore the "bad" work histories that prevented some individuals from getting any employment but demeaning labor. The effectiveness of the staff's treating a man with "unemployment problems" like any other human being is demonstrated by the following example. A twenty-five-year-old resident with a long history of employment transiency and "drinking" came to the Neighborhood House in search of "any job that'll pay a few bucks." His frankly stated reason for wanting a job was to earn enough money to buy a "full bottle." He didn't specify the kind of work he wanted, because he was convinced that he would, as always, "end up carrying out the slop, anyway." The staff members wouldn't go along with his view of himself; they told him they thought he was worth more than he thought. Working his way through stages of negativism, confusion, and sarcastic humor, the man finally agreed to take on what the House staff offered straightforwardly as a "challenge." Mr. Y and the applicant together found an employment situation which offered the clearest opportunity and highest wages he had ever experienced. The employer, Mr. Y, and the applicant himself openly discussed his potentials, and limitations, and all agreed that he should not be hindered by his past record. The man was hired, and for four-and-one-half months maintained steady and successful employment—the longest period of time he had remained on any job in his working life. However, the holiday season was approaching, and he was afraid he was going to succumb to temptation. But he liked his job, and he didn't want to "foul up." Having on a number of occasions shared his pride in himself with Mr. Y for "making it on the job," he now went to him with his dilemma. He knew he couldn't get by the Christmas holidays without "hitting the bottle"; it had been a habit pattern for too many years of his short life. Yet he did not want to give up all he had finally gained. Once again, Mr. Y, employer, and employee got together and honestly confronted his problem. On the strength of his work record on the job, the employer agreed to grant him a two-week leave of absence without pay during the Christmas holidays. Promptly at 8:30 on the morning when his leave of absence had elapsed, the employee, after two rousing weeks, returned to the job. "Man," he confided to Mr. Y, "it didn't seem to be as much fun anymore. I'm glad to be back." He has been steadily and satisfactorily on the job since that time. For this man, the Neighborhood House had provided a neutral ground upon which the burdens of his past could, at his own pace and by his own choosing, be shed with dignity for a more productive future.

Along with making contacts, building programs, and providing services in such a way that the dignity of Neighborhood residents was enhanced, the House staff members were firmly establishing themselves, and the whole concept of a Neighborhood House, as worthy of trust. No price, material or psychological, had to be paid for help from the Neighborhood House. Assistance conformed to the individual, not vice versa. The House was on Neighborhood "turf" and staffed by "our own people." Support, in whatever form wanted, was there when and however often wanted. No restrictions, no criticisms, implicit or explicit, were associated with assistance—unless the individual "tried to sell himself short." The increasing trust in the Neighborhood House, and realization of its usefulness, are reflected in its hours of operation. When it first began, the House was open from 8:00 A.M. until 5:00 P.M., five days a week. Six months later, the residents insisted that it remain open from 8:00 A.M. until 9:00 P.M., five days a week. At this writing, the residents have decided the House should remain open from 8:00 A.M. until 9:30 P.M. during the work week, and all day Saturday and Sunday. (Informally, the House is usually always open after official closing time.

Furthermore, members of its staff are considered, by the residents, to be on call twenty-four hours a day.)

Approximately twenty meetings a week are held at the Neighborhood House. Among those are included the following classes: youth and adult education, cooking, sewing, health, hat making, gardening, landscaping, and arts and crafts. Weekly "Neighborhood meetings" are held in which relaxed, informal discussion takes place concerning Neighborhood needs, problems, and activities. At least monthly the HPP Neighborhood Committee conducts its official meeting in the House. An increasing number of impromptu "get togethers" form in the House as it steadily becomes "the place to meet."

When asked for whom he worked, Mr. Y quickly and sincerely would respond, "for us, for the Neighborhood people." When he had been an Extension Worker, he felt that he had to "meet the needs of the agency more than the needs of the people." Now he was more clearly able to identify with those whom he served. When he first began working with agency officials as director of the Neighborhood House, he tended to be suspicious of their motives and somewhat defensive. For example, often he would appear in an official's office without an appointment, hoping to "catch him off guard" and not giving "the opposition a chance to dig in and maintain its defenses." His early philosophy, as he himself described it, was "attack rather than tact." However, as time went on, he realized that "hostility got me hostility in return." He concentrated on the structure and procedures of the agencies, and became acquainted with those areas of flexibility within the organizational systems. Gradually Mr. Y came to interpret an agency response, "That's impossible," to mean, "I've got to try another way." When he would discover a way in which an agency could render an innovative service to someone in the Neighborhood, the agency official, as reported by Mr. Y, would "be thankful as hell. Some of those guys're as happy as we are when someone points out to them a new way to use their own system." Mr. Y became less willing to impute malevolent motivation to agency officials, and more prone realistically to assess the useful but complex and sometimes self-defeating nature of bureaucratic procedure. He saw the Neighborhood House staff, along with those whom he accepted as colleagues in the service organizations, as faced with the task of "using the system to our best advantage." On occasion, though he identified himself clearly with the Target Neighborhood residents, Mr. Y experienced the stresses of marginality—of being a bridge between the poor and the not-poor. He felt pressured by conflicting expectations for his performance by Neighborhood residents on the one hand, and agency officials on the other. As he became more expert in "playing the role" in an agency setting, and more resourceful in reaching and effectively helping Neighborhood residents, he became more comfortable with his often marginal operating position. He philosophized that stresses resulting from conflicting expectations for his performance were "just part of the job." Mr. L, the HPP Committee chairman, who himself had experienced the pressures of marginality, was instrumental in the director's adjusting to that philosophy.

The role model and informal training provided by the House's social worker (from the supporting agency) profoundly influenced Mr. Y's effectiveness with agency representatives. Similarly, the role model and informal training provided by Mr. Y profoundly influenced the social worker's effectiveness with Neighborhood residents. At first guardedly, but soon openly, they shared with each other frustrations, satisfactions, and strategies associated with social innovation. This sharing erased earlier feelings each had that the other "might just con him." The evolution of their relation, and consequently the evolution of the relation between Neighborhood House and supporting agency, demonstrated the feasibility of indigenous leaders and organizations working closely and beneficially with professional leaders and organizations—so long as experiences can be shared by functional *equals* in a co-operative rather than a competitive climate.

CREATING A NEIGHBORHOOD

Prior to the organization of the HPP Committee and the establishment of the House, Highland Park–Pierce was a "neighborhood" primarily because of city-determined geographical boundaries and a relatively unstable sense of out-group cohesion—"This is one of the areas where us Negroes can live." There was no "neighborhood" in the organized, purposive, and self-determined connotation of the word. Initially, as pointed out, the HPP Committee and the House staff were committed to facilitating services for needy residents, in a fashion that would not impinge upon their dignity. The House staff had not systematized its thoughts about organizing the Neighborhood or Neighborhood groups toward social action. Similarly, the residents were initially most concerned about what the House could do for them, not what they could do for themselves in organized groups beyond but focused by the House.

By the end of November, 1966, the beginnings of group organization toward social-change goals could be observed. The residents had decided they wanted another, unstructured, "Neighborhood meeting" on the last Thursday of every month. This meeting was open to all members of the Neighborhood, would co-ordinate with the HPP Neighborhood Committee, but was to be without agenda or designated chairman. Discussions were to be concerned with whatever the attending participants would, at the time, see fit to discuss. At one of those meetings, a resident suggested to the group, "Let's get out in to the Neighborhood, the bunch of us, and do something together. I mean something constructive and not just a picnic or a party." The participants were enthralled by this idea, and after some discussion agreed that a suitable first project would be to "get out as a group and clean up some of these weed-ridden yards and empty lots that make our blocks look like slums." Another resident recommended that the man who had made the suggestion to clean lots be established as chairman of the "Clean-up Committee." The chairman-nominee audibly choked and exclaimed, "Me! I've never done anything like that before! I can't be a chairman! I can't lead that thing!" His wife strongly agreed, saying, "Yeah, that's right! He can't do that! He's never done anything like that!" After considerable encouragement from other members of the group, the chairman-nominee acceded, and became the chairman-elect. On several Saturdays thereafter, he convened his small work force (ranging from four to twelve men) at prechosen work sites. Volunteers would chop and rake weeds, gather and haul off litter, and when finished, plant a sign which read: "This Lot Cleared by the Highland Park–Pierce Neighborhood House." Several lots were improved by the men, and as a result of their example, a number of other families spontaneously cleared the weeds from their own yards. Most important, however, was the fact that this was the first, the precedent-setting, spontaneous organization, through the House, of Neighborhood residents toward an agreed-upon group goal.

Several of the committees and classes meeting regularly in the Neighborhood House evolved toward broader goals than those for which they were first intended by the members. One committee, for example, was begun by residents to seek new ways to help elder citizens. Shortly, however, consideration of the problems of these citizens expanded to consideration of the problems of the Neighborhood residents in general. The meetings became general forums on social problems. Regular attendance grew to forty members, not necessarily because the group was resolving issues at this time, but because it gave members a chance to define those issues, in many cases for the first time in their lives. The topics for their discussions began to crystallize. Subgroups were spawned to deal with more specific problems, and to develop action toward solutions. The subcommittees were concerned with politics, recreation, employment, legislative change, and education. Representatives of the subcommittees consulted with city officials who could advise them on matters relative to their interests, problems, and proposals. Later, this forum replaced the monthly Neighborhood House business meetings, thus affording an opportunity for continuous community dialogue and a staging ground for Neighborhood-based social action.

Mr. L, chairman of the Highland Park–Pierce Neighborhood Committee, expressing the growing change-orientation of the membership, spoke of "the importance of our rehabilitating our Neighborhood." Somewhat fearful of urban renewal and stimulated by the striking changes in the landscape brought about by the Clean-up Committee, many of the residents began talking about what they could do "to make our Neighborhood a prideful place." This sense of neighborhood was further sharpened by the community-wide publicity, in the form of newspaper feature stories, editorials, and television reports that Highland Park–Pierce was receiving through the activities of its Neighborhood House. Through the various programs, classes, services, and field activities of the House, residents were interacting more frequently and in new ways with one another. "I was reminded of the old days," reflected an eighty-two-year-old man who was among the first residents of the area. "We all used to get together down at the general store. We'd sit around and talk, and share our troubles with one another, and go out and do things together if they had to be done. That kind of store isn't around here anymore, but the Neighborhood House sure seems just like one." The Neighborhood House actually was beginning to function as a focus for Neighborhood integration, and the HPP Committee continued to be a guiding influence.

Increasingly, residents themselves emphasized the need for Neighborhood "organization." "What makes a big voice," proclaimed a participant in the monthly Neighborhood meeting, "is not one man screaming all alone. It's a hundred voices together. That's what's heard!" Other participants commented less graphically about "the strength of organization for getting things done." The potential for political and economic organization was acknowledged, and specific measures, such as voter registration and credit unions, were discussed.

The director of the Neighborhood House, continuing to be influenced by the desire of residents, similarly began to see the House as being able to fulfill a purpose beyond helping specific individuals in a nonthreatening way. Commented Mr. Y:

"I'm getting the feeling that at first the House was really only able to hand out band-aids to people one at a time, when what was really needed was a blood transfusion for the whole Neighborhood. The services, when they're gotten in the right way, are necessary, and we're going to continue taking advantage of them. But if poverty and inequality are really going to be ended here, we're going to have to change two things. First, our images as 'no-good poverty types' and second, those parts of the system which support poverty and inequality. You can do both those things with the organization of responsible people. I think we're getting that kind of organization out here."

In June, 1967, Neighborhood residents suggested to the House staff that a weekly newsletter be published and distributed as "another way to let us communicate with one another." The staff acted upon the suggestion, and each week prepared a two-page mimeographed "Newsletter" listing House and general activities, schedules, volunteer services, wanted or for-sale items, rentals, baby-sitting services, etc. The papers were distributed to each home in the Neighborhood by children of the residents. Only five weeks after its first distribution, the "Newsletter" was much in demand, as evidenced by the number of telephone calls of concern when for one reason or another the paper was a day late or missing. Furthermore, a number of community residents immediately outside the boundaries of Highland Park–Pierce requested that it be delivered to them, as well as to residents inside the boundaries. The implementation of, and reaction to, the Highland Park–Pierce "Newsletter" manifested a growing perception of a cohesive neighborhood. Its contents indicated the broadening scope of Neighborhood House functioning. The publication announced newly available services, listed personal announcements, and gave other "newsy" items. In addition, moreover, the "Newsletter" editorialized on civil-rights legislation, stimulated concern about public housing and voter registration, and reported Mr. Y's suggestion concerning the city's proposed Model Police Force. The concept of a united Neighborhood making concerted efforts toward social action was becoming explicit.

"Action, Together!"

As shared Neighborhood identity increased, residents, under the stimulation of the HPP Committee and the House, became more convinced of the importance of rehabilitating and maintaining the Neighborhood as a residential area. They did not want Highland Park–Pierce to be considered a "slum section." They were aware of the need for better streets, more adequate lighting, more efficient sewerage disposal, and for the provision of adequate low-cost housing. But they were fearful of compulsory urban renewal in which plans would be made *for* them, independent from the Neighborhood's own involvement and needs. As a result of this concern, and an increased appreciation of their Neighborhood, for the first time in Topeka's history a low-income area began to work, under its own stimulation and initiation, for urban development which could be funded by a co-operative city and federal program. In December, 1966, Mr. L and the HPP Committee invited the director of Urban Renewal to meet with them at the Neighborhood House to discuss ways for "us to rehabilitate our Neighborhood." The residents refused to be discouraged by the complexities of city, state, and federal Urban Renewal policies as explained to them. A number of them, including the Neighborhood House staff, have now become familiar with urban-renewal legislation, what can and cannot be accomplished by implementation of the law, and participant responsibilities in the planning and development of local projects. Although no operational plan has yet been evolved by Highland Park–Pierce residents through governmental channels, they continue their efforts toward acquiring official recognition of their desire to rehabilitate the Neighborhood at their own direction and without arbitrary relocation.

The House staff and the Target Neighborhood Committee are presently launched upon a campaign to stimulate: (1) rehabilitation of blighted but serviceable homes; (2) destruction and clearing of homes already condemned; (3) the building of new homes in the Neighborhood ("building homes in a low-income area is a good investment"); (4) rent subsidy or the building of low-rent units; (5) the development of a class on "how to take care of property"; (6) the establishing of a Neighborhood housing corporation to be run by Highland Park–Pierce residents. At one of the HPP meetings, the residents concluded, "Our neighborhood has the highest potential of all the others in Shawnee County. We've got more and better land available than anywhere else. Let's find better ways to use it, or else we're liable to lose it."

Later in December, 1966, the residents took advantage of an opportunity to reinforce their consensus about rehabilitating and maintaining Highland Park–Pierce as a residential area. Furthermore, they had an opportunity to demonstrate to the community at large that they identified with their Neighborhood and wished to "have some say" about changes that were made within it.

A local service-station owner wanted to expand his business by building a branch in Highland Park–Pierce. He had located suitable property, and had filed a request with the Board of City Commissioners for rezoning the property from residential to commercial designation. The Neighborhood House staff, in its routine review of published city business, learned of the businessman's intention and took the matter to the Neighborhood residents for discussion. After considerable debate and deliberation, the residents unanimously agreed that commercial rezoning would not be compatible with their goals for residential rehabilitation. The Advisory Council, urged by the HPP Committee, directed the Neighborhood House to send the following letter to the Board of City Commissioners:

Board of City Commissioners
City Building
Topeka, Kansas

GENTLEMEN:

This letter is written in behalf of the people of the Highland Park–Pierce Neighborhood in protest of rezoning the corner of 25th and Adams for a service station.

It is the feeling of the Advisory Board that such a step would be a detriment to the area and would be in direct opposition to what we are trying to achieve in the way of bettering the neighborhood and general surroundings for the neighborhood people. Commercial zoning would mean encouragement of other types of business nearby, and thus, lower the property value and at the same time lessen the hope of developing this area into a desirable residential neighborhood.

The general feeling of those who live in this area is unfavorable toward rezoning and they have submitted protest thru petitions.

Your consideration in this matter will be greatly appreciated.

As a follow-up to the letter, thirty-five Neighborhood residents, led by Mr. L, chairman of the HPP Committee, attended a meeting of the Board of Commissioners at City Hall, and verbally registered their objections to the rezoning.

In order to give the businessman an opportunity to present "his side of the story," the Neighborhood residents invited him to meet with them in the Highland Park–Pierce House. He told the attending residents and Neighborhood House staff that his studies and discussions with the commissioners "showed" that, within five to ten years, the street on which he wished to build his new service station would be a major thoroughfare, and would be zoned commercially. He talked about the advantages of having a service station in the area, and passed around a picture of one of his stations in a middle-class section of town. His major arguments were that the service station would complement the Neighborhood and that eventually the property would be rezoned anyway.

When he had finished his presentation, the residents expressed their specific objections. Some felt that the establishment of a service station would lower the property value of surrounding houses. Others felt that one service station would bring with it a proliferation of similar businesses and associated noise unsuitable to a residential area. A Negro woman worried that a service station would bring in the "motorcycle crowd." One of the men systematically pointed to the number of service stations readily accessible in the nearby shopping and business areas, and questioned why one had to be put up in the middle of their "living places."

The businessman reiterated his argument that change was going to take place inevitably, and that progress shouldn't be stopped. Mr. L responded:

"We know the area will develop. We want it to. There's growth all around us. We know this. We want to develop with the rest of the city, but we feel we want to develop our Neighborhood as we see fit. Now, if you're willing to help our Neighborhood as you say, then you should be willing to see our point. You're interested in the Neighborhood for your station's sake; we're interested in the Neighborhood for the Neighborhood's sake. We know that street will be a major thoroughfare someday, and we know that major thoroughfares offer good commercial sites. But we'd like to keep our area strictly residential, and develop it into a place where people can be proud to live."

The businessman stated that he thought he would have a good chance to build the station even if the people didn't agree, but, he added, "I'm going to withdraw my application for the rezoning. I don't want to offend you; I would want your business." He then stated, "I have a proposition for you to consider. Would you review this request, say, in another two or three years? It may be that you'll be willing to have a station then." Mr. L responded, "Sir, I have a proposition for you. Would you be willing to join our committee? Would you be willing to help us plan the development of our Neighborhood in the way that we would like to have it, and in a way that would be beneficial to all?" The businessman accepted, and the session adjourned. After the meeting, one of the Neighborhood residents told the businessman that he had "made a mistake." You shouldn't have bought the land, requested a zoning permit, and *then* told the people about it. You should've come to us first, and you could've saved yourself that trouble."

As a result of their experience with the rezoning case, the Neighborhood residents had learned something more about the workings of "the system" in the community, and about effective means to communicate one's desires within that system. More importantly, they were now convinced, by the success of their own action, that "people, no matter how poor, can get something done if there's action together!" Through petition, personal appearances, and direct confrontation with the issues, the residents had influenced the "unbeatable power structure." The "system" seemed to them far less formidable now; far less alien. With a strong case rationally and forcefully presented by numbers, they knew now that representatives of the Establishment could be stopped from making arbitrary decisions. From firsthand experience of the workings of complex social structures, they were gaining insight concerning how the structure affects them, and, more importantly, how they could affect the social structure. Their encounters, some successful and some unsuccessful, with powers before believed to be unapproachable and unmovable, yielded increasing self-confidence and a sense of their own competency and power.

After the success in blocking the rezoning attempt, the HPP Committee and House staff launched upon a series of endeavors toward Neighborhood improvement. They petitioned the Board of City Commissioners for increased attention to "our nonroads in Highland Park–Pierce." They requested that additional street lights be installed in their Neighborhood. They approached the Fire Department and asked it to raze the houses which had previously been condemned by the city. Representatives of the Neighborhood House volunteered testimony and support for a controversial Minimum Housing Code under review by the city commisioners. The Neighborhood House staff, at the prompting of the residents, registered disillusionment with the city's attempt to implement a "Model Police Force Program" when, in its view, "first we ought to take steps toward having a 'Model City,' and try to eliminate the social problems which cause police problems." A committee from the House approached the Kansas State Legislature, requesting legislative change which would broaden the existing cosmotology training program to make it more accessible and useful to residents. Each of these social-action endeavors was conducted in an orderly, purposive, but forcefully united manner. The outcome of most of these attempts is still pending at this writing, but the residents, aware of their new-found "clout," are steadily "maintaining pressure" to get what they think is best for themselves and the Neighborhood.

As action evolved, so also did new sets of stated goals for the Neighborhood House. The first set of goals, developed by the TOEO, the Advisory Council, and the HPP Committee, stressed facilitating available services. The second set stressed more centrally purposive social change: (1) to provide psychosocial first aid to large numbers of people experiencing stress from both external and internal causes; (2) to transform passive, uninvolved, apathetic receivers of others' beneficence into helpers and active citizens; (3) to develop

362

Poverty Warriors

independence, autonomy, and better over-all functioning on the part of the people in the Neighborhood; (4) to demonstrate that indigenous nonprofessionals can provide meaningful service for their population; (5) to initiate changes in services—emphasizing the importance of the impact of the helper on the helped; (6) to affect the Neighborhood by developing greater social integration and cohesion among its residents.²

"Rub out the Imaginary Boundaries"

Initially, as the Neighborhood House began to develop, the residents were concerned about what the programs could do for them as individuals. As a sense of neighborhood grew, they began to see the value of, and to become involved in, group efforts toward social action which would have impact upon Highland Park–Pierce. The proliferation of self-initiating contacts with agencies, and involvement in concerted social action, generated among the residents a new realization of their dignity, worth, and potency. Reinforced by their now-demonstrated competencies and strengthened by awareness of membership in a cohesive Neighborhood, the participants were willing to extend themselves beyond their own ground. The experience of control of, and responsibility for, self and Neighborhood began to dispose them toward the community at large.

At a later HPP Committee meeting, the participants discussed "the role of the Neighborhood House in the city of Topeka." They agreed that the House's first obligation was to Highland Park–Pierce, but they also agreed that "we should be neighbors to everyone in the city of Topeka. We should be willing to help anyone who needs it, whether he's black or white. We have a problem with poverty, but so does the city of Topeka. We should share what we've learned about poverty, the hard way, with those who really want to do something about it."

Some of the social action with which residents had already been

<hr/>

² The HPP Committee and House staff were influenced in this revision of House goals by Frank Riessman and Emanuel Hollowitz, "The Neighborhood Service Center: An Innovation in Preventive Psychiatry," *American Journal of Psychiatry*, 123, 11 (May, 1967), 1408–1413.

involved concerned the community at large—for example, their support of the Minimum Housing Code for the city of Topeka, their statements in support of a Model City project, and their criticism of the Model Police Force Program. The adult-education class conducted at the House included students from areas *outside* Highland Park–Pierce. A day-care center had been established in the Neighborhood, and parents from other Neighborhoods had been invited to enroll their children. The Highland Park Pierce residents' emphasis upon Neighborhood rehabilitation rather than relocation emphasized potential benefit for Topeka. "Improving and increasing residential property in our Neighborhood would be a benefit to the city," suggested Mr. L, "because they'd be able to get more tax revenue that way. Right now, they're only getting farm-land taxes from right here in the middle of the city. They could use that extra tax money for better streets and more lighting in Highland Park Pierce, but also for other areas, too." Plans for the House's first anniversary party included an open invitation to "all citizens of Topeka. We want to let everyone know we're developing our Neighborhood, but we're not developing it like an island," explained Mr. Y. Mr. L agreed, adding, "We need the help of other people in Topeka, there's no question about that. But we've also learned now that the people of Topeka need *our* help in meeting this poverty problem. It's time we rub out the imaginary boundaries between us."

A number of citizens in the community at large asked the House to schedule meetings in which problems of poverty and prejudice could be discussed with city-wide participation. The House responded and, at 7:30 P.M. on August 22, 1967, the first meeting of "Let's Talk" was held. For three hours, thirty participants, black and white, poor and not-poor, discussed issues relevant to "a movement toward better racial understanding." The meeting, described by a newspaper reporter as having "never really ended," was thereafter scheduled to be held each Monday night in the Neighborhood House.

In August, 1967, Mr. Y manifested again his and the residents' widening concept of community responsibility. He learned from some of the residents that "trouble is about to begin" in another

part of the city. Some Negro working men had been subject to unilateral and "unfair" work changes, resulting in a loss of accumulated
vacation time without compensation. Feeling that they had no other
way to express their grievances, the men decided to "mess up the
landscape a little bit." Mr. Y, agreeing with Highland Park–Pierce
residents that he "should try to do something about it," rushed to
the area and "let those guys know there might be a better way to
solve their problems than getting people hurt." Mr. Y, who had
years before been a member of a "corner gang" in the same area,
convinced the men to "try it my way first, and if that doesn't work,
then do it your way." He and the men met with the employers, presented the grievances, and worked out a solution satisfactory to all.
Several Topeka citizens credit Mr. Y's action as having "prevented
the beginning of a riot."

Successful and recognized involvement in city-wide affairs further
enhanced the identities of the participants and increased the number of their functional social roles. Residents increasingly commented about "our community" as well as "our Neighborhood." The
growing feeling of belongingness and responsibility is well exempli-
fied by the following statement, made by Mr. L as he reflected upon two years of involvement as a Target Neighborhood Officer in
the poverty program:

"I sometimes wonder how I got involved in all this! People ask
me how I got started, and I really can't give a very good answer. I
can only say that no other program has made such an impression
on me in all my life.

"It's hard for me to explain. Maybe it's that it's hard for a Negro
man to find a place in the mainstream of the society. But now I have
a feeling that I've found a slot in life for myself. This program offered me an opportunity to create that slot that I've been looking
for maybe all my life. I was a pretty quiet guy, never wanting to get
into the limelight. I always wanted to stay out of the way, because
it was safer that way. I'm in a position now where I can really help
other people, and I can see the results of my work and it makes me
feel good. It makes me feel I'm really somebody. Sure, there're still

people who I depend on for help. Everybody needs somebody. But now I can see that others need me, too—people in the Neighborhood and people in Topeka. I'm listened to with respect now in some places that maybe wouldn't have let me through their door two years ago. They don't always agree with me, but I wouldn't want that, either. What's important is that people now think that I, and the people I represent, are worth listening to. That makes you feel worth more. Makes you feel more like a man. These last two years of happiness in the program, of being able to find myself, have been worth more than all my other adult years."

The HPP Committee could have foundered at the Testing Stage (VII) when the members assessed that they had indeed lost meaningful participation in the Extension Worker Program they had developed. Mr. L at times encountered considerable criticism from his followers concerning the loss of the program. However, he apparently was able to endure the stress of "walking the tightrope" by drawing upon his conviction that "good things are not easy." Resolutely, he, and soon the other HPP Committee members, sought another proposal—the Neighborhood House—with determination not to lose their "maximum feasible participation." The Neighborhood House provided the members with a sense of control, identity, and pride, and the means whereby they could inaugurate other self-determined, short-range, and rapid-payoff programs for residents. Gradually, with the help of nonrestricting delegate agencies, they became interested in long-range activities, and in change as well as service functions. Ultimately, they began to look beyond the boundaries of the HPP Neighborhood into endeavors that concerned the community at large.[3]

While chairman of the HPP Committee, Mr. L deliberately and carefully developed his own training as an indigenous leader. He explained to me how he watched the moves of the "pros" in the meetings of the Economic Opportunity Board and other meetings, and learned from their successes and mistakes. He had read several

---

[3] See Louis A. Zurcher, Jr., and Alvin E. Green, *From Dependency to Dignity: Individual and Social Consequences of a Neighborhood House.*

books on leadership and on social problems. He emphasized the importance of such training:

"Our biggest problem is not entirely the lack of facilities and opportunities here in Topeka. Our main trouble is that we're not in the mainstream of the community. We don't know what's going on, what's available. We just don't know the techniques for using community services and local government like other people do. Having lumber and nails doesn't help you build a house unless you have some idea how to swing the hammer and where to put the pieces."

He was able, by his own determination, to learn the *process* as well as the *content* aspects of poverty-program indigenous leadership. Some indigenous leaders are unable to do so on their own. The poverty-intervention organization that provides such training for its indigenous leaders would undoubtedly thereby increase the likelihood of accomplishing its purposes.

Furthermore, it is apparent from the case history of the Highland Park–Pierce Target Neighborhood Committee that the reaching of the Purposive Stage (VII) by a target group depends upon the opportunity for it to develop a concrete and reachable group goal (program). The members must feel that they had a significant role not only in the planning but in the implementation and operation of the activity they have chosen. On the other hand, as indicated in the case history of the Indian Target Neighborhood Committee, to "shoot for the moon" and not come near, or to have a target group struggle to organize itself without some idea about the how and the why of organizing simply compounds the miseries of the participants. If the poverty-intervention organization solicits as a part of its over-all program the development of neighborhood-action groups, it has the obligation unobtrusively to provide training and alternative activities which will stimulate that development.

CHAPTER 15

Perception of the Leadership Role: Revisited

In order to assess shifts in Target Neighborhood Officer perception of the indigenous-leader "bridge" role since the first administration of the Role Perception Scale in November, 1966 (Admin I; see Chapter 11), the scale was included as part of the questionnaire readministered to TNOs in May, 1967 (Admin II).

Among the eighteen TNOs who completed the Role Perception Scale for Admin II were: seven males, eleven females; three Anglo-Americans; ten Negro-Americans; three Mexican-Americans; and two American Indians. The median time as a TNO was seventeen months, and the median Economic Opportunity Board attendance was ten meetings. Seven months of participation had elapsed between Admin I and Admin II.

SHIFTS IN PERCEPTION

Table 6 presents comparisons of Admin I with Admin II median Orientation and Marginality Scale scores for all TNOs, and for sex, ethnic, and participation categories.

TABLE 6. Comparison of Administration I with Administration II Orientation and Marginality Median Scale Scores for all TNOs, and for Sex, Ethnic, and Participation Categories (N = 18)

	Orientation Scale			Marginality Scale		
Classification	*Admin I*	*Admin II*	*Change*	*Admin I*	*Admin II*	*Change*
All TNOs	5.41	5.60	+	3.78	3.61	−
Males (N = 7)	5.27	5.45	+	4.18	4.00	−
Females (N = 11)	5.55	5.73	+	3.73	3.45	−
Anglos (N = 3)	4.82	5.36	+	3.73	4.00	+
Negroes (N = 10)	5.55	5.73	+	3.73	3.50	−
Mexicans (N = 3)	5.45	5.59	+	4.14	3.84	−
Indians (N = 2)	5.10	5.73	+	3.46	4.10	+
Actives (N = 13)	5.27	5.73	+	3.73	3.50	−
Inactives (N = 5)	5.55	5.36	−	4.00	4.00	0
Stayers (N = 10)	5.50	5.84	+	3.73	3.43	−
Leavers (N = 8)	5.37	5.33	−	3.96	4.00	+

As revealed in Table 6, TNOs as a group showed an increase in Orientation Scale scores, indicating a tendency to increase orientation toward Neighborhood residents and to decrease orientation toward the TOEO. Assessment of field observation and interviews suggests two factors which may have influenced the shift in orientation. Some TNOs initially seemed to perceive identification with the TOEO to be more status-enhancing than identification with Neighborhood residents. However, later positive local and national publicity for indigenous leaders, urgings from Neighborhood residents, and the controversy and general uncertainty surrounding OEO as an enduring formal organization served to enhance the status of "leaders of the poor." Secondly, increased orientation toward the poor moved

TNOs from the marginal role, and from stresses associated with being a bridge. TNOs' tendency to perceive their roles as being less marginal is reflected in the decreased Marginality Scale scores, reported in Table 6, for TNOs as a group. Though the number of respondents is quite small and the scale findings in need of further research substantiation, it can cautiously be concluded that the marginal indigenous-leader role expected by the TOEO was not comfortably enacted by TNOs. It can also be cautiously concluded that TNOs found it more acceptable to reorient their role perceptions toward the poor, rather than toward the TOEO. Apparently, orientation toward the poor was a more workable and rewarding role perception (it must be remembered that TNOs were not paid employees of the TOEO). These conclusions are substantiated by the observational data presented in other chapters, especially Chapters 12, 13, and 14. These conclusions are further supported by Orientation and Marginality Scale changes reported in Table 6 for Actives, Inactives, Stayers, and Leavers. As indicated in Table 6, Actives showed an increase in Orientation scores and a decrease in Marginality scores. Inactives, on the other hand, showed a decrease in Orientation scores and no change in Marginality scores. Also, their Marginality scores were on both Admin I and II higher than those of the Actives. It might be speculated that their lack of deep involvement in the processes of poverty intervention kept their original perceptions of the indigenous-leader role isolated from challenge and, in fact, encouraged them further to shift in orientation toward the TOEO.

Those TNOs who were "Stayers" showed an increase in Orientation scores and a decrease in Marginality scores. The Leavers, conversely, showed a decrease in Orientation scores and an increase in Marginality scores. Whether the direction of Leaver changes existed prior to, and contributed to, their leaving, or are *ex post facto* changes, is problematical. However, interview data support the conclusion that at least some of the Leavers tried in earnest to enact the marginal TNO role, met with frustration or rejection, and left the program before shifting their orientations as did the Stayers.

The patterns of correlations between social-psychological variables and Orientation and Marginality Scale scores were not so con-

sistent for Admin II as for Admin I (see Table 5). By Admin II, the
high Orientation scorers no longer seemed to be as much "like the
poor" nor the high Marginality scorers as much "like middle-class
types" as they had in Admin I. It is suggested that TNOs who
evolved a more viable role perception (one less stressful and more
rewarding than the bridge role expected by the TOEO) were stimulated by participation toward positive social-psychological changes.
TNOs who did not modify their role perception—the Inactives and
Leavers—showed little positive social-psychological change.

The smallness of the number of respondents in each ethnic category makes it difficult to draw conclusions about differences and
changes in Orientation and Marginality scores among TNOs according to ethnic membership. As indicated in Table 6, Negroes showed
the highest and Anglos the lowest Orientation scores in both Admin
I and II. All four TNO ethnic groups showed increases in Orientation scores from Admin I to Admin II. Negroes and Mexicans
showed decreases, Anglos and Indians increases, in Marginality
scores. It appears, therefore, that Negroes showed the most, and
Anglos the least, orientation toward the poor, and that Negroes and
Mexicans were less willing that Anglos and Indians to maintain a
perception of marginality for the TNO leadership role. However,
the size of the groups for which data were available of necessity re-
stricts the drawing of conclusions concerning ethnicity and scale
scores. The findings are further complicated by the facts that both
Indians and all but one Anglo were Leavers, and most of the Active
TNOs were Negroes. Thus the variations in Marginality score
changes could be more a reflection of degree of participation than
of subcultural influences associated with ethnic membership. These
confounding factors demand that the interpretations offered for
TNO ethnic-group role perception must be considered primarily as
hypotheses for further research.

As indicated in Table 6, male and female TNOs showed the same
pattern of changes revealed for TNOs as a group. Males, however,
seemed less oriented toward the poor than were females, and tended to perceive the indigenous-leader role to be more marginal.

The shifts in role perception as presented and interpreted raise some question concerning the feasibility of the bridge expectation for indigenous leaders. Differences in expectations for the leader role can and do exist between the staff of a poverty-intervention organization and the indigenous leaders themselves. Furthermore, it is apparent that enactment of a bridge role can engender considerable stress for the incumbent—stress which he may attempt to avoid by dropping out, or by modifying his perception of the leadership role. If a poverty-intervention organization is structured to involve indigenous leaders in marginal roles, findings here suggest that continuous training programs, emphasizing the dynamics of marginality, be included in the programing. The staff of a poverty-intervention organization might also anticipate that indigenous leaders, encountering conflict, may resolve their marginality by increased orientation either to the poor or to the organization itself. An essential question to be considered by the staff is which of those alternative orientations will contribute to the most productive social change and to the amelioration of poverty in a particular community.

PART IV
Conclusions

CHAPTER 16

Functionally Marginal or Marginally Functional?

I N   A N   A T T E M P T to implement the
mandate of the Economic Opportunity Act of 1964, the Topeka poverty program espoused a strategy for social intervention which I
have conceptualized here as the Overlap Model. Representatives
from among the community's poor and not-poor were to meet on an
equal-status basis, and together develop and supervise specific OEO
poverty projects. The dynamics of the interaction were expected to
break down stereotypes, to open lines of communication, and, by
"maximum feasible participation," to develop indigenous leadership
among the poor. The ultimate goal was to bring about, through a
community-wide effort, significant amelioration of poverty and enduring social change.

As the poverty-intervention organization designed to operationalize the Overlap Model, the TOEO labored to maintain a position of
"Functional Marginality" between the poor and the not-poor, and
to be the meeting ground for representatives in Neighborhoods,
Study Committees, and the Economic Opportunity Board.

It seems apparent that the intentions of the Topeka social planners were noble, their attempts admirable, but that they did not
fully anticipate either the complexity of poverty intervention or the
profound impact the *process* experience would have upon the participants, both poor and not-poor.

Target Neighborhood Committees became something more than
"forums for the expression of residents' needs and problems." The
committees became social processes in themselves, and manifested
discrete stages of development. Each stage provided the participants with a different type of process experience, and the Target
Neighborhood Officers with a different kind of leadership problem.
Committee autonomy, attainability of reachable goals, opportunity
for speedy knowledge of results concerning the efficacy of participation, and differences in expectations between TOEO and Neighborhood residents became crucial issues. The degree to which those
issues could be resolved determined the longevity of the Target
Neighborhood Committee, and the facility with which it could
evolve through the stages of development. Depending upon the kind
of interaction a Target Neighborhood Committee would have with
the poverty-intervention organization and other not-poor representatives, it could evolve either a purposefulness which served well the
goals of the poverty program, or a terminal catharsis which served
to negate those goals.

The bridge role expected of the indigenous leader—the Target
Neighborhood Officer—was found to be quite stressful for him. Differences between the expectations of the TOEO and the expectations
of the leader's followers often were extensive, and not easily resolv-
able. He almost always was able to acquire information which
would help him solve problems of program *content*, but seldom was
he able to acquire information which would help him understand
the stress of his marginality. After experience as a Target Neighbor-

hood Officer, his own view of the leadership role often changed, and he became more oriented toward the expectations of his followers. Ironically, this shift in view often was not in harmony with the expectations of the poverty-intervention organization for indigenous leaders.

Differences between the poor and the not-poor representatives on the Economic Opportunity Board in relevant social-psychological variables were far more striking than anticipated. Those differences influenced the way members perceived program content, and served to generate much more conflict than the planners had anticipated. The planners had expected a certain amount of dissension during Board meetings, but they did not expect the meetings to be as volatile as in fact they were.

The Functional Marginality position planned for the TOEO was far more stressful to its staff members than anyone had imagined it would be. Virtually every action taken by TOEO staff was under the scrutiny of other participants, and inevitably one group or another, one individual or another, would be vocally and vociferously dissatisfied. Members of the TOEO staff found themselves buffeted among often conflicting expectations of TNOs, agency representatives, citizens at large, and representatives of regional and national OEO. The "middle ground" the TOEO staff attempted to maintain turned out to be not unlike a zone of combat.

The unanticipated degree of dissension and conflict in expectations is not necessarily dysfunctional to the poverty-intervention organization that follows a strategy similar to the Overlap Model, and maintains a position of Functional Marginality between the poor and the not-poor. Such dissension and conflict may be a functional part of, or a prelude to, social change. The point to be emphasized is that when a poverty organization chooses such a strategy and such an operating position, *all its participants*, professional and indigenous, poor and not-poor, should be prepared for, and have an understanding of, the *process* experiences which will obtain. Hour upon hour, lesson after lesson, is offered to poverty-intervention organization staff and indigenous leaders concerning the content of OEO poverty programs intended to stimulate social change. At least the same attention should be given to social and psychological aspects of that social change.

Essentially, this training, which must be continuous, should prepare the participant for the stresses and conflicts he inevitably will experience as a poverty warrior. Consequently, it might be called "marginality training."[1] An important part of such training might include regular sessions in which the participants could gather together, in an unstructured meeting, simply to discuss freely and openly the stresses they are presently encountering in their roles as change agents. If the Research Committee's (see Appendix A) and research staff's interaction with TOEO staff is any indication, both intervention-organization personnel and indigenous leaders need a closed environment in which they can simply "let off steam" about their jobs and their process experiences. Perhaps social scientists could usefully contribute their expertise in such a setting.

Despite the lack of formal training for TOEO staff, Board members, and TNOs, the Topeka poverty program through its Overlap Model did accomplish several of its goals. It encouraged the emergence of some thirty indigenous leaders, provided them with "maximum feasible participation," and thereby gave "a voice to the poor." Yankelovich comments that of all OEO's national objectives, the attempt to give visibility and a voice to the poor has come closest to achievement.[2] The interaction of the poor and the not-poor on the Economic Opportunity Board did challenge some stereotypes, tended to open lines of communication, and engendered some relevant social-psychological changes among Target Neighborhood Officers, as a function of their involvement. Furthermore, those changes provided empirical support for OEO's speculation that "maximum feasible participation" could be socially therapeutic for the involved

---

[1] Goldfarb and Riessman have written a program of role-playing for indigenous leaders. See Gene Goldfarb and Frank Riessman, "Role Playing with Low-Income People," Washington, D.C., Tutorial Assistance Center, 1966, mimeograph.

[2] Daniel Yankelovich, "CAP Programs and Their Evaluation: A Management Report," prepared for the Office of Economic Opportunity, September, 1967, lithograph.

poor. Finally, through the Overlap Model, the Topeka program implemented over a million dollars in poverty-intervention projects.

Whether the Overlap Model will yield any enduring social change is difficult to say at this point. Certainly some changes in individuals, particularly the TNOs, were observed. Changes, some major but most minor, in the policies of agencies and helping organizations were also observed. Most importantly, a fairly extensive complex of formal and informal interactions among agency representatives, citizens at large, and TNOs evolved. That network has a potential for enduring social change. Most of the long-range poverty-intervention impact of the Topeka program is contingent, however, upon the success of such projects as Head Start, the Neighborhood House, Neighborhood Youth Corps, and Manpower Training.

The Overlap Model involved as active participants very few of Topeka's poor. None of the so-called "hard-core poor" assumed positions of indigenous leadership. However, some of the TNOs, having schooled themselves to be change agents, seemed to be reaching deeply into the community's poverty pockets, especially through such vehicles as the Neighborhood House.

The essential question is: By what alternative model might a community like Topeka have implemented poverty intervention? By an approach similar to the Alinsky strategy? It had not the financial resources, the ghetto poverty, nor the low-income militancy generally prerequisite for that strategy. At the other extreme, the "City Hall" approach would probably not have allowed for participation of the poor. It may be, therefore, that in relatively complacent communities, where poverty is largely "unseen" and "well behaved," the Overlap Model can be an effective first step. It can make the community aware of poverty as a social problem, stimulate the development of indigenous leadership, bring federal antipoverty funds in for local use, and, if flexible enough, set the stage for increasing autonomy and self-direction within the target neighborhoods. The Overlap Model can, when operationalized by an effective poverty-intervention organization and buttressed with adequate training programs for the participants, yield purposive autonomy among the poor, rather than cathartic autonomy. In this

way it can, perhaps, avoid the kind of cathartic fall-out and program disruption and demise cited by Lawrence Davis in his recent
critique of Alinsky's Syracuse Crusade for Opportunity.[3]

The TOEO implemented the Overlap Model by Functional Marginality. Again, the "middle ground" may be a workable first position for a poverty-intervention organization to take in a relatively
complacent community. Though stressful to the staff, the Functional
Marginality position brings already existing community resources to
bear on the amelioration of poverty, and can, as a relatively neutral
"third party," at least hold up a reflective mirror to those who resist
social change. But can a poverty-intervention organization maintain
a Functional Marginality position as its programs evolve, and as
the poor become increasing involved and increasingly sophisticated?

Can a poverty-intervention organization like the TOEO endure a
position of Functional Marginality for any length of time without its
staff becoming defensive and inflexible? There would be times when
such an organization would be called upon to be an advocate of,
and identified with, the poor. And there would be times when the
organization would be called upon to be an advocate of, and identified with, the Establishment. Martin Rein suggests that OEO poverty-intervention organizations have the potential for becoming
ideal redistributive mechanisms. As such, they could mediate federal action through a planning executive responsive to their own
constituencies and provide the "social reform which America has so
desperately lacked." To do so, he concludes that such organizations
must be "somewhat detached from the politics of city hall or any
sectional interests, yet responsive to them all. . . . They must be free
to arbitrate disinterestedly between national and local demands,
pursuing long-term needs through the tangle of immediate pressures. . . . Their ability to negotiate the political issues depends
upon a professional neutrality which alone earns them the trust of
all parties."[4]

[3] Lawrence Davis, "Syracuse: What Happens When the Poor Take Over?"
The Reporter, 38 (March, 1968), 19–21.

[4] Martin Rein, "Community Action Programs: A Critical Reassessment," *Poverty and Human Resources Abstracts: Trend*, 3 (May–June, 1968), 6–7. For

Such an organization, to be "functionally marginal," calls for a staff that is young, resilient, and specially trained. Perhaps such organizations call for establishing a relatively autonomous corps of professional "change agents," with their own career line, their own ideology, their own *esprit*. Like an ombudsman, the professional change agent would be relatively unhindered by undue bureaucratic controls.

The Overlap Model, the TOEO and its Functional Marginality, the TNOs, the Economic Opportunity Board, and the Target Neighborhood Committees are all part of a particular poverty program in a particular community. The generality of the findings is limited, consequently, to the judgment of the reader. It is hoped, however, that practitioners and researchers will see parallels between the process experiences of Topeka's poverty warriors and the experiences of those involved in social-intervention endeavors with which they are familiar. Clearly there is need for comparative research involving intervention programs representative of different social problems, geographical locations, organizational styles, member characteristics, and expectations for indigenous leaders. Current federal programming continues to call nation-wide for the involvement of citizens in intervention projects, and planned social intervention increasingly is becoming a national technique. The question to be asked anew in each community planning such projects and intervention is: What strategy toward what goals?

---

other perspectives, see: Amitai Etzioni, *The Active Society*; Sarajane Heidt and Amitai Etzioni (eds.), *Societal Guidance*; Ralph M. Kramer, *Participation of the Poor*; Daniel Patrick Moynihan, *Maximum Feasible Misunderstanding: Community Action in the War on Poverty*; Frank Riessman, *Strategies Against Poverty*; and Hans B. C. Spiegel, *Citizen Participation in Urban Development*, Vol. 1, *Concepts and Issues*.

APPENDICES

The Research Role and the Research Staff

I began this study of the Topeka poverty program shortly after my arrival at the Menninger Foundation in September, 1965. Significant events concerning the formation of the TOEO prior to that time had been reconstructed from interviews with the TOEO staff and program participants, with members of the Topeka Welfare Planning Council, and by the analysis of applications, records, and reports of the poverty-intervention organization.

Earlier in 1965, Michael Brooks had in a seminal paper written that "the emerging community action programs offer unprecedented opportunities not only to the Nation's poor, but to a second category of persons as well—namely to students of the structure and dynamic processes of the community." He added, "While the ideal sample may continue to elude us, we are nevertheless confronted with a research opportunity unparalleled in the history of American community study."[1] Brooks suggested that research associated with community-action programs was important for the following reasons:

(1) To inform the funding agent as to the value being received per dollar spent (the accounting function); (2) To refine and improve the program being evaluated, through a continuous feedback of its results to the planning process (the feedback function); (3) To make available to other interested communities, whether involved in community action programs or not, the results of the program being evaluated (the dissemi-

---

[1] Michael P. Brooks, "The Community Action Program as a Setting for Applied Research," *Journal of Social Issues*, 21, 1 (January, 1965), 29–40.

nation function); and (4) To clarify, validate, disprove, modify, or otherwise affect the body of theory from which the hypotheses underlying the program were derived (the theory-building function).[2]

He differentiated between studies which would emphasize the program productivity (whose analysis could be quantitative) and the program process (whose analysis would be largely qualitative).[3]

The study of the Topeka poverty program primarily emphasized "theory-building." It focused upon the program process and the social-psychological impact of that process on those community members who were participants (see Preface). It was decided that those processes and experiences could, at least at first, best be assessed by the field techniques of observation and unstructured interviews.

Whyte comments that there is no one best way to do field research. The methods that an investigator chooses must depend upon the nature of the field situation and the research problem.[4] A study which focuses upon the human aspects of social change, particularly when concerned with poverty programs, presents a very special field situation. Human beings who are entrapped in poverty generally are suspicious of, and resistant to, formal research probings. Tape recorders, structured interviews, and the like can easily seem threatening to the respondent, bringing refusals to co-operate or, worse, passivity manifested by the respondents' giving the "right" answers to the investigator. Furthermore, individuals who are poor generally are slow to trust, and therefore to confide in, people with whom they have not had continued interpersonal association. They certainly will not, as likely would members of the middle socio-economic class, "open up" to investigators simply because they are representatives from a reputable organization or agency. These considerations, based upon much evidence from field researchers,[5] provided part of the rationale for using the field

---

[2] *Ibid.*, p. 34.

[3] *Ibid.*, p. 35.

[4] William Foote Whyte, "The Slum: On the Evolution of Street Corner Society," in A. J. Vadich, J. Bensman, and M. R. Stein (eds.), *Reflections on Community Studies*, pp. 3–69.

[5] See, for example: Richard Adams and J. J. Preiss (eds.), *Human Organization Research*; Robert K. Bain, "The Researcher's Role: A Case Study," in *Human Organization Research*, pp. 140–152; John Gullahorn and George Strauss, "The Field Worker in Union Research," in *Human Organization Research*, pp. 153–165; Joseph R. Gusfield, "Field Work Reciprocities in Studying a Social Movement," *Human Organization*, 14, 3 (1955), 29–33; Oscar Lewis,

techniques that we adopted. Another important reason for the choice was that little is known concerning the dynamics of social change among the poor, particularly when such change is stimulated by a poverty-intervention organization. Therefore it was felt that the research should maximize the possibility of discovery and be frankly exploratory in nature.

The same methods—observation and unstructured interviews—were chosen for gathering data from the TOEO staff and the not-poor participants of the poverty program. This was not because the TOEO Director, his staff, or the not-poor participants might have felt threatened by more obvious research methods, but because such techniques could add to, and perhaps confound, the already difficult action task which the rather delicate poverty-intervention organization was striving to accomplish. Furthermore, the use of more flexible field techniques allowed research access to a wide range of significant change phenomena related to the poverty-intervention organization itself.

If sufficient rapport was established with the participants, and both occasion and necessity arose, it was determined that attitude questionnaires might be administered. It was expressly postulated, however, that no research technique would be used which was felt by the researchers or the TOEO staff to be detrimental to the efficacy of the poverty-intervention organization and its associated programs.

The observation used in this study was similar to Gold's typology "observer-as-participant."[6] That is, the observers attended meetings and sat with the members but did not take an active part, and we remained as inconspicuous as possible. Each observer was introduced into a meeting by the Assistant Director of the TOEO or by an observer who had already been accepted by, and was familiar to, the group. The first such observer was myself, and my being there was explained to the members as "a researcher friend who wants to learn about community action." I, and the seven research assistants who subsequently joined the project as the number of meetings increased, answered in-meeting inquiries about the study in very general terms—for example, "We're interested in groups and how

---

The Children of Sanchez; George J. McCall and J. L. Simmons, *Issues in Participant Observation*; Rosalie H. Wax, "Reciprocity as a Field Technique," *Human Organization*, 11, 3 (1952), 31–34; William Foote Whyte, *Street Corner Society*.

[6] Raymond L. Gold, "Roles in Sociological Field Observations," *Social Forces*, 36 (March, 1958), 217–223.

they grow." In a relatively short time, we attended the meetings unnoticed and our research was taken for granted.

Tape recorders and other formal data-gathering devices were eschewed out of consideration for the fragility of the developing target committees and the sensitivity of the members. Notes were taken at the discretion of the observers—not at all if they thought that their writing would distract the group. The observations and impressions, written or not, were nonetheless recorded in private and followed a standardized form (see Appendix B) no later than twenty-four hours after the meeting. (Actually, there were relatively few meetings where note-taking was adjudged by observers to be imprudent. Usually some members were themselves jotting down information, thus providing precedents for pad and pencil.)[7]

The observation began in September, 1965, and terminated in May, 1967. During that time more than two hundred meetings of TOEO committees had been attended and documented by the research staff. Approximately four hundred unstructured interviews had been conducted with participants. Since the research field station was in the same set of buildings as the offices of the TOEO, daily contact had been maintained with the TOEO staff.

The research technique of observation afforded access to staff and participants that would have been impossible with more objective but

[7] Some supportive arguments for, and examples of, these procedures are: Howard S. Becker, "Problems of Inference and Proof in Participant Observation," *American Sociological Review*, 23 (December, 1958), 652–660; Severyn T. Bruyn, *The Human Perspective in Sociology: A Methodology of Participant Observation*; Harold Garfinkel, *Studies in Ethnomethodology*; Barney G. Glaser and Anselm L. Strauss, *The Discovery of Grounded Theory: Strategies for Qualitative Research*; Buford H. Junker, *Field Work: An Introduction to the Social Sciences*; Ned Polsky, *Hustlers, Beats, and Others*; Mortimer Sullivan, Stuart Queen, and Ralph Patrick, "Participant Observation as Employed in the Study of a Military Training Program," *American Sociological Review*, 23 (December, 1958), 660–670; Eugene J. Webb, Donald T. Campbell, Richard D. Schwartz, and Lee Sechrest, *Unobtrusive Measures: Non-Reactive Research in the Social Sciences*; Louis A. Zurcher, Jr., David Sonenschein, and Eric Metzner, "The Hasher: A Study of Role Conflict," *Social Forces*, 44 (June, 1968), 505–514; Louis A. Zurcher, Jr., "The Sailor Aboard Ship: A Study of Role Behavior in a Total Institution," *Social Forces*, 43 (March, 1965), 389–400; Louis A. Zurcher, Jr., "The Naval Recruit Training Center: A Study of Role Assimilation in a Total Institution," *Sociological Inquiry*, 31, 1 (Winter, 1967), 85–98; Louis A. Zurcher, Jr., "The Social Psychology of Ephemeral Roles: A Disaster Work Crew," *Human Organization*, 27, 4 (Winter, 1968), 281–297.

more seemingly threatening data-gathering methods, especially at the beginning of the study, when the poverty program was young. Furthermore, the rapport that evolved through the observation allowed the research staff to continue its observing over the course of nineteen months with very few missed meetings, and to approach members at will for impromptu, unstructured interviews. The research strengths and richness of data gained by this sustained observer closeness to staff and participants were accompanied, however, by the potential problems of subjectivity and unreliability.

Several steps were provided in the research design to minimize the impact of subjectivity and maximize the reliability of the data. Meeting reports were standardized by systematic recording, and each observer maintained full and continuous knowledge of evolving working hypotheses and their associated specific variables (see Appendix C). This knowledge, as suggested by Lippitt, served to increase reliability.[8] Two staff meetings a week were held to remind the observers of the study variables and frames of reference, or to discuss changes. In the majority of cases each field meeting was attended by two observers whose parallel observations, independently recorded without prior mutual discussion, were subsequently compared. Following every meeting, at least one of the committee's officers was informally interviewed by an observer, and notes or impressions substantiated. Similarly, after every meeting a member of the TOEO staff was informally interviewed for substantiation of data. In those cases where only one observer had been present, a TOEO staff member was again consulted after the meeting report had been prepared for final draft. Every observer attended and reported all Economic Opportunity Board meetings, thus providing a sweeping reliability check among the entire research staff. As a final control, the project's chief research assistant and I read every completed report for inconsistencies or inaccuracies.

Once the meeting and interview reports had been typed in final form and circulated among all the research staff, they were assigned to a separate file for each Target Neighborhood Committee, each Study Committee, the Economic Opportunity Board, files for other relevant meetings, and special files for such substantive topics as Neighborhood Committee elections, indigenous-leadership problems, the views of co-operating agencies, etc. This filing system approximated Whyte's organization of

[8] Ronald Lippitt, *Observation and Interview Methods of the Leadership Training Study.*

field notes according to discrete social groups.[9] Cross-references were included in each file when necessary. Part of the task of the research staff was to expand the cross-filing system according to revelant categories, and thus further organize the data.[10] Finally, the data were organized by the regular and frequent preparation of working and formal papers, each attempting to tie together the observational data conceptually, according to the evolving research questions. Those papers served as the basis for staff discussion, the generation of ideas, and as part of the progress reports submitted to the granting agency.

An information retrieval system was developed by assigning a punch card to each observer's meeting report and each unstructured interview, and coding the material according to the substantive variables presented in Appendix C.

In research of this type, based as it is upon observation and unstructured interviews and assessing as it does a sequence of social phenomena over time, the onset postulating of specific hypotheses was difficult. Rather, as Becker and Geer point out, such research is aimed at discovering problems and generating an hypothesis as it goes along, and therefore the design should not hinder the possibility of discovery by rigidly establishing predetermined hypothesis.[11] Becker and Geer, in the study they described, were entering the unfamiliar social world of the medical student, and wanted initially to learn enough about that world, through observation, to be able to make analyses which would lead to the formulation and testing of hypotheses. The procedure they recommended suggested that the gathering of observational data should lead to the conceptualizing of organizational models, whose assumptions can be further tested.

This is essentially the procedure that was followed in the present research. The research staff entered the unfamiliar world of poverty intervention and wanted initially to learn enough about the world, through observation, to be able to make analyses which would lead to the con-

9 William Foote Whyte, "The Slum," p. 27.
10 The organization of files was also influenced by Robert H. Guest, "Categories of Events in Field Observation," in Richard N. Adams and J. J. Preiss (eds.), *Human Organization Research*, pp. 225–239; and Kurt H. Wolff, "The Collection and Organization of Field Materials: A Research Report," *Ohio Journal of Science*, 52, 2 (March, 1952), 49–61.
11 Howard S. Becker and Blanche Geer, "Participant Observation: The Analysis of Qualitative Field Data," in Adams and Preiss (eds.), *Human Organization Research*, pp. 267–289.

ceptualizing of models and the postulating of hypotheses for further testing. As Becker and Geer had indicated, and as illustrated in Chapters 1 and 2 of the present work, models (The Overlap Model and Functional Marginality) did in fact emerge from the accumulating data. Throughout the book, the reader has seen other models and hypotheses emerge and, it is hoped, will be stimulated to test them in comparative settings.[12]

The Research Assistants

A few comments must be made concerning the characteristics of the persons who served as observers in the study, and the kinds of roles they played.

The individuals chosen for the observer role would have to be non-

[12] For descriptions of research approaches in other social-intervention studies, see: Gilbert R. Barnhart, "A Note on the Impact of Public Health Service Research on Poverty," *Journal of Social Issues*, 21 (January, 1965), 142–149; Brooks, *Journal of Social Issues*, 21 (January, 1965), 29–40; Donald T. Campbell, "Factors Relevant to the Validity of Experimentation in Social Settings," *Psychological Bulletin*, 54 (July, 1957), 297–311; Eleanor K. Caplan, "Evaluation of a Program Involving Multiple Community Agencies," paper presented at the American Sociological Association Meetings, Miami Beach, Florida, September 1, 1966; William W. Cooper, Harold J. Leavitt, and Maynard W. Shelley, II (eds.), *New Perspectives in Organization Research*; Arthur G. Cosby, "An Experimental Approach to the Study of Poverty," *Sociology and Social Research*, 53 (January, 1969), 163–170; Arthur G. Cosby, "A Reassessment of Experimental Designs for Sociological Research," Mississippi State University, 1966, mimeograph; Arthur G. Cosby and George Oettinger, III, "The Possibility for Experimental Poverty Studies," Mississippi State University, 1967, mimeograph; George W. Fairweather, *Methods for Experimental Social Innovation*; Howard E. Freeman and Clarence C. Sherwood, "Research in Large Scale Intervention Programs," *Journal of Social Issues*, 21 (January, 1965), 11–28; Norman B. Henderson, "Cross-Cultural Action Research: Some Limitations, Advantages, and Problems," *Journal of Social Psychology*, 73 (October, 1967), 61–70; Herbert Hyman, Charles Wright, and T. K. Hopkins, *Applications of Methods of Evaluation: Four Studies of the Encampment for Citizenship*; Berton H. Kaplan, "Social Issues and Poverty Research: A Commentary," *Journal of Social Issues*, 21 (January, 1965), 1–10; Ralph M. Kramer, *Participation of the Poor*; Peter Marris and Martin Rein, *Dilemmas of Social Reform*; Edward A. Suchman, "Intervention and the 'Intervening' Variable: A Conceptual and Methodological Model for Evaluative Research," paper presented at the meeting of the American Sociological Association, Miami Beach, Florida, September 1, 1966; and Carol H. Weiss, "Utilization of Evaluation: Toward Comparative Study," paper presented at the meeting of the American Sociological Association, Miami Beach, Florida, September, 1966.

threatening to the participants, able to assume the neutral research position, sensitive to the ongoing processes of social intervention, able to
discern the impact of the process upon the participants, capable of helping
to expand conceptualization and to develop working hypotheses, and able
to write concise reports on observations. The task of finding such persons
was not easy. All too often candidates were uneven in their skills—for
example, strong on conceptualizing and writing ability, but weak on establishing rapport with indigenous participants, or vice versa.

The final crew of research assistants consisted of four males and three
females between the ages of twenty and twenty-seven. Two of the females
and one of the males were Negro-American; the rest were Anglo-American.
All the research assistants had had some college experience, and three of
them were recent drop-outs. Their college majors ranged from mathematics
to music, but all of them had had some contact with the social sciences.
The chief research assistant had had some graduate work in sociology.
Each of the observers was interested in, or had at one time tried, creative
writing, and two thought of it as a potential profession. They all had
dabbled with the fine arts in one form or another. All the research assistants
came from more or less disrupted families, and seemed extremely sensitive
to the emotional qualities of interpersonal relations. Four of them knew
poverty from firsthand experience. Three had been active in civil-rights
endeavors. Most importantly, all the research assistants manifested considerable empathy for others, and instantaneously seemed to grasp what it
meant to observe the process experience of participants in a poverty-
intervention program. During the research project, all but one of the
observers lived in a Target Neighborhood.

As mentioned above, the research staff met formally twice weekly to
discuss current observations in light of the working hypotheses, to focus
attention upon any emerging trends, to isolate new research problems, and
to point out inconsistencies in the findings. However, the staff interacted
with each other informally each day, and almost daily there were impromptu meetings concerning some relevant research item. The research
team became very close-knit, and since their observational tasks could and
did demand attention during all hours of the day, most of them became
close personal friends and spent considerable amounts of leisure time
together.

At times it was difficult for members of the research staff to maintain
a neutral position and avoid getting directly involved in community action.
It was necessary for them to become familiar with, if not friendly with,

the Target Neighborhood Officers and several of their followers. As that process of involvement took place, and as the research assistants became more empathetic with, and sensitive to, the reactions of the Neighborhood people, they also became more caught up in the action aspects of the program. Often they felt frustrated that they couldn't "do something" to help the program work better at the grass-roots level. Furthermore, specific research assistants became very much attached to specific Target Neighborhood Committees and Target Neighborhood Officers, and often were quite hesitant to shift to other observational duties when it became necessary. Since at the onset it had been determined that the research findings would not be pumped directly back into the action system until after the completion of the project and all the data were in, the importance of the neutral research role was a continual topic for staff discussion. Not surprisingly, following the completion of the research period, five of the seven observers accepted jobs in action-oriented social-change organizations.

The Research Committee

The Research Committee was perhaps a unique aspect of the study of the Topeka poverty program. Early in the research it became apparent that the persons who best knew what the impact of the TOEO was upon the Target Neighborhoods were the elected officers of the Target Neighborhood Committees. Those officers were deeply involved in the poverty program, spent many of their off-work hours directing and attending the various meetings, and were the weather vanes for "maximum feasible participation" of the poor. Furthermore, if the mandate of the Economic Opportunity Act meant involvement of the poor at all levels of poverty intervention, then it would be consistent to encourage them to participate as well in the research and evaluation of that program.

Consequently, after sounding out the interest of Target Neighborhood Officers, I invited their participation in what was to be called the "Research and Program-Evaluation Study Committee." The committee was to be sanctioned by the TOEO as one of its legitimate Study Committees, and therefore the chairman of the committee would have a vote on the Economic Opportunity Board. On November 30, 1965, the Research Committee was formed. I briefly chaired its first meeting until the election of officers—I was not, of course, a candidate—was completed. The members then voted to close meetings to everyone except Target Neighborhood Officers, research personnel, and invited guests. Subsequent meetings were held at least once, but usually twice, a month, eschewed rigid agenda, were held in the conference room of the research field station, and had an average attendance of about seventeen members.

The topics discussed at the meetings, which started at 7:30 P.M. and often lasted until 11:30, were many and varied. Often one of the members would suggest an idea for discussion, and a good part of the evening would be spent on a topic such as: work; religion; welfare; what it means to be an indigenous leader; what "research" is; what "social change" is; what "mental health" is, and what psychiatrists really do. At least once during each evening the research staff would introduce for discussion one of the research variables, and ask the members for their opinions, reactions, etc. The research design was discussed in general terms with the members, as were the evolving conceptualizations of the Overlap Model and Functional Marginality. The research staff made every effort to analyze for the group, in understandable terms, any experience or problem described by one of the participants. Similarly, if the members wished to hear a social-science treatise on a substantive issue (for example, prejudice), the research staff would quickly respond. The procedure for grant applications, and the sources of funding for research grants, were explained to the group. Summary reports of papers written and reports submitted were presented to the members of the Research Committee, but again in very general terms so as not to confound the research or unduly interfere with the evolution of the poverty program.

During those meetings, perhaps more than anywhere else, members of the research staff were sorely tempted to pass on specific study findings to the participants. Taught now by hindsight, it might be concluded that it would have been better to do exactly that. There were many areas where specific research findings could have been helpful not only to Target Neighborhood Officers, but to TOEO staff and agency representatives as well. However, hindsight also testifies that there were a number of instances where our advice, if given, would have at that time been precisely in error. At any rate, the stance of the research staff during the period of the study was that we would as silently as possible gather as much information as we could, analyze and systematize the results, and hope that the findings would ultimately be of use not only to the TOEO but to other intervention organizations as well.

Ironically, the neutral stance of the research staff was better tolerated by the Target Neighborhood Officer members of the Research Committee than by the staff members themselves. They saw the wisdom of the observers' not becoming committed to one group or another in the poverty program, and even advised the observers to "play it cool" so "nobody'll slam doors in your face." They realized that neutrality provided the staff with access to all participants. On several occasions, when one of the research observers would be asked by someone to express an opinion on a particular action issue or to give advice concerning a decision to be made, a member of the Research Committee would protest, "He shouldn't answer that yet! He's a researcher!" That neutral stance, and a rigid policy of maintaining the confidentiality of interviews, served the observers well throughout the study. Several times meetings of various other committees would be considered private, and all nonmembers would be asked to leave —all nonmembers that is, except "the researchers." When, as a matter of information, I presented my intention to conduct a study of the Topeka poverty program to the Economic Opportunity Board and requested its vote of approval, the Target Neighborhood Officers lent their support and stimulated a unanimous affirmative vote.

The Research Committee, therefore, provided Target Neighborhood Officers with participation at another level of the poverty program. It allowed them to contribute directly to a research endeavor in a fashion other than as passive respondents. Furthermore, meetings of the Research Committee, in contrast to other committee meetings, provided a relaxed, unstructured setting in which Target Neighborhood Officers could freely, comfortably, and in confidence express their views about various aspects of the poverty intervention, including the rewards and stresses of their own roles in the program. They found themselves in a climate where no topic was taboo, and everyone's opinion was equally accepted. At the same time, their off-hand remarks, their humor, anger, joy, frustration, reflections, arguments, and criticisms yielded to this study some of its richest data.

Format for Recording Observation Data

I. *Designation of date, location, time, and researchers.*

II. *A physical description:*
   a) Of the meeting place.
   b) Of the seating arrangement.
   c) Of the style of dress of the participants.
   d) Other important factors which may affect the meeting (e.g., bad weather may cause low attendance).

III. *Pre-meeting comments:*
   a) Expectations of what may occur; agenda.
   b) Recording of conversations with participants or between participants before the beginning of the meeting.
   c) Additional information gathered between the last meeting held and the present meeting.

IV. *Tabulation of persons present:*
   a) Target Neighborhood Officers (TNOs).
   b) Target Neighborhood residents.
   c) Topeka Office of Economic Opportunity.
   d) Agency representation and citizens at large.
   e) Researchers.
   f) Others (visitors, children, etc.).
   g) Ethnic breakdown.
   h) Number of female and male.

V. *Actual meeting process:*
   a) Recording of statements.
   b) Items discussed.
   c) Proposals made.
   d) Other pertinent information relevant to the variables under study.
   e) Key figures in meeting.
   f) Agenda for future meeting.

VI. *Post-meeting comments:*
   a) Recording of conversation with participants or between participants after the close of the meeting.

VII. *Researchers' comments* (to be parenthetical if included in the body of the report):

a) Interpretations in contrast to expectations.

b) Interpretations of the effects of the meeting on future developments.

c) Interpretations of the meeting itself (mood, etc.).

Major Variables and Coding Categories

I. *Quasi-stationary equilibrium of Topeka:*
  1. Power structure.
  2. Demography.
  3. Ecology.
  4. Index of industrialization and technical organization.
  5. History of social change.
  6. History of social habits and group standards.

II. *Topeka Office of Economic Opportunity* (TOEO):
  7. History of its inception.
  8. Philosophy, rationale, goals (Overlap Model—in the abstract).
  9. Bureaucratization.
  10. Social expedient for involvement.
  11. Managerial succession.
  12. Consultation from without.

  Organizational structure
  13. Internal.
  14. External.

  Interaction with Target Neighborhood Committees (TNC)
  15. Co-operation.
  16. Conflict.

  Interaction with delegate agencies
  17. Co-operation.
  18. Conflict.

  Interaction with power structure
  19. Co-operation.
  20. Conflict.

  Director role
  21. Self-image and expectations.
  22. Stresses.
  23. Changes.

Assistant Director role

24. Self-image and expectations.
25. Stresses.
26. Changes.

Functional Marginality

27. Tactics.
28. Stresses.

Organizational style

29. Political model.
30. Ministerial model.

Programs

31. Output—community-action programs funded.
32. Decision-making process.

Interaction with City Hall

33. Co-operation.
34. Conflict.

Views of

35. Board (Economic Opportunity Board).
36. OEO, national and regional.

III. *TOEO and TNC*:

37. Involvement with politics.
38. Interaction with local businesses.

IV. *TNC*:

39. Histories of inception.
40. Expressed (by participants) goals, rationales, etc.
41. Changes in expressed (by participants) goals, rationales, etc.
42. Meeting places—descriptions of environment, etc.
43. Neighborhood participation, degree of.
44. Indices of dependence upon TOEO and staff.
45. Program output—programs sponsored.

Stages of development

46. Orientation.
47. Catharsis.
48. Focus.
49. Action.
50. Limbo.
51. Testing.
52. Purposive.

Indigenous leadership

53. Emergence.

54. Elections.
55. Marginality and responses to marginality toward OEO.
56. Attitudinal base and attitudinal shifts (toward middle class, toward self, etc.).
57. Behavioral base and behavioral shifts (toward middle class, toward self, etc.).
58. Evidences of increasing or decreasing involvement in TOEO complex.
59. Issue of power and control.
60. Conflicts with other TNOs or Target Neighborhood residents.

Indices of autonomy
61. Purposive- or accomplishment-based.
62. Disenchantment.

Interaction with other TNCs
63. Co-operation.
64. Conflict.

V. *Target Neighborhood residents*:
65. Attitudes toward work.
66. Negro data.
67. Indian data.
68. Mexican-American data.
69. Anglo data.

Indices of
70. Future orientation—present orientation.
71. Alienation.
72. Achievement motivation.
73. Activity-passivity.

Views of
74. OEO, national.
75. TOEO.
76. Agencies.
77. Delegate agencies.
78. City Hall.
79. Board.
80. Leadership Training Sessions.
81. Poverty and the poor.

VI. *Middle-class participants' and others' view of*:
82. TOEO complex.
83. Target Neighborhood residents.
84. Board.

VII. *The role of the research and the researchers vis-à-vis*:
    85. The poor.
    86. The TOEO.

VIII. *Miscellaneous*:
    87. Universalism *vs.* particularism.
    88. Neighborhood House.

Opinion Questionnaire, Administered to Poverty Board Members to Assess Social-Psychological Characteristics (See pp. 66–68 for references.)

INSTRUCTIONS:

Will you please express your opinion about the following statements. Read each statement, see to what extent you agree or disagree with it, then check-mark the space following the answer that best tells how you feel.

1. The secret of happiness is not expecting too much out of life, and being content with what comes your way.
Strongly agree_____ Agree_____ Undecided_____ Disagree _____ Strongly disagree_____

2. Nowadays a person has to live pretty much for today and let tomorrow take care of itself.
Strongly agree_____ Agree_____ Undecided_____ Disagree _____ Strongly disagree_____

3. I don't get to visit friends as often as I'd like to.
Strongly agree_____ Agree_____ Undecided_____ Disagree _____ Strongly disagree_____

4. All I want out of life in the way of a career is a secure, not too difficult job, with enough pay to afford a nice car and eventually a home of my own.
Strongly agree_____ Agree_____ Undecided_____ Disagree _____ Strongly disagree_____

5. People are just naturally friendly and helpful.
Strongly agree_____ Agree_____ Undecided_____ Disagree _____ Strongly disagree_____

6. Everything is relative, and there just aren't any definite rules to live by.
Strongly agree_____ Agree_____ Undecided_____ Disagree _____ Strongly disagree_____

7. It's hardly fair to bring children into the world with the way things look for the future.
Strongly agree_____ Agree_____ Undecided_____ Disagree _____ Strongly disagree_____

8. If you have the chance to hire an assistant in your work, it is always better to hire a relative than a stranger.
Strongly agree_____ ___ Agree_____ Undecided_____ Disagree
_____ Stron~~~ ~~~ree_____

9. Sometimes I ~ ~ the world.
Strongly agree__ _____ Undecided_____ Disagree
_____ Strongly __

10. Nothing in life is woı. ~ of moving away from your parents.
Strongly agree_____ Aͫ~~ ~~ndecided_____ Disagree
_____ Strongly disagree__

11. There is little or nothing I can ι. ~nting a major "shooting" war.
Strongly agree_____ Agree_____ _____ Disagree
_____ Strongly disagree_____

12. We are just so many cogs in the machineɾ, ɟf life.
Strongly agree_____ Agree_____ Undecided_____ Disagree
_____ Strongly disagree_____

13. It's silly for a teen-ager to put money into a car when the money could be used to get started in business or for an education.
Strongly agree_____ Agree_____ Undecided_____ Disagree
_____ Strongly disagree_____

14. Real friends are as easy as ever to find.
Strongly agree_____ Agree_____ Undecided_____ Disagree
_____ Strongly disagree_____

15. People's ideas change so much that I wonder if we'll ever have anything to depend on.
Strongly agree_____ Agree_____ Undecided_____ Disagree
_____ Strongly disagree_____

16. When looking for a job, a person ought to find a position in a place located near his parents, even if that means losing a good opportunity elsewhere.
Strongly agree_____ Agree_____ Undecided_____ Disagree
_____ Strongly disagree_____

17. It is important to make plans for one's life and not just accept what comes.
Strongly agree_____ Agree_____ Undecided_____ Disagree
_____ Strongly disagree_____

18. Most people today seldom feel lonely.
Strongly agree_____ Agree_____ Undecided_____ Disagree
_____ Strongly disagree_____

19. There is little chance for promotion on the job unless a man gets a break.
Strongly agree_____ Agree_____ Undecided_____ Disagree _____ Strongly disagree_____

20. The best kind of job to have is one where you are part of an organization all working together even if you don't get individual credit.
Strongly agree_____ Agree_____ Undecided_____ Disagree _____ Strongly disagree_____

21. With so many religions around, one doesn't really know which to believe.
Strongly agree_____ Agree_____ Undecided_____ Disagree _____ Strongly disagree_____

22. One can always find friends if he shows himself friendly.
Strongly agree_____ Agree_____ Undecided_____ Disagree _____ Strongly disagree_____

23. The end often justifies the means.
Strongly agree_____ Agree_____ Undecided_____ Disagree _____ Strongly disagree_____

24. When a man is born, the success he is going to have is already in the cards, so he might just as well accept it and not fight against it.
Strongly agree_____ Agree_____ Undecided_____ Disagree _____ Strongly disagree_____

25. Even when teen-agers get married, their main loyalty still belongs to their fathers and mothers.
Strongly agree_____ Agree_____ Undecided_____ Disagree _____ Strongly disagree_____

26. It is frightening to be responsible for the development of a little child.
Strongly agree_____ Agree_____ Undecided_____ Disagree _____ Strongly disagree_____

27. How important is it to know clearly in advance your plans for the future?
Very important_____ Important_____ Undecided _____ Unimportant_____ Very Unimportant_____

28. When you are in trouble, only a relative can be depended upon to help you out.
Strongly agree_____ Agree_____ Undecided_____ Disagree _____ Strongly disagree_____

29. In spite of what some people say, the lot of the average man is getting worse, not better.
Strongly agree_____ Agree_____ Undecided_____ Disagree _____ Strongly disagree_____

30. When the time comes for a boy to take a job, he should stay near his parents, even if it means giving up a good job opportunity.
Strongly agree_____ Agree_____ Undecided_____ Disagree _____ Strongly disagree_____

31. Sometimes I have the feeling that other people are using me.
Strongly agree_____ Agree_____ Undecided_____ Disagree _____ Strongly disagree_____

32. The future looks very dismal.
Strongly agree_____ Agree_____ Undecided_____ Disagree _____ Strongly disagree_____

33. There are so many decisions that have to be made today that sometimes I could just "blow up."
Strongly agree_____ Agree_____ Undecided_____ Disagree _____ Strongly disagree_____

34. It doesn't make much difference whether the people elect one candidate or another, for nothing will change.
Strongly agree_____ Agree_____ Undecided_____ Disagree _____ Strongly disagree_____

35. These days, a person doesn't really know whom he can count on.
Strongly agree_____ Agree_____ Undecided_____ Disagree _____ Strongly disagree_____

36. I often wonder what the meaning of life really is.
Strongly agree_____ Agree_____ Undecided_____ Disagree _____ Strongly disagree_____

37. I worry about the future facing today's children.
Strongly agree_____ Agree_____ Undecided_____ Disagree _____ Strongly disagree_____

38. Planning only makes a person unhappy, for your plans hardly ever work out anyway.
Strongly agree_____ Agree_____ Undecided_____ Disagree _____ Strongly disagree_____

39. We're so regimented today that there's not much room for choice even in personal matters.
Strongly agree_____ Agree_____ Undecided_____ Disagree _____ Strongly disagree_____

40. The only thing one can be sure of today is that he can be sure of nothing.
Strongly agree_____ Agree_____ Undecided_____ Disagree _____ Strongly disagree_____

41. There are few dependable ties between people anymore.
Strongly agree_____ Agree_____ Undecided_____ Disagree _____ Strongly disagree_____

42. I don't get invited out by friends as often as I'd really like.
Strongly agree_____ Agree_____ Undecided_____ Disagree
_____ Strongly disagree_____
43. There's little use writing to public officials because they often aren't really interested in the problems of the average man.
Strongly agree_____ Agree_____ Undecided_____ Disagree
_____ Strongly disagree_____
44. The world in which we live is basically a friendly place.
Strongly agree_____ Agree_____ Undecided_____ Disagree
_____ Strongly disagree_____

The Stouffer-Toby Role Conflict Scale was also administered, but it is not reproduced here (see p. 68).

Role-Perception Scale

Consider for a moment what you feel the job of a Target Neighborhood Officer to be. Then please express your opinion about the following items. Each item presents two possible tasks, labeled **A** and **B**, for the Target Neighborhood Officer. Weigh the two tasks (**A** and **B**) together, and indicate the balance of their importance, as you can see it, by marking the appropriate response.

1.

A	B
To get information from the Topeka OEO office to the Target Neighborhood residents	To get information from the Target Neighborhood residents to the Topeka OEO office

A *exclusively* important, **B** unimportant	A *very much* more important than **B**	A *much* more important than **B**	A *slightly* more important than **B**	A and **B** equally important	**B** *slightly* more important than A	**B** *much* more important than A	**B** *very much* more important than A	**B** *exclusively* important, A unimportant

2.

A	B
To spend time with the Topeka OEO staff in order to learn what can be done about poverty problems	To spend time with the Target Neighborhood residents in order to learn what can be done about poverty problems

A *exclusively* important, **B** unimportant	A *very much* more important than **B**	A *much* more important than **B**	A *slightly* more important than **B**	A and **B** equally important	**B** *slightly* more important than A	**B** *much* more important than A	**B** *very much* more important than A	**B** *exclusively* important, A unimportant

3.

A
To educate the Target Neighborhood residents about the services available through the Topeka OEO office

B
To educate the Topeka OEO office about the needs of the Target Neighborhood residents

A *exclusively* important, B unimportant	A *very much* important than B	A *much* more important than B	A *slightly* more important than B	A and B equally important	B *slightly* more important than A	B *much* more important than A	B *very much* more important than A	B *exclusively* important, A unimportant

4.

A
To talk with the Topeka OEO staff before making decisions about community-action proposals

B
To talk with Target Neighborhood residents before making decisions about community-action proposals

A *exclusively* important, B unimportant	A *very much* important than B	A *much* more important than B	A *slightly* more important than B	A and B equally important	B *slightly* more important than A	B *much* more important than A	B *very much* more important than A	B *exclusively* important, A unimportant

5.

A
To represent the Topeka OEO office to the community at large

B
To represent the Target Neighborhood residents to the community at large

A *exclusively* important, B unimportant	A *very much* important than B	A *much* more important than B	A *slightly* more important than B	A and B equally important	B *slightly* more important than A	B *much* more important than A	B *very much* more important than A	B *exclusively* important, A unimportant

6.

A
To help the "poor" learn about the "middle class"

B
To help the "middle-class" learn about the "poor"

A *exclusively* important, B unimportant	A *very much* important than B	A *much* more important than B	A *slightly* more important than B	A and B equally important	B *slightly* important than A	B *much* more important than A	B *very much* more important than A	B *exclusively* important, A unimportant

7.

If we put the Topeka OEO office on one end of a line and the Target Neighborhood residents on the other end, where would you put the Target Neighborhood Officer? The position you mark indicates your opinion about the working position he should generally take in order to do the best job, as you see it.

Topeka OEO office _____ _____ Target Neighborhood residents

8.

As a Target Neighborhood Officer, where do you see yourself on the line? The position you mark should indicate your opinion about your general working position as a Target Neighborhood Officer.

Topeka OEO officer _____ _____ Target Neighborhood residents

9.

If we put the agencies on one end of a line and the Target Neighborhood residents on the other end, where would you put the Target Neighborhood Officer? The position you mark should indicate your opinion about the working position he should generally take in order to do the best job as you see it.

Agencies _____ _____ Target Neighborhood residents

10.

As a Target Neighborhood Officer, where do you see yourself on the line? The position you mark should indicate your opinion about your general working position as a Target Neighborhood Officer.

Agencies _____ _____ Target Neighborhood residents

11.

On a line from "rich" to "poor," where would you place yourself?

"Rich" _____ _____ "Poor"

BIBLIOGRAPHY

Abrahams, J. "Group Psychotherapy: Implications for Direction and Supervision of Mentally Ill Patients," in Theresa Muller (ed.), *Mental Health in Nursing*. Washington, D.C.: Catholic University Press, 1949, pp. 77–83.

Adams, Richard N., and J. J. Preiss (eds.). *Human Organization Research*. Homewood, Illinois: Dorsey Press, 1960.

Alinsky, Saul D. *Reveille for Radicals*. Chicago: University of Chicago, 1946.

————. "The War on Poverty—Political Pornography," *Journal of Social Issues*, 21 (January, 1965), pp. 41–48.

American Community Development: Preliminary Reports by Directors of Projects Assisted by the Ford Foundation in Four Cities and a State. New York: Ford Foundation, Office of Reports, 1964.

Bach, G. R.: *Intensive Group Psychotherapy*. New York: Ronald Press, 1954.

Bain, Robert K. "The Researcher's Role: A Case Study," in Richard N. Adams and J. J. Preiss (eds.), *Human Organization Research*. Homewood, Illinois: Dorsey Press, 1960, pp. 23–28.

Bales, R. F. "The Equilibrium Problem in Small Groups," in Talcott Parsons, R. F. Bales, and E. A. Shils, *Working Papers in the Theory of Action*. New York: Free Press, 1953, pp. 111–161.

Bales, R. F., and F. L. Stodtbeck. "Phases in Group Problem Solving," *Journal of Abnormal and Social Psychology*, 46 (October, 1951), pp. 485–495.

Ball, Richard A. "A Poverty Case: The Analgesic Subculture of the Southern Appalachians," *American Sociological Review*, 33 (December, 1968), pp. 885–895.

Barnhart, Gilbert R. "A Note on the Impact of Public Health Service Research on Poverty," *Journal of Social Issues*, 21 (January, 1965), pp. 142–149.

Beal, George M. "How Does Social Change Occur?" Ames, Iowa: RS-384, Cooperative Extension Service, Iowa State University, February, 1962.

Beck, Burtram M. "Knowledge and Skills in Administration of an Anti-Poverty Program," *Social Work*, 11, 3 (July, 1966), pp. 102–106.

Becker, Howard S. "Problems of Inference and Proof in Participant Observation," *American Sociological Review*, 23 (December, 1958), pp. 652–660.

Becker, Howard S., and Blanche Geer, "Participant Observation: The Analysis of Qualitative Field Data," in Richard N. Adams and J. J. Preiss (eds.), *Human Organization Research*. Homewood, Illinois: Dorsey Press, 1960, pp. 267–289.

Bee, Robert L. "Patterns of Acceptance and Integration of Development Programs in an American Indian Community: An Interim Analysis," University of Connecticut, 1968, mimeograph.

Beilin, H. "The Pattern of Postponability and Its Relation to Social Class Mobility," *Journal of Social Psychology*, 44 (August, 1956), pp. 33–48.

Beiser, M. "Poverty, Social Disintegration and Personality," *Journal of Social Issues*, 21, 1 (January, 1965), pp. 56–78.

Bell, Wendell. "Anomie, Social Isolation and Class Structure," *Sociometry*, 29 (June, 1957), pp. 105–116.

Bell, Wendell, and Maryanne Force. "Urban Neighborhood Types and Participation in Formal Associations," *American Sociological Review*, 21 (February, 1956), pp. 146–156.

Bennis, Warren G., Kenneth D. Benne, and Robert Chin (eds.). *The Planning of Change: Readings in the Applied Behavioral Sciences*. New York: Holt, Rinehart and Winston, 1961.

Bennis, Warren G., and Shepard, H. A. "A Theory of Group Development," Human Relations, 9, 4 (November, 1956), pp. 415–437.

Bernstein, B. "Language and Social Class," *British Journal of Psychology*, 11 (1960), pp. 271–276.

Bion, W. R. *Experience in Groups*. New York: Basic Books, 1961.

Blau, Peter M., and W. Richard Scott. *Formal Organization*. San Francisco: House, 1956.

Blau, Peter M., and W. Richard Scott. *Formal Organization*. San Francisco: Chandler, 1962.

Boose, B. J., and S. S. Boose. "Some Personality Characteristics of the Culturally Disadvantaged," *Journal of Psychology*, 65 (March, 1967), pp. 157–162.

Bradford, L. P. "Membership and the Learning Process," in L. P. Bradford, J. R. Gibb, and K. D. Benne (eds.), *T-group Theory and Laboratory Method*. New York: Wylie, 1964, pp. 190–215.

———. "Trainer-Intervention: Case Episodes," in L. P. Bradford, J. G. Gibb, and K. D. Benne (eds.), *T-group Theory and Laboratory Method*. New York: Wylie, 1964, pp. 136–137.

Bradford, L. P., J. R. Gibb, and K. D. Benne (eds.), *T-group Theory and Laboratory Method*. New York: Wylie, 1964.

Brager, George. "The Indigenous Worker: A New Approach to the Social Work Technician," *Social Work*, 10 (April, 1965), pp. 33–40.

———. "New Concepts in Patterns of Service: The Mobilization for Youth Programs," in Frank Riessman, Jerome Cohen and Arthur Pearl (eds.), *Mental Health of the Poor*. Glencoe, Illinois: Free Press, 1964, pp. 412–421.

———. "Organizing the Unaffiliated in a Low-Income Area," in Louis A. Ferman, Joyce L. Kornbluh, and Alan Haber (eds.), *Poverty in America*. Ann Arbor: University of Michigan Press, 1965, pp. 390–395.

Brager, George, and Frances P. Purcell (eds.). *Community Action Against Poverty*. New Haven, Connecticut: College and University Press, 1967.

Bredemeier, Harry C. "New Strategies for the War on Poverty," *Trans-Action*, 2 (November–December, 1964), pp. 3–8.

———. "Suggestions to Communities for Participation in the War on Poverty," New Brunswick, New Jersey: Urban Study Center, Rutgers University, 1964, mimeograph.

Brooks, Michael P. "The Community Action Program as a Setting for Applied Research," *Journal of Social Issues*, 21, 1 (January, 1965), pp. 29–40.

Bruyn, Severyn T. *Communities in Action: Pattern and Process*. New Haven, Connecticut: College and University Press, 1963.

———. *The Human Perspective in Sociology: A Methodology of Partici-pant Observation*. Englewood Cliffs, New Jersey: Prentice-Hall, 1966.

Burgess, M. Elaine. "Poverty and Dependency: Some Selected Charac-teristics," *Journal of Social Issues*, 21 (January, 1965), pp. 79–97.

Burke, Edmund. "Citizen Participation in Renewal," *Journal of Housing*, 23 (January, 1966), pp. 18–25.

Callender, Charles. "Social Organization of the Central Algonkian In-dians," *Milwaukee Public Museum Publications*, No. 7, 1962.

Campbell, Donald T. "Factors Relevant to the Validity of Experimenta-tion in Social Settings," *Psychological Bulletin*, 54 (July, 1957), pp. 297–311.

Caplan, Eleanor K. "Evaluation of a Program Involving Multiple Com-munity Agencies," paper presented at the meeting of the American Sociological Association, Miami Beach, Florida, September, 1966.

Carter, Barbara. "Sargent Shriver and the Role of the Poor," *The Reporter*, 35 (May 5, 1966), pp. 18–19.

Caudill, Harry M. *Night Comes to the Cumberlands.* Boston: Little, Brown, 1962.

Chin, Robert. "The Utility of System Models and Developmental Models for Practitioners," in Warren G. Bennis, Kenneth D. Benne, and Robert Chin (eds.), *The Planning of Change: Readings in the Applied Behavioral Sciences.* New York: Holt, Rinehart and Winston, 1961, pp. 201–214.

Clifton, James A. "Culture Change, Structural Stability and Factionalism in the Prairie Potawatomi Reservation Community," *Midcontinent American Studies Journal,* 6, 2 (1965), pp. 101–122.

Clifton, James A., and Barry Isaac. "The Kansas Prairie Potawatomi: On the Nature of a Contemporary Indian Community," *Transactions* of the the Kansas Academy of Science, 67, 1 (1964), pp. 1–24.

Cloward, Richard A. "The War on Poverty: Are the Poor Left Out?" *The Nation* (August 2, 1965), pp. 55–60.

Coch, L., and J. R. P. French. "Overcoming Resistance to Change," *Human Relations,* 1, 4 (1948), pp. 512–532.

Cohen, A., and H. Hodges. "Characteristics of the Lower Blue Collar Class," *Social Problems,* 10, 4 (1963), pp. 303–334.

Cohen, Yehudi A. "Patterns of Friendship," in Yehudi A. Cohen (ed.), *Social Structure and Personality.* New York: Holt, Rinehart and Winston, 1961, pp. 353–354.

——— (ed.). *Social Structure and Personality.* New York: Holt, Rinehart and Winston, 1961.

Cohnstaedt, Martin L., and Peter Irons. "A Head Start for Community Organizations," paper presented to the Society for the Study of Social Problems, American Sociological Association, Miami Beach, Florida, August, 1966.

Cooper, William W., Harold J. Leavitt, and Maynard W. Shelley, II (eds.). *New Perspectives in Organization Research.* New York: Wylie, 1964.

Corsini, R. J. *Methods of Group Psychotherapy.* New York: McGraw-Hill, 1957.

Cosby, Arthur G. "A Reassessment of Experimental Designs for Sociological Research," Mississippi State University, 1966, mimeograph.

———. "An Experimental Approach to the Study of Poverty," *Sociology and Social Research,* 53 (January, 1969), pp. 163–170.

Cosby, Arthur G., and George Oettinger, III. "The Possibility for Experimental Poverty Studies," Mississippi State University, 1967, mimeograph.

Coser, Lewis. *The Social Functions of Conflict.* Glencoe, Illinois: Free Press, 1956.

Criminger, George. "A Neighborhood House Leads the Way," in R.

Franklin (ed.), *Patterns of Community Development*. Washington, D.C.: Public Affairs Office Press, 1966, pp. 97–704.

Davis, Lawrence. "Syracuse: What Happens When the Poor Take Over?" *The Reporter*, 38 (March, 1968), pp. 19–21.

Dean, Dwight G. "Alienation: Its Meaning and Measurement," *American Sociological Review*, 26 (October, 1961), pp. 753–758.

Deutsch, M. P. "The Disadvantaged Child and the Learning Process," in A. H. Passow (ed.), *Education in Depressed Areas*. New York: Columbia University Press, 1963, pp. 163–179.

Dozier, Edward P. "Folk Culture to Urbanity: The Case of Mexicans and Mexican-Americans," University of Arizona, 1964, mimeograph.

Dubey, D. C., and Willis Sutton. "A Rural 'Middle Man in the Middle': The Indian Village Level Worker in Community Development," *Human Organization*, 24 (Summer, 1965), pp. 148–151.

Economic Opportunity Act of 1964, 78 Stat. 508, Sec. 202 (*a*).

Economic Opportunity Amendments of 1966, 80 Stat. 1451, Sec. 203 (*c*) 2.

Economic Opportunity Amendments of 1966, 80 Stat. 1451, Sec. 203 (*c*) 3.

Economic Opportunity Board of Shawnee County, Kansas, Inc., By-laws of.

Empey, Lamar J. "Social Class and Occupational Aspirations: A Comparison of Absolute and Relative Measurements," *American Sociological Review*, 21 (December, 1956), pp. 703–709.

Etzioni, Amitai. *Modern Organizations*. Englewood Cliffs, New Jersey: Prentice-Hall, 1964.

——. *The Active Society*. New York: Free Press, 1968.

Etzioni, Amitai, and Eva Etzioni (eds.). *Social Change: Sources, Patterns and Consequences*. New York: Basic Books, 1964.

Fairweather, George W. *Methods for Experimental Social Innovation*. New York: John Wiley and Son, 1967.

The Federal Delinquency Program: Objectives in Operation Under the President's Committee on Juvenile Delinquency and Youth Crime. Washington, D.C.: U.S. Government Printing Office, 1962.

Ferman, Louis A., Joyce L. Kornbluh, and Alan Haber (eds.), *Poverty in America*. Ann Arbor: University of Michigan, 1965.

Fishman, Jacob R., and Frederic Solomon. "Youth and Social Action: Perspectives on the Student Sit-In Movement," *American Journal of Orthopsychiatry*, 33, 5 (October, 1963), pp. 872–882.

Fishman, Leo (ed.). *Poverty Amid Affluence*. New Haven, Connecticut: Yale University Press, 1966.

Florence Heller Graduate School for Advanced Studies in Social Welfare.

"Community Representation in Community Action Programs," Report No. 1 (February, 1968), Waltham, Massachusetts: Brandeis University.

Franklin, R. (ed.). *Patterns of Community Development*. Washington, D.C.: Public Affairs Office Press, 1966.

Freeman, Howard E., and Clarence C. Sherwood. "Research in Large Scale Intervention Programs," *Journal of Social Issues*, 21 (January, 1965), pp. 11–28.

Gamson, William A. "Community Power Research and Community Action," paper presented before the American Sociological Association, San Francisco, California, September, 1967.

Gans, Herbert J. "Redefining the Settlement's Function for the War on Poverty," *Social Work*, 9, 4 (October, 1964), pp. 3–12.

————. "Subcultures and Class," in Louis A. Ferman, Joyce L. Kornbluh, and Alan Haber (eds.), *Poverty in America*. Ann Arbor: University of Michigan, 1965, pp. 302–311.

Gardner, Burleigh B., and William F. Whyte. "The Man in the Middle: Position and Problems of the Foreman," *Applied Anthropology*, 4, 1 1945), 1–28.

Garfinkle, Harold. *Studies in Ethnomethodology*. Englewood Cliffs, New Jersey: Prentice-Hall, 1967.

Gerth, Hans H., and C. Wright Mills (trans. and eds.). *From Max Weber: Essays in Sociology*. New York: Oxford University Press, 1946.

Glaser, Barney G., and Anselm L. Strauss. *The Discovery of Grounded Theory: Strategies for Qualitative Research*. Chicago: Aldine Publishing Company, 1967.

Glazer, Nona Y., and Carol F. Creedon, *Children and Poverty*. Chicago: Rand McNally, 1968.

Gold, Raymond L. "Roles in Sociological Field Observations," *Social Forces*, 36 (March, 1958), pp. 217–223.

Goldfarb, Gene, and Frank Riessman. "Role Playing with Low-Income People." Washington, D.C.: Tutorial Assistance Center, 1966, mimeograph.

Goldner, Fred H. "Organizations and Their Environment: Roles at Their Boundary," paper presented before the American Sociological Association, New York, September, 1960.

Golembiewski, R. T. *The Small Group*. Chicago: University of Chicago Press, 1962.

Gordon, Margaret. *Poverty in America*. San Francisco: Chandler, 1966.

Gossen, Gary H. "A Version of the Potawatomi Coon-Wolf Cycle: A Traditional Projection Screen for Acculturative Stress," *Search: Selected Studies by Undergraduate Honors Students at the University of Kansas*, No. 4 (1964), pp. 1–21.

Bibliography 415

Gottesfeld, Harry, and Gerterlyn Dozier. "Changes in Feelings of Power-lessness in a Community Action Program," *Psychological Reports*, 19 (December, 1966), p. 978.

Gould, Rosiland. "Some Sociological Determinants of Goal Striving," *Journal of Social Psychology*, 13 (May, 1941), pp. 461–473.

Green, James W., and Selz C. Mayo. "A Framework for Research in the Actions of Community Groups," *Social Forces*, 31 (May, 1953), pp. 323–326.

Grey, Alan L. *Class and Personality in Society.* New York: Atherton, 1969.

Grosser, Charles F. "Community Development Programs Serving the Urban Poor," *Social Work*, 10 (July, 1965), pp. 15–21.

————. "Local Residents as Mediators Between Middle-class Professional Workers and Lower-class Clients," *Social Service Review*, 40, 1 (March, 1966), pp. 56–63.

Guest, Robert H. "Categories of Events in Field Observation," in Richard N. Adams and J. J. Preiss (eds.), *Human Organization Research.* Homewood, Illinois: Dorsey Press, 1960, pp. 225–239.

Gullahorn, John, and George Strauss. "The Field Worker in Union Research," in Richard N. Adams and J. J. Preiss (eds.), *Human Organization Research.* Homewood, Illinois: Dorsey Press, 1960, pp. 28–32.

Gurin, Arnold, and Joan Levin Ecklein. "Community Organization for What? Political Power or Service Delivery?" Waltham, Massachusetts: Brandeis University, 1966, mimeograph.

Gusfield, Joseph R. "Field Work Reciprocities in Studying a Social Movement," *Human Organization*, 14, 3 (1955), pp. 29–33.

Haggstrom, W. C. "The Power of the Poor," in Frank Riessman, Jerome Cohen, and Arthur Pearl (eds.), *Mental Health of the Poor*, New York: Free Press, 1964, pp. 205–223.

Harrington, Michael. *The Other America: Poverty in the United States.* New York: MacMillan, 1963.

Harvey, O. J. (ed.). *Motivation and Social Interaction.* New York: Ronald Press, 1963.

Heidt, Sarajane, and Amitai Etzioni (eds.), *Social Guidance.* New York: Crowell, 1969.

Henderson, Norman B. "Cross-Cultural Action Research: Some Limitations, Advantages, and Problems," *Journal of Social Psychology*, 73 (October, 1967), pp. 61–70.

Herbert, Eléonore L., and E. L. Trist. "The Institution of an Absent Leader by a Students' Discussion Group," *Human Relations*, 6, 3 (August, 1953), pp. 215–248.

Herzog, E. "Some Assumptions About the Poor," *Social Service Review*, 37, 4 (December, 1963), pp. 391–402.

Holland, John B., Kenneth E. Tiedke, and Paul A. Miller. "A Theoretical Model for Health Action," *Rural Sociology*, 22 (June, 1957), pp. 149–155.

Hunter, Floyd, Ruth C. Schaffer and Cecil G. Sheps. *Community Organization: Action and Inaction*. Chapel Hill: University of North Carolina Press, 1956.

Hyman, Herbert, Charles Wright, and T. K. Hopkins. *Applications of Methods of Evaluation: Four Studies of the Encampment for Citizenship*. Berkeley: University of California Press, 1962.

Irelan, Lola M., and Arthur Besner. "Low-Income Outlook on Life," *Welfare in Review*, 3 (September, 1965), pp. 13–19.

Junker, Buford H. *Field Work: An Introduction to the Social Sciences*. Chicago: University of Chicago Press, 1960.

Kahl, Joseph A. "Some Measurements of Achievement Motivation," *American Journal of Sociology*, 70, 6 (May, 1965), pp. 669–681.

Kahn, Robert L., Donald M. Wolfe, Robert P. Quinn, J. Diedrick Snoek, and Robert A. Rosenthal. *Organizational Stress: Studies in Role Conflict and Ambiguity*. New York: Wylie, 1964.

Kaplan, Berton H. (ed.). "Poverty Dynamics and Interventions," *Journal of Social Issues* (entire issue), 21 (January, 1965), pp. 1–153.

———. "Social Issues and Poverty Research: A Commentary," *ibid.*, pp. 1–10.

———. "The Structure of Adaptive Sentiments in a Lower Class Religious Group in Appalachia," *ibid.*, pp. 126–141.

Kaplan, Howard B. "Implementation of Program Change in Community Agencies," *Milbank Memorial Fund Quarterly*, 45 (July, 1967), pp. 321–332.

Keller, Suzanne. "The Social Role of the Urban Slum Child: Some Early Findings," *American Journal of Orthopsychiatry*, 33, 5 (1963), pp. 823–831.

Key, William H. "Controlled Intervention—The Helping Professions and Directed Social Change," *American Journal of Orthopsychiatry*, 36, 3 (April, 1966), pp. 400–409.

———. "An Urban Renewal Relocation Program," in Milton F. Shore and Fortune B. Mannino (eds.), *Community Mental Health: Problems, Programs, and Strategies*. New York: Behavioral Publications, 1969, pp. 22–37.

Kirschner Associates. "A Description and Evaluation of Neighborhood Centers." Albuquerque, New Mexico: December, 1966, mimeograph.

Klein, Woody. "People vs. Politicians: Defeat in Harlem," *The Nation*, July 27, 1964, pp. 27–29.

Knoll, Erwin, and Jules Whitcover. "Fighting Poverty—and City Hall," *The Reporter*, 32 (June 3, 1965), pp. 19–22.

———. "Policies and the Poor: Shriver's Second Thoughts," *ibid.*, 33 (December 30, 1965), pp. 23–25.

Kramer, Ralph M. "Ideology, Status and Power in Board-Executive Relationships," *Social Work*, 10, 4 (October, 1965), pp. 107–114.

———. *Participation of the Poor*. Englewood Cliffs, New Jersey: Prentice-Hall, 1969.

Kramer, Ralph M., and Clare Denton. "Organization of a Community Action Program: A Comparative Case Study," *Social Work*, 12, 4 (October, 1967), pp. 68–80.

Krause, Elliott A. "Functions of a Bureaucratic Ideology: 'Citizen Participation,'" *Social Problems*, 16 (Fall, 1968), pp. 129–143.

Kuenstler, Peter. "Urban Community Center Work in Underdeveloped Countries," *Community Development*, 1 (1958), pp. 27–31.

Lance, Squire. Speech to the Catholic Interfaith Council, Catholic Chancellory, Kansas City, Missouri, March 23, 1966.

Lane, Ralph, Jr. "Sociological Aspects of Mental Well Being," in R. Brockbank and D. Westby-Gibson (eds.), *Mental Health in a Changing Community*. New York: Grune and Stratton, 1966, pp. 43–45.

LaPiere, Richard T. *Social Change*. New York: McGraw-Hill, 1965.

Leighton, Alexander H. "Poverty and Social Change," *Scientific American*, 212 (1965), pp. 21–27.

Leon, Robert L. "Maladaptive Interaction Between Bureau of Indian Affairs Staff and Indian Clients," *American Journal of Orthopsychiatry*, 35, 4 (July, 1965), pp. 723–728.

LeShan, L. "Time Orientation and Social Class," *Journal of Abnormal and Social Psychology*, 47, 3 (July, 1952), pp. 589–592.

Levine, J., and J. Butler, "Lecture vs. Group Discussion in Changing Behavior," *Journal of Applied Psychology*, 36, 1 (February, 1952), pp. 29–33.

Levinson, Perry, and Jeffry Schiller. "Role Analysis of the Indigenous Nonprofessional," *Social Work*, 11 (July, 1966), pp. 95–101.

Levitan, Sar A. "The Design of Antipoverty Strategy," in Ben B. Seligman, *Aspects of Poverty*. New York: Crowell, 1968, pp. 238–287.

Lewin, Kurt. *Field Theory in Social Science*. New York: Harper, 1951.

———. "Group Decision and Social Change," in T. H. Newcomb and E. L. Hartley (eds.), *Readings in Social Psychology*. New York: Holt, 1947, pp. 330–344.

———. "Problems of Group Dynamics and the Integration of the Social Sciences: I, Social Equilibria," *Journal of Human Relations*, 1, 1 (1947), pp. 5–41.

Lewis, Hylan. "Child Rearing Among Low Income Families," in Louis A. Ferman, Joyce L. Kornbluh, and Alan Haber (eds.), *Poverty in America*. Ann Arbor: University of Michigan, 1965, pp. 342–353.

Lewis, Oscar. *The Children of Sanchez*. New York: Random House, 1961.

———. *La Vida*. New York: Random House, 1966.

Liebow, Elliot. *Tally's Corner*. Boston: Little, Brown, 1967.

Lippitt, Ronald. *Observation and Interview Methods of the Leadership Training Study*. New York: Boy Scouts of America, 1943, mimeograph.

Lippitt, Ronald, Jeanne Watson, and Bruce Westley. *The Dynamics of Planned Change*. New York: Harcourt, Brace, and World, 1958.

Litterer, Joseph A. *Organizations: Structure and Behavior*. New York: Wylie, 1963.

Loomis, Charles P., and J. Allan Beegle, *Rural Social Systems*. Englewood Cliffs, New Jersey: Prentice-Hall, 1950.

Maier, N. R. F. "'The Quality of Group Decisions as Inflenced by the Discussion Leader," *Human Relations*, 3, 2 (June, 1950), pp. 155–174.

Mann, J. "Group Therapy with Adults," *American Journal of Orthopsychiatry*, 23, 2 (April, 1953), pp. 332–337.

Marris, Peter, and Martin Rein. *Dilemmas of Social Reform: Poverty and Community Action in the United States*. New York: Atherton, 1967.

Martin, E. A., and W. F. Hill. "Toward a Theory of Group Development: Six Phases of Therapy Group Development," *International Journal of Group Psychotherapy*, 7, 1 (January, 1957), pp. 20–30.

McCall, George J., and J. L. Simmons. *Issues in Participant Observation*. Reading, Massachusetts: Addison-Wesley, 1969.

McClosky, H., and J. Schaar. "Psychological Dimensions of Anomie," *American Sociological Review*, 30, 1 (February, 1965), pp. 14–40.

Maccoby, Eleanor, Joseph Johnson, and Russell Church. "Community Integration and the Social Control of Juvenile Delinquency," *Journal of Social Issues*, 14, 3 (1958), pp. 38–51.

McCord, William, John Howard, Bernard Friedberg, and Edwin Harwood. *Life Styles in the Black Ghetto*. New York: Norton, 1969.

McDonald, Dwight. "Our Invisible Poor," in Louis A. Ferman, Joyce L. Kornbluh, and Alan Haber (eds.), *Poverty in America*. Ann Arbor: University of Michigan, 1965, pp. 6–24.

MacGregor, H. "Task Force on Indian Affairs," *Human Organization*, 21, 2 (1962), pp. 125–137.

Marsh, C. Paul, and Minnie M. Brown. "Facilitative and Inhibitive Factors in Training Program Recruitment Among Rural Negroes," *Journal of Social Issues*, 21 (January, 1965), pp. 110–125.

Meadow, Arnold, and David Stoker. "A Comparison of Symptomatic Behavior of Mexican-American and Anglo-American Hospitalized Patients," *Archives of General Psychiatry*, 12, 3 (1965), pp. 267–277.

Meissner, Hanna H. (ed.), *Poverty in the Affluent Society*. New York: Harper and Row, 1966.

Merton, Robert K. "The Role-Set," *British Journal of Sociology*, 8 (June, 1957), pp. 106–120.

Messinger, Sheldon L. "Organization Transformation," *American Sociological Review*, 22 (February, 1965), pp. 3–10.

Miller, Paul A. *Community Health Action*. East Lansing: Michigan State College Press, 1953.

Miller, S. M. "The American Lower Class: A Typological Approach," in Arthur B. Shostak and William Gomberg (eds.), *New Perspectives on Poverty*. Englewood Cliffs, New Jersey: Prentice-Hall, 1966, pp. 22–40.

Miller, S. M., Frank Riessman, and Arthur Seagull. "Poverty and Self-Indulgence: A Critique of the Non-Deferred Gratification Pattern," in Louis A. Ferman, Joyce L. Kornbluh, and Alan Haber (eds.), *Poverty in America*. Ann Arbor: University of Michigan, 1965, pp. 285–302.

Miller, S. M., and Martin Rein. "The War on Poverty: Perspectives and Prospects," in Ben B. Seligman, *Poverty as a Public Issue*. New York: Free Press, 1965.

Miller, W. B. "Focal Concerns of Lower Class Culture," in Louis A. Ferman, Joyce L. Kornbluh, and Alan Haber (eds.), *Poverty in America*. Ann Arbor: University of Michigan, 1965, pp. 261–270.

Minuchin, Salvador, Braulio Mantalvo, Bernard Guerney, Bernice Rosman, and Florence Schumer. *Families of the Slums*. New York: Basic Books, 1967.

Mischel, Walter. "Preference for Delayed Reinforcement and Social Responsibility," *Journal of Abnormal and Social Psychology*, 62, 1 (January, 1961), pp. 1–7.

Modlin, H. C., and Mildred Faris. "Group Adaptation and Integration in Psychiatric Team Practice," *Psychiatry*, 19, 1 (February, 1956), pp. 97–103.

Mogulof, Melvin B. "A Developmental Approach to the Community Action Program Idea," *Social Work*, 12, 2 (April, 1967), pp. 12–20.

Moynihan, Daniel Patrick. *Maximum Feasible Misunderstanding: Community Action in the War on Poverty*. New York: Free Press, 1968.

Muller, Theresa (ed.). *Mental Health in Nursing*. Washington, D.C.: Catholic University Press, 1949.

Newcomb, T. H., and E. L. Hartley (eds.). *Readings in Social Psychology*. New York: Holt, 1947.

Office of Economic Opportunity. "Community Action Program Fact Sheet." Washington, D.C.: 1965, mimeograph.

Parker, S. "Leadership Patterns in a Psychiatric Ward," *Human Relations,* 11, 4 (November, 1958), pp. 287–301.

Parsons, Talcott, R. F. Bales, and E. S. Shils. *Working Papers in the Theory of Action.* New York: Free Press, 1953.

Parsons, Talcott, and Edward A. Shils (eds.). *Toward a General Theory of Action.* Cambridge: Harvard University Press, 1959.

Passow, A. H. (ed.). *Education in Depressed Areas.* New York: Columbia University Press, 1963.

Pearl, Arthur, and Frank Riessman. *New Careers for the Poor.* New York: Free Press, 1965.

Pearlman, Helen. "Self-Determination: Reality or Illusion?" *Social Service Review,* 39, 4 (1965), pp. 410–422.

Perlman, Robert, and David Jones. *Neighborhood Service Centers.* Washington, D.C.: U.S. Department of Health, Education, and Welfare, 1967.

Pettigrew, Thomas F. *A Profile of the Negro-American.* Princeton, New Jersey: Van Nostrand, 1964.

Pinkney, Alphonso. *Black Americans.* Englewood Cliffs, New Jersey: Prentice-Hall, 1969.

Piven, Frances. "Participation of Residents in Neighborhood Community Action Programs," *Social Work,* 11, 1 (January, 1966), pp. 73–80.

Polsky, Ned. *Hustlers, Beats, and Others.* Chicago: Aldine Publishing Company, 1967.

Preston, M. G., and R. K. Heintz. "Effects of Participatory vs. Supervisory Leadership on Group Judgment," *Journal of Abnormal and Social Psychology,* 44, 3 (July, 1949), pp. 345–355.

Rainwater, Lee. "Neutralizing the Disinherited: Some Psychological Aspects of Understanding the Poor." St. Louis, Missouri: Washington University, 1967, mimeograph.

Redfield, Robert. "The Folk Society," *American Journal of Sociology,* 52 (January, 1947), pp. 301–315.

Reiff, Robert, and Frank Riessman. "The Indigenous Non-Professional: A Strategy of Change in Community Action and Community Mental Health Programs," *Community Mental Health Journal,* Monograph No. 1, 1965.

Rein, Martin. "Community Action Programs: A Critical Reassessment," *Poverty and Human Resources Abstracts: Trend,* 3 (May–June, 1968), pp. 6–7.

Rein, Martin, and Frank Riessman. "A Strategy for Anti-Poverty Community Action Programs," *Social Work,* 11 (April, 1966), pp. 3–12.

Richardson, Steven A. "A Framework for Reporting Field-Relations Experiences," pp. 124–139, in Richard N. Adams and J. J. Preiss (eds.), *Human Organization Research*. Homewood, Illinois: Dorsey Press, 1960, pp. 124–139.

Ridgeway, James. "Saul Alinsky in Smugtown," *The New Republic*, 152 (June 26, 1965), pp. 15–17.

Riessman, Frank. "A Comparison of Two Social Action Approaches: Saul Alinsky and The New Student Left." New York: Albert Einstein College of Medicine, Department of Psychiatry, September, 1965, mimeograph, p. 9.

———. "The 'Helper' Therapy Principle," *Social Work*, 10 (April, 1965), pp. 27–32.

———. "New Approaches to Mental Health Treatment of Low-Income People," in *Social Work Practice*. New York: Columbia University Press, 1965, pp. 174–187.

———. "New Possibilities: Services, Representation in Careers," presentation to Planning Session for the White House Conference "To Fulfill these Rights," November, 1965, mimeograph.

———. "Strategies and Suggestions for Training Non-Professionals." New York: Albert Einstein College of Medicine, Department of Psychiatry, 1968, mimeograph.

———. *Strategies Against Poverty*. New York: Random House, 1969.

———. "The Strengths of the Poor," in Arthur Shostak and William Gomberg (eds.), *New Perspectives on Poverty*. Englewood Cliffs, New Jersey: Prentice-Hall, 1966, pp. 40–47.

Riessman, Frank, Jerome Cohen, and Arthur Pearl. *Mental Health of the Poor*. New York: Free Press, 1964.

Riessman, Frank, and Emanuel Hollowitz. "The Neighborhood Service Center: An Innovation in Preventive Psychiatry," *American Journal of Psychiatry*, 123, 11 (May, 1967), pp. 1408–1413.

Rodman, Hyman. "The Lower Class Value Stretch," in Louis A. Ferman, Joyce Kornbluh, and Alan Haber (eds.), *Poverty in America*. Ann Arbor: University of Michigan, 1965, pp. 270–284.

Roethlisberger, Fritz J. "The Foreman: Master and Victim of Double Talk," *Harvard Business Review*, 23, 3 (Spring, 1945), pp. 285–294.

Rosen, Bernard C. "The Achievement Syndrome: A Psychocultural Dimension of Social Stratification," *American Sociological Review*, 21 (April, 1956), pp. 203–211.

Rosen, B., and A. D'Andrade. "Psycho-social Origins of Achievement Motivation," *Sociometry*, 22 (September, 1959), pp. 185–218.

Ross, Murray G. *Case Histories in Community Organization*. New York: Harper and Brother, 1958.

Rossi, Peter, and Robert A. Dentler. *The Politics of Urban Renewal: The Chicago Findings.* New York: Free Press of Glencoe, 1961.

Rotter, J. B. "Generalized Expectancies of Internal vs. External Control of Reinforcement," *Psychological Monographs,* 80 (1966), No. 609.

Rubin, Lillian. "Maximum Feasible Participation: The Origins, Implications and Present Status," *Poverty and Human Resources Abstracts,* 2 (November–December, 1967), pp. 5–18.

Rutledge, Aaron L., and Gertrude Zemon Gass. *Nineteen Negro Men.* San Francisco: Jossey-Bass, 1967.

Sanford, David. "The Poor in Their Place," *The New Republic,* 153 (November 20, 1965), pp. 5–6.

Sauer, Christopher, John Holland, Kenneth Tiedke, and Walter Freeman. *Community Involvement.* Glencoe, Illinois: Free Press, 1957.

Schneider, Louis, and S. Lysgaard. "The Deferred Gratification Pattern: A Preliminary Study," *American Sociological Review,* 18, 2 (April, 1953), pp. 142–149.

Schroder, H. M., and O. J. Harvey. "Conceptual Organization and Group Structure," in O. J. Harvey (ed.), *Motivation and Social Interaction.* New York: Ronald Press, 1963, pp. 134–166.

Schultz, W. C. *FIRO: A Three Dimensional Theory of Interpersonal Behavior.* New York: Rinehart, 1958.

Searcy, Ann. "Contemporary and Traditional Prairie Potawatomi Child Life," *K. U. Potawatomi Study Research Report Number Seven.* Lawrence, Kansas: University of Kansas, Department of Anthropology, September, 1965, mimeograph.

———. "The Value of Ethnohistorical Reconstructions of American Indian Typical Personality: The Case of the Potawatomi," *Transactions of the Kansas Academy of Science,* 68, 2 (1965), pp. 274–282.

Segalman, Ralph. "Dramatis Personae of the Community Action Program: A 'Built-In' Conflict Situation," *Rocky Mountain Social Science Journal,* 4 (October, 1967), pp. 140–150.

Seigel, Sidney. *Non-Parametric Statistics for the Behavioral Sciences.* New York: McGraw-Hill, 1956, pp. 184–194.

Seligman, Ben B. *Aspects of Poverty.* New York: Crowell, 1968.

———. *Poverty as a Public Issue.* New York: Free Press, 1965.

Selover, William C. "Federal Pressure Felt: U.S. Poor Gain Foothold in Local Programs," *Christian Science Monitor,* August 2, 1966, p. 10.

———. "Old Ways Bind Poverty Drive," *Christian Science Monitor,* August 3, 1966, p. 1.

Selznick, Philip. *TVA and the Grass Roots.* Berkeley: University of California Press, 1949.

Shamin, Ibrahim. "The Role of Lay Leaders," *Community Development,* 3 (1959), pp. 81–87.

Shore, Milton F., and Fortune B. Mannino (eds.). *Community Mental Health: Problems, Programs and Strategies.* New York: Behavioral Publications, 1969.

Shostak, Arthur B. "Promoting Participation of the Poor: Philadelphia's Anti-Poverty Program," *Social Work,* 11 (January, 1966), pp. 65–72.

————. "Containment, Co-Optation, or Co-Determination?" *American Child,* November, 1965, pp. 1–5.

Shostak, Arthur B., and William Gomberg (eds.). *New Perspectives on Poverty.* Englewood Cliffs, New Jersey: Prentice-Hall, 1966.

Sigel, Roberta. "Citizen Committees—Advice vs. Consent," *Trans-Action,* 4 (May, 1967), pp. 47–52.

Silberman, Charles E. *Crisis in Black and White.* New York: Vintage Books, 1964.

Simpson, R. L., and M. Miller. "Social Status and Anomia," *Social Problems,* 10, 3 (Winter, 1963), pp. 256–264.

Sjoberg, Gideon, R. Brymer, and B. Farris. "Bureaucracy and the Lower Class," *Sociology and Social Research,* 50, 3 (April, 1966), pp. 325–337.

Spiegel, Hans B. C. *Citizen Participation in Urban Development, Vol. 1, Concepts and Issues,* Washington, D.C.: NTL Institute for Applied Behavioral Science, 1968.

————. *Neighborhood Power and Control: Implications for Urban Planning,* Document No. PB 183176. Springfield, Virginia: U.S. Department of Commerce, 1967.

Spindler, George, and Louise Spindler. "American Indian Personality Types and Their Sociocultural Roots," *Annals* of the American Academy of Political and Social Science, 311 (1957), pp. 147–157.

Spinley, E. M. *The Deprived and the Privileged.* London: Routledge and Kegan Paul, 1953.

Srole, Leo. "Social Integration and Certain Corollaries: An Exploratory Study," *American Sociological Review,* 21 (December, 1956), pp. 709–717.

Stirrings in the Big Cities: The Great Cities Projects. New York: Ford Foundation, Office of Reports, 1964.

Stone, I., D. Leighton, and A. H. Leighton. "Poverty and the Individual," in Leo Fishman (ed.), *Poverty Amid Affluence.* New Haven, Connecticut: Yale University Press, 1966, pp. 72–97.

Stouffer, Samuel A., and Jackson Toby. "Role Conflict and Personality," *American Journal of Sociology,* 56 (March, 1951), pp. 395–406.

Stoute, A. "Implementation of Group Interpersonal Relationships Through Psychotherapy," *Journal of Psychology*, 30 (July, 1950), pp. 145–156.

Strauss, M. "Deferred Gratification, Social Class, and the Achievement Syndrome," *American Sociological Review*, 27 (June, 1962), pp. 326–335.

Suchman, Edward A. "Intervention and the 'Intervening' Variable: A Conceptual and Methodological Model for Evaluative Research," paper presented before the American Sociological Association, Miami Beach, Florida, September, 1966.

Sullivan, Mortimer, Stuart Queen, and Ralph Patrick. "Participant Observation as Employed in the Study of a Military Training Program," *American Sociological Review*, 23 (December, 1958), pp. 660–670.

Topeka Daily Capital, Monday, January 31, 1966, p. 24.

Topeka Office of Economic Opportunity. *Annual Report for 1965–1966*. Topeka, Kansas: Topeka Office of Economic Opportunity, 1966.

Topeka-Shawnee Regional Planning Commission. "Neighborhood Analysis for the Topeka-Shawnee County Regional Planning Area," Master Plan Report No. 5. Topeka, Kansas: September, 1965.

Tuckman, Bruce W. "Developmental Sequence in Small Groups," *Psychological Bulletin*, 63, 6 (1965), pp. 384–399.

Turner, John B., and Arthur Blum. "Action and Knowledge Gaps in Neighborhood Organization," paper presented before the National Association of Social Workers' Council on Community Planning and Development, Cleveland, Ohio, December, 1968.

Vadich, A. J., J. Bensman, and M. R. Stein (eds.). *Reflections on Community Studies*. New York: Wylie, 1964.

Valentine, Charles A. *Culture and Poverty*. Chicago: University of Chicago Press, 1969.

Vogt, E. Z. "The Acculturation of American Indians," *Annals* of the American Academy of Political and Social Science, 311 (1957), pp. 137–146.

Warren, Roland L. *The Community in America*. Chicago: Rand McNally Company, 1963.

———. "Types of Purposive Social Action at the Community Level," No. 11, *Papers in Social Welfare*. Waltham, Massachusetts: Brandeis University, 1965, pp. 17–30.

———. *Perspectives on the American Community*. Chicago: Rand McNally, 1966.

Wax, Rosalie H. "Reciprocity as a Field Technique," *Human Organization*, 11, 3 (1952), pp. 31–34.

———. "Twelve Years Later: An Analysis of a Field Experience," in

Richard N. Adams and J. J. Preiss (eds.), *Human Organization Research*. Homewood, Illinois: Dorsey Press, 1960, pp. 166–178.

Webb, Eugene J., Donald T. Campbell, Richard D. Schwartz, and Lee Sechrest. *Unobtrusive Measures: Non-Reactive Research in the Social Sciences*. Chicago: Rand McNally, 1966.

Weiss, Carol H. "Utilization of Evaluation: Toward Comparative Study," paper presented before the American Sociological Association, Miami Beach, September, 1966.

Wellman, David. "The Wrong Way to Get Jobs for Negroes," *Trans-Action*, 5, 5 (May, 1968), pp. 9–18.

Wheeler, John H. "Civil Rights Groups—Their Impact Upon the War on Poverty," *Law and Contemporary Problems*, 31 (Winter, 1966), pp. 152–158.

Whitman, R. M. "Psychodynamic Principles Underlying T-group Processes," in L. P. Bradford, J. R. Gibb, and K. D. Benne (eds.). *T-group Theory and Laboratory Method*. New York: Wylie, 1964, pp. 310–335.

Whyte, Donald R. "Sociological Aspects of Poverty: A Conceptual Analysis," *Canadian Review of Sociology and Anthropology*, 2, 4 (November, 1966), pp. 175–189.

Whyte, William Foote. "The Slum: On the Evolution of Street Corner Society," in A. J. Vadich, J. Bensman, and M. R. Stein (eds.), *Reflections on Community Studies*. New York: Wylie, 1964, pp. 3–69.

———. *Street Corner Society*. Chicago: University of Chicago Press, 1943.

Wilcoxon, Frank, S. K. Katti, and Roberta A. Wilcox. *Critical Values and Probability Levels for the Wilcoxon Rank Sum Test and the Wilcoxon Signed Rank Test*. American Cyanamid Company and Florida State University, August, 1963.

Wilson, Charles E., and Adrienne S. Bennett. "Participation in Community Action Organizations: Some Theoretical Insights," *Sociological Inquiry*, 37, 2 (Spring, 1968), pp. 191–203.

Wilson, James Q. "Planning and Politics: Citizen Participation in Urban Renewal," *Journal of the American Institute of Planners*, 29 (November, 1963), pp. 47–52.

Witmer, Lawrence, and Gibson Winter. "Strategies of Power in Community Organizations." Chicago: University of Chicago, 1968, mimeograph.

Wittenberg, Rudolph M. "Personality Adjustment Through Social Action," *American Journal of Orthopsychiatry*, 18, 2 (April, 1948), pp. 207–221.

Wolf, A. "The Psychoanalysis of Groups," *American Journal of Psychotherapy*, 3, 4 (October, 1949), pp. 525–528.

Wolff, Kurt H. "The Collection and Organization of Field Materials: A Research Report," *Ohio Journal of Science*, 52, 2 (March, 1952), pp. 49–61.

Wray, Donald E. "Marginal Man of Industry: The Foreman," *American Journal of Sociology*, 54 (January, 1948), pp. 298–301.

Wright, C., and H. Hyman. "Voluntary Association Memberships of American Adults," *American Sociological Review*, 23, 3 (June, 1958), pp. 284–294.

Yankelovich, Daniel. "CAP Programs and Their Evaluation: A Management Report," prepared for the Office of Economic Opportunity, September, 1967, lithograph.

Zald, Mayer N. *Organizing for Community Welfare*. Chicago: Quadrangle Books, 1967.

Zurcher, Louis A., Jr. "The Sailor Aboard Ship: A Study of Role Behavior in a Total Institution," *Social Forces*, 43 (March, 1965), pp. 389–400.

————. "Functional Marginality: Dynamics of a Poverty Intervention Organization," *(Southwestern) Social Science Quarterly*, 48 (December, 1967), pp. 411–421.

————. "The Leader and the Lost: A Case Study of Indigenous Leadership in a Poverty Program Community Action Committee," *Genetic Psychology Monographs*, 76 (August, 1967), pp. 23–93.

————. "The Naval Recruit Training Center: A Study of Role Assimilation in a Total Institution," *Sociological Inquiry*, 31, 1 (Winter, 1967), pp. 85–98.

————. "The Social Psychology of Ephemeral Roles: A Disaster Work Crew," *Human Organization*, 27, 4 (Winter, 1968), pp. 281–297.

————. "Poverty Program Indigenous Leaders: A Study of Marginality," *Sociology and Social Research*, 53, 2 (January, 1969), pp. 147–162.

————. "Stages of Development in Poverty Program Neighborhood Action Committees," *Journal of Applied Behavioral Science*, 5, 2 (April, 1969), pp. 222–258.

————. "The Poverty Board: Some Consequences of 'Maximum Feasible Participation,'" in press, *Journal of Social Issues*.

Zurcher, Louis A., Jr., and Alvin E. Green, with Edward Johnson and Samuel Patton. *From Dependency to Dignity: Individual and Social Consequences of a Neighborhood House*. New York: Behavioral Publications, 1969.

Zurcher, Louis A., Jr., and William H. Key. "The Overlap Model: A Comparison of Strategies for Social Change," *Sociological Quarterly*, 8, 4 (Winter, 1967), pp. 85–97.

Zurcher, Louis A., Jr., and Arnold Meadow. "On Bullfights and Baseball:

An Example of the Interaction of Social Institutions," *International Journal of Comparative Sociology*, 8 (March, 1967), pp. 99–117.

Zurcher, Louis A., Jr., Arnold Meadow, and Susan Zurcher. "Value Orientation, Role Conflict, and Alienation from Work," *American Sociological Review*, 30, 4 (1965), pp. 539–548.

Zurcher, Louis A., Jr., David Sonenschein, and Eric Metzner. "The Hasher: A Study of Role Conflict," *Social Forces*, 44 (June, 1968), pp. 505–514.

INDEX

Acting Director (TOEO): responsibilities and problems of, 49–50
Adult Basic Education Program: achievements of, 55; considerations of Board in processing proposal for, 78–79; TNOs on, 196; classes of; held in Neighborhood House, 363
Advisory Council: as immediate supervisor of Neighborhood House, 338; meets with Neighborhood House staff and HPP Committee, 342; directs Neighborhood House to send letter of protest to Board of City Commissioners, 358; mentioned, 340
aged: Indian respect for, 305; Indian interest in home for, 305–306. SEE ALSO Medicare Alert
agencies: contributing to local share of OEO funding, 56–57. SEE ALSO delegate agencies; specific agencies
agency representatives. SEE non-Target Neighborhood Officers
Alinsky, Saul, Model: and power for poor, 13, 16; social-action tactics of, 13; and nonviolent conflict, 14–15; organizational structure of, 15; and attitudes toward community, 15–16; involvement of poor in, 16; TOEO Director and Assistant Director on, 39; mentioned, 12, 17, 379, 380
Assistant Director (TOEO): previous experience of, 20–21, 29–30; in TOEO recruitment, 29–30, 36; criticism of,

because of conflicting expectations, 36–37; role of, 38; on relations with TNOs, 38; on relations with Director, 38–39; on Alinsky approach, 39; disagreements of, with Director, 39; demands upon time of, 46; on stress of job, 49; as Acting Director, 49–50; resignation of first, 50; role of, in Board meetings, 84, 99–100, 105; on ideal TNO role, 230; in organizing TNC's, 237, 240–241, 243–244, 245, 248, 249, 251, 253–254, 256, 257; in organizing Indian Committee, 271, 272, 273–274, 275–276, 280–282, 283–287 passim, 295, 299, 303, 305, 311–312, 313; Indian opinion of, 276, 277, 300; statements of, on organizing Indian Committee, 281, 283; as influenced by Mexican-American value orientation, 282; on Indian Committee and chairman, 323; attempts to reactivate Indian Committee, 330; in organizing Highland Park–Pierce Neighborhood Committee, 333. SEE ALSO Topeka Office of Economic Opportunity, staff of

Becker, Howard S.: on need for flexibility in research, 388, 389
beneficiaries: of formal organizations, 33; of TOEO, 33–34
Bennett, Adrienne S., on poverty-intervention organizations: organizational characteristics of, 27; goals of, 34

434   *Index*

gram, 226–227; problems of, 227.
SEE ALSO Target Neighborhood Officers
In-School Neighborhood Youth Corps
Program: compared with Out-of-School Program, 103. SEE ALSO
Neighborhood Youth Corps Program
interviews, with Board members: non-TNO results, 118–144; TNO results, presented and contrasted with
non-TNO, 146–176

Job Corps Center: TNO on, 195
jobs: TNOs on, 208–212, 215–216;
TOEO programs relevant to, 215;
non-TNOs on, 216–217; Neighborhood House director on, 348; role
of Neighborhood House staff in securing, 348–350; Negro problems
with discrimination in, and Neighborhood House director, 364
Juvenile and Probate Courts: work
with Neighborhood House, 345
juvenile delinquency: TNOs on, 198–199

Kahl Activism Scale: and Integration
with Relatives Scale: use of, in
social-psychological study, 66, 67
Kansas Neurological Institute: works
with Neighborhood House, 345
Kansas State Cooperative Extension
Service: contributes to local share
of OEO funding, 56
Kansas State Legislature: influence
of, on background experience of
Director, 26; approached by Neighborhood House committee, on cosmotology training program, 361
Kansas State Technical Assistance
Office: works with Neighborhood
House, 345
Kansas Teachers Association: works
with Neighborhood House, 345
Kansas Welfare Department (State):
director of, speaks at Indian Mission, 308–309

Labor Department: works with Neighborhood House, 345
Lance, Squire: on Alinsky Model social-action program, 13

Leadership Training Sessions: inaugurated by TOEO, 247, 307; Indian
Committee chairman at, 308; mentioned, 322
Legal Aid Society: contributes to local
share of OEO funding, 57; representative of, speaks to Board meeting, 89–90
Leon, Robert L.: on Indian interaction with Bureau of Indian Affairs, 277, 278
"Let's Talk": first meeting of, 363
Levinson, Perry: study of, on indigenous nonprofessionals, 227

Manpower Training: importance of
success of, 379
"maximum feasible participation"
mandate: TOEO goals for implementing, 33; determining limits of,
42–43; Economic Opportunity Act
insists upon, 63; opinions of non-TNOs on, 121–124, 142; opinions of
TNOs on, 150–152, 174–175; dilemma of amount of participation
and possible dangers of, 151; opinions of TNOs and non-TNOs on,
evaluated and compared, 151–152;
stressed, in organizing TNCs, 240;
conflicting interpretation of, 336;
determination of Highland Park–Pierce Committee to retain, 365;
Overlap Model in implementing,
375; TOEO achievements as support
for, 378; and Research Committee
participation by TNOs, 391. SEE
ALSO Overlap Model; Topeka Office of Economic Opportunity,
Functional Marginality position of,
Overlap Model adopted by
Mayetta, Kansas: location of Prairie
Potawatomi Reservation, 270
Medicare: Indian questions about,
306, 309
Medicare Alert Program: achievements of, 55; Board considerations
in processing proposal for, 78–79
Menninger Foundation: influence of,
on social-science orienttaion of TOEO,
11; contributes to local share of
OEO funding, 57; provides most of
local share of Neighborhood House

funding, 338; works with Neighborhood House, 345; mentioned, 7
mental-health programs: TNOs on, 223–224
mental illness: TNOs on, 221–224
Merton, Robert K.: on role relations and expectations, 36
Methodist Indian Mission: minister of, and TOEO, 271, 275; building of, described, 284
Mexican-Americans: value orientation of, 282; speech on organization of, made to Indian Committee, 296–297
Miller, Paul A.: on prerequisites for action, 32–33
Minimum Housing Code: supported by HPP residents, 361, 363
ministers: as representatives of poor, 220, 221
modal group dynamics. SEE Target Neighborhood Committees, stages of development of
Model City Project: supported by HPP residents, 361, 363
Model Police Force Program: HPP residents object to, 361; mentioned, 356
Mogulof, Melvin B.: on disparity between goals of Economic Opportunity Act and realistic expectations, 35

National Association for the Advancement of Colored People (NAACP): role of, in Topeka, 8
Neighborhood Aide Program: achievements of, 55; problems created by Indian aide selected for, 323–324
Neighborhood Extension Worker Program. SEE Extension Worker Program
Neighborhood House: achievements of, 56, 365; Board considerations in processing proposal for, 78–79; Board ratifies selection of personnel for, 92; seen as accomplishment of TOEO, by TNOs, 155, 164, 165; evolution of, 260; formal goals for, 337; unwritten purpose of, 338; local funding for, 338; organizational structure of administration of,

338; Advisory Council for, 338; approval of proposal for, 339; qualifications of Neighborhood aide for, 340; selection of staff members for, 341; "Open House" of, 344; problems confronted and solved by, 345; community agencies and service organizations working with, 345; content-orientation of staff of, 345; staff of, assists Neighborhood residents in dealing with agencies, 346; aide of, and cooking class, 347–348; staff of finds employment for Neighborhood residents, 348–350; success of, described, 350; open hours of, 350–351; meetings held at, 351; social-action group evolves from, 354; as focus for Neighborhood integration, 355; "Newsletter" of, 356; Neighborhood rehabilitation campaign of, 357; letter on rezoning sent by, for HPP residents, 358; staff of, registers disillusionment with Model Police Force Program, 361; supports Minimum Housing Code, 361; committee from, approaches Kansas Legislature on cosmotology training program, 361; new goals for, 361–362; role of, in city of Topeka, 362; day-care center of, 363; adult education class of, includes non-Neighborhood students, 363; plans for first anniversary party of, 363; "Let's Talk" program of, 363; importance of success of, 379. SEE ALSO Highland Park-Pierce Neighborhood Committee
—building for: Board approves lease of, 91, 93; location and acquisition of, 339–340; furnishing and stocking of, 342; described, 343
—director of: qualifications of, 340; experience of, described, 341; on Extension Worker Program, 341–342; assists resident with financial problem, 346–347; views of, on employment, 348; and relations with agency officials, 351–352; and pressures of marginality, 352; relationship of, with social worker, 352; on role of Neighborhood

tion" mandate; Topeka Office of Economic Opportunity, Overlap Model adopted by

parliamentary procedure: TNO and non-TNO views on, 88; TNO problems with, 109; problems of second Board president with, 113 ff.; need for training in, 176; problems of TNCs with, 245, 246, 257; problems of Indian Committee chairman with, 299, 307
Personnel Committee: report on, presented at Board meeting, 94
Pettigrew, Thomas F.: on aggressive meekness of minority groups, 280
Planning and Development Grant: reasons for selection of, for Topeka, 9; date received in Topeka, 19; achievement of, 54
"poor whites": special problems of, 201, 207
poverty-intervention organizations: OEO funding of, 5–6; Alinsky and Overlap Models for, compared, 13–16; strategies for, 17; organizational characteristics of, 27; goals of, 34; disparity between OEO goals and realistic expectations of, 35; TOEO Director on lack of precedents for, 40; vulnerability of, during managerial succession, 49; as bridge between poor and not-poor, 72–73; and problems of uncertainty concerning, 139; role of press in community evaluation of, 143; and dilemma of amount of power for poor, 151; suggestions for Board meetings of, 159; size and voting proportions of, 169; process-experience determinants of, 176–177; social-psychological changes in poor as result of participation in, 179–180; areas of participation in, of indigenous nonprofessionals, 188, 226–227; need for short-range stimulating activities for, 255, 366; in sustaining TNCs through stages of development, 262–263; need for attention by, to social-psychological aspects of social change, 377–378; potential of, 380; staff for, 381;

need for research on strategy of, 381. SEE ALSO community-action programs; social-action programs
—training programs for: suggestions for, 73, 139, 143–144, 149, 150, 236, 378; need for, 150, 152–153, 162, 169–170, 175, 176–177, 247–248, 331, 366, 371
power structure: in Topeka, 7; Alinsky Model and Overlap Model views of, 16
Pow-Wow Club: 325
Prairie Potawatomi. SEE Indian residents; Mayetta, Kansas
prejudice: TNOs on, 200–202, 363
Pre-School Study Committee: and Day Care Centers, 86, 89
process experience: as goal of TOEO, for poor, 33; lack of information on, 52; distinctions in, and duplication of content, 106; determinants of, 176–177; failure of TOEO to anticipate complexity of impact of, 376
program content: as goal of TOEO, through community-action proposals, 33; availability of information on, 52; problems in duplication of, when process experiences differ, 106
psychiatrists: TNOs on, 222–224
Public Health Service: works with Neighborhood House, 345

questionnaires: used in Admin I and Admin II, reproduced, 400–404
Quie Amendment (to Economic Opportunity Act): problems caused by, 45–46; as attempt to define "maximum feasible participation," 64; and elimination of non-TNOs, 118–120; hostility of non-TNOs toward, 136

recruiting: universalistic approach in, 29 and n. 9; particularistic approach in, 29 and n. 10; bureaucharisma in, 30; importance of charisma of recruiters for, 30 and n. 11
—use of division of labor in: problems solved by, 29–30; problems created by, 39–40
Redfield, Robert: on familial society, 282